# 200 kilometres around
# MELBOURNE

## Your essential guide to Melbourne and surrounds

GW00502575

**A Caddick, K Firth**                    **1st edition**

Published in Australia by Gregory's Publishing Company
(A division of Universal Press Pty Ltd)
ACN 000 087 132

Marketed and distributed by Universal Press Pty Ltd

**New South Wales**: 1 Waterloo Road, Macquarie Park 2113

Ph: (02) 9857 3700 Fax: (02) 9888 9850

**Queensland**: 1 Manning Street, South Brisbane 4101

Ph: (07) 3844 1051 Fax: (07) 3844 4637

**South Australia**: Freecall: 1800 021 987

**Victoria**: 585 Burwood Road, Hawthorn 3122

Ph: (03) 9818 4455 Fax: (03) 9818 6123

**Western Australia**: 38a Walters Drive, Osborne Park 6017

Ph: (08) 9244 2488 Fax: (08) 9244 2554

The Publisher would be pleased to receive additional or updated material, or suggestions for future editions. Please address these to the Publishing Manager at Universal Press Pty Ltd.
If you would like to use any of the maps in this book please contact the CMS Manager at Universal Press Pty Ltd.

**National Library of Australia Cataloguing-in-Publication data**

Caddick, Alison
Gregory's 200 kilometres around Melbourne : your essential
guide to Melbourne and surrounds.

1st ed.
Includes index.
ISBN 0 7319 1146 6.

1. Victoria - Guidebooks. 2. Melbourne (Vic.) - Guidebooks.
3. Victoria - Tours. 4. Melbourne (Vic.) - Tours I.
Firth, Kellie. II. Gregory's Publishing Co. III. Title :
200 kilometres around Melbourne. IV. Title : Two hundred
kilometres around Melbourne.

919.45104

Publishing Manager: Greg Reid

Production Manager: Harold Yates

Editorial Manager: Kathy Metcalfe

Editor: Shelley Kenigsberg

DTP/Layout Artist: Vivien Valk

Photographic Researcher: Kathleen Gandy

Cartographic Design: Laurie Whiddon, Map Illustrations

Cartography: Laurie Whiddon, Map Illustrations

Cartographic Researcher: Ray Kerkin

Artist, Victorian flora and flauna emblems: Brian Johnston

Reproduction by: Graphic Skills

Printed by: Australian Print Group

**Disclaimer**
The authors and publisher disclaim any responsibility to any person for loss or damage suffered from any use of this guide for any purpose. While considerable care has been taken by the authors and the publisher in researching and compiling the guide, the authors and the publisher accept no responsibility for errors or omissions. No person should rely upon this guide for the purpose of making any business, investment or real estate decision.

The representation of any maps of any road or track is not necessarily evidence of public right of way. Third parties who have provided information to the author and publisher concerning the roads and other matters did not warrant to the author and publisher that the information was complete, accurate or current or that any of the proposals of any body will eventuate and, accordingly, the author and publisher provide no such warranty.

# Contents

# Acknowledgments

The Publisher would like to gratefully acknowledge the following organisations and individuals for their generosity in supplying photographs and images, and for their permission to reproduce photographic material used in this book.

**All photographs supplied by Tourism Victoria, with the exception of the following:**

'Como', National Trust 67 (T).
Alpine Toboggan Park p. 48 (T)
Balloon Flights Vic. p. 210.
Banyule City Council p. 50 (B).
Barringo Equestrian Centre p. 81 (B).
Bruce Postle, South Gippsland Shire Council p. 163 (T).
Bundoora Park p. 47 (BR).
Cathy's Farm Market Orchard p. 109 (B).
Ceres p. 38 (TL).
Chocolate Box p. 68 (B).
City of Yarra pp. 35 (BL), 35 (TR), 36 (BL), 37 (TR), 41 (TR), 45 (TL), 45 (BR), 49 (B), 51 (B), 53 (BR), 53 (BL).
Country Perennials p. 169 (B).
Dallas Montgomery, Lynne Bullen & Adrian Dwyer p. 285 (TL).

David Shermer p. 267 (T).
David Traeger Wines p. 221 (B).
Eilean donan Gardens p. 169 (T).
Fitzroy Pool p. 53 (TR).
Flagstaff Hill Maritime Museum p. 252 (T).
Geelong Otway Tourism pp. 121 (B), 121 (T), 124 (B), 126 (B), 132 (BL).
Gippsland Art Gallery p. 157 (T).
Gippsland Country Tourism p. 157 (B).
Graham Drummond p. 210 (B).
Greater Shepparton Council p. 216 (T).
Hedgend Maze p. 108 (B).
Jacques Reymond p. 61 (TR).
Jeff Thomson, Heide Gallery p. 60 (B).
Kyneton Daffodil Festival p. 77 (B).
La Mama theatre p. 39 (BR).
Lavender Patch p. 282 (T).

Melbourne Museum p. 40 (TL).
Milawa Cheese Company p. 275 (TR).
Mornington Peninsula Tourism pp. 54, 128 (B), 129 (T), 129 (B), 130 (T), 132 (BR), 135 (B), 136 (B), 141 (B), 144 (T), 145 (T), 147 (T).
Mornington Vineyard Estate p. 131 (B).
Mountain-Top Experience p. 152 (B).
Mt Buffalo Chalet p. 287 (B).
National Holden Motor Museum, Echuca p. 208 (T).
Norgates Plant Farm p. 94 (T).
NSW NPWS Ch. 7 icon, pp. 150–177 (T).
Otway Herb Nursery and cottage Garden p. 246 (B).
Parks Victoria pp. 58 (T), 69 (T), 113 (B)
Promway p. 152 (M).
Red Bears 65 (T).
Richmond Hill Cafe p. 45 (TR).
Rochester Business Services. p. 212.

Roger King, The Boite p. 46 (BL).
Scienceworks p. 140 (T).
Serigraph Gallery p. 156 (B).
Seymour Alternative Farming Expo p. 206 (T).
South Gippsland Shire Council pp. 153 (B), 153 (T), 156 (T), 162 (T), 166 (T).
Surfworld Surfing Museum p. 251 (B).
The Gamekeeper's Secret p. 85 (B).
Timboon Farmhouse cheese p. 257 (B).
Tourism QLD Ch 6 icon pp. 120–147 (T).
Tramway Museum Society of Victoria p. 95 (T).
Transaero p. 95 (B).
Victorian Antique Centre p. 84 (T).
View's End, Bellarine p. 142 (B).
Wangaratta Visitor Info Centre p. 275 (BR).

**Pink Heath,**
**Victorian flora emblem.**

**Leadbeaters Possum,**
**Victorian fauna emblem.**

# It's easier to be well travelled when you're well read.

Melbourne
VICTORIA • AUSTRALIA

Macedon Ranges & Spa Country
VICTORIA • AUSTRALIA

Yarra Valley, Dandenongs & The Ranges
VICTORIA • AUSTRALIA

The Bays & Peninsulas
MELBOURNE • VICTORIA • AUSTRALIA

Phillip Island & Gippsland Discovery
VICTORIA • AUSTRALIA

Goldfields
VICTORIA • AUSTRALIA

Goulburn Murray Waters
VICTORIA • AUSTRALIA

The Grampians
VICTORIA • AUSTRALIA

The Great Ocean Road
VICTORIA • AUSTRALIA

Lakes & Wilderness
EAST GIPPSLAND • VICTORIA • AUSTRALIA

Legends, Wine & High Country
VICTORIA • AUSTRALIA

Murray Outback
VICTORIA • AUSTRALIA

Victorian Tourism Information Service

For any two of these comprehensive guides to the regions of Victoria or for more information on touring around Victoria, call the *Victorian Tourism Information Service* on 132 842. When touring through Victoria, look out for our accredited *Visitor Information Centres*. *i*

Tourism Victoria
You'll love every piece of Victoria

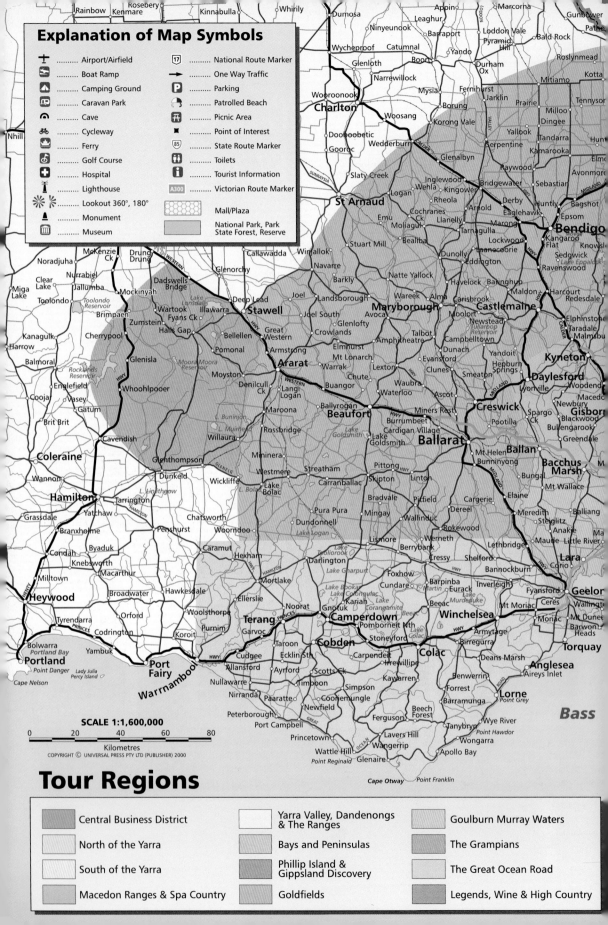

## Explanation of Map Symbols

| Symbol | | | Symbol | |
|---|---|---|---|---|
| ✈ | .......... Airport/Airfield | | [17] | .......... National Route Marker |
| 🛥 | .......... Boat Ramp | | → | .......... One Way Traffic |
| ⛺ | .......... Camping Ground | | P | .......... Parking |
| 🚐 | .......... Caravan Park | | 🏊 | .......... Patrolled Beach |
| 🕳 | .......... Cave | | ⊞ | .......... Picnic Area |
| 🚴 | .......... Cycleway | | 85 | .......... State Route Marker |
| ⛴ | .......... Ferry | | 🚻 | .......... Toilets |
| ⛳ | .......... Golf Course | | i | .......... Tourist Information |
| ✚ | .......... Hospital | | A300 | .......... Victorian Route Marker |
| ⚲ | .......... Lighthouse | | ⬡⬡ | .......... Mall/Plaza |
| ✳ ✳ | .......... Lookout 360°, 180° | | | National Park, Park |
| ▲ | .......... Monument | | | State Forest, Reserve |
| 🏛 | .......... Museum | | | |

SCALE 1:1,600,000

0    20    40    60    80

Kilometres

COPYRIGHT © UNIVERSAL PRESS PTY LTD (PUBLISHER) 2000

# Tour Regions

| | | | | | |
|---|---|---|---|---|---|
| | Central Business District | | Yarra Valley, Dandenongs & The Ranges | | Goulburn Murray Waters |
| | North of the Yarra | | Bays and Peninsulas | | The Grampians |
| | South of the Yarra | | Phillip Island & Gippsland Discovery | | The Great Ocean Road |
| | Macedon Ranges & Spa Country | | Goldfields | | Legends, Wine & High Country |

## Region, Tour and District Maps

| | |
|---|---|
| ▭▭▭▭ | .......... Dual Roadway |
| ▬▬▬▬ | .......... Through Route |
| ▭▭▭▭ | .......... Major Road |
| ▭▭▭▭ | .......... Minor Road |
| sealed   unsealed | .......... Minor Road (Tour Maps Only) |
| ├──┼──┤ | .......... Railway |
| ├──⋀──┤ | .......... Walking Track |

## Street Maps

| | |
|---|---|
| **WEST GATE FWY** | .....Dual Roadway |
| **ST KILDA    RD** | .....Through Route |
| FLINDERS      ST | .....Major Road |
| KAVANAGH      ST | .....Minor Road |
| ├──┼──┤ | .....Railway |
| ├──⋀──┤ | .....Walking Track |

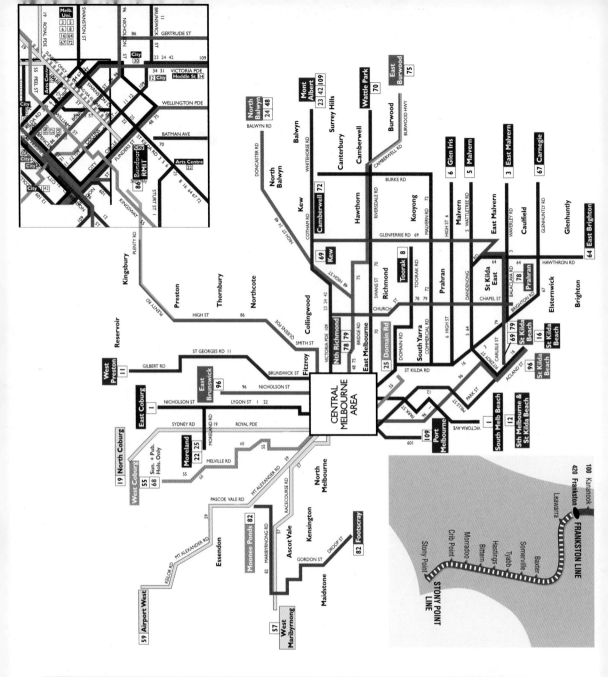

## CITY TRAMS

### Swanston Street

- **1** East Coburg – Sth Melb Beach
- **3** East Malvern
- **5** Malvern
- **6** Glen Iris
- **8** Toorak
- **16** St Kilda Beach
- **22** Moreland
- **25** Moreland – Domain Rd (AM peak only)
- **64** East Brighton
- **67** Carnegie
- **72** Camberwell

### Elizabeth Street

- **19** North Coburg
- **57** West Maribyrnong
- **59** Airport West
- **68** West Coburg (Sun + Pub. Hols. only)

### William Street

- **55** West Coburg – Domain Rd

### Latrobe Street

- **23** Mont Albert
- **24** North Balwyn
- **23** Latrobe Street – Brunswick Street
- **34** Hoddle Street

### Bourke Street

- **86** Bundoora RMIT
- **95** Exhibition Building – Burke & Spencer Sts
- **96** St Kilda Beach – East Brunswick

### Collins Street

- **11** West Preston
- **12** Sth Melb & St Kilda Beach
- **31** Spencer Street – Brunswick St
- **42** Mont Albert
- **109** Mont Albert – Port Melbourne

### Flinders Street

- **48** North Balwyn
- **75** East Borwood

### Batman Avenue

- **70** Wattle Park

### CITY CIRCLE TRAM

## SUBURBAN TRAMS

- **69** St Kilda Beach – Kew
- **78** Prahran – Nth Richmond
- **79** St Kilda Beach – Nth Richmond
- **82** Footscray – Moonee Ponds

Pink Numbers – Extra and Peak Services Only

Zone 2

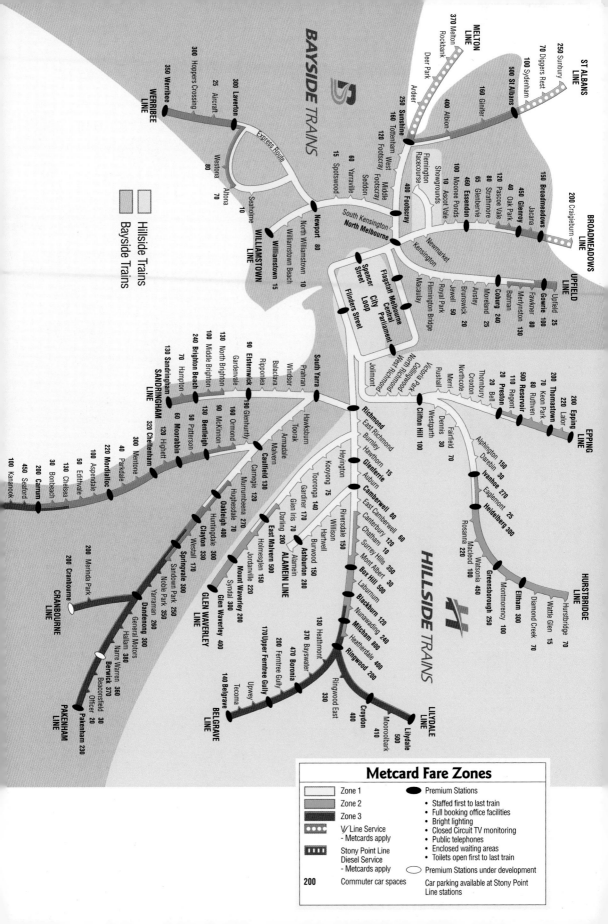

**BAYSIDE TRAINS**

**HILLSIDE TRAINS**

**ST ALBANS LINE**
370 Melton
Rockbank
250 Sunbury
70 Diggers Rest
100 Sydenham
500 St Albans
160 Ginifer
400 Albion
250 Sunshine
160 Tottenham
120 Footscray West
Middle Footscray
10 Footscray
Seddon

**MELTON LINE**
Deer Park
Ardeer

**BROADMEADOWS LINE**
200 Craigieburn
150 Broadmeadows
120 Pascoe Vale
80 Strathmore
65 Glenbervie
460 Essendon
100 Moonee Ponds
Ascot Vale
Showgrounds
Flemington Racecourse
400 Footscray
450 Glenroy
Jacana
40 Oak Park

**UPFIELD LINE**
Upfield 25
Gowrie 100
70 Fawkner
Merlynston
130 Batman
240 Coburg
Moreland 25
Anstey
Brunswick
Jewell 50
Royal Park
Flemington Bridge
Macaulay
North Melbourne

**EPPING LINE**
200 Epping
220 Lalor
200 Thomastown
70 Keon Park
80 Ruthven
500 Reservoir
110 Regent
20 Preston
20 Bell
Thornbury
Croxton
Northcote
Merri
Rushall

**HURSTBRIDGE LINE**
Hurstbridge 70
Wattle Glen 15
Diamond Creek 70
300 Eltham
Montmorency 100
Greensborough 250
Watsonia 450
Macleod 100
Rosanna 220
Heidelberg 300
Eaglemont 25
Ivanhoe 270
Darebin 30
Alphington 150
Fairfield 70
Dennis 30
Westgarth
Clifton Hill 100

**WERRIBEE LINE**
350 Werribee
300 Hoppers Crossing
300 Laverton
25 Aircraft
80 Westona
70 Altona
Seaholme
15 Spotswood
60 Yarraville
Newport 80
North Williamstown
Williamstown Beach

**WILLIAMSTOWN LINE**
Williamstown 15

**SANDRINGHAM LINE**
130 Sandringham
130 Hampton
70 Brighton Beach
100 Middle Brighton
240 North Brighton
Elsternwick 90
Gardenvale
Ripponlea
Balaclava
Windsor
Prahran
Hawksburn
South Yarra
130 Glenhuntly
160 Ormond
90 McKinnon
50 Bentleigh
60 Patterson
120 Moorabbin
320 Cheltenham
300 Highett

**CRANBOURNE LINE**
200 Cranbourne
200 Merinda Park

**PAKENHAM LINE**
230 Pakenham
20 Officer
30 Beaconsfield
360 Berwick
380 Narre Warren
General Motors
300 Hallam
300 Dandenong
260 Yarraman
350 Noble Park
250 Sandown Park
300 Springvale
170 Westall
330 Clayton
300 Huntingdale
70 Oakleigh
270 Murrumbeena
120 Hughesdale
130 Carnegie
Malvern
Armadale
Toorak

**GLEN WAVERLEY LINE**
400 Glen Waverley
200 Syndal
500 Mount Waverley
220 Jordanville
150 Holmesglen
Darling 200
70 Glen Iris
170 Gardiner
140 Tooronga
75 Kooyong
Heyington

**ALAMEIN LINE**
170 Upper Ferntree Gully
Tecoma
Upwey
140 Belgrave

**BELGRAVE LINE**
Alamein 280
Burwood 150
Hartwell
Willison
Riversdale 150
Mont Albert 30
Surrey Hills 350
Chatham 10
Canterbury 120
East Camberwell 60
Camberwell 80
Auburn
Glenferrie 15
Hawthorn
Burnley
East Richmond
Richmond

**LILYDALE LINE**
Lilydale 500
Mooroolbark 410
Croydon 400
Ringwood East
330 Ringwood
200 Heathmont
400 Bayswater
470 Boronia
130 Heathmont

**East Malvern 500**
Laburnum
Box Hill 500
Blackburn 120
Nunawading 240
Mitcham 800
Heatherdale
Ringwood 200
Ashburton 280

Clifton Hill 100

**Metcard Fare Zones**

| | |
|---|---|
| Zone 1 | Premium Stations |
| Zone 2 | • Staffed first to last train |
| Zone 3 | • Full booking office facilities |
| V/Line Service - Metcards apply | • Bright lighting |
| | • Closed Circuit TV monitoring |
| Stony Point Line Diesel Service - Metcards apply | • Public telephones |
| | • Enclosed waiting areas |
| | • Toilets open first to last train |
| **200** Commuter car spaces | Premium Stations under development |

Car parking available at Stony Point Line stations

South Kensington
North Melbourne
Newmarket
Kensington
Spencer Street
Melbourne Central
Parliament
City Loop
Flinders Street
Flagstaff
Jolimont
West Richmond
North Richmond
Collingwood
Victoria Park

Express Route

Left: **Melbourne tram.**
Right: **The Yarra River.**

# Melbourne CBD

**A**ustralia's second largest city, Melbourne is Australia's cultural capital – a place of style and innovation, represented in the city's mix of elegant Victorian buildings and cutting-edge architecture, its long established cultural institutions and innovative arts and entertainment scene. It is famous for shopping and food; its trams and glorious gardens; its music and theatre scene; and major sporting events.

Melbourne will delight the discerning traveller. The CBD, explored on foot and by tram, offers an intricate system of arcades and laneways, with diverse historical and cultural precincts and hidden haunts where theatre and music thrive and good food abounds. This large cosmopolitan city is renowned for its friendly atmosphere – 'London without the hassle'. A city of the seasons, Melbourne can be cold in winter, but wood fires burn in many pubs and restaurants. In summer visit Port Phillip Bay – not far away. At any time of the year the city's cycling paths are ideal for active sightseeing, while its parks offer beautiful picnic settings.

Melbourne is an event city, hosting major Australian and international sporting, arts and trade extravaganzas. These include the Australian Tennis Open, the Qantas Australian Grand Prix, the Melbourne International Arts Festival and the Fosters Melbourne Cup. Melbourne is truly 'marvellous' – the term used to describe it as far back as the 1880s.

## ℹ Tourist information

**Victorian Tourism Info Service**
13 28 42

**Melbourne Info Line**
for weekly events
Ph: 1300 655452

**City Experience Centre**
Melbourne Town Hall
Cnr Swanston and Collins Sts
Melbourne 3000

**Victorian Visitor Info Centre**
Cnr Swanston and Little Collins Sts
Melbourne 3000

**Info Booths**
Flinders St Stn
Cnr Flinders and Swanston Sts
Melbourne 3000

Bourke St Mall
Between Swanston and Elizabeth Sts
Melbourne 3000

**Websites**
www.melbourne.org
www.tourism.vic.gov.au
www.melbourne.vic.gov.au

## Must see, must do

- ★ **Melbourne Central** (p.19)
- ★ **National Gallery of Victoria on Russell** (p.21)
- ★ **Rialto Towers Observation Deck** (p.26)
- ★ **Royal Botanic Garden** (p.30)
- ★ **Southgate** (p.27)
- ★ **Victorian Arts Centre** (p.27)

## Radio stations

**3AW:** 1278 AM

**3LO:** 774 AM

**3RRR:** 102.7 FM

**FOX FM:** 101.9 FM

**Radio National:** 621 AM

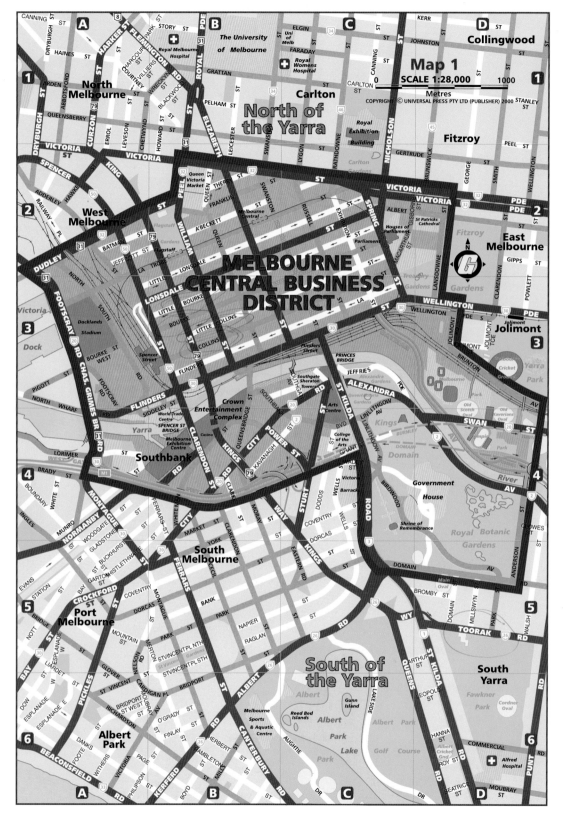

## Natural features

Melbourne lies on the Yarra River at the northern tip of Port Phillip Bay. East lie the Dandenongs; west, the basalt plains, extending into Victoria's western district. The CBD occupies hilly ground north of the river. The modern CBD was constructed on a grid turned away from its waterways. This has changed with the development of Southbank on the Yarra, and will alter further with the opening of Docklands over coming years.

The Yarra River was Melbourne's lifeblood. The first Europeans to arrive in 1835 moored their vessels at the CBD's south-western corner near Flinders and Spencer Sts intersection. Many of Melbourne's original natural features are no longer visible – hills have been flattened, the river's path altered, but the Yarra continues as a major focus. Especially lovely from the SE Arterial and Alexandra Ave, its gracious 19th century bridges can be viewed against a backdrop of modern Melbourne.

## History

Two Aboriginal tribes have special claims as Melbourne's original custodians. The Woiworung and Bunurong peoples – of the Kulin nation – inhabited the area for 40 000 years, fishing the river, and hunting bountiful populations of kangaroo and smaller animals. In 1835, John Batman entered Port Phillip to survey it for his private consortium, the Port Phillip Association.

Batman is famous for his supposed treaty with the Aborigines, now thought to have been a hoax, exchanging knives and blankets for land. Private entrepreneurs nevertheless invaded north and west of Melbourne, establishing sheep stations and building the settlement which was to become Melbourne. The 'Port Phillip District' was considered an illegal occupation by the Crown, and brought under the control of New South Wales. Victoria became a separate colony in 1851, with Melbourne as its capital.

In 1851 Melbourne had a population of 23 000. With the discovery of gold the first dramatic expansion occurred. By 1861, it had grown to 140 000; by 1880 to 283 000, far surpassing Sydney. Gold fuelled the boom which saw the construction of the first grand civic buildings. Described in the 1880s as 'Marvellous Melbourne', it was a thriving metropolis. In 1901, with federation of the colonies, Melbourne became the seat of national government, Federal Parliament moving to Canberra in 1927.

A further boom in the post-war period transformed Melbourne from a British outpost to the multicultural centre it is today. Immigrants from southern Europe, and later the Middle East and Asia arrived to provide labour for the burgeoning factories. Today's city skyline is testament to further booms in the 1980s and 1990s. Melbourne is undergoing a massive transformation, with many redevelopment projects and buildings currently underway.

**Rivals for founder's title**
Controversy reigns over who rightly wears the mantle of founder of Melbourne. Despite the rival claims of John Batman and John Pascoe Fawkner, Captain Lancey of the *Enterprize* seems to have been the first European to set foot on the site.

*Andersons Bridge crossing the Yarra River.*

**Only one in the world!**

Dine a la carte aboard a 1927 tram as you travel through Melbourne's leafy avenues and busy streets. The distinctive burgundy Colonial Tramcar Restaurant is a winner of coveted tourism awards for its unique service.
Ph: (03) 9696 4000

# Getting there
## Airport links
Melbourne Airport at Tullamarine, 20min from Melbourne, is well-serviced by both private and public buses and taxis. The Sky Bus leaves every 30min for Melbourne, linking the airport to various city locations, ending at either Spencer St Stn or the Melbourne Transit Centre in Franklin St. Hire cars are available at the airport, and the Tullamarine Fwy is an efficient route into the north-western end of the city.

## By public transport
Visitors should get hold of the Met's handy public transport maps, available at info centres, train stations and on trams. Tram and train routes to and from the city and terminal points within the CBD grid are clearly indicated. The Met, as well as numerous suburban companies, also coordinates suburban bus lines.

The main city station for suburban trains is Flinders St Stn, in the heart of the city, with many lines directly linked into the underground City Loop, stopping at Flinders St, Spencer St, Flagstaff, Melbourne Central and Parliament. V/Line country trains and buses pull into Spencer St Stn, at the city's western end. (See maps pp. 8, 9.)

*Melbourne Arts Centre spire at night.*

# By road
For drivers entering Melbourne for the first time, it is important to note that on certain main arteries connected into the City Link tollway system, automatic electronic tolling occurs. Various toll options, including day passes, are available, and visitors should ring the City Link info line for details. Ph: 13 26 29

# Getting around
## The Met
The Met is Melbourne's integrated system of suburban trams, trains and buses. A new ticketing system has recently been introduced and various ticket alternatives are available. Short trip tickets can be purchased on trams and buses. Two-hr and 1-day tickets can be purchased in newsagents, milk bars and post offices, as well as from ticket machines at train stations and on board trams. Monthly tickets are available from major train stations. Note that tram machines only take coins. Ph: 13 16 38

## Trams
Melbourne's trams are one of the city's enduring icons and a very pleasant way to travel. Various routes intersect the CBD grid, giving excellent access to all points of interest. Many run great distances out to Melbourne's far-flung suburbs. Self-guided tram tours are a great way to get a feel of the city.

The **City Circle** tram – a distinctive maroon colour – is a free service, picking up passengers at tram stops in Spring, Flinders, Spencer and Latrobe Sts. Ringing the CBD area, it gives direct access to the Flagstaff, Carlton and Treasury Gardens, to Melbourne Central and the State Library, to Parliament House, Flinders and Spencer Sts Stns, as well intersecting with the various tram lines spanning out to other destinations. The round trip takes 40min.

## Buses
Buses leave from various points around the city for routes not covered by trams and trains. Buses provide alternative access to some bayside locations, as well as to many rural fringe suburbs, but play

*Melbourne's trams are an efficient and fun way to visit the city and outlying suburbs.*

**Face off or face-to-face?**
They say one of the differences between Melbourne and Sydney is that in trams passengers sit face-to-face, while in buses you only see the back of other people's heads. Could this explain Melbourne's less harried, more friendly demeanour?

only a small role within the CBD itself. The Russell St bus gives access to the CBD's Greek quarter, and provides an alternative route to Carlton and Fitzroy.

### Taxis

An efficient taxi system operates throughout Melbourne and its suburbs. City hotels will call taxis for their guests, and there are major taxi ranks at key locations, in particular, Flinders and Spencer Sts Stns. Silver Top Taxi Service is Melbourne's largest operator. Ph: 13 10 08

### By road

While it is preferable to take public transport in and around Melbourne, especially on major events days, car travel to and from the city is possible. Avoid peak hours.

Melbourne is well-serviced with multi-level carparks signposted throughout the CBD, costing approx $16 a day. The Southbank precinct is especially well-catered for, with undercover parking behind Southgate and in the Casino complex. Good street meter parking on the CBD fringe is also available along Victoria St in the north, around the Treasury and Fitzroy Gardens to the east, and in the Kings Domain area to the south of the CBD. But beware, Melbourne's parking officers brook no

argument. Visitors should study the parking signs before heading off on foot.

### River ferries and cruises

Various craft ply the waters of the Yarra River, departing from Southbank. **Southbank Cruises** can deliver passengers to various waterside locations, including Melbourne Park, the MCG, the Royal Botanical Gardens and even to Flemington Race Course on Melbourne Cup day. Lunch and dinner cruises are

*Melbourne Tennis Centre and city skyline.*

**Southbank footbridge.**

available on their *Lady Chelmsford*, a refitted Sydney Harbour ferry. This trip takes passengers through the busy Port of Melbourne and into the new Docklands precinct. Ph: (03) 9645 9944. Regular sightseeing tours leave every 30min, mid-morning–mid-afternoon with **Melbourne River Cruises**. Ph: (03) 9629 7233. A regular ferry service operates between Southgate and Williamstown.

### City Explorer

The City Explorer, a double-decker bus, can be joined at any of 16 stops around the city. Taking in many of the city's major attractions, visitors can take the round trip or hop on and off as they wish. It departs daily on the hour from 10am–4pm, with a break at 1pm, from Melbourne Town Hall, where tour guides can help visitors plan their day. Discounts on entry fees to some attractions are offered to City Explorer patrons. Ph: (03) 9563 9788.

### Tours

Harley Davidson, Chevrolet convertibles, double-decker buses and bicycles are just some of tour options available in Melbourne. Check with visitor info centres for details.

There are also tours specialising in particular features of Melbourne life.

**Programs! Programs!**
For Melbourne's program of free summer entertainment — art, music, kids activities and open air cinema — get the brochure 'Summer Fun in the Parks', available at visitor info centres.

**Melbourne Alive** offers Night Life Activity Tours, stopping at bars, jazz haunts, nightclubs and restaurants. Ph: (03) 9525 0025. **City Pub Tours**, meeting under the Flinders St Stn clocks, takes visitors on an enjoyable walk through Melbourne's infamous and entertaining watering holes. Ph: (03) 9384 0655

There are also tours for children, freeing parents for their own activities, with **Kids Tours Melbourne**, Ph: 0416 110 899. And there are several options for guided tours of Melbourne's artist studios and galleries, including the **Melbourne City Art Galleries Walk and Tram Tour**. Ph: (03) 9897 3174

### Self-guided walks

The City of Melbourne's Heritage Walks are outlined in the their excellent pamphlets complete with expert commentary on the social and architectural history of the city, available at info centres. The 7 walks cover the various city precincts in detail, exposing the city's rich cultural heritage and sometimes infamous past.

## Festivals and events
### Sidney Myer Free Concerts

In high summer, under the stars, visitors are treated to a program of wonderful concerts by the Melbourne Symphony Orchestra. Held over several weeks, in the unique outdoor venue, the Sidney Myer Music Bowl, the concerts are a time when families take picnic dinners to revel in the music and surrounds of the Kings Domain.

### Australian Open Tennis Championships

The Australian Open is a Grand Slam partner to the French Open, Wimbledon and the US Open. Held in the spectacular Tennis Centre in Melbourne Park in the last two weeks of Jan, it attracts 1000s of visitors. Tickets are available through Ticketmaster.

### Chinese New Year Festival

The festival procession, centred on Melbourne's Chinatown, includes dragons wending their way down Little Bourke St to the sound of drums, gongs and fire crackers. The crowds gather to watch the noisy celebrations and sample the exquisite food of this intimate quarter.

### Woolmark Melbourne Fashion Festival

Held in late Feb, the Woolmark Melbourne Fashion Festival showcases autumn and winter fashions by Australian designers at locations within the CBD and across greater Melbourne. There are fashion parades, exhibitions and workshops. Ph: (03) 9826 9688

### Antipodes Festival

Melbourne is the third largest Greek city in the world, and its thriving Greek community comes out in force to celebrate both its ancient and modern-Australian heritage. Events are held over 6 wks, and include a street parade and a program of arts events, with plenty of dancing, food and ouzo.

### Melbourne Moomba Festival

Australia's largest outdoor festival, Moomba is Melbourne's people's festival held over 10 days in early March. For generations families have watched its fabulous street parade and decamped to the banks of the Yarra for its outdoor

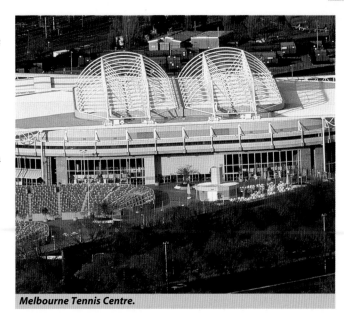

*Melbourne Tennis Centre.*

carnival, water skiing championships and spectacular fireworks display.

### Melbourne Food & Wine Festival

Food is one of *the* reasons to visit Melbourne, regarded as Australia's culinary capital. During the 3 wks of the Melbourne Food and Wine Festival in Mar, mouth-watering events take place at venues throughout the city. The city's chefs are given full license to tantalise and educate, against a backdrop of Melbourne's rich multicultural mix.

### Melbourne International Comedy Festival

Laugh your socks off at the Melbourne International Comedy Festival over 3 wks in Apr. Mainstream and feral, in big and tiny venues around town, comedians from all over the world stand up with Australia's funniest men and women. Ph: (03) 9417 7711

### Anzac Day Parade

Much of Melbourne comes to a standstill for the Anzac Day Parade on 27 Apr, which commemorates what many consider to be the nation's true founding moment – the battle of Gallipoli fought by the ANZACs in WWI. It commemorates today the fallen of all wars, centred on the imposing Shrine of Remembrance.

*Greek dancers at the Antipodes Festival.*

*Fashion parade.*

*Flemington.*

*Flemington Racecourse is home to the famous horserace, Fosters Melbourne Cup.*

### Melbourne Film Festival

Held in late Jul–early Aug, the Melbourne Film Festival has been a feature of the Melbourne calendar for over 40 yrs. Over 2 wks, film aficionados hunker down for marathon film-viewing in venues across the city, featuring the latest in innovative film-making from across the world.
Ph: (03) 9417 2011

### Royal Melbourne Show

This grand agricultural show held in Sept is etched into the memories of all Melbourne children and is the culmination of the year for many in rural Victoria. In this meeting of city and country, visitors can view showjumping and dressage, sheep dog trials and thoroughbred judging, boil a billy and sample damper or visit the many exhibitions.

### Melbourne Spring Fashion Week

Spring Fashion Week held in the 1st week of Sept, has a 7-day calendar packed with events. Focused on the CBD's retailers and stockists, it attracts large numbers to its catwalk shows, film festival, workshops, and its intriguing fashion walk, where visitors get a behind-the-scenes look at the city's fashion industry. With a focus on education, and with many events free of charge, Melbourne Spring Fashion Week is a unique opportunity to enjoy and learn about fashion. For program details,
Ph: (03) 9654 2288

### Melbourne Festival

Centred on the Southbank precinct, this international festival of the arts held in mid-Oct–Nov, brings together non-stop entertainment of the highest calibre. The Melbourne festival covers the full range of artistic offerings by including opera, music, dance, theatre and the visual arts. The festival abounds in free arts events, as well as offering a range of ticket options suited to visitors' particular arts interests.
Ph: (03) 9662 4242

### Fosters Melbourne Cup

At the height of the spring racing festival, the Melbourne Cup is the horse race that brings the nation to a standstill every year. Because of the race, there is a public holiday in Melbourne on the 1st Tues in Nov, and most people 'have a flutter'. It attracts visitors from all over Australia as well as international visitors. The Melbourne Cup, which is run at Flemington Racecourse, is also an occasion for high fashion and silly hats amidst champagne-induced revelry.

### Carols by Candlelight

Another occasion on which to pack a picnic tea and sit under the stars on the lawns of the Kings Domain at the Sidney Myer Music Bowl is Carols by Candlelight. The concert features well-known Australian artists who play to the wrapt attention of candle-holding children.

# Main CBD localities and suburbs

With the creation of Melbourne's new Docklands precinct, Melbourne will divide into 3 major areas: Melbourne CBD, Docklands and Southbank.

## Melbourne CBD
### Central Retail District Map 1

The Central Retail District, bounded by Russell, Latrobe, William and Flinders Sts, is the hub of Melbourne's retail trade, incorporating part of Chinatown and the Greek quarter, as well as major historical features and attractions. It is crisscrossed by the city's famous arcades and laneways where cafes, fashion outlets and unique shops provide the visitor with an array of options for eating, browsing and buying.

At the heart of the CBD, Swanston St meets the Bourke St Mall. **Myer** and **David Jones** department stores, next door to the Melbourne GPO, open onto the Mall, where buskers ply their trade in this pleasant pedestrian precinct. Both Myer and David Jones extend north over Little Bourke St, joined at several levels by suspended walkways. On Lonsdale St Myer is connected by walkway to Melbourne's most recent retail development, **Melbourne Central**, located on the corner of Swanston St and Latrobe St.

Here the opportunities for browsing and shopping expand exponentially. **Daimaru** department store is located here, as is a massive complex of shops, cafes and restaurants in ambient surrounds. Now a favourite meeting place for Melburnians, Melbourne Central is distinguished by a 20-storey conical glass tower which encloses the **Shot Tower**, built in 1889, a fascinating sight from below in the complex's main plaza. On the hour the **Marionette Watch** plays Waltzing Matilda, opening out to display two minstrels and their Australian bush friends.

From the **Bourke St Mall**, the historic arcades which extend south towards Flinders St, can be explored. The **Royal Arcade** and **Centre Way** are especially lovely. Stylish cafes abound, as well as intriguing specialty shops — candy makers,

jewellers, lingerie specialists, specialty wool shops.

The Royal Arcade is watched over by two elaborate 19th century figures, Gog and Magog, who strike the hour, to the delight of passersby.

The **Royal Arcade** and **Causeway** connect to Little Collins St, the Royal Arcade facing Block Place, which meets the **Block Arcade**. Here the tone is distinctly upmarket, with chic boutiques lining the way out to Collins St. Browsing in this beautiful tiled walkway, shoppers are often accompanied by live chamber music being played in the central plaza. Several lanes give access to Collins St from Little Collins St. **Howey Place** is another favourite laneway, while **Australia on Collins**, at 234 Collins St, is another spectacular multi-level complex with fine shops and eateries.

Crossing Collins St, visitors will enter one of the CBDs most sought-after residential locations. The **Centre Way** meets Flinders Lane, where a more bohemian quarter has sprung up in recent years. Close to the Council for Adult Education building, which offers short courses in everything from Indian cooking to the meaning of postmodern art, and to

**Melbourne Cinemas**

**Greater Union**,
131 Russell St

**Hoyts Cinema Centre**,
140 Bourke St

**Village Centre**,
206 Bourke St

**Village at Crown**,
Crown Entertainment Complex

**Village Gold Class**,
Crown Entertainment Complex

**Kino Cinema**,
45 Collins St

**Lumiere Cinema**,
108 Lonsdale St

*There are many fine and varied foods to buy in Melbourne's CBD.*

**Yummy yum cha and more**

One of Chinatown's most popular restaurants is **Dragon Boat**, 203 Little Bourke St. It specialises in yum cha and fine a la carte dining. **Mask of China**, at 117 Little Bourke St, is another fine eating establishment, winning the *Age Good Food Guide* consistently over a decade. For something cheaper, try the **Supper Inn**, upstairs at 15 Celestial Ave, off Little Bourke.

the many galleries in this Flinders Lane precinct, the atmosphere is 'cool' but cosy. In **Degraves St**, with its tables and umbrellas, and in the Centreway, visitors will find cheap gastronomic pleasures, from chic Italian to macrobiotic health food and sushi in the tiny bars that line the lanes.

### Chinatown *Map 2*

Melbourne has had a significant Chinese population since the 1850s when thousands of Chinese poured in to find their fortunes in the goldfields. Little Bourke St has long been the centre of Chinese commerce and culture, and is today a treasure trove of restaurants, grocery stores and various Australian-Chinese institutions. The street is lined with restaurants, while many of the laneways off Little Bourke St offer intriguing locations and more unusual dishes. Some Malaysian and Japanese restaurants can also be found in Chinatown.

Yum cha is a popular meal for the Chinese community, a tradition of breakfast or brunch taken to with gusto by Australians of many ethnic backgrounds.

On Sunday mornings especially, visitors flock to Little Bourke St to take their pick of the delectable dim sum, spring rolls, buns, and other dishes offered to them on trolleys.

The **Museum of Chinese Australian History**, 22 Cohen Pl, off Little Bourke, houses various artefacts, including Dai Loong, the dragon who emerges each year for Chinese New Year celebrations, and an audio-visual display of the history of the Chinese in Australia. Open daily, 10am–4.30pm. Walking tours of Chinatown also leave from here. Ph: (03) 9662 2888

### Greek quarter *Map 1 C2*

For coffee and honey-soaked cakes, Lonsdale St, between Russell and Swanston Sts, is the place to go. Restaurants, Greek music shops and travel agents offering the glittering Aegean Sea tempt passersby. Tables line the pavement and it is a pleasant spot to stop and bask in the northern sun. This section of Lonsdale St is the focus for festivities associated with the Antipodes Festival (p.17).

### Swanston St *Map 1 B2–C3*

Swanston St, once the city's major north-south thoroughfare, has been reborn as a day-time pedestrian precinct, from Flinders St to Latrobe St. Pavement cafes and shops line the street, with many of Melbourne's historic civic buildings marking the way.

**Flinders St Stn** stands in all its Victorian glory beside the Princes St Bridge, a great 'mouth' consuming commuters at peak hour. Opposite the stn, **Young and Jackson's Hotel** is also a time-worn meeting place. Lonely travellers seeking the solace of its famous bar have for generations been able to gaze up at the pub's infamous nude, *Chloe*, now located in the upstairs bar.

**St Pauls Cathedral**, sits on another corner of this busy intersection. Noted as an example of Gothic Revival architecture, it was completed in 1892. It is open to the public daily and on occasions provides a magnificent venue for organ, choral and other musical events. Several services are held on Sun, as well as daily throughout the week. Ph: (03) 9650 3791

Guided tours of the stately **Melbourne Town Hall**, on the corner of Collins St, reveal a wealth of historical

*Flinders Street Station at night.*

detail. This building replaces an earlier modest civic centre, its grand style more in keeping with the aspirations of Marvellous Melbourne. Completed in 1870, there are a number of features of interest, including its fabulous *Grand Organ*, with over 6000 pipes, its ornate meeting rooms and portico, and extensive collection of Australian paintings. Ph: (03) 9658 9658. The town hall is a major venue for visiting speakers, musical events and the Melbourne Comedy Festival.

Swanston St intersects with the Bourke St Mall, marked by several intriguing sculptural identities, including Jim Pitsas's short little weird guys in suits, and some high-flying pigs. It proceeds past Chinatown and the Greek quarter to Latrobe St, where the **State Library of Victoria** sits opposite Melbourne Central.

Visitors should peruse the State Library's publication *What's On*. Exhibits often coincide with major Melbourne events, such as St Patricks Day and the Victorian Heritage Festival, while regular sessions in genealogy, Internet training, tours and special lectures are also offered. The library's magnificent domed reading room is a fabulous cocoon for those who wish to search out a favourite volume and read it in peace. Librarians will assist visitors with any request.

The **National Gallery of Victoria on Russell** is located in the same complex of buildings as the library. It opens onto Russell St. Relocated here while redevelopment proceeds at the gallery's St Kilda Rd address, it continues to exhibit a large number of works from its permanent collection, as well as hosting visiting collections.

The **RMIT University** in Swanston St opposite the State Library, is renowned for its postmodern architectural creation, **Storey Hall**, at 344 Swanston St. An example of architectural pastiche, it is a bejewelled medieval fantasy in shiny modern materials. Storey Hall is home to the **RMIT Gallery**, which runs a changing exhibition program of contemporary art, installations, mixed media, new media

**Marvellous Melbourne – by the book**
*Melbourne's Architecture*, by Philip Goad, is the authoritative text on Melbourne's architectural history. Filled throughout with magnificent photos, the book traces the beginnings of Marvellous Melbourne and the booms and busts that were to shape the city.

# Melbourne's churches

St Patricks Cathedral (p.24) and St Pauls Cathedral (p.20) are landmark edifices in the city of Melbourne. But Melbourne has many lovely smaller churches of architectural note. They are also a striking indication of the social and religious mix of colonial Victoria. Most are open for part or all of the day, and welcome visitors.

A walk up Collins St hill will take visitors past the Baptist Church (1862), Scots Church (1874), and St Michaels Uniting Church (1867). St Michael's interior is especially intriguing and beautiful. Its rounded space, with coved ceiling and horseshoe gallery is very theatrical, and its stained glass windows, both traditional and contemporary, are stunning. Tours daily, 10.30am–1.30pm.

St Peters (1848) sits on the corner of Albert and Gisborne Sts, opposite St Patricks Cathedral. This High Anglican church has been associated with many significant Melbourne figures. Dame Nellie Melba learnt the organ here as a child, while Henry Handel Richardson, recalling the church from her childhood, renamed it 'St Stephens' in her classic, *The Getting of Wisdom*.

The Holy Trinity Lutheran Church (1874) is also in this vicinity, at 22 Parliament Pl. The Wesley Church (1858) at 148 Lonsdale St, and St Francis Catholic Church (1845) at 326 Lonsdale St are also of interest. St Francis' conducts 6 masses daily — the busiest church in Australia.

# Melbourne's historic theatres

The Uptown Precinct is home to Melbourne's historic theatres. Many have been preserved or restored and are wonderfully theatrical statements in their own right. International and Australian comedy hits, blockbuster musicals, exotic dance companies and a variety of other stage shows come to this part of town. Exhibition St is abuzz with activity when the **Comedy Theatre** and **Her Majestys** switch on their street lights and patrons gather on the pavements.

The **Princess Theatre**, in Spring St, is a magnificent Victorian fantasy, with elaborate ironwork and graceful dome. Inside, the atmosphere is electric. This building is full of atmosphere, and great show-biz stories abound, including the one about the ghost in the dressing rooms, which any number of actors will tell you is true. The **Regent Theatre** in Collins St was fully restored after many years battling against demolition, reopening in 1996. Originally built in 1929, its design was inspired by the New York Capitol Theatre, then considered to be the most lavish theatre in the world. The Regent is again its old self — a fabulous concoction of Hollywood glamour, lavishly opulent!

If you cannot get to a show, there is a very entertaining walking tour of the Regent and Forum Theatres, Tues and Thurs, 10am–2pm. Ph: (03) 9820 0239

and architecture. Exhibitions change every 6 wks, and admission is free. Open Mon–Fri, 11am–8pm; Sat, 2pm–5pm. Ph: (03) 9925 1717

Close by, the **Old Melbourne Gaol,** Victoria's oldest penal establishment, is open to the public, graphically displaying what life was like between those cold bluestone walls in the 19th century. Its fascinating exhibition includes the death masks of many of the criminals – including Ned Kelly, Australia's most controversial bushranger – hanged at this location. Open daily, 9.30am–4.30pm. Visitors can also attend the very popular night tour and performance which brings to life the last days of poor old Ned. Ph: (03) 9663 7228

The historic **Melbourne Baths** are located close by (p.31).

### North Melbourne *Map 1 B2*

The **Queen Victoria Market** is a Victorian beauty. A mainly outdoor market, protected by high rounded iron gables, the hurly burly of this busy trading centre with more than 1000 stalls attracts large numbers of Melburnians and tourists alike.

As well as a tumultuous array of fresh produce, visitors will find clothing, leather goods and manchester. In its fabulous deli area, Polish, Greek and Italian stalls vie for attention. A favourite with regular shoppers is coffee and a hot continental sausage at one of the stand-up food stalls.

*Melbourne's historic Regent Theatre.*

*Old Melbourne Goal.*

## QUEEN VICTORIA MARKET

*With over 1000 different types of stalls, Queen Victoria Markets is a fascinating place to shop.*

The market is open Tues and Thurs, 6am–2pm, Fri, 6am–6pm, Sat, 6am–3pm. On Sun, the food stalls close and additional craft and bric-a-brac stalls open from 9am–4pm.

In summer, Nov–Mar, the **Gaslight Market** runs Wed, 6.30pm–10.30pm. Bands, bars, quality arts and crafts, and stalls offering aromatherapy products and massage are mingled with multicultural food stalls offering everything from generous seafood platters and paella to Thai and Vietnamese delicacies. The market also runs popular tours – its 'Foodies Dream Tour' speaks for itself. Ph: (03) 9320 5835

### Uptown *Map 1 C2*

At the eastern end of the city, Uptown is a lively, urbane area, dominated by Parliament House and the Old Treasury, as well as extensive modern State Government offices. It is also Melbourne's live theatre hub with its huddle of historic theatres and the location of several fine churches.

The Parliament of Victoria first met in 1856 in the first two parliamentary chambers completed in that year. The original design envisaged 'a building of colossal proportions', including a 45m dome rising above the present vestibule, and two additional wings – this excess seemed fitting in Melbourne's first 'great boom'. The building was completed in

1892 without these features, at the beginning of the 1890s depression.

Built in neo-classical style, Parliament House's various chambers feature magnificent columns and ornate ceilings, fine wood panelling and plush upholstery. The public are welcome to witness the business of the house from the viewing galleries of both the Legislative Assembly and Legislative Council. When Parliament is not sitting, visitors can view the elegant Queens Hall and wonderful domed Parliamentary Library, as well as the Premiers Corridor which houses the busts and portraits of former premiers. Free tours leave from the Vestibule Mon–Fri, at 10am, 11am, noon, 2pm, 3pm 3.45pm. Ph: (03) 9651 8569

The **Old Treasury** building in Spring St, facing Collins St, was also built at the height of gold fever and is considered a masterpiece in the Renaissance Revival style. It is now the **Old Treasury Museum**, which hosts a program of visiting exhibitions. A substantial centralised treasury was necessitated by the huge wealth generated in the 1850s – between 1851 and 1862 the Victorian goldfields produced gold worth $40 billion in today's terms. The Treasury's once famous gold vaults are now on display. Open Mon–Fri, 9am–5pm, weekends, 10am–4pm.

Tucked away at 39 Gisborne St, the **Fire Services Museum** is a great find.

**'About Books'**
This free guide to Melbourne's book world covers the range of bookshops from middle and high brow, to antiquarian and religious, by name, location and subject matter. Get hold of one from a visitor info centre or bookshop.

*Old Treasury Museum.*

Open Fri, 9am-3pm. It attracts large numbers of children to its intriguing historical displays of antique fire engines and shiny brass hats, the Fire Chief's room – as it was in 1893 – and a collection of uniforms dating back to the Great London Fire of 1666. Demonstrations of ladders, hoses and fire engines run from 10.30am-11.30am. Ph: (03) 9662 2907

The top ends of Bourke and Collins Sts are busy with office workers and theatre patrons dining at the many pavement cafes and stylish restaurants. **Pellegrinis** in Bourke St is a favourite coffee bar. **Florentinos**, also in Bourke St, is an exclusive restaurant with a long history in this once bohemian quarter of Melbourne. Opposite Parliament House, the **Windsor Hotel**, another fine 19th century establishment, offers exclusive accommodation, as well as genteel afternoon teas amidst the potted palms and more youthful entertainment at its **Hard Rock Cafe**.

This precinct has a number of good book and fine music stores with helpful staff – **Hill of Content** and **Thomas Music** being just two. **Haighs Chocolate Shop** at 26 Collins St is a must for the discerning chocoholic.

The top end of Collins St, sometimes referred to as the 'Paris end', is elegantly lined with plane trees, illuminated at night. Many of the small 19th century buildings or at least their facades remain.

This is Melbourne's centre of *haute couture*. **Collins Place**, beneath the imposing modern Collins Towers, is a large internal plaza with several levels of cafes and restaurants, gift and fashion shops. The **Kino Cinema**, renowned for showing art house movies, is also here.

101 Collins St is well worth visiting. Two large classical columns rise up as if to support the portico but have no functional supporting role in this, another of Melbourne's postmodern architectural creations. Inside, visitors will pass by internal waterways with fabulous gold-leaf covered recesses on their way to Flinders lane, with its bevy of cafes and almost-hidden haunts.

The **Alcaston Gallery** at 2 Collins St specialises in Aboriginal art from Central and Western Australia, and often holds public lectures. Ph: (03) 9654 7279. At 321 Exhibition St, the **Postmaster Gallery**, refurbished in a sleek modern style, houses the most significant collection of stamps and philatelic artwork in Australia. Rare colonial and federation material is on display, as well as changing exhibitions and an interactive display, 'Think Design', especially designed for children and teenagers. Open Tues-Fri, 10am-5pm, Sat-Mon, noon-5pm.

**St Patricks Cathedral**, on the corner of Albert and Gisborne Sts, is a magnificent building, regarded as one of the world's great Gothic Revival churches. It was designed by Wilkinson Wardell, a pupil of the founder of the Gothic Revival movement, August Pugin. Commenced in 1850, and consecrated in 1897, its 3 imposing spires were added in 1937 under the guidance of Archbishop Mannix – a prominent figure in the political history of Melbourne, whose statue stands in the forecourt. Open daily.

### West End *Map 1 A2–B2*

The West End, from William to Spencer Sts, is the commercial end of town, incorporating the legal precinct. In its south-west corner, Spencer St Stn forms a barrier to the docklands, and railway viaducts shield the Yarra River. Railways mark the edge of the western end of the city, although the redevelopment of

**Find art the easy way**
The **Art Almanac** is the essential guide to the visual arts in Melbourne. A free monthly publication, it provides a comprehensive listing of current exhibitions with full descriptions and handy map references.

Docklands will re-establish the CBD's connection to its waterways.

The blocks close to the Flinders and Spencer Sts intersection provide fascinating insights into the early history of European settlement. Many of the old warehouses and woolstores survive, as well as some of the cramped little pubs once frequented by sailors and travellers as they disembarked from the sailing ships tied up at Flinders St.

A pavement plaque outside the old **Customs House**, marks the point where John Batman is said to have set foot in 1835, declaring it 'the place for a village'. Spencer St Stn sits on what was Batmans Hill, not far from where Batman's arch rival John Pascoe Fawkner built Melbourne's first pub on the corner of Williams St and Flinders Lane, now demolished. The flavour of the mid 1800s is perhaps best evoked in **Highlander Lane**, where several small rough stone warehouses dating from the 1850s remain.

The Customs House at 400 Flinders St is today the **Immigration Museum**. This sophisticated museum explores the journeys made by immigrants over the last

*St Patricks Cathedral.*

200 yrs through audiovisual displays and a fine collection of memorabilia. The fears and hopes of those come to a foreign land are eerily projected through voices accompanying the various displays. The Schiavelli Gallery provides a venue for Melbourne's many ethnic communities to tell their personal stories of hope and hardship in special exhibitions. Open daily, 10am–5pm.

# Flinders Lane

Once the centre of Melbourne's rag trade, Flinders Lane's alleyway abounds with tucked-away cafes, art galleries and innovative dress designers' shopfronts. From Spring to Elizabeth Sts it intersects with many other little lanes to produce a beehive of activity.

For superb Aboriginal art, wander in to **Aboriginal Art Galleries of Australia**, 31 Flinders Lane or the **Gallery Gabriel Pizzi**, 141 Flinders Lane, both international art dealers renowned as experts in their field. With direct links to Aboriginal communities in Arnhem Land, Central and Western Australia, they have been at the forefront of bringing Aboriginal art to the attention of a world market.

**Span Galleries 1 2 and 3**, 45 Flinders Lane, is an exciting gallery located in an historic warehouse. If you want the latest in contemporary Australian art practice, this is the place to come. Span runs a full exhibition program, with special exhibits often coinciding with the major arts festivals, as well as a program of talks and seminars, occasional dance performances and literary readings. Its audiovisual room explores the burgeoning multimedia field.

**The trail begins here**

Melbourne's **Golden Mile Heritage Trail** starts at the Immigration Museum. A $1 guide can be purchased here. The trail, marked by golden plaques in the pavement, takes in the city's key 'Gold Era' buildings and places of historical note. It ends at the Exhibition Building (above).

On the 2nd floor of Customs House the **Hellenic Antiquities Museum**, confirming Melbourne's special relationship with Greece, features exhibitions of antiquities loaned by the Greek Government. Open daily, 10am–5pm.

A number of architecturally interesting commercial buildings line Collins and Bourke Sts. The Gothic Revival splendour of the former ES&A Bank and Stock Exchange, now the **ANZ Bank** at 376–392 Collins St, should not be missed. Pamphlets available in the foyer provide notes for a self-guided tour of the building.

For a comprehensive guide to the history of the West End, see the Melbourne City Council's Heritage Walk No. 6, a 2-hr walking trail. Break for lunch, or start with breakfast at the grand Renaissance Revival **Railways Administration Building** on Spencer St, now a hotel with a pleasant outdoor cafe or at **The Rialto Block**, in Collins St between William and King Sts. Behind the lovely facades of this 19th century row of buildings are chic cafes and restaurants.

Above them towers the southern hemisphere's tallest building, the **Rialto Towers** which house the **Rialto Towers Observation Deck** on the building's 55th floor. The deck gives 360° views of Melbourne. A 20min video explains the development of Melbourne. There is a café and other amenities here too. Open daily, 10am till late.

Down from the Rialto, between Queen and Elizabeth Sts lies the **Hardware Precinct**, centred on Hardware Lane. A favourite of the legal fraternity, this area has a village atmosphere, with pavement cafes, bars and sandwich shops, and an array of specialist retailers. Photography, music and art shops mingle with travel agents and outdoor stores ready to equip travellers heading to Victoria's wilderness areas and ski resorts.

The **Royal Mint**, corner of William and Latrobe Sts is another fine example of the architecture of Marvellous Melbourne. It is the home of the **Royal Historical Society**. The society has a specialist collection of books, manuscripts, photographs, postcards and maps, and a vast array of material relating

*Rialto Towers.*

to the history of Melbourne and Victoria. It offers research advice and tours, as well as hosting lectures of public interest. Open Mon–Fri, 10am–4pm. Guided tours are held on Tues and Thurs at 11am. Ph: (03) 9670 1219

### Docklands Map 1 A3

Still under construction, Docklands will open Melbourne out to its natural waterfront at Victoria Harbour and the Yarra River. This huge development involves construction of over 2000 new dwellings, a marina, a technology park and 'Yarranova' — an entertainment precinct featuring a movie-based theme-park, a 20-screen megaplex, and film and TV studios. **Colonial Stadium**, opening early 2000, is a state of the art sporting complex seating 52 000 patrons, providing Australian Rules football and other sports with another spectacular venue.

The striking new **Bolte Bridge**, which spans both Victoria Harbour and the Yarra River, and the massive **Westgate Bridge** can be viewed here.

### Southbank Map 2 A1

Southbank is Melbourne's major arts and entertainment precinct located south of the Yarra River. **Southgate**, a stylish multi-levelled shopping precinct with scores of cafes and restaurants, shops and small galleries, fronts directly onto the river. Pleasure craft leave from here, and the atmosphere is one of lively activity. Walkways connect to either side of the river and under St Kilda Rd to the parklands lining Alexandra Ave and Kings Domain. Outdoor performances are frequent on the generous pavements and plazas in this area.

Further west, Southgate is connected by riverside walkways to the **Melbourne Casino and Entertainment Complex**. Upmarket designer label boutiques mingle with a host of shops, and the food court here offers an array of quality multicultural fare at low cost. The Casino is open 24-hrs. Pokie machines extend as far as the eye can see, while for the high rollers, luxury gaming rooms offer more discreet places to win or lose vast quantities of money. There are several cinemas, as well as bars and music venues in the finest traditions of Chicago jazz haunts and Las Vegas night clubs.

Behind the glitz lies the heart of Southbank. International performers and Australia's leading performing arts companies appear here at the **Victorian Arts Centre**, with its several theatre spaces, the **Melbourne Concert Hall** and the **Malthouse Theatre**. The **Melbourne Festival** is centred here (p.18).

The **Melbourne Symphony** runs an exciting program of classical and popular concerts from Feb-Nov. For a free program, Ph: (03) 9626 1111. The **Australian Ballet** performs at the Arts Centre's State Theatre in Feb, Mar, Jun and Sept, Ph: (03) 9684 8600. **Opera Australia** visits from Mar-Apr and Nov-Dec. Ph: (03) 9686 7477

The **Melbourne Theatre Company**, Victoria's leading theatre company, presents 11 productions each year, spanning classical and contemporary drama and comedy in the Arts Centre Playhouse and George Fairfax Studio. Ph: 1800 810 356. **Playbox** at the CUB

**Malthouse** is dedicated to the promotion of Australian theatre, offering a lively program of new plays and performance works. Ph: (03) 9685 5111

The Arts Centre and Concert Hall both offer tours – the buildings are themselves worthy of a visit. Designed by John Truscott, the Concert Hall's glowing interior – its pink marble walls evoking the colours of Central Australia – and its works by major Australian painters, speak eloquently of Australia's unique cultural heritage. Tours Mon-Fri, noon and 2.30pm from the Arts Centre shop.

The **Australian Centre for Contemporary Art** will relocate from its present address in Dallas Brooks Dve to the Malthouse Plaza Precinct, late 2000. Housed in a stunning red steel building, the centre will show visiting Australian and international contemporary visual art. It will also house the rehearsal studios of Melbourne's premier dance company, Chunky Moves. Ph: (03) 9654 6422

Visitors can also browse through the **Performing Arts Museum** at the Victorian Arts Centre. Whether it is gowns worn by famous divas or the shoes of chorus girls, the jackets of pop idols or elaborate stage sets, the museum has it all. Open Mon-Sat, 9am-11am and Sun, 10am-5pm, free of charge.

**Eat your way around**
Southgate's winter program of progressive dinners is a great way to sample this precinct's fine restaurants. Ph: (03) 9699 4311

*Melbourne casino and Entertainment Complex.*

**EG** will entertain you
For info about entertainment in Melbourne, the *Age* newspaper's *EG* is a must. A weekly publication, out on Fridays, it reviews and lists the range of Melbourne's music, film, theatre and dance events.

# Nightlife in Melbourne

As the sun sets and the lights go on, Melbourne's many bars and music venues — piano bars, jazz venues, alternative music lounges, nightclubs, friendly pubs — come alive across the CBD.

Near theatres in the Uptown precinct and on Southbank, late night bars abound. For pre- or post-theatre drinks try the **Gin Palace** at 190 Little Collins, or **Jacks Piano Bar**, a stylish cocktail bar, in the Crown Entertainment Complex. Try **Barfly's Cafe Bar** at 16 Bourke St, which has a 24-hr licence or **Rockman's Regency Hotel** bar, cnr Exhibition and Lonsdale Sts, open every night, till midnight. There are lots of options, and it's worth cruising around these precincts to get a feel for what's on offer.

**Bennetts Lane**, 25 Bennetts La, is the top venue for contemporary jazz, showcasing the work of Australian and international artists. Ph: (03) 9663 2856. **Ruby Red**, at 11 Drewery Lane, off Little Lonsdale St, is another intimate bar and music venue with a great atmosphere — usually playing funky jazz.

The **Stork Hotel**, 504 Elizabeth St, attracts a young clientele — backpackers and locals alike — to its Rhythm and Blues nights, while **The Lounge** at 243 Swanston St and **The Venue** at 168 Russell St also attract a young clientele. Here they feature a cool lounge atmosphere with alternative music.

The other major nightlife location is King St. Once quite seamy, this area has been revamped and now small, quieter bars can be found and enjoyed. There are several lively nightclubs — **Inflation**, **The Grainstore Tavern** and **Heaven** to name a few — side by side.

*Outside the National Gallery is Deborah Halpern's sculpture, 'Angel'.*

The **National Gallery**, which sits beside the Art Centre, is presently closed for redevelopment but is scheduled to reopen 2002. Until then a walk beside its famous moat to see Deborah Halpern's startling sculpture 'Angel' is recommended. This 2-headed, 3-legged sculpture has become a Melbourne icon. The **Victorian College of the Arts**, across Southbank Boulevard at 234 St Kilda Rd, is Victoria's premier arts college, with schools in art, drama, film and television, and music. Performances, screenings and exhibitions of students' work are open to the public throughout the year. Ph: (03) 9685 9300

The other major Southbank attraction is the **Polly Woodside Melbourne Maritime Museum**. Housed in some of the few remaining historic cargo sheds beside the ultramodern **Melbourne Exhibition Centre**, visitors can relive

Melbourne's maritime history. View photographs of graceful schooners tied up at Flinders St, and learn about the huge volume of trade that passes through the Port of Melbourne. *Polly Woodside* is the beautifully restored sailing ship, built in Belfast in 1885, and now moored in the Yarra River. It is open for inspection daily. Ph: (03) 9699 9760

## Parks and gardens

### *Flagstaff Gardens Map 1 B2*

At the northern end of the city, opposite the Queen Victoria Market, sit the Flagstaff Gardens. Here, on the hill, the early colonists could look out to Hobsons Bay and watch the sailing ships arrive. These gardens have extensive tended garden beds and lush lawns, as well as shady elms. There are tennis courts and a bowling club in the grounds.

### *Kings Domain Map 1 C4*

Lining St Kilda Rd south of the CBD, this expansive area of public parkland is a graceful setting for many historical monuments, fountains and Melbourne's floral clock. **Government House**, a national Trust property and residence of the Governor, stands high above the Domain with its imposing white tower. Tours Mon, Wed and Sat. Booking is essential. Ph: (03) 9654 5528

*Polly Woodside Melbourne Maritime Museum.*

The **Shrine of Remembrance** dominates this area. Built to commemorate the fallen of WWI, it is the focus of the ANZAC Day Parade. A perpetual flame burns outside, while inside the names of the war dead are listed. A visit to the Shrine is invariably moving. On the 11th hr of the 11th day of the 11th month, light strikes the grave of the unknown soldier entombed at the Shrine's centre. The public are welcome to climb the Shrine and take a guided tour. Open daily, 10am–5pm. The famous sculpture Simpson and his Donkey, portraying a WWI stretcher bearer, is a short distance away.

Close to the National Herbarium on Birdwood Ave sits **La Trobes Cottage**, 'Jolimont'. It speaks eloquently of Melbourne's humble beginnings. A prefabricated cottage, timber-clad with a shingle roof, it was brought from London by Governor La Trobe in 1839. Original furniture and period decor are on display. Open Mon, Wed, Sat and Sun, 11am–4pm.

### *Parliament House Gardens Map 1 C2*

Tucked away behind Parliament House are 9ha of glorious gardens. In classical European design, the gardens' curving paths, extensive lawns and colourful flower beds are a delight. Unfortunately, they are open to the public only once a year, usually in spring, as part of Parliament House open day.

A small section of Parliament Gardens, on the corner of Spring and Albert Sts, is reserved for the public. For visitors wanting

*Flagstaff Gardens.*

**We were framed first**

A new dining room was added to La Trobe's cottage in the 1830s by a local builder. Relocated to its present site in 1998, its stud walls were revealed. Now historians argue that Australia originated the timber stud frame, a technique used throughout the world. It was previously thought to have been an American invention.

## Open-air fun

The Royal Botanic Gardens run open-air cinema and theatre productions in summer, including performances of *Wind in the Willows*.

## Ancestral land

Aboriginal guides lead tours of the Royal Botanical Gardens along the Aboriginal Heritage Walk. They talk about ancestral land that the gardens now occupy and also traditional plants.

to take a load off their feet, there are seats and inviting lawns. Coles Fountain, a modern water sculpture, provides a cooling backdrop on a hot summer's day.

### Royal Botanic Gardens

Acclaimed as the most beautiful and botanically interesting botanical garden in Australia, the Royal Botanic Gardens cover 36ha, tucked behind the Kings Domain. Established in 1846, its design and botanical history is synonymous with Baron Ferdinand von Mueller, whose imprint on Australian botany has been profound.

Magnificent vistas have been created around a series of lakes, populated by black swans and other water fowl. Many kms of paths curve past sweeping lawns, through fine avenues of European and other exotic trees and shrubs, to groves of Australian trees and to rare specimens, as well as to the romantic nooks and crannies which make this garden such a delightful retreat.

There are entrances close to the Sidney Myer Music Bowl, Domain Rd,

*The tranquil Royal Botanic Gardens.*

and at the corner of Alexandra Ave and Anderson St, South Yarra. **Observatory Gate** on Birdwood Ave is the best point for visitors wanting to orient themselves, and is the place to book tours. Visitors can browse the literature here while having coffee in the Observatory Gate Café. The Royal Botanic Gardens Tea Rooms is located in the middle of the gardens, looking out across the lake. The

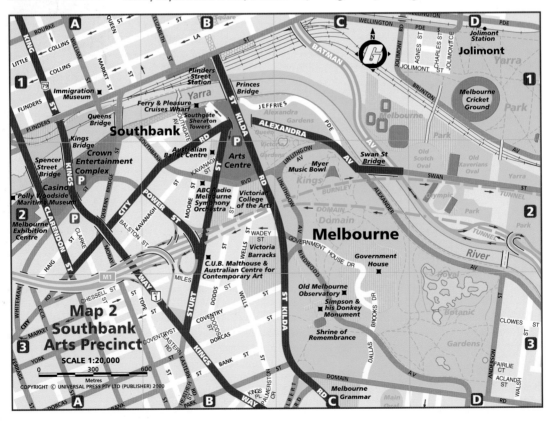

*The historic Royal Arcade.*

City Cycle Tours offers another way to see Melbourne by bike. Short and long tours to various destinations are offered, passing through many of Melbourne's varied precincts, with rests at major historical attractions. Ph: (03) 9585 5343

### Health and fitness centres
There are numerous gyms within the CBD. The Victorian Fitness Industry Association recommends the **City Club Health and Fitness Centre** at 123 Collins St, Ph: (03) 9653 4894, **Lifestyle Fitness Centre**, at 500 Bourke St, Ph: (03) 9670 9291, where casual visits cost around $20 a session. Check the *Yellow Pages* for other health and fitness centres. See also, Melbourne City Baths (below).

### Shopping complexes and arcades
For detailed information on Melbourne's famous shopping complexes and arcades, see Melbourne's CBD (p.19).

### Swimming
The historic **Melbourne City Baths** (*Map 1, B2*) at 420 Swanston St is a great place to get into the swim. Its 2 pools and private baths offer both relaxation and the chance to keep up that exercise regime. The baths have a fully equipped gym with affordable casual rates. Open weekdays, 6am-10pm, weekends 8am-6pm. Ph: (03) 9663 5888

**Find yourself a possum in the park**
Summer Fun in the Parks, a program of the Melbourne City Council, runs possum tours in the Fitzroy Gardens each summer. Ph: (03) 9658 8713

*City Baths.*

gardens are open daily, 7.30am-5.30pm, Apr-Oct, and 8.30pm Nov-Mar.

From Observatory Gate visitors can also take a tour of the observatory and learn about the crucial astronomical work done by Australian scientists in mapping the southern skies. Ph: (03) 9252 2300

### Treasury Gardens
Sitting beside the old Treasury Building, these gardens adjoin the Fitzroy Gardens (p.50). They are an ideal retreat from the busy city. The John F Kennedy Memorial is located here. Possums abound in the elm trees, and can be seen in the early evening.

## Recreational activities
### Ballooning
Fabulous hot air balloons are often seen floating across the Melbourne skyline. What a great way to get a view of the busy metropolis beside the bay. **Balloon Sunrise** operates flights daily, weather permitting, leaving around 5am. Ph: (03) 9427 7596

### Cycling
Melbourne is an ideal city for cycling. The paths that snake along the Yarra River and around the Kings Domain are especially scenic. Maps available from visitor info centres show access points onto the **Capital City Trail** and **Main City Trail** bike path and to other paths leading out of the city. These extensive cycling paths extend for many kms in several directions.

For bike hire, try **Fitzroy Cycles** at 224 Swanston St. Ph: (03) 9639 3511, or **Hire a Bike** at Southgate. Ph: 019 429 000

## Fun for the young
★ City Circle Tram (p.14)
★ Cycling along the Yarra (p.31)
★ Fire Services Museum (p.23)
★ Kids Tours Melbourne (p.16)
★ Melbourne City Baths (p.31)
★ Old Melbourne Gaol (p.22)
★ Polly Woodside Melbourne Maritime Museum (p.28)
★ Postmaster Gallery (p.24)
★ Rialto Towers Observation Deck (p.26)
★ River Cruises (p.15)

Left: **AFL at the Melbourne Cricket Ground.**
Right: **Royal Exhibition Building.**

# North of the Yarra

**M**elbourne's inner north exudes creative energy. Part sophistication, part bohemian grunge, part old working-class and overwhelmingly multicultural, it is a fascinating urban mix. There are vibrant shopping strips in Brunswick, Fitzroy, Richmond and Collingwood, as well as an array of entertainment venues and cultural activities. Galleries and theatres, music and comedy venues, not to mention good bookshops and a vast array of eating houses, are the attractions of this vibrant area. Lively ethnic cultures – Arab, Turkish, Greek, Italian, Vietnamese – distinguish its various neighbourhoods, the origin of many of the area's well-known festivals.

The inner north is also known for its gracious Victorian architecture, its elm-lined 19th century parks and gardens, and some major sporting and recreational facilities. The Melbourne Cricket Ground, the Melbourne Museum, the Royal Exhibition Building and Melbourne Zoo are all located in the inner north.

In the outer north, suburbia nestles into the hills. There are a number of pretty little towns on the rural fringe, with creeks and trails to explore, as well as local markets, galleries and places of historical interest. While hardly on the tourist trail, the industrial west of Melbourne – the location of Australia's largest port – provides a different angle on the sprawling conurbation of Melbourne. Its docks and waterways, heavy industrial complexes and working-class suburbs have their own story to tell.

## ℹ Tourist information

**Victoria Tourism Info Service**
Ph: 13 28 42

**Bundoora Park Visitor Info Centre**
Bundoora Park
Plenty Rd, Bundoora
Ph: (03) 9462 4079

**City Experience Centre**
Melbourne Town Hall
Cnr Swanston and Little Collins Sts
Melbourne 3000

**Victorian Visitor Info Centre**
Cnr Swanston and Little Collins Sts
Melbourne 3000

**Whittlesea Visitor Info Centre**
Cnr Beech St and Church St
Whittlesea 3757
Ph: (03) 9716 1866

**Yarra Community Access Points**
Ph: (03) 9205 5433

**Websites**
www. melbourne org
www.tourism.vic.gov.au
www.melbourne.citysearch.com.au

## Must see, must do

★ **Australian Gallery of Sport and Olympic Museum** (p.43)
★ **Brunswick St** (p.43)
★ **Fitzroy Gardens** (p.50)
★ **Lygon St** (p.39)
★ **Melbourne Zoo** (p.44)
★ **Melbourne Wholesale Market Experience** (p.48)
★ **Melbourne Museum** (p.40)

## Radio stations

**3AW:** 1278 AM
**3LO:** 774 AM
**3RRR:** 102.7 FM
**FOX FM:** 101.9 FM
**Radio National:** 621 AM

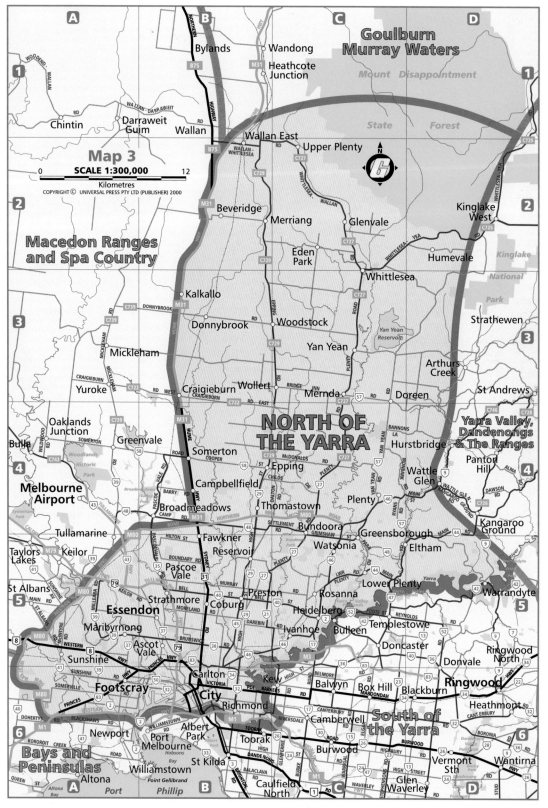

## Natural features

The Yarra River is the area's dominant natural feature, wending its way down from the Gt Dividing Range in the east, meeting with numerous smaller tributaries and making its way slowly through flat inner Melbourne. At Yarra Bend in Kew and Fairfield, it has cut a dramatic meandering path through wattle-studded cliffs and remnant yellow-gum woodlands. The Merri and Darebin Creeks, meeting the Yarra in Clifton Hill and Fairfield, provide more welcome green relief in this urban landscape. In recent years the regeneration of these waterways close to the city has led to the return of native birds and animals, notably the azure kingfisher and swamp wallaby. In the north-east, the Plenty River joins the Yarra at Templestowe, where river flats provide a number of recreational possibilities.

Directly north of Melbourne, the rural shire of Whittlesea is set in gentle undulating countryside, rising to the Gt Dividing Range near Kilmore and Kinglake. Small creeks and nature reserves together with state forest preserve native bushland and its precious flora and fauna. In the west, the Maribyrnong River has cut its path over thousands of years through the dry Keilor plains, known for their deep creek and river bed gorges.

*Fitzroy is Melbourne's oldest suburb.*

## History

'North of the Yarra'. It has never competed with 'South of the Yarra' and all that this phrase connotes for Melburnians. Historically, the *nouveau riche* moved south and east of the river, taking up the high ground. From Toorak and Kew, where the big houses were built along the river, the middle classes could literally look down upon the travails of Collingwood, Richmond and Fitzroy, where textiles factories, breweries, foundries and printeries all jostled one beside the other.

These inner north suburbs are some of the oldest parts of Melbourne, Fitzroy its oldest suburb. While traces of early rural settlement remain, the Victorian

*Fairfield Boat House at Yarra Bend is a great place to relax and have a picnic.*

**The brown is tannin — promise!** Melburnians joke about their river flowing upside down — with the mud at the top. Its muddy colour is caused by run-off, but it is considered a healthy river. Before settlement it was a glassy dark brown, caused by tannin leaching from the bush around it.

architecture which so defines this area is testament to Melbourne's early urban sprawl, triggered by the great bursts of development associated with the goldrush and 'Marvellous Melbourne'. Fine terraces grace the streets of East Melbourne, Carlton and Fitzroy, the residences of local patricians. In Collingwood and Richmond some of the tiniest workers cottages still remain. These working-class suburbs, home of the Irish and Anglo poor, were to become home to successive waves of post-war migrants – Italian, Greek, Lebanese, Turkish, Vietnamese, and more.

Today, while much of the inner north is gentrified, areas like Brunswick and Coburg, on Sydney Rd, remain strongly working-class. In the west, Melbourne's docklands were to grow up close to the mouths of the Yarra and Maribyrnong rivers, superseding the historic port town of Williamstown. The west would also see massive mid 20th century industrial development, making it Melbourne's industrial heartland.

## Getting there

### By public transport
**Inner north**

The inner north is well-serviced by trams, trains and buses. Visitors should consult the Met's Melbourne Tram and Train Maps, which are available from info centres and train stations and are also reprinted on pp.8, 9.

For Carlton, visitors should take the Swanston St tram to Melbourne University. For Richmond, trams leave Collins St for Victoria St; and Flinders St for Swan St and Bridge Rd. For Fitzroy, the no. 11 tram from Collins St travels along Brunswick St, while the no. 86 tram from Bourke St will take visitors to Smith St and Clifton Hill, and all the way to Bundoora Park. (p.51).

**Outer north**

Trains regularly leave the City Loop for Epping. on the Epping line, and for Eltham on the Hurstbridge Line. For Whittlesea, take the no. 86 tram to Bundoora, and Dysons connecting bus no. 562. Dysons Bus Lines, ph: (03) 9467 6111

*Fringe Parade.*

*The Melbourne International Flower Show.*

### By road

Plenty Rd, the main route to Whittlesea, is reached via the middle suburbs of Northcote and Preston along Lower Plenty Rd. For some of the smaller towns, and for direct access to Mt Disappointment, take the Hume Hwy, via Sydney Rd.

## Getting around

Several tour operators offer cultural tours of the inner north. **Creatours** take interesting walking tours, visiting galleries and artist studios in Richmond and Fitzroy. Ph: (03) 9822 0556. **Cultural Capitol Tours** offers ½-1 day tours, including the 'Bohemian Ramble', which introduces visitors to the delights of inner suburban cafe society. Ph: (03) 9347 3039

## Festivals and events

### Midsumma Festival

Melbourne's Gay and Lesbian Festival, held over Jan each year, features a street parade and ball, and various arts events. Ph: (03) 9525 4746. These include **Movies Under the Stars, the Melbourne Queer Film and Video Festival**, screened at the Amphitheatre, Fairfield Park. Ph: (03) 9510 5576

### Victoria St Lunar New Year Festival

In the heart of the Vietnamese quarter, this lunar New Year festival is a lively affair, with dragons, music and plenty of exotic streetside food. Check the daily press for an exact date in Jan. Ph: (03) 9428 9078

### Brunswick Music Festival and Brunswick Street Party

The Brunswick Music Festival is a showcase for ethnic, folk, acoustic and traditional music, with local, interstate and international musicians. Three wks of events start with the Brunswick Street Party – in Sydney Rd, Brunswick – on the first Sun in Mar. Ph: (03) 9388 1460

### The Melbourne International Flower and Garden Show

This international horticultural event, held mid-Apr, attracts 1000s of visitors to its 100s of stalls, spectacular flower displays, demonstrations and seminars. Held at the Royal Exhibition Building and surrounding Carlton Gardens, it is a beauty to behold. Ph: (03) 9639 2333

### Boite Winter Festival

Many of the Boite Winter Festival's 80 plus events are held in venues in the inner north. International artists, together with local musicians and ethnic communities explore the rich roots of world music in performance and workshops. A large component of the festival is devoted to acapella singing. Ph: (03) 9417 3550

### Melbourne Fringe Festival

The epitome of Brunswick St, Fitzroy, this quirky, creative, energetic festival comes to town in Sept–Oct each year. The young and hopeful trial their plays, comedy, poetry, fashion and art. The infamous street parade reflects the street back to itself – provocative floats, grunge fashion, the Brunswick St Waiter's Race, avant-garde food and music. Don't miss it! Ph: (03) 9481 5111

### Yarra Moonlantern Festival

Held around Sept on the occasion of the full moon, the Yarra Moonlantern Festival echoes the traditional Indo-Chinese harvest celebration in which families make moon lanterns, eat special moon cakes, and tell traditional stories. It is held on the Nth Richmond Housing

Estate on the cnr of Lennox and Highett Sts, Richmond. Ph: (03) 9429 5477

### Lygon St Festa

Held in late Oct the Lygon St Festa is one of Melbourne's oldest street festivals, reflecting the long history of Italian migration to Melbourne. A real atmosphere of Carnivale takes over, with street performances, food and more food, activities for children, and a program of stage performaces. Ph: (03) 9348 1299

### Hispanic Fiesta

One large block of Johnston St Fitzroy is closed off in Nov for this small but lively fiesta. Located in the Hispanic quarter beside the flamenco bars, Spanish restaurants and Iberian food shops, it is a great opportunity to watch a little tango, listen to fabulous guitar playing, and eat paella. Ph: (03) 9417 6151

### Whittlesea Show

The Whittlesea Show is one of the closest country agricultural shows to Melbourne. Held over the first weekend in Nov, it is a great family day out. Ph: (03) 9716 2835

### Hmong New Year Festival

Six hundred Hmong people from the Indochinese highlands of Laos live in the inner northern suburbs. At the end of the 12th lunar month they get together to

**Let's shed light**
Twice awarded the Australia Day Event of the Year, the **Yarra Moonlantern Festival** is devoted to community understanding and cultural diversity. Thousands of people come to enjoy lantern-making workshops, multicultural performances, food and art.

*Brunswick St, Fitzroy, hosts the annual Melbourne Fringe Festival.*

**Family fun at CERES.**

celebrate their language and culture with traditional ballgames, food and music. They welcome others to join them at Deep Rock Oval, Yarra Park. Ph: (03) 9417 2553

# Main localities and towns
## *Inner north*
### Brunswick *Map 3 B5*

Sydney Rd is the heart and soul of Brunswick and its northern neighbour, Coburg. This long shopping strip, while depressed in places, provides a fascinating window onto a part of Melbourne's intriguing multicultural mix. Where the Italians and Greeks once dominated in these suburbs, the Lebanese, Turkish and Arabic communities are now very prominent.

This means great food shopping, cheap exotic restaurants, cafes and cake shops, as well as cheap shopping generally. Ali Baba's Variety Store sits beside Melbourne's best Turkish restaurants, dark Greek tavernas, Franco Cozzo's modern rococo bedroom furniture and boutiques displaying extravagant Italian wedding dresses!

At the **Mediterranean Food Store**, an Italian supermarket at 482 Sydney Rd, there is a huge selection of cheap, authentic Mediterranean produce. **Alaysha**, at 555 Sydney Rd, Sydney Rd, is a very popular Turkish restaurant offering great family meals at good prices. The most sublime *baklava*, or Lebanese pastries, are available at **Balha's Pastry** at 478 Sydney Rd.

For visitors walking the strip, **AI Bakery** at 643 Sydney Rd is a welcoming place to have a coffee and freshly baked Lebanese herb bread. Lebanese music plays in the background as the baking goes on in a large wood-fired oven.

Belly dancing is the other great attraction of Sydney Rd. Visitors could try the **The Golden Terrace** restaurant, or the **Eastern Nights Restaurant** which holds a regular Bellydance Club Night, at 874 Sydney Rd. Ph: (03) 9383 4488. There are fresh produce markets too, in both Brunswick and Coburg.

The **Mechanics Institute Performing Arts Centre**, at the intersection of Sydney

Rd and Glenlyon Rd, is at the centre of the renowned Brunswick Music Festival (p.37), and runs an exciting program of theatre, dance and music, usually with a multicultural flavour. Ph: (03) 9388 1460. The new **Counihan Gallery in Brunswick**, 233 Sydney Rd, houses an extensive collection of visual art, and will continue the Mechanics Institute tradition of sponsoring special exhibitions, often coinciding with community festivals such as the Koorie and women's festivals. Ph: (03) 9240 2498

There is access to bike and walking paths along the **Merri Ck Trail** in East Brunswick, connecting to Nth Fitzroy and Clifton Hill. **CERES**, or the Centre for Education, Research and Environmental Strategies, sits on the bank of the Merri Creek, at 8 Lee St, East Brunswick. Ph: (03) 9387 2609. Open daily from 9am–5pm. This is a terrific place for a family outing. Visitors can learn about innovative horticultural techniques and new energy technologies. There is an African village here too, vegetable gardens and various farm animals. **CERES Nursery** is open daily 10am–5pm, and CERE'S whole food café, 10am–3pm.

**Pentridge Gaol** is located in Coburg on the corner of Sydney Rd and Bell St. The old 'bluestone college' is a formidable 19th century building, with high stone walls and guards' towers. Recently closed, it will be redeveloped as a new housing development, with a tourist precinct.

### Carlton *Map 4*

Once Melbourne's bohemian quarter, full of student digs and seedy cafes, today Carlton is an upmarket shopping centre, stylishly Italian. It sports many wonderful Italian cafes and restaurants. Italian shoes and men's and women's fashions are on display in trendy boutiques. There are icecream shops and gift shops, cinemas and bookshops.

**Readings**, at 309 Lygon St, is one of Melbourne's premier bookstores, and is open late for those people who like night-time browsing. The **Nova Cinema** in Lygon St is known for its arthouse, as well as general release, movies.

**La Mama** theatre, at 205 Faraday St is a tiny venue seating around 40 people. Important in the renaissance of Australian theatre in the 1970s, it continues to run an exciting program of experimental theatre by up and coming new talent. Ph: (03) 9347 6948. The **Bridget McDonnell Gallery** is around the corner at 130 Faraday St. A commercial gallery, it specialises in modern Australian painting. Ph: (03) 9347 1700

Carlton offers so many options if you're looking to eat. **Papa Ginos** is a much-loved, traditional *pizzeria*. **Brunetti's Cakes** in Faraday St is a fine place to lunch on *calzone*, or to indulge that craving for little cakes and icecream. Part of Melbourne's 1970s wine renaissance, **Jimmy Watsons Wine Bar**, near the cnr of Elgin St, is now a Melbourne institution.

The University of Melbourne sits on Carlton's border with Parkville (p.44). Taking a walk north past the university colleges under an avenue of elm trees or a tram ride from Elgin St, visitors will come to the **Melbourne General Cemetery** in **Nth Carlton**. Sublime angels hover over the graves of early settlers in many weed-covered corners of the cemetery. In contrast to this ethereal view, the Elvis Presley memorial, erected by local fans, is an eccentric attraction to which many make the pilgrimage.

**Melbourne Cemetery Tours** offers a range of fascinating theme tours of the cemetery, all very '19th century'. Try 'The Gentle Sex', 'Trade Unionists and the 8-hr Day', 'Law and Order' and 'Medicos and Misadventure'. Ph: (03) 9872 5492

The cemetery borders extensive playing fields, including public tennis courts and a terrific children's playground on the cnr of Princes Park Dve and MacPherson St in Princes Hill, also home to the Carlton Football Club at **Optus Oval**. The *Nth Carlton and Princes Hill Walk*, a map with photos and architectural notes, is available from the Community Access Pt on the cnr of Rathdowne and Fenwick Sts, Nth Carlton, or from the City of Yarra. Ph: (03) 9205 5063

In Nth Carlton, the **Rathdowne St** village has a very pleasant ambience. Not

*Alfresco dining in Lygon St.*

as busy as Lygon St, its cafes, book and antique shops offer a full afternoon's browsing. The **Rathdowne St Food Store**, 617 Rathdowne St, is an ideal place to take a break, serving an exceptional breakfast and gourmet eat-in or take-away lunches.

**Sth Carlton** borders the CBD and has a number of places of interest. In a suburb renowned for its lovely Victorian terrace houses, **Drummond St**, Sth Carlton has many outstanding Victorian buildings. Around the corner, the dour old **Victorian Trades Hall** sits opposite the **Eight Hour Day Memorial**, the starting place of many a Melbourne street demonstration. The **New International Bookshop**, located in the Trades Hall building at the corner of Victoria and Lygon Sts, offers a good capuccino while you browse through its collection of texts.

The **Royal Exhibition Building**, spanning the block between Rathdowne and Nicholson Sts, is a Melbourne icon. Set in the lovely Carlton Gardens (p.50) and built in 1880 for the World Fair, its strikingly beautiful dome sits high on the northern skyline. Today it is an events venue, housing concerts and balls, as well as many expos, like the Melbourne International Flower and Garden Show and the Contemporary Arts Fair. A place of architectural interest and many an

**Treading the boards**

La Mama opened its doors in 1967, cresting the wave of Australia's New Wave Theatre. Jack Hibberd, David Williamson, Barry Oakley and John Romeril all had plays performed at La Mama in its early years.

*The ultra modern Melbourne Museum.*

and *Everest* on its huge screen, it is a favourite with children. Ph: (03) 663 5454

## Clifton Hill *Map 3 B5*

Clifton Hill is a pretty Victorian neighbourhood. Its small shopping area on Queens Pde is gracefully arranged under wide Victorian verandahs. There are antique shops and children's toy shops, gourmet fish and chips shops and many cafes. Merri Ck is accessible at the High St Bridge, or better, from the Esplanade close to where the Merri Ck meets the Yarra River. Walk, cycle, rollerblade or drive to **Dights Falls** beside Trenery Cres (p.49). The **Quarries Park Play Space**, an adventure playground, is located on the bike path near Ramsden St.

## Collingwood *Map 3 B6*

One of Melbourne's old working-class suburbs, Collingwood is not Melbourne's first tourist destination. But it has its charm. **Smith St** is a hub of activity – some of it seedy – with cheap shopping, eccentric specialty shops and some terrific cafes and restaurants.

Melissa's is a local favourite for a lunch of Greek *spanikopita*. The **Grace Darling** is a lovely restored pub on the corner of Smith and Peel Sts, which often has jazz at night. The shocking pink, postmodern hairdresser **Lure** isn't cheap, but the unhealthy pink glow is mesmerising and the cutting first class. North of Johnston St, a bevy of

intriguing historical anecdote, it is well worth taking a tour. Ph: (03) 9270 5000

The Exhibition Building dome might be high, but as every local resident will say, not high enough to compete with the thrusting 'blade' of the new **Melbourne Museum** next door. This ultra modern construction sits side by side with ornate Victoriana. The Museum, opening in 2000, will house state of the art exhibitions with an emphasis on interactive displays, including an extensive Aboriginal collection and performances with a focus on the Koorie culture of south-eastern Australia. Ph: (03) 9651 6777

The **IMAX Cinema** is also located in the museum complex. Showing a range of documentaries like *Mysteries of Egypt*

*Fitzroy Gardens in East Melbourne is a beautiful park for walking and relaxing.*

high-quality factory shops, including **Nike** and **Piping Hot**, stretch down to Alexander Pde.

There are several galleries close by. **Oxcart** is a large warehouse refurbished as an artist-run studio complex. Its **Pre-View Gallery**, at 64 Wellington St, allows visitors to sample resident artists' work at special exhibitions. Ph: (03) 419 370 880. **Australian Galleries**, at 35 Derby St, is a large commercial gallery, one of the first in Melbourne, dealing in contemporary Australian art. It is open Tues–Sat, 10am–6pm. Ph: (03) 9417 4303

The **Collingwood Children's Farm** offers a dramatic break from the inner urban scene. It occupies 7ha of paddocks and gardens located in the grounds of the old Abbotsford Convent on the banks of the Yarra River. Children can wander by the pig pens and rabbit hutches, joust with the goats or take a tumble in the long grass. The cows are milked at 10am and 4pm. Open 9–5pm daily, at St Helliers St, Abbotsford. Ph: (03) 9205 5469

*Children's Farm.*

### East Melbourne *Map 1 D2*

This small pocket of prime real estate, with its large Victorian homes, is a most sought after residential location and a very charming area through which to

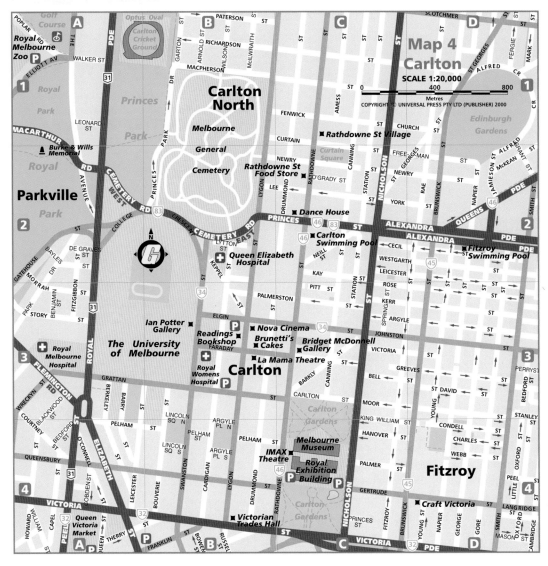

**Delicious indulgences**

Cafe affogatto is a Brunswick St specialty. A scoop of vanilla icecream in double expresso, doused in Frangelico or any other liqueur of your choice, it is superb. At the Gypsy Bar it costs $7, but it's worth it.

*The Melbourne Cricket Ground (MCG) is home to cricket and Australian Rules Football.*

stroll. It is home to Melbourne's glorious **Fitzroy Gardens**, as well as **Yarra Park** at Jolimont.

To see the interior of one of East Melbourne's elegant residences, visitors can do no better than visit the **Johnston Collection**. This magnificent collection of fine furniture and decorative arts, is the legacy of William Robert Johnston, an international antique dealer. It can be viewed unimpeded by restraining ropes in the house just as William Johnston left it.

Open Mon-Fri. For times, ph: (03) 9416 2515.

The **Melbourne Cricket Ground**, temple to Australian Cricket and Australian Rules Football, is also located in East Melbourne. One of the world's great stadiums, it has a capacity of over 100 000 people. It has some great

# The Melbourne Cricket Ground

Cricket was a passion from the earliest days of European settlement. The Melbourne Cricket Club played at various locations before the MCG was established on its present site in 1854. Australia's first international cricket match was played here in 1862, won by the English, and the first Australian Test match in 1877. Meanwhile, the Melbourne Football Club, formed in 1858, had taken up residence at the MCG in that year and was to become the Melbourne establishment's pride and joy.

The MCG is a crucial part of the iconography of Australia's unique game of football. Australia's most famous ground, it has traditionally staged the Grand Final, every team's holy grail. The origins of Australian Rules Football are obscure, but today the scholars suggest that it has both Gaelic and Aboriginal origins. The Koories of south-eastern Australia are said to have played a game remarkably like the game we see today, using a ball made out of possum skins.

For those who want to sample Melbourne's twin grand passions, tickets can be purchased through Ticketmaster, Ph: (03) 136 100, or at the gate by general admission. Football commences the first weekend in Apr, with passions rising to Grand Final on the last Sat in Sept. Cricket takes up on 1 Oct with Sheffield Shield matches and occasional 1-day matches, including international 1-day games late in the season. The highlight of the cricket season is the Test, traditionally played from Boxing Day over 5 days.

architecture too. The **Great Southern Stand** was redesigned for the World Cup Final by Melbourne's Daryl Jackson and opened in 1992, and is well worth viewing from Brunton Ave.

The **Australian Gallery of Sport and Olympic Museum** is located at the MCG. Open daily, 10am–4pm, its has 3 levels of expert displays, including the Australian Cricket Hall of Fame and an IOC-endorsed exhibition tracing the history of the modern Olympics. Tours of the stadium and gallery are also available. Ph: (03) 9657 8879

### Fitzroy *Map 4 D4*

Cheaper and more relaxed than Lygon St – where it helps to look elegant – Brunswick St's emphasis is on cool. The passions that drove the residents of Carlton in its bohemian heyday, have transferred here long ago, and it is vibrant with young fashion, cheap, innovative food, galleries and quirky boutiques, selling everything from designer coffee to handmade furniture.

The retro look is everywhere. Window shop at the **Ministry of Style** at 348 Brunswick St or **Out of the Closet** across the road at 237 Brunswick St. Take a strong cafe latte at the original postmodern cafe, **Marios**, just north of Johnston St, which doubles as a small gallery space featuring the work of young artists. The **Gypsy Bar** at 334 Brunswick St is a great late night haunt.

Brunswick St's favourite lunch and breakfast house is **Babka Bakery Cafe**, at no. 358. This Central European establishment serves blintzes and dumplings, Russian hors d'oeuvres and borscht. For picnicking try the **Edinburgh Gardens** in Nth Fitzroy or **Carlton Gardens** just a block away (p.50).

**Casa Iberica** on the corner of Johnston and Fitzroy Sts is a Spanish and Portuguese grocery, ideal for purchasing picnic food. It sits in Fitzroy's small Hispanic quarter where flamenco bars open late, and several good Spanish restaurants serve exotic dishes.

Brunswick St also has plenty to offer the overseas traveller looking for unusual gifts. **On Shore**, at 247 Brunswick St, sells

*Fitzroy Nursery.*

the 'produce of Australia' – everything from Australian chocolates featuring Wattle Seed and Illawarra Plum, to happy little winged cushions, cards, and fine woodwork in Australian timbers.

Across the street, visitors shouldn't miss **Vasette** – avant-garde florist – with its huge fibreglass honey bees swarming up the wall and an overpowering scent trailing onto the street. The **Fitzroy Nursery**, 390 Brunswick St, is another floral delight.

There are also a number of book and music shops. The **Brunswick St Bookstore**'s trendy selection and shiny leather couch beckon weary travellers, while the **Grub St Bookshop** offers the chance to find that long-lost favourite or

*Marios cafe in Brunswick St features strong coffee and works of art.*

**Uni of Melbourne.**

out-of-print edition in its extensive secondhand book collection.

At the **Mary Mackillop Centre**, 11 Brunswick St, visitors can peruse memorabilia associated with Australia's only beatified saint, who worked with the poor of Fitzroy. Ph: (03) 9419 9273

### Parkville *Map 4 A2*

Parkville is an island of pristine Victorian architecture, bordered by the University of Melbourne to the east and **Royal Park** to the west.

The **University of Melbourne**, the city's most prestigious, is an interesting melange of architectural styles, from mock Oxford, dating from the late 19th century, to 1960s skyscrapers and late 1990s pastiche. The university's **Ian Potter Museum of Art** illustrates the latter. This vibrant gallery exhibits both touring shows and pieces from the university's extensive collection. Entrance is via Swanston St, under a large relief sculpture, a tumble of torsos and architectural motifs that jut out above the pavement. Open Tues–Sun, 10am–5pm; Thurs open till 9pm.

The several university gardens, especially the **System Garden** beside the Botany School, offer very pleasant places to sit and relax. The university cafetaria and coffee lounge offer an array of affordable, satisfying meals with a multicultural flavour.

The **Royal Melbourne Zoo** is located in Royal Park (p.50). Australia's oldest zoo, it has also been at the forefront of reform. Its new habitat zones are especially appealing. The Butterfly House and Gorilla Rainforest are key attractions, as are its giant pandas and Australian native fauna reserve. The Royal Melbourne Zoo is one of Melbourne's premier attractions. Open daily, 9am–5pm, and Thurs–Sun in Jan and Feb, 9am–7pm. Ph: (03) 9285 9300

The Zoo also stages the very popular open-air 'Zoo Twilights' program in Jan and Feb, featuring jazz and big band artists. It is wonderful outing for the whole family.

### Richmond *Map 3 B6*

Once known as 'Struggletown', this old working-class suburb is another Victorian quarter, graciously gentrified in many areas, but retaining its old charm and multicultural dynamism. Richmond sits beside the Yarra River, and it was along the river that early settlement proceeded in the 1840s.

Close to the river old factories have been refurbished as the glamour showrooms of a number of international companies. Houses in this area close to Swan and Chapel St are often the smallest of the working-men's cottages. A walk down **Richmond Hill** on the now upmarket Bridge Rd reveals what must

**A deadly trail**
Fired by the thought of crossing the unknown interior of Australia, Burke and Wills set off from Melbourne in 1860 to reach the Gulf of Carpentaria. By Sept 1861 the two heroes and all but one of their party were dead, perished in the desert near Coopers Creek.

**Bargain buying by the book**
The *Bargain Shoppers Guide to Melbourne*, available at newsagencies, lists cut-price markets, auctions, warehouses, factories and bazaars.

*The Melbourne Zoo's Butterfly House features many beautiful species.*

*Shopping in Victoria St, Richmond.*

*Richmond Hill Cafe.*

Bridge Rd, offers a pleasant break from the fashion trail.

Visitors to Melbourne should not miss the **Richmond Hill Cafe and Larder**, 48–52 Bridge Rd. Run by Melbourne's doyenne of good food, Stephanie Alexander, it is a very special place to have breakfast, brunch or dinner. Visitors can also browse in the larder and cheese shop or flip through one of Alexander's gorgeous food books. Ph: (03) 9421 2808

Victoria St is the central focus of Melbourne's Vietnamese quarter. Vietnamese music floats on the air, as do the pungent, earthy aromas that emanate from the various retailers. Fresh, even live, fish and exotic shellfish are a specialty. Live crabs, flown in from Darwin each Sun, are a great treat. Hearty bowls of noodle soup from the many small cafes cost around $6.

**Thy Thy Restaurant** at 142 Victoria St is a busy, inexpensive eating house. **Thy Thy 2**, 116 Victoria St, provides a more upmarket setting for the same great food.

Richmond is also a thriving arts precinct. Numerous small galleries are within walking distance between Swan St and Bridge Rd. The *Richmond Gallery Walk*, a pamphlet put out by Yarra City Council, features five galleries specialising in Australian and international painting, sculpture, Aboriginal art, works on paper and photography. Entry to the galleries is free, but remember, these galleries are closed in Jan. The pamphlet is available from the Richmond Town Hall in Bridge Rd or the Richmond Library in Church St.

*Richmond Heritage Walk* is also available from the same locations.

The **Capital City Bike Trail** (p.31) passes through Richmond along the river around **Burnley**, taking in many scenic views of the Yarra. The **Yarra Scenic Drive**, which commences in the Kings Domain area, also follows this route along the river, past the **Burnley Sidings**, a series of riverbank parks and playing fields. The **Burnley Golf Course** and **Burnley Gardens** (p.52), beside the Burnley Horticultural College, are located here. These are very pretty

have been a bustling trading centre in the 1850s. Plaques on shops and stores give the names of retailers and tradesmen and the goods and services once on offer there.

The three major centres in Richmond are **Swan St**, **Bridge Rd** and **Victoria St**. Sat and Sun are both busy shopping days. Swan and Bridge are famous for designer label shopping, especially designer-label clearance shops.

Near the cnr of Swan and Chapel Sts, Jag, Diesel, Kamikazee and many other young labels offer their out-of-season stock at affordable prices. Heading towards the city on Swan St, the perilously domed old-style variety store **Dimmeys** offers the biggest bargains on earth. Visitors wanting gourmet coffee and cake can't do better than **Cafe La Barbera**, just across the road.

At the East Melbourne end of Bridge Rd, trendy designer boutiques sell the latest women's and men's fashions. What seems to be an endless line of upmarket shops, cafes and warehouse clearance stores stretches down the hill. Anthea Crawford sits close to R M Williams Boots and Moleskins. Esprit is just up from the Paddington Coat Company and down from Bendon. **The Bookshelf**, 116

**Finding Aboriginal texts**

**The Bookshelf** on Bridge Rd carries the world's largest selection of books by and about Aboriginal people. It also sells audiocassettes, tribal area maps, posters and cards, many illustrated by Aboriginal artists.

# Nightlife in the inner north

This area hosts art and general release cinemas, comedy venues, music pubs, live theatres, dance studios, even stand-up poetry nights. Fitzroy, Carlton and Richmond are brimming with creative energy. Here is a selection of venues.

### Cinema

**Cinema Nova**, Lygon Court, 380 Lygon St, Carlton.
Ph: (03) 9347 5331
**Westgarth Theatre**, with its original wide screen, 89 High St, Northcote. Ph: (03) 9482 2001

### Comedy

**Comedy Club**, 380 Lygon St, Carlton.
Ph: (03) 3481622
**Prince Patrick Hotel**, 135 Victoria Pde, Collingwood. Ph: (03) 9419 4197

### Dance

**Dance House**, Centre for Contemporary Movement. Rear, 150 Princes St. Ph: (03) 9347 2860

### Theatre

**La Mama**, 205 Faraday St, Carlton.
Ph: (03) 9347 6948
**The Universal Theatre**, 19 Victoria St, Fitzroy.
Ph: (03) 9419 3777

### Music

*Irish/Folk*
**Dan O'Connell Hotel**, 225 Canning St, Carlton.
Ph: (03) 9347 1502

*Jazz*
**The Night Cat**, 141 Johnston St, Fitzroy.
Ph: (03) 9417 0090

*Cover bands*
**Royal Derby Hotel**, 446 Brunswick St, Fitzroy
Ph: (03) 9417 2321

*Rock*
**Central Club**, 293 Swan St, Richmond.
Ph: (03) 94281480
**Corner Hotel**, 57 Swan St, Richmond.
Ph: (03) 9427 7300
**Punters Club**, 376 Brunswick St, Fitzroy.
Ph: (03) 9417 3006
**Evelyn Hotel**, 351 Brunswick St Fitroy.
Ph: (03) 9419 5500

*Roots*
**The Rainbow**, cnr David and Young Sts, Fitzroy.
Ph: (03) 419 4193

*World music*
**The Boite, World Music Cafe**, Mark St Hall, Mark and Falconer Sts, Fitzroy Nth. Ph: (03) 9417 3550
**The Stage**, Smith St, Collingwood. Ph: (03) 9417 2703

---

locations for walking, cycling and picnicking, a short distance from the Swan St shopping centre.

### Rural fringe
#### Eltham *Map 3 D5*

Eltham, set in a pretty bush location by Diamond Creek, is famous for the artistic communities that have made it their home. **Montsalvat**, at 7 Hillcrest Ave, is its best-known artists community. Built in the 1930s and 40s as an artists commune, its stone buildings evoke a romantic village-like atmosphere. It is said to be in the French provincial style. There is a farmhouse, a block of artists 'cells' and the grand gothic Great Hall. Hand-wrought jewellery, ceramics and textiles are on display and for sale. Ph: (03) 9439 7712. There are many other artisans' workshops and galleries in the Eltham area. Visitors should get hold of the pamphlet *Discover Millumbik* from visitor info centres.

**Craft markets** are another way to sample the artistic offerings and local produce of this area. The **Eltham Community Art and Craft Market** is a large affair held on the banks of Diamond Creek on the 1st and 3rd Suns, Nov and Dec 9am–2pm. The **St Andrews**

*The Boite Cafe.*

*Montsalvat Artists Colony, Eltham, displays and sells jewellery, ceramics and textiles.*

**Market**, a further 30 min drive along the Heidelberg-Kinglake Rd, makes for an ideal day-outing from Melbourne. This unique market is quirky, earthy and friendly, selling homemade and homegrown goods of all kinds. Opposite the St Andrews Hotel, it is held every Sat, 8am-1.30pm.

There are lots of options for **car touring** once visitors pass through the increasingly suburban Eltham. Excursions to Research, to Kangaroo Ground, or across to Warrandyte, offer many delightful opportunities for picnicking beside creeks and rivers. Visitors can continue on to the Christmas Hills and the Yarra Valley along very scenic routes, stopping at small galleries, scenic lookouts, and an increasing number of fine restaurants in the little towns along the way. **Adams** of North Riding at 1726 Heidelberg-Kinglake Rd St Andrews, is an award-winning a la carte restaurant. Ph: (03) 9710 1461. **Weller Restaurant** in Kangaroo Ground, offers magnificent views and a picturesque garden setting for lunches and afternoon teas.

Ph: (03) 9712 0266. These are both ideal ways to break your journey.

### Whittlesea *Map 3 C2*

Whittlesea is a pretty country town beside the Plenty River, rimmed by the Gt Dividing Range. It gives its name to the Whittlesea Shire, which takes in several outer northern suburbs and an array of small country towns in the Plenty Ranges district. The Hume Hwy lies to the west, Mt Disappointment to the north and the **Kinglake NP** to the east.

Whittlesea is an ideal place from which to tour this section of the Gt Diving Range, sample farmgate produce and visit the studios of local craftspeople.

There are several ideal picnic spots and scenic outlooks — at **Toorourrong Park, Yan Yean Reservoir, Yarrambat Park** and **Mt Disappointment**. At Toorourrong Park there is the special attraction of the **Australian Platypus Conservancy**. On Sat and Sun, in the late afternoon, visitors can take a Platypus Insight Tour, which includes a walk to

**Farmgate sales**
**Donnybrook**
**Farmhouse Cheese**,
Donnybrook.
Ph: 9745 2315
**Floridia Cheese**, for
soft cheeses, 327
Settlement Rd,
Thomastown.
Ph: 9464 2600
**Hellenic Cheese Farm**,
for sheep and goat's
cheese, 55 Cotters Rd,
Epping. Ph: 9408 1539
**Just Picked Berries
and Fruit**, Arthurs Ck
and Old Plenty Rds,
Yan Yean.
Ph: 9716 2292
**Sugarloaf Peach
Orchards**, 255
Eaglesnest Rd, Arthurs
Creek. Ph: 9714 8260

*The Alpine Toboggan Park is a wonderful place for a family day.*

spot a platypus in the wild. Bookings essential. Ph: (03) 9716 1664

Whittlesea is also the location of some active recreational pursuits ideal for children. The **Alpine Toboggan Park** is a must. With 1.2km of toboggan track, a state of the art mini-car course, a water slide and pleasant mini-golf course for the family, it is sure to be a hit. Ph: (03) 9716 1078

**K & J Thomas**, at 2110 Plenty Rd, are motor cycle specialists. They run a non-competitive 'two-wheeled pony club' – the Mavrickhana – where kids aged 5-12 can learn to ride safely. K & J

Thomas also sponsor regular ride days in the surrounding country, loan bikes, run workshops and teach adult beginners. Ph: (03) 9716 2019

For something quieter, kids might like to see the **Model Railway Museum** in Yarrambat, open Wed, Sat and Sun, and daily during school holidays, 10am–4pm. Ph: (03) 9436 1112

### The west
### Footscray *Map 3 A6*
To the west of the city lies Melbourne's industrial heartland. The dock areas along Footscray and Dynon Rds handle Melbourne's huge container trade – many times the volume of Sydney's docks – and harbour many of old Melbourne's secrets. Once there were glorious wetlands here, home to the great flocks of birds John Batman observed in 1835. During the Great Depression this area was a conspicuous home to the destitute who set up a shanty town on high ground along Footscray Rd.

Today the **Wholesale Fruit and Vegetable Market** and **National Flower Centre** are situated in this vicinity. Tours by **Melbourne Wholesale Market Experience** are highly recommended. Visitors experience the hustle and bustle of this huge complex at 6am with breakfast served at the **Flower Centre**. Ph: (03) 9620 2089

Along the **Maribyrnong River**, which flows into the Yarra at **Fishermans Bend**,

*Melbourne's Wholesale Fruit and Vegetable Market.*

*Port of Melbourne at night.*

small craft are moored and there are several fishing platforms. Just downstream from the Dynon Rd Bridge, visitors can take a pleasure cruise of the river with **Maribyrnong River Cruises**. Ph: (03) 9689 6431

Footscray shopping centre is lively and cheap, with a large indoor produce market. Footscray has many Vietnamese restaurants in this, another of Melbourne's Vietnamese quarters.

**Footscray Community Arts Centre**, at 45 Moreland St, runs workshops in all art forms as well as a concert and theatre program. Much of the work it presents originates in the communities of the western suburbs. The Centre's **Gabriel Gallery** is open Mon–Thurs, 9.30am–4.30pm; Fri, 9.30am–5.30pm; weekends, noon–4pm. Ph: (03) 9689 5677. **Hendersons Cafe** overlooking the Maribyrnong River, is open for breakfast and lunch Mon–Sat.

## National Parks and State Forests

### Mt Disappointment SF *Map 3 C1*

The explorers Hume and Hovell named the mountain in 1824 on their trail-blazing trip south over the Gt Dividing Range. To their disappointment they could not see Port Phillip Bay from the summit. Close to Whittlesea, the forest covers 15 870ha, and is a popular location for walking and horse riding, as well as car and motorcycle touring.

There are extensive tracks and a number of picnic areas. Blairs Hut and Andersons Garden are picturesque spots to picnic, with toilets, BBQs, tables and running water. Camping is permitted at several locations. Maps are available from visitor info centres and the Dept of Natural Resources and Environment. Ph: (03) 9637 8325

### Yan Yean Reservoir Park *Map 3 C3*

Yan Yean Reservoir is Melbourne's oldest reservoir, built in 1857. River red gum, she-oaks and kangaroo grass surround a very pleasant picnic area, and there are magnificent views across the reservoir to the Gt Dividing Range. There are wood-fired BBQs, with wood supplied, and other facilities.

### Yarra Bend Park *Map 5*

Yarra Bend was reserved as parkland in 1877. It was even considered a possible location for Government House. This large park has 16km of river frontage, including rugged escarpments, open woodlands and formal parkland, with walking paths following the river, and cycling paths. Kanes Bridge, or the old 'swing bridge', joins the northern and southern sides of Yarra Bend Park. **Dights Falls** sits at the junction of the river with Merri Ck, where the ruins of the Dight brothers flour mill and bluestone water channel can still be seen today.

**Ancient fishing grounds**
Dights Falls, in Yarra Bend Park was an important meeting and fishing site for the Wurundjeri people.

**Magical carvings**

The **Fairy Tree** in Fitzroy Gardens was carved by **Ola Cohn** in 1934. It depicts fairies and gnomes and bush animals — the laughing jackass, flying foxes and possums. She used the irregular features of the old river red gum to produce an enchanting bush reverie.

This patch of urban bush is a very popular location for Melburnians, who come here to walk, canoe, and socialise at one or other of the boat houses at Studley Park and Fairfield. Yarra Bend Park joins **Fairfield Park** on the northern side of the river. Parkland follows the river through Ivanhoe and Heidelberg to Templestowe. There are a number of sports grounds, walking paths and golf courses along the river flats, accessible from those suburbs. The **Main Yarra Trail** cycling path passes through this corridor.

## Parks and gardens

### Carlton Gardens *Map 4 C3–C4*

One of Melbourne's many lovely Victorian gardens bordering the CBD, the Carlton Gardens are the setting of the Melbourne Museum and Royal Melbourne Exhibition Building. On either side of these buildings are dense elm avenues, ideal spots for relaxing. Spectacular flowerbeds by the Rathdowne St entrance lead to a classic fountain. There is a public tennis court north of the Exhibition Building on the Nicholson St side.

### Edinburgh Gardens *Map 4 D1*

Visitors will find another extensive elm tree-lined 19th century garden located in Nth Fitzroy. The gardens' picturesque band rotunda faces Brunswick St, and

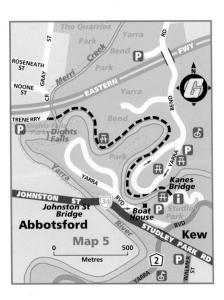

there are two playgrounds for small children. This is a favourite place for walking dogs, lounging on the lawns and picnicking. The gardens sit beside the Petersen Oval, once the Fitzroy Football Club ground, with its restored Victorian football stand. There are tennis courts, basketball rings and a skateboarding rink all discreetly tucked into the gardens. You can get a spectacular view of the city skyline from the hill by the oval.

### Fitzroy Gardens *Map 1 D2*

These wonderful gardens should not be missed. They are distinguished by their sweeping lawns and huge elm tree avenues, which provide dense shade on hot summer days, and many intriguing smaller gardens and historic features. **Cooks Cottage**, built in 1775 in Great Ayton, England, is a major attraction, but remains a simple English cottage, a reminder of the modest origins of Australia's European discoverer, Captain James Cook. The **Conservatory** is also popular, with continuous displays of colourful exotic plants.

Close by sit the whimsical **Fairy Tree** and a miniature **Tudor Village**. The **Dolphin Fountain** to the west of the main path is a favourite with children.

### Royal Park *Map 4 A1*

This huge area of open parkland is great for jogging and dog walking, kite flying and picnicking. Several large sports

*Heidelberg School Artists' Trail is an interesting and relaxing walk.*

facilities are located here, as well as a public golf course at its north-western end. BBQs are located on Macarthur Rd opposite the Melbourne Zoo. An interesting place to see is the Burke and Wills memorial cairn in Macarthur Rd where that ill-fated exploration to Central Australia left Melbourne in 1860. A small native Australian garden occupies Royal Park's north-eastern corner on Royal Pde near the intersection with Gatehouse St.

## Other attractions

### Bundoora Park and Coopers Settlement *Map 3 C5*

An urban farm, an historic village, an exciting adventure playground and educational facility sits beside parkland with BBQ facilities. Take a scenic drive to the top of Mt Cooper. You'll also find a public golf course at Bundoora Park. Situated only 15kms from Melbourne, Bundoora Park is a great place to unwind and be transported back to another era. Bundoora Park Visitors Centre is open daily, 8.30am–5pm. The park is open from sunrise to sunset, and Coopers Settlement from 10am–4.30pm. Ph: (03) 9462 4079

### Fairfield Boathouse *Map 3 B6*

The Fairfield Boat House is set in pretty bushland overlooking the Yarra River on Fairfield Park Dve, accessible from Heidelberg Rd. Visitors can feed the many waterbirds, hire canoes or rowing boats, take devonshire teas or picnic close by.

### Heidelberg School Artists Trail *Map 3 C5*

This trail comprises 12 colour signs featuring the paintings of six artists from the Heidelberg School. The signs have been erected at the *plein air* sites along the Yarra River where such famous artists as Arthur Streeton and Tom Roberts worked in the 1880s and 1890s. This fascinating trail is accessible at Yarra Flats Park and a number of other points. For a map and interesting walking notes contact the Banyule City Council. Ph: (03) 9490 4222

### Melbourne's Living Museum of the West *Map 3 A5*

Located at Pipemakers Park, Van Ness Ave, Maribyrnong the museum is Australia's first eco-museum – a community-based regional museum focused on the heritage, environment and culture of the western region. Open Mon–Thurs, 10am–4pm, weekends, 11am–5pm. Ph: (03) 9318 3544

### Westgarthtown *Map 3 B4*

This remarkable relic of German settlement in Australia is located in suburban Melbourne at 100 Gardenia Rd, Thomastown. Several families settled here after their 6-mth trip from Hamburg in 1850. This precinct features 2 farmhouses, a Lutheran church, and a cemetery. It has been restored by the Shire of Whittlesea and is on the Victorian Heritage Registry. Open only for tours by appt. Ph: (03) 9217 2293

## Recreational activities

### Boating

Nothing can be more relaxing than rowing down the Yarra. Canoes and dinghys are available for hire at Fairfield and Studley Park boathouses (p.50).

### Cycling

Melbourne and its northern suburbs offer great cycling beside Melbourne's two main rivers. The **Main Yarra Trail** follows the Yarra from Southbank

*Studley Boathouse.*

*There are fun cycling trails along the Yarra.*

through the inner north to Yarra Bend Park and on to Westerfold Park in Templestowe, some 33.5km in total. For shorter rides, travel the 12.5kms to Dights Falls, or 13.5kms to Fairfield Boathouse, which has tea and luncheon available.

The **Merri Ck Trail** branches off at Dights Falls, passing through Clifton Hill, Brunswick and Coburg. It passes the environment centre, CERES (p.38). The **Darebin Ck Trail** starts at the Darebin Parklands in Alphington and ends close to Bundoora Park (p.51).

For a western adventure along the **Maribyrnong River**, take the path from Southbank or pick it up at the Footscray or Dynon Rd bridges. From the city to the lovely Brimbank Park, it is 28kms. The path also passes the Living Museum of the West, about half-way. Parks Victoria/Bicycle Victoria maps are available from info centres.

### Golf

A number of private and public golf courses are located along the Yarra River in the inner northern suburbs. The **Yarra Bend Golf Course** is located in Fairfield, Ph: (03) 9481 3729. The **Burnley Golf Course** is adjacent to Swan St, Richmond. Ph: (03) 9205 5048. Further north are the **Bundoora Park Golf Course**, Ph: (03) 9469 3880 and the very picturesque **Yarrambat Park Golf Course** near Whittlesea. Ph: (03) 9436 2201

### Gyms and fitness centres

Check the *Yellow Pages* locality guides for the many health and fitness centres located in the inner north. Yarra City Council runs two well-equipped and friendly gyms, at **Collingwood Leisure Centre**, Ph: (03) 9205 5522, and **Richmond Recreation Centre**. Ph: (03) 9205 5032

### Horseriding

**Upper Plenty Trail Rides** on the Wallan-Whittlesea Rd, Upper Plenty offer trail rides, moonlight hay rides and tuition in riding and driving. Ph: (03) 5783 1310. At the **Victorian Showjumping Stables**, in Whittlesea, Olympian Russell Johnstone gives expert under-cover tuition. Ph: (03) 9716 2229

### Indoor rock climbing

The **Mill Indoor Rock Climbing Centre**, Australia's largest, is for serious climbers, offering great facilities and the chance to join group expeditions. It is located only 2km from the city at 78 Oxford St, Collingwood. Ph: (03) 9419 4709

### Swimming

Often the only relief in the northern suburbs on a hot summer's day is to be found at the local pool. There are outdoor olympic-size pools at Brunswick, Fitzroy, and Nth Melbourne. The **Brunswick Baths** in Dawson St is heated

*Melburnian's have a lifelong passion for Australian Rules Football.*

and open all year. Ph: (03) 9381 1840. The **Fitzroy Pool**, just off Brunswick St, is part of local lore, a great place to laze in the sun or under a tree during summer. Ph: (03) 9417 649. There are indoor pools that are open all year, from early in the morning, at the **Collingwood Leisure Centre** in Clifton Hill, Ph: (03) 9205 5522, the **Richmond Recreation Centre**, Ph (03) 9205 5032, and **Brunswick Baths**.

## Tennis

Public tennis courts can be found in most neighbourhoods. These courts are often managed by adjacent leisure centres, as are the facilities at Richmond and Clifton Hill. Fitzroy Tennis Club has a particularly lovely location in the Edinburgh Gardens, Nth Fitzroy, Ph: (03) 9482 3269. In Carlton, visitors are welcome at the Nicholson St courts in the Carlton Gardens, and at Princes Park, corner of Princes Park Dve and Macpherson St, Princes Hill. For other public courts, ring local council recreation services.

## Walking

There are abundant walking trails in the inner and outer north. See the various entries under NPs and Parks (pp.49, 50).

# Fun for the young

★ Alpine Toboggan Park (p.480)

★ Bundoora Park (p.51)

★ Canoeing on the Yarra (p.51)

★ CERES (p.38)

★ Collingwood Children's Farm (p.40)

★ Cycling on the Main Yarra Trail (p.51)

★ Fitzroy Swimming Pool (p.53)

★ Footy at the MCG or Optus Oval (pp.42, 39)

★ IMAX Cinema (p.40)

★ Indoor Rock Climbing (p.52)

★ MCG Gallery of Sport tours (p.43)

★ Quarries Park Play Space (p.40)

★ Rollerblading on the Merri Ck Trail (p.52)

★ Royal Melbourne Zoo (p.44)

**Swimming and stories**
Fitzroy Pool is part of local lore. It features in Helen Garner's novel *Monkey Grip*. It was also the subject of a community musical by Hannie Rayson, *Aqua Profonda*, after huge local protests in 1997 saved it from the developers.

*Quarries Park Play Space is an adventure playground in Clifton Hill.*

**Anyone for tennis?**
Public tennis courts often have off-peak rates for games before 6pm. Racquet hire costs around $5; court hire around $11 for 1hr.

Left: **Sailing, Port Phillip Bay.**
Right: **Chris Graf's on Chapel St, South Yarra.**

# South of the Yarra

Stretch your legs (and your mind) out beyond Melbourne's compelling CBD and you'll soon discover that vibrant centres of culture, fashion, art and good eating are also found in the south-eastern parts of the city.

Seaside St Kilda provides the perfect entree – somewhere to experience the beach, frolic at a fair, stroll by some history, and somewhere to eat, drink and soak in the ambience. South and Port Melbourne too profit from rich histories and diverse attractions including a temple, tapestry weavers, a market, and a mammoth playhouse owned by a friendly red bear. Enjoy a coffee and a certain style and scene in the urban villages of South Yarra (famous for its fashion houses) and Armadale (famous for its antiques and art) or get in the groove in nearby funky Prahran.

Pick a park – inner city at Albert Park Lake, home to the Grand Prix, or outer suburb, in Templestowe and Warrandyte, or elsewhere along the Yarra River where you can stop to sample modern art or antique apples. Take time too to hear the tales history has to tell, at the region's many museums and historic homes. You'll be surprised how full a day can be when you venture south at the Yarra.

## ℹ Tourist information

**City Experience Centre**
Melbourne Town Hall
Cnr Collins and Swanston Sts,
Melbourne 3000

**Victorian Visitor Info Centre**
Melbourne Town Hall
Cnr Little Collins and Swanston Sts,
Melbourne 3000

**City of Melbourne Info Booths**
Flinders St Station, Bourke St Mall,
Queen Victoria Market (market days only)

**Information Victoria**
356 Collins St, Melbourne 3000
Ph: 1 300 366 356
(Extensive suburban history book section)

**City Activities Info Line**
Ph: 1 300 655 452 (local call cost Aus wide)

**Victoria Tourism Info Service**
Ph: 13 28 42

**Websites**
www.melbourne.org
www.tourism.vic.gov.au

## Must see, must do

★ **Albert Park Lake** (p.59)
★ **Chapel St, South Yarra** (p.67)
★ **Como Historic House and Garden** (p.67)
★ **Museum of Modern Art at Heide** (p.69)
★ **South Melbourne Market** (p.65)
★ **St Kilda foreshore and pier** (p.63)

## Radio stations

**ABC Classic:** FM 105.9
**3AW:** AM 1278
**3LO:** AM 774
**Radio National:** AM 621
**3RRR:** FM 102.7
**Triple M:** FM 105.1

## Natural features

Logically, the northern boundary of this region is the Yarra River which rises east of Warburton, travelling through the hilly, treed eastern suburbs towards its destination, Port Phillip Bay. En route the river supports an atlas of wildlife, including the shy platypus, and small and large parks which are dotted along its course, including Warrandyte State Park, Studley Park and Westerfolds Park.

The second natural border, the Bay is its own impressive (and picturesque) statistic: 35 times larger than Sydney Harbour with a 25km cubic volume, equivalent to the capacity of 1 million olympic-size swimming pools. Two of its rare residents are the little penguins and the native water rats, the Rakali. Both find shelter in the rocks and rubble of the St Kilda breakwater. Further east, the hilly terrain provides views of the low-lying city before reaching the region's border just short of the foothills of the Dandenong Ranges.

## History

As early as 1868, author H Laurie pronounced that 'The suburbs of Melbourne are now nearly as important as the city itself'. That this land south of the Yarra had already been highly valued by its original inhabitants, the Aboriginal peoples, was as yet unacknowledged.

Gold-rich, Melbourne in the 1880s dawned as an era of real estate as ambitious land speculators sought new subdivisions, soon serviced by government funded railway lines. Monies were spent creating suburban municipal landmarks like the South Melbourne Town Hall and individuals with pounds to spend established hilltop estates in Toorak, Hawthorn and Kew — one witty English visitor nicknamed some of the lavish sheep-funded estates 'Muttonswool'. Factories flourished in Port Melbourne and South Melbourne, home to the working class, while others on better incomes moved south and east to more pleasant acres. The Depression of the 1890s further consolidated poverty's hold on the inner city and encouraged others to move to the outer 'ring'.

Fortunes eventually rallied and Melbourne's extensive public transport network was later supported by the motor car, which brought city access even closer — it was possible to work in the city and live happily in the suburbs. Each suburb developed its own extensive community and post WWII immigration brought a bounty of migrants who have added much to the local culture, cuisine, architecture and spirit.

Recreation today, as it was in the past, is often found seaside at places like St Kilda (p.62) or by water at Albert Park

(p.62)

**Breakwater wildlife**

To learn more about St Kilda's colony of 100 **Little Penguins** (who can sleep in the water on their stomachs) and small group of native water rats, **Rakali**, call for a copy of the *St Kilda Pier Park Notes* from Parks Victoria. Ph: 13 19 63

*Studley Park on the Yarra River.*

**Historical wit**

In the 1880s G A Sala christened the city 'Marvellous Melbourne', though some other observers, remarking on the lack of a sewerage system, changed the title to 'Marvellous Smellbourne'.

*Pettys Orchard.*

Lake and along the length of the Yarra. Trends toward inner city living have brought new life to Port and South Melbourne, and the urban villages excel in casual and fine dining, innovative galleries, fashion and interiors.

## Getting there

### By road

The 4 major roads reaching into the region are the E Fwy, the SE Fwy, the Princes Hwy and the Nepean Hwy. Peak hour traffic times are to be avoided.

### By tram, train and bus

Continuing its tradition of extensive public transport, Melbourne runs frequent tram, train and bus services in and around the suburbs. An invaluable reference for visitors is the Met's Melbourne Tram and Train Maps, which are available from train stations and info centres, and are reproduced on pp.8, 9.

Swanston St is the central city departure point for trams destined for Sth Melbourne, St Kilda, Sth Yarra, Toorak, Armadale and Camberwell (via Prahran and Malvern). Alternative tram services to St Kilda and Sth Melbourne depart along Bourke and Collins Sts.

Trains run regularly and efficiently to Sth Yarra, Toorak, Armadale and Prahran, and reach further south through to Glen Waverley, Alamein, Belgrave and Lilydale.

Bus services cover most of the south including areas like Templestowe and Doncaster where there is little other public transport available.

For additional details of timetables and services pick up a copy of the free pamphlet *City and Suburbs Tram Fares and Travel Guide* available from visitor info centres, Ph: 13 16 38 or visit the following excellent websites: www.victrip.vic.gov.au and www.melbbuslink.com.au

## Getting around

For a different perspective of the inner suburban sights try a leisurely guided bicycle tour with **City Cycle Tours**. Based at the NE cnr of Treasury Gardens, on Lansdowne St, CBD, these tour guides not only cover city territory, they tour south of the Yarra on their St Kilda by The Bay and other rides. Bookings req. Ph: (03) 9585 5343

Catering to those with an affection for the arts, **Creatours** operate small group tours visiting professional artists and craftspeople in their studios. In this region they offer St Kilda Studio Walks and other tours by arrangement. 1 Elm Grove, Armadale. Ph: (03) 9822 0556

**Culture Capital Tours** know well the routes to Melbourne's most interesting art outcrops and centres. Depart on one of their ½- or 1-day tours including Melbourne's Artist Colonies, Craft Centre and Edwardian Village, or Bohemian Ramble. Ph: (03) 9347 3039

## Festivals and events

### St Kilda Festival

Home to creative artists of every imaginable medium, St Kilda hosts a seaside celebration of life and the Arts during early Feb. Fine food and wine complement the exhibits, street parties, concerts and summer festivities. Ph: (03) 9209 6777

### Qantas Australian Grand Prix

Held in early Mar (dates confirmed annually by the FIA), the Australian Grand Prix spotlights Melbourne on the world sports stage as Albert Park's 5.26km circuit becomes the venue for the

*Grand Prix racing action.*

first event in the Formula 1 racing calendar. Four days of racing action and entertainment. Ph: 13 16 41

## Antique Apple Orchard Festival Days

Autumn's harvest (Mar) provides a rare chance to sample antique apples (no longer commercially available) at Pettys Antique Apple Orchard (p.69). Events include guided tours of the trees, an apple produce market, antique apple tree sales, children's activities, music and other festivities. Small admission fee applies. Ph: 13 19 63

## St Kilda Film Festival

Be challenged, stretched, awed and entertained at St Kilda's highly respected film festival held Apr or May at The George cinemas. Featuring Australia's premier Short Film Competition, screenings, presentations and free forums. Ph: (03) 9209 6777

## Chapel Street Festival

Once a year in early Nov, Chapel and Greville Sts, Prahran close to traffic and erupt into a street fiesta of live bands, fabulous food, entertainment and a cacophony of personality. Ph: (03) 9529 6331

## Oppy Family Fun Ride

Families bring out their bikes Melbourne Cup weekend in Nov and enjoy a healthy 'fun-ride' around an extensive section of bike paths just west of the Dandenongs, known as **Knox Cycleway**. Ph: (03) 9298 8000

## Main localities

### Albert Park Map 6 A4, 7 B1

City-reach recreation has been Albert Park's drawcard since Melbourne's early days. Conveniently located close to the CBD, the area has a lake, 18-hole public golf course and 270m driving range, one of the largest aquatic and sports centres in the southern hemisphere, home ground for a roll-call of sports clubs, plus, as any motor enthusiast would know, the track venue for the Qantas Australian Grand Prix.

**Boating on Albert Park Lake.**

Named after the consort of Queen Victoria, **Albert Park** and its **Lake** (formerly a lagoon) are today a 225ha parkland and picturesque built-lake. Dug to a depth of 1-1.5m, the lake provides perfect conditions for **boating**, sailing, canoeing and rowing (p.71). Joggers and casual strollers share the **5km walking track**, others enjoy lunch at one of 11 picnic areas within park boundaries – some with BBQs and playgrounds. A variety of restaurants, cafes, kiosks and nightclubs offer alternative fare and entertainment. Within the boundaries of the park there are 25 sporting fields, plus the **Albert Park Hockey/Tennis Centre** and the **Melbourne Sports and Aquatic Centre**, fun for all ages, with a wave pool, waterslide and seemingly infinite facilities (p.70). For more info phone Parks Victoria: 13 19 63.

Once the site of a coal gas production plant, **Gasworks Park** at 21 Graham St today offers a creative centre for art and its appreciation. A theatre company, artists' studios, bookshop and gallery of original children's book illustrations (**Books Illustrated**) are located within the historic buildings (built in 1873). Additional features include public access pottery kilns, darkroom and art classes. Books Illustrated is open Sun–Thurs, 12am–5pm. Ph: 9209 6207. If you're hankering for coffee and cake or

**Team tradition**
Until 1982, Lake Oval, Albert Park was home-ground to the red and white sporting AFL team South Melbourne, today known as the Sydney Swans.

# Some galleries south of the Yarra

Regarded as a cultural capital, Melbourne's contribution to the arts extends well beyond the CBD. Though centres like Armadale are replete with galleries for buyers, you will find some excellent exhibitions throughout the southern suburbs (see also the **Museum of Modern Art at Heide**, p.69). Phone ahead for details of current programs.

**East and west gallery** specialises in antiquities from SE Asia, China and Japan and contemporary works in clay. 665 High St, E Kew, Open Mon–Fri, 10am–5pm, Sat, 10am–2pm, free admission. Ph: (03) 9859 6277

**Glen Eira city gallery** houses a permanent collection of paintings, sculpture and ceramics, including works by the Boyd Family, Noel Counihan, Isabel Davies, plus a range of exhibitions throughout the year. Cnr Glen Eira and Hawthorn Rds, Caulfield. Mon–Fri, 10am–5pm, Sat–Sun, 1pm–5pm. Ph: (03) 9524 3287

**Kingston art centre** has a gallery for contemporary art, sculpture garden, plus Sunday concerts, 979 Nepean Hwy, Moorabbin. Open Mon-Fri, 10am–6pm, Sun, 2pm–5pm. Ph: (03) 9556 4440

**Linden art centre and gallery** has contemporary exhibitions, experimental work by emerging artists, children's sculpture garden and play area, 26 Acland St, St Kilda. Open Tues–Sun, 1pm–6pm, free admission. Ph: (03) 9209 6560

**Mia Mia Gallery** displays Aboriginal art by local and central desert artists in-residence, Westerfolds Park, Fitzsimons Ln, Templestowe. Open Wed–Sun, 9.30am–6pm (summer), 10am–5pm (winter). Ph: (03) 9846 4636

**Monash University gallery** houses Australian and international contemporary art, installations, performance and 2-dimensional art, plus artists talks and forums, Building 55, Monash University, Wellington Rd, Clayton. Open Tues–Fri, 10am–5pm, Sat, 2pm–5pm, free admission. Ph: (03) 9905 4217

At **Waverley City gallery**, there are changing exhibitions of historical and contemporary art, craft and design and an outstanding collection of Australian photography, 170 Jells Rd, Wheelers Hill. Open Tues–Fri, 10am–5pm, Sat–Sun, 12pm–5pm. Ph: (03) 9562 1569

*Modern sculpture by Jeff Thomson, 1987.*

something more substantial, head to **Bridport St** (between Montague and Merton Sts) and enjoy both the food and the friendly atmosphere.

### Armadale *Map 6 B4*

**High St**, Armadale complements its sophisticated neighbouring suburbs of Toorak and South Yarra with a reputation for well-established style. Here there are more than **100 antique dealers, rare book specialists** and at least **20 art galleries** exhibiting and selling works ranging from paintings by Australia's most famous artists, to ceramics, Near Eastern artifacts and modern prints. **Vogue fashion** and **furnishings** attract a certain

class of buyer and for would-be brides, High St assembles the calling cards of some of Australia's best known wedding dress couturiers. *Wedding Walks in Stonnington*, available from local retail bridal outlets, provides a map of services and products in the extended area. Once you've finished exploring, an array of good coffee shops and restaurants make Armadale a complete day's destination. For more information, check www.highstreet.com.au

### Port Melbourne *Map 6 A4*

In 1839, 4 yrs after the first permanent settlement of Melbourne, a gentleman by the name of Captain Willbraham Liardet

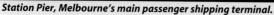

*Station Pier, Melbourne's main passenger shipping terminal.*

chose Port Melbourne as his place of residence. He then promptly built a hotel and jetty and set up a mail service to the city. It was fitting that Liardet foresaw the importance of 'the pub' as by 1876 the working class port district boasted 48 hotels. Though at least half of these venues closed as the suburb transformed from its dock-serving heritage to a popular bayside address, you can still take a **self-guided walking tour** of some of these historic drinking houses. The Port Melbourne Historical and Preservation Society have produced, *The Pubs of Port*, a pamphlet available from any of the 8 hotels on **Bay St**. The street, 'a vintage village', is also popular for coffee, cake or a great meal.

For those impressed by the bulk and buoyancy of a ship, Melbourne's main passenger shipping terminal, **Station Pier**, is the place to see the departing *Spirit of Tasmania* and *The Devil Cat* — two passenger services to Tasmania, plus occasional visiting naval ships. Consider also parts of the pier's long history — as point of departure for soldiers sent to war and a welcoming dock for thousands of post-war immigrants. Several convenient tearoom/ kiosks sell refreshments. **Steamtug Wattle** run a ferry service to Williamstown from the pier,

Sun 10.30am, noon, 1.30pm and 3pm, Feb-May, Oct-Dec. Ph: (03) 9328 2739

### Prahran *Map 6 B4*

Contrasting with the Sth Yarra arm of the street, **Chapel St** Prahran has a personality of preferences — sometimes alternative and grunge, sometimes extroverted and groovy. Hairdressers, fashion shops and 'junk' stores are known for their charisma, while the eating options at this end are often diverse and economical — ranging from gourmet fish and chips, to Indian, Polish, Thai, Sri Lankan or Nepalese.

In spite of its name, **Commercial Rd**, off Chapel St, is better known for its flamboyant drag queens and gay nightlife than for its commerce, though there are a number of interesting enterprises along the street. Running geographically parallel, **Greville St** contributes alternative appeal with a stretch of lounge bars, restaurants, cafes and second- and first-hand stores. A market with flair is held in Greville St each Sunday, noon–5pm.

Discover market fare, food and the occasional roving musician at **Prahran Market** (established in 1864), located at 177 Commercial Rd, open Tues, dawn–5pm, Thurs-Fri, dawn–6pm, Sat, dawn–5pm, ph: (03) 9522 3301, or for a

**Esplanade alive**

Come to the St Kilda Upper Esplanade Sun, 10am-5pm and you'll discover one of the best art and craft markets in the city. More than 220 artists set up their stalls, with wares ranging from handcrafted jewellery and mirrors, to sculpture, pottery and chopping boards. Ph: 9209 6209

preview of local talent and cultural endeavour, visit **Chapel off Chapel** at 12 Little Chapel St, which hosts theatre, music, dance exhibitions and other events. Ph: (03) 9522 3382. A surprising escape from the city surrounds is **Victoria Gardens** on High St, where behind the big grey stone wall you'll find a beautifully landscaped reserve, ornamental fountain, plenty of play area, plus a playground.

### St Kilda *Map 7*

St Kilda is more than a palm-fringed bayside suburb, it is a vibrant, cosmopolitan mood that inevitably draws you back. You are sure to find your niche somewhere here among the buzzing cafes, restaurants and cake shops, in the secluded gardens and galleries or frolicking in the sun on the beach.

Reputedly named sometime in 1841–42 when the captain of the anchored cargo yacht 'Lady of St Kilda' enjoyed a pleasant seaside picnic here, the area has since enjoyed a rich and rowdy history. Initially attracting the affluent and well-to-do during the buoyant goldrush days, the 1890s depression brought a change of fortunes as the wealthy moved to Toorak, and brothels and such seedy trades began to flourish. But St Kilda's reputation for assorted

entertainments persisted: a foreshore fair opened in 1912 (now Luna Park), St Moritz's ice-skating rink opened in 1939 (on the site of the Novotel), and through various incarnations the suburb established itself by the 1990s as a premier tourist destination.

Today St Kilda's streets have a flavour of their own. Start on **Fitzroy St**, where you can suit your appetite and enjoy a great souvlaki or pizza, or experience more sophisticated dining at one of the many stylish restaurants and bars. During summer the footpaths are full of alfresco coffee drinkers soaking up the sun. Close by, **Acland St** expands the menu with an eclectic range of places to eat. Its most tempting offerings are the continental cakes sold at a string of European delicatessens and cafes. The street's mix of retail shops is equally diverse and appealing, including a hair salon famous for its vivacious rooftop sculpture. For those who love second-hand books, clothing and furniture stores it is also worth strolling the surrounding side streets where you'll find curiously named establishments like Junkarucci and Mondo Thrasho.

Situated between Fitzroy and Acland Sts, **The Esplanade**'s historic entertainment venues still draw crowds to their varied calendar of performances and

*Alfresco dining, Acland Street.*

events. In 1927 the **Palais Theatre** on the Lower Esplanade was Australia's grandest suburban picture palace, and with a seating capacity of 3000 it was also the world's largest. Today it hosts live entertainment, from rock to opera. Ph: (03) 9534 0651. One of St Kilda's most notable establishments is the **Esplanade Hotel**, affectionately known as 'The Espy'. Originally built in 1880, the hotel has been a haunt for musicians and artists for decades. Today you can catch a live band (some for free) or stand-up comedy in the *Waiting Room* (Gershwin Room). For details of times and performers Ph: (03) 9534 0211. Despite a succession of courtroom dramas, developers have fortunately failed thus far in their attempts to overhaul, obscure or remove this local icon.

*St Kilda's alluring foreshore.*

The true face of fun in St Kilda is undeniably **Luna Park**. Located on the Lower Esplanade, the park's smiling mouth and motto 'Just for Fun' provide plenty of reason to visit, though kids are easily convinced by the attractions, including the Tunnel of Terror, Sky Rider, Games Arcade, Dodgem Cars and the Scenic Railway (in spite of its name, this is no sedate way to see the scenery). Entry is free and rides are paid for by purchased coupons. Open Fri, 7pm–11pm, Sat, 1pm–11pm, Sun, 1pm–9pm, daily during school and public holidays, 1pm–9pm. Ph: (03) 9525 5033. Nearby on Newton St (follow the signs off Grey St) is a slightly unconventional community playground, also popular with children. The **St Kilda Adventure Playground** features a flying fox, real chooks, a reading room, and various wooden constructions to explore. Admission is free though adult supervision is required. Open Mon–Fri, 3.30pm–5.30pm, Sat–Sun and holidays, 10am–5pm.

**St Kilda's foreshore** boasts sea, sand, a long sealed stretch of path plus a pier, restaurants with a history and more. In-line skaters, cyclists, skateboarders and other outdoor enthusiasts (or novices) make use of a designated 10km trail from Port Melbourne to Elwood, though there is still plenty of room for casual walkers.

Two historic buildings, one a turn-of-the-century tea-house (now **The Stoke House**), the other a public bathing pavilion (**Donovans** restaurant) are popular places to eat while watching the passing ships. The **St Kilda Pier**, built in 1853 to assist settlers unloading their construction materials, reaches out into the bay providing a different view of the city. The historic kiosk at the end of the pier provides the perfect place to rest.

Another way to enjoy the bay is to take a ferry to Williamstown. The Southern Spirit and John Batman Ferry depart from the 1st low landing on St Kilda Pier on a 25min trip Sat, Sun and public hols, departing hourly from 11.30am–3.30pm. Ph: 9506 4144. Enjoy a free BBQ while penguin-watching with **Penguin Waters Cruises**, launching from St Kilda Pier (and Berth 7, Southgate). Regular departures day and night. Ph: (03) 9645 0533

At the cnr of Carlisle and Barkly Sts, the **National Theatre** hosts an array of both community-based and professional dance and musical performances. Ph: (03) 9525 4611 (box office). Located across the Nepean Hwy, an outing to **The Astor** theatre is much more than a night at the movies. Although the constantly changing calendar includes both classic and contemporary films (double features most nights), the feel of the place is distinctively 1920s-1930s. Art deco, with comfy couches and mood lighting, a

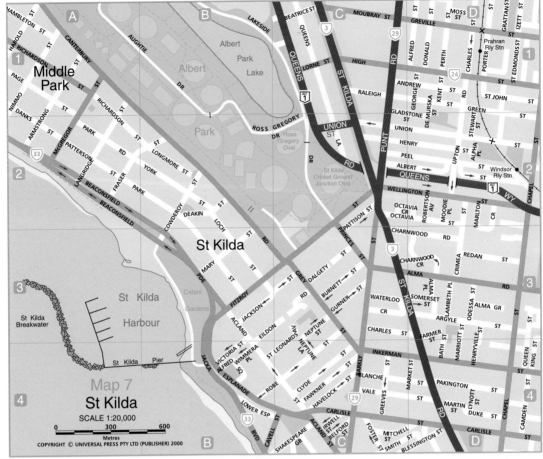

Map 7
## St Kilda
SCALE 1:20,000

0    300    600
Metres
COPYRIGHT © UNIVERSAL PRESS PTY LTD (PUBLISHER) 2000

**Walk into history**
For those in search of
history's landmarks
you can walk the
streets of Sth Yarra,
Toorak, Malvern,
Armadale and Prahran
armed with a copy of
*12 Great Walks in
Stonnington* available
from Stonnington City
Council. Ph: 9823 1333

resident pianist is sometimes known to play before screenings. 1 Chapel St, St Kilda. Ph: (03) 9510 1414

Also across the Nepean Hwy, at 26 Alma Rd, the **Jewish Museum of Australia** provides cultural context in an area central to Melbourne's Jewish community. Changing exhibitions explore such varied topics as 'People of the Precious Legacy: Australian Jews from Czechoslovakia' and 'The Days of Creation' in photographs, while permanent displays include 'The Jewish Year', a scrolling 'Story of Esther' and a listening post playing snippets of Talmudic debate. The **Jewish Museum Shop** is stocked with items of Judaica, cards and posters, ceramics, glassware and specialty books. Open Tues–Thurs, 10am–4pm, Sun 11am–5pm. Ph: (03) 9534 0083. **Synagogue Tours** are run Tues–Thurs, 12.30pm, Sun, 12.30pm and

3pm. Nearby **Carlisle St** is well known for its kosher food stores and eateries (including Kosher Express).

## Sth Melbourne *Map 6 A3*
To Melbourne's early settlers the lush volcanic outcrop then known as Emerald Hill offered a gently elevated vantage of the city and surrounding swampland. Renamed, but still enriched by its history, Sth Melbourne is today an upwardly mobile inner-city suburb with an eclectic array of attractions.

Start with a stroll along **Clarendon St**, increasingly popular for its cafes and restaurants. Many buildings in the street have retained or restored their Victorian fronts and verandahs and the Emerald Hill area between Clarendon, Park, Cecil and Dorcas Sts is heritage classified. The grand **Sth Melbourne Town Hall** (1880) on Bank St is a notable landmark, while one essential destination is the **See Yup Guan Ti Temple** (1866). Hidden among residences at 76 Raglan St, the temple is the oldest non-Christian place of worship in Australia, embodying the religious beliefs of Taoism and the philosophy of Confucius. Beautiful artefacts inside and outside the temple have significant meaning and have been imported from Guangzhou in China. As a practising place of worship appropriate respect is requested. An info sheet is available. Open daily, 9am–4pm. At 399 Coventry St are 3 **Iron Houses**, National Trust classified kit homes manufactured in Manchester and sent to Australia in the 1850s to help ease the goldrush housing shortage. Open Sun, 1pm–4pm.

For those with a love affair with food (and cooking) **The Vital Ingredient** at 206 Clarendon St is a treasure trove of ingredients, usual and unusual, cookbooks and culinary equipment, servicing both restaurants and the general public. Classes are taught here by some of Australia's most notable chefs. Open Mon–Fri, 9am–5.30pm, Sat, 9am–4pm. Ph: (03) 9696 3511. You can purchase fresh produce amongst other goods at the **Sth Melbourne Market** (1867), cnr Cecil and Coventry Sts. With more than 200 undercover stalls, its aisles are stocked

*Playtime at Red Bears Playhouse.*

with plenty of distractions, from art prints, candles and clothing to health food, handmade soaps and more. Open Wed, 8am–2pm, Fri, 8am–6pm, Sat–Sun, 8am–4pm. Ph: (03) 9209 6295. Nearby, at 260 Park St, is the **Victorian Tapestry Workshop** where you can watch skilled artists weaving their works, purchase a small or large tapestry or buy wool for your own masterpiece. A free *Tapestry Map* guides you to 25 tapestries displayed around the CBD. Open for viewing Mon–Fri, 10am–4pm. Tours by appt. Wed and Thurs. Admission fee charged. Ph: (03) 9699 7885

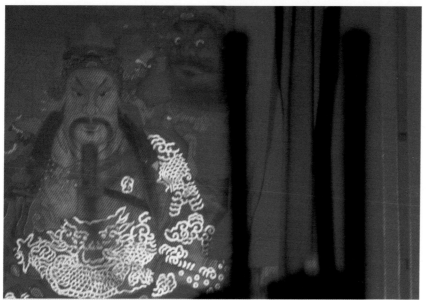

*Interior, See Yup Guan Ti Temple, Sth Melbourne.*

**Cooks tour**

For a small fee, Sth Melbourne Market's in-house chef will tour you through its aisles of fresh food, giving tips on purchasing and preparing fresh market food. Hot drink, calico shopping bag and discount card included. Ph: (03) 9209 6295

## Cinema Centres

| NAME | ADDRESS | PHONE |
| --- | --- | --- |
| **Cinema Europa** | | |
| Jam Factory | 500 Chapel St, Sth Yarra | Ph: (03) 9827 2440 |
| Southland | The Street, Westfield Shoppingtown, 1239 Nepean Hwy, Cheltenham | Ph: (03) 9582 5050 |
| **Hoyts Cinemas** | | |
| Chadstone | Chadstone Shopping Centre, 1341 Dandenong Rd, Chadstone | Ph: (03) 9563 1988 |
| Forest Hill | Cnr Mahoneys and Canterbury Rds, Forest Hill | Ph: (03) 9894 2000 |
| Croydon | 3-5 Hewish Rd, Croydon | Ph: (03) 9725 6544 |
| **Palace** | | |
| Cinema Como | Cnr Toorak Rd and Chapel Sts, Sth Yarra | Ph: (03) 9827 7533 |
| The George | 135 Fitzroy St, St Kilda | Ph: (03) 9534 6922 |
| Trak | 445 Toorak Rd, Sth Yarra | Ph: (03) 9827 9333 |
| Balwyn | 231 Whitehorse Rd, Balwyn | Ph: (03) 9817 1277 |
| Cameo Belgrave | 1628 Burwood Hwy, Belgrave | Ph: (03) 9754 7844 |
| **Village** | | |
| Jam Factory | 500 Chapel St, Sth Yarra | Ph: (03) 9825 4688 |
| Glen Waverley | Century City Walk, 289 Springvale Rd, Glen Waverley | Ph: (03) 9550 8688 |
| **Independents** | | |
| Astor | 1 Chapel St, St Kilda | Ph: (03) 9510 1414 |
| Classic Cinema | 9 Gordon St, Elsternwick | Ph: (03) 9523 9739 |
| Longford | 59 Toorak Rd, Sth Yarra | Ph: (03) 9867 2700 |

*Astor cinema.*

*Stylish South Yarra.*

Kids and adults are catered for at **Red Bears Playhouse**, a giant colourful indoor playground, restaurant and cafe where the motto is 'Where kids can be kids and adults can be ... either'. Highlights include a labyrinth of equipment, ball pit, art and craft activities and other endless play possibilities — either supervised by a parent/adult or by the Playhouse staff, though child-minding is only available for children over 5yrs. Holiday programs and birthdays are specialties. Located at 134 York St, the playhouse is open Mon–Fri, 9.30am–6.30pm, Sat–Sun, 8.30am–7.30pm. Ph: (03) 9645 0788.

(A smaller **Red Bears Playhouse** is also located at the Glen Waverley Century City Walk, 289 Springvale Rd, Glen Waverley).

A free outdoor supervised alternative is **Skinners Adventure Playground**, 211a Dorcas St (entrance between 209 and 211). Open Mon–Fri, 3.30pm–5.30pm, Sat–Sun, 10am–5pm. Ph: (03) 9209 6352

Formerly the malting house of the Castlemaine Brewery, the **CUB Malthouse** at 113 Sturt St is today home to **Playbox**, one of Australia's best known contemporary theatre companies. The complex houses 2 theatres, a cafe, bar and restaurant. Box office hours Mon–Sat, 9am–5pm. Ph: (03) 9685 5111.

Next door is the extraordinary copper-clad complex that is permanent home to the **Australian Centre for**

**Como Historic House and Garden.**

**Contemporary Art**. Exhibition space, amphitheatre, sculpture garden, cafe and bookshop broaden the appeal of this arts village.

### Sth Yarra and Toorak *Map 6 B4*

**Toorak Rd**, Sth Yarra is where the bevy of cafe lattes, boutiques, restaurants and BMWs begins. **Chapel St**, boldly intersecting, is Melbourne's definitive contemporary fashion strip where shops artfully flaunt their desirable wears — cuts and cloths created by both Australian and international designers. One popular all-weather destination is the **Jam Factory** at no. 500 where cinemas, retail and eating outlets and the state's biggest bookstore are housed in one convenient complex which, truthfully named, was previously the manufacturing site of the Australian Jam Company.

Fittingly found in this prestigious neighbourhood is **Como Historic House and Garden**, a magnificent mansion built only 12 yrs after Melbourne was permanently settled. Named after the lake in Italy where the first owner proposed to his wife, the home has hosted generations of Melbourne's high society. Today owned by the National Trust, the property has been faithfully refurnished, from the stables and servants quarters to the extravagant gold ballroom and tower. The 1st Sat each month the National Trust conduct escorted Como Twilight Tours showing off the night-time charm of the residence (including a secret bedroom), followed by a champagne supper. Located cnr Williams Rd and

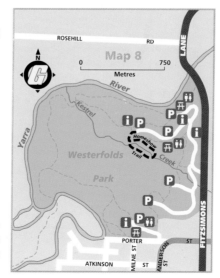

*A Nolan 'Ned Kelly' at Heide.*

Lechlade Ave. Open daily, 10am–5pm. Ph: (03) 9827 2500

Decorously dressed in its Gucci best, Toorak is known for its **village** of prestigious boutiques, stylish cafes and elegant dining, and as Melbourne's elite residential address. Here you can purchase haute couture, collectable art, antiques and furnishings or simply drive the streets admiring the monumental homes.

### Warrandyte *Map 6 D2*

A lucky strike in July 1851 changed the face of Warrandyte, then known as Andersons Creek, as a deluge of miners descended to the site of Victoria's first government rewarded gold-find (now marked with a **memorial cairn**).

Today the region promoted as 'country in the suburbs' not only boasts a beautiful **state park** along the Yarra, it also supports a tradition of craft, pottery and art, established since the 1890s. Among the **Yarra St** district stores you'll find Australiana Aspect, Earth Art Gallery, Essence of Australia, Scandles World of Candles, The Claypot Gallery, Potters Cottage Gallery and others too numerous to mention. There is a selection of suitable places to dine and for those interested in history the **Warrandyte Historical Museum** in the old post office building at 111 Yarra St features local photos and memorabilia from the past. Open Sat-Sun, 1pm–4pm. Ph: (03)

9844 3662. The 1st Sat each month from 9am–1pm the **Warrandyte Community Market** sets up Yarra-side at Stiggants Reserve, cnr Stiggant and Yarra Sts. Ph: (03) 9844 4495

## State Parks

### Warrandyte SP *Map 6 D2*

Though the goldrush of the 1850s saw vegetation sacrificed to the search for gold, bushland eventually returned and today the 620ha SP not only shows historic marks of mining, it has also been replenished with box eucalypts, manna gums, silver wattles, wildflowers and orchids, and is home to platypus, koalas, kangaroos and wombats. Linked together by the flow of the Yarra River, the park is popular for canoeing, bushwalking, horseriding, gold panning, abseiling and rockclimbing at Whipstick Gully Quarry (by arrangement with the ranger). Picnic facilities are at **Pound Bend**, **Jumping Creek**, **Sandy Bay** and **Whipstick Gully**. Open daily, 9.30am–7pm (daylight savings), 9.30am–5pm. Ph: 13 19 63

## Parks and gardens

### St Kilda Botanical Gardens *Map 6 A4*

Established in 1859, these gardens are a pleasant mix of order and seclusion featuring towering palm trees, sprawling lawns, a small duck pond, giant chess board, hot-house style conservatory, playground and seasonal memorial rose garden. Off Blessington St. Locked daily at sunset.

### Westerfolds Park *Map 8, 6 C2*

Originally part of the Wurundjeri tribe territory, and later home to the Heidelberg School artists, this 123ha bushland park features Yarra River views, wide open spaces, 6.1km of bitumen trails suitable for walking, cycling and in-line skating, playground equipment, canoe ramp, trails for horseriding (with a permit), **Mia Mia Gallery** (p.60) plus BBQs and picnic tables. The 1km, 30min **Homeshow Trail**, starting from Manna Gum carpark tours you through the 'homes'

**Chocolate treat**

Chocaholics will love **The Chocolate Box**, a cornucopia of dark, milk and white delights at 765 Burke Rd, Camberwell. Open Mon-Sat, 8am-6pm. Ph: (03) 9813 1377

of the local wildlife. Only 15km from the CBD, entrances are Fitzsimons Ln or Porter St, Templestowe. Open daily, 8.30am-8pm (summer), 8.30am-5pm (winter). Access for the disabled. Ph: 13 19 63

## Other attractions

### Australian Racing Museum *Map 6 B4*

It is appropriate that a city held spell-bound each Nov by a horserace should be host to the Australian Racing Museum. Located through Gate 22 at the Caulfield Racecourse, Station St, Caulfield, the museum relives racing history through art, photos, stunning silks, memorabilia and trophies. There is also a shop and small racing related library. Open Tues-Thurs, 10am-4pm, race days 11am-4pm, and by appt. Free admission. Ph: (03) 9257 7279

### Jewish Holocaust Museum and Research Centre *Map 6 B4*

A sobering witness against one of history's darkest epochs, the Jewish Holocaust Museum at 13 Selwyn St, Elsternwick graphically records the Jewish experience in WWII through photographs, newspapers, art and video. Guides at the museum are survivors of the Holocaust and tell of their personal experiences. The centre is a memorial, aiming to 'combat racism and preserve the Australian tradition of tolerance and acceptance'. Open Mon-Fri, 10am-2pm, Sun, 11am-3pm. Ph: (03) 9258 1985. Admission is free.

### Kew Traffic School *Map 6 B3*

During school holidays, the Kew Traffic School offers young kids the chance to learn the road rules the fun way, riding its circuit of simulated roads, complete with working traffic lights. Children must be accompanied by an adult. BYO helmet (and bike if preferred). Located cnr Grange and Cotham Rds, Kew. Open Mon-Fri, 10am-3pm. Ph: (03) 9278 4770

### Museum of Modern Art at Heide *Map 6 B3*

The Museum of Modern Art at Heide is the former home of art patrons John and Sunday Reed whose generosity to

Melbourne's radical art coterie during the 1940s-50s encouraged the work of such artists as Arthur Boyd, Albert Tucker, John Percival and Sidney Nolan (who painted his famous Ned Kelly series here). Bordering the Yarra River in a beautiful garden setting, the gallery features both changing exhibitions and an excellent permanent collection, Sunday's kitchen garden, a sculpture park plus a licensed cafe and shop. Located at 7 Templestowe Rd, Bulleen. Open Tues-Fri, 10am-5pm, Sat-Sun and public holidays, 12pm-5pm. Ph: (03) 9850 1500

*Pettys Orchard.*

### Pettys Antique Apple Orchard *Map 6 C2*

What do Winter Bananas, Cleopatras, Bonzas and Peasgood's Nonsuch have in common? All are creatively named antique apples, some of the more than 200 types no longer commercially available that are grown and displayed at the 44ha Parks Victoria antique apple orchard at Templestowe. The best time to visit is autumn (around Mar) when Festival Days are held (p.59), though the orchard can be enjoyed in all its seasons. Enjoy too the parkland, walking trails, bird hide and orchard museum. Phone for *Park Notes*. Ph: 13 19 63

*Australian Racing Museum, Caulfield.*

*In-line at St Kilda.*

### Rippon Lea Historic House and Garden *Map 6 B4*

Secluded in its suburban setting at 192 Hotham St, Elsternwick, Rippon Lea Historic House and Garden is an extraordinary example of a once privately-owned city estate. Originally built in 1868 by Sir Frederick Sargood, there are over 5ha of landscaped gardens with a lake, ornate bridges, waterfall, orchard and fernery. Tours of the 33-roomed Romanesque-style mansion operate every 30 min; tours of the garden are at 2pm daily. Open Tues–Sun, 10am–5pm. Ph: (03) 9523 6095

### Studley Park Boathouse *Map 6 B3*

In 1863 the Burn family established the Yarra River's first boathouse, then known as 'Riversdale', situated in what was to become Studley Park (1877). Although this riverside retreat has been Melbourne's most popular picnic spot for more than 130 yrs, today the eating options have broadened as the renamed Studley Park Boathouse at 1 Boathouse Rd now houses a kiosk, cafe and fine dining restaurant – all open daily, though hours vary. Ph: (03) 9853 1828. Recreational diversions include ½hr hire of row boats, kayaks and canoes (or longer if you'd prefer to paddle futher), walks through the beautiful bushland and

access to cycling paths. Nearby **Kanes Bridge**, a suspension bridge built in 1934, provides access over the river to the greater Yarra Bend Park (p.49).

## Recreational activities

### Cycling

The most popular cycling paths in the region follow scenic stretches of water – the Yarra River (p.58) and St Kilda foreshore. Bikes for hire around St Kilda are: **Bicycle Hire**, foreshore near St Kilda Pier, open daily, 10am–sunset in summer, Sat–Sun, 10am–4pm, weather permitting in winter, Ph: 0412 445 575; and **St Kilda Cycles**, 11 Carlisle St, St Kilda, open Mon–Fri, 9am–6pm, Sat, 9am–5pm, Sun, 10am–4pm. Ph: (03) 9534 3074

Further afield, Knox City Council have established **Knox Cycleway** – over 60km of cycling paths, including sections named after Sir Hubert Opperman who spent the last years of his life in the area. Ph: (03) 9298 8000 for map and info.

### In-line skating

Conveniently located close to one of the city's best in-line skating paths are a number of in-line skate hire outlets:

**Albert Park In-Line**, 179 Victoria Ave, Albert Park, Open daily, 9am–late (summer), 9am–7.30pm (winter) till dusk. Ph: 9645 9099

**Apache Junction**, 21 Carlisle St, St Kilda. Open daily, 10am–8pm (summer), 10am–5pm (winter). Ph: (03) 9534 4006

**Fun Factory** (indoor skating centre), 257 Toorak Rd, Sth Yarra, Open daily, 10.30am–6pm. Ph: (03) 9826 8274

**Rock'n N Roll'n**, 11a Fitzroy St, St Kilda. Open Mon–Fri, 9am–late (summer), 9am–6pm (winter), Sat–Sun, 10am–late (summer), 10am–6pm (winter). Ph: (03) 9525 3434

### Leisure centres

### Melbourne Sports and Aquatic Centre

Choose from a field full of sports ranging from basketball, badminton, squash, European handball, table tennis, netball, martial arts, volleyball, diving, underwater hockey, water polo and a 1000m$^2$ fitness centre. Water fun is

*A popular cycling path is along the Yarra River.*

*Luna Park, 'Just for Fun', Lower Esplanade, St Kilda.*

found in many forms, with facilities ranging from a wave pool, waterslide, spas and sauna to a 25m lap pool and toddlers pool. A creche and kiosk are also on-site. Located on Aughtie Dve, Albert Pk. Open Mon-Fri, 6am-10pm, Sat-Sun, 6am-8pm. Ph: (03) 9926 1555

**Waves Leisure Centre** *Map*

Further south, in Highett, is a suburban leisure centre for kids. Waves Leisure Centre, 111 Chesterville Rd, promotes fun and fitness. Facilities include a wave pool, lap pool, toddlers pool, spas, gymnasium, indoor K2 climbing wall, indoor team sports, cafe and creche. Open Mon-Fri, 6am-10pm, Sat-Sun and public holidays, 7am-7pm. Ph: (03) 9553 1038

*On the water*

**Jolly Rogers School of Sailing**, Boat Hire and Kiosk, Aquatic Dve, Albert Park Lake. Offer boat and aquabike hire and lessons. Open daily, 9am-5pm. Ph: (03) 9690 5862

**Albert Park-Sth Melbourne Rowing Club** (Ph: (03) 9682 4440) and **YWCA Rowing Club** (Ph: (03) 9529 8596) offer Learn to Row sessions, Sun mornings.

**St Kilda Marina Complex** at Marine Parade, Elwood run fishing and other charters, Yarra River cruises and a sailing school. A restaurant is also on site. Open daily. Bookings Ph: (03) 9534 0448

**YachtPro**, Royal Melbourne Yacht Squadron, St Kilda Pier. 'Sail Port Phillip Bay and see Melbourne from the sea, with your crew or ours'. Ph: (03) 9525 5221

**Adventure Canoeing**, Yarra River, Warrandyte State Park, guided or self-guided 2hr tours or full-day hire including shuttle, safety gear and instruction. Ph: (03) 9844 3223

# Fun for the young

★ Canoeing on the Yarra (p.71)

★ In-line skating, St Kilda Beach (pp.63, 70)

★ Kew Traffic School (p.69)

★ Luna Park (p.63)

★ Melbourne Sports and Aquatic Centre (p.70)

★ Red Bears Playhouse (p.66)

★ St Kilda Adventure Playground (p.63)

*'Sail Port Phillip Bay'.*

*Left:* **Lake Daylesford boathouse.**
*Right:* **Daylesford.**

# Macedon Ranges and the Spa Country

From the mystery of Hanging Rock, to the undulating pastoral lands by the Campaspe River, to the spa towns bordering rugged bushland, this region offers a wonderful diversity of landscapes and local culture.

Renowned for its luxury B&B accommodation — in secluded bush and farmland settings — the region offers myriad possibilities for gentle rambling and quiet pottering through bookshops, antique stores, and galleries. The legendary Mt Macedon is a sightseer's delight and gardener's mecca. Woodend, Kyneton and Daylesford are sophisticated regional towns supporting vibrant local arts communities and fine regional food production. For those who take relaxation seriously the regional specialties include taking the waters, herbal baths or engaging one of the many masseurs who work in the spa country. Tour the region's famed wineries, many of which offer weekend lunches in superb bluestone farmhouses, or visit the region's coffee shops and bakeries, delicatessens and outstanding restaurants.

Opportunities for family fun and active recreation also abound. Visitors can explore bush tracks and old gold diggings, go fishing and picnicking in local reserves, horse ride through magnificent forests and enjoy inexpensive fare at some of the region's great old pubs.

## Tourist Information

**Daylesford Tourist Info Centre**
Vincent St, Daylesford 3460
Ph: (03) 5348 1339

**Kilmore Info Centre**
Kilmore Library
12 Sydney St, Kilmore 3764
Ph: (03) 5781 1319

**Kyneton Visitor Info Centre**
Jean Hayes Reserve
High St, Kyneton 3444
Ph: (03) 5422 6110

**Sunbury Info Centre**
The Old Courthouse
43 Macedon Rd, Sunbury 3429
Ph: (03) 9744 2291
Freecall 1800 677 995

**Woodend Tourist Info Centre**
High St, Woodend 3442
Ph: (03) 5427 2033

**Websites**
www.macedon-ranges.vic.gov.au
www.humetourism.com.au
www.melton.vic.gov.au

## Must see, must do

★ **Daylesford** (p.79)
★ **Hanging Rock** (p.90)
★ **Hepburn Springs Spa Resort** (p.81)
★ **Lavandula lavender farm** (p.82)
★ **Mt Macedon gardens** (p.92)
★ **Mt Macedon summit** (p.86)

## Radio stations

**3LO:** 774 AM
**RN:** 621 AM
**JJJ:** 90.3 FM
**3CCC:** 89.5 FM
**3BO:** 93.5 FM
**KLFM:** 96.5 FM
**3CV:** 1071AM

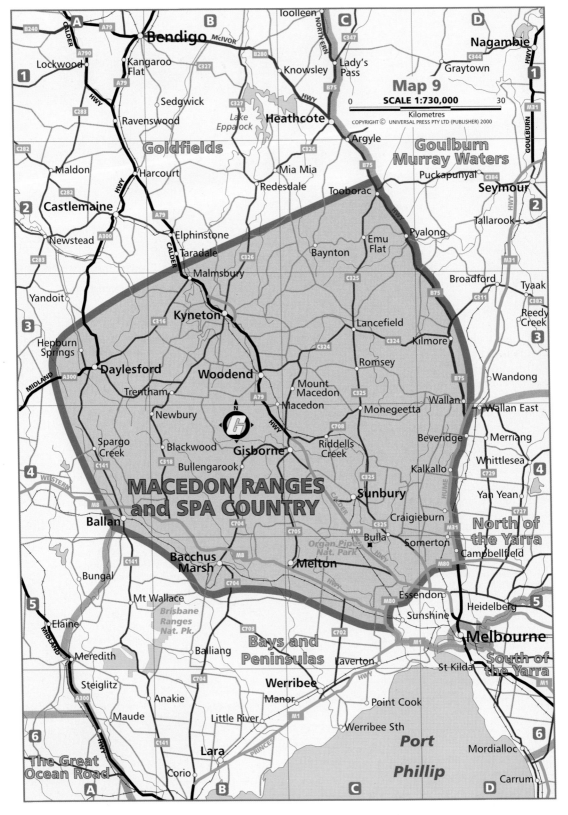

Map 9
SCALE 1:730,000
0       30
Kilometres
COPYRIGHT © UNIVERSAL PRESS PTY LTD (PUBLISHER) 2000

**Goldfields**

**Goulburn Murray Waters**

**MACEDON RANGES and SPA COUNTRY**

**North of the Yarra**

**Bays and Peninsulas**

**South of the Yarra**

**The Great Ocean Road**

*Port Phillip*

Bendigo, Toolleen, Nagambie, Lockwood, Kangaroo Flat, Knowsley, Lady's Pass, Graytown, Sedgwick, Ravenswood, Lake Eppalock, Heathcote, Argyle, Maldon, Harcourt, Mia Mia, Redesdale, Tooborac, Puckapunyal, Seymour, Castlemaine, Tallarook, Newstead, Elphinstone, Taradale, Baynton, Emu Flat, Pyalong, Broadford, Tyaak, Malmsbury, Yandoit, Kyneton, Lancefield, Kilmore, Reedy Creek, Hepburn Springs, Romsey, Wandong, Daylesford, Woodend, Mount Macedon, Wallan, Wallan East, Trentham, Macedon, Monegeetta, Beveridge, Merriang, Newbury, Whittlesea, Spargo Creek, Blackwood, Riddells Creek, Kalkallo, Yan Yean, Bullengarook, Gisborne, Sunbury, Craigieburn, Ballan, Bulla, Somerton, Campbellfield, Bacchus Marsh, Melton, Essendon, Bungal, Mt Wallace, Brisbane Ranges Nat. Pk., Organ Pipes Nat. Park, Heidelberg, Elaine, Sunshine, Meredith, Balliang, Laverton, Melbourne, St Kilda, Steiglitz, Anakie, Werribee, Maude, Little River, Manor, Point Cook, Werribee Sth, Lara, Mordialloc, Corio, Carrum

*View of Daylesford from Mt Franklin.*

## Natural features

The flat plains encountered on entering the region are the result of one of the world's largest lava flows. Deep creek beds cut dramatically through this landscape, and though some of the area is sadly degraded, the creek beds give way to gentle grazing land that rises to the Macedon Ranges along the Calder Hwy, to the Lerderderg Gorge SP along the Western Fwy, and the foothills of the Gt Dividing Range outside Kilmore. Ancient volcanic activity gave birth to many of the region's notable formations: Mt Franklin near Daylesford, Mt Macedon itself, and the unique Hanging Rock, Camels Hump and Organ Pipes.

The Macedon Ranges mark a distinct break in the region's climate and geology. They are home to lush vegetation, including mountain ash, fern gullies, and twisted snow gums at Camels Hump. A dryer climate prevails north where the Campaspe and Loddon rivers flow to the Murray River, meandering through the lowlands, rich grazing lands and prosperous country towns. West, around Melton the unique limestone country is ideal for breeding thoroughbreds, while the rugged terrain of the Lerderderg and Coliban rivers, confirm that remote area as real 'lizard country'.

## History

The territories of several Aboriginal tribes once intersected this region around Kyneton. The Djadjawurung people occupied the area to the west around Daylesford, the Daunwurung extended north-east through the Cobaw area, and the Woiworung occupied the area around Mt Macedon and Lancefield. John Batman explored parts of the region in 1835, and claimed to have purchased land, including Mt Macedon, Mt Kororoit and the Jackson and Kororoit Ck areas via a treaty with members of the Woiworung tribe in 1835.

Sheep runs were quickly taken up, from Sunbury to Yandoit. A wealthy landed gentry grew, and hugely profitable enterprises flourished. The mansion Rupertswood in Sunbury remains testament to the fabulous fortunes made by a few in this period.

Gold, however, was the greatest spur to development, from the 1850s onward. The Calder Hwy follows one of the first gold routes – through Diggers Rest, one day from Melbourne by foot, past 'Shorts Hotel', a coach stop, now an archeological dig, on the way to the Bendigo goldfields. The Western Hwy passing through Melton and Bacchus Marsh marked the way to the Ballarat goldfields. Gold fever saw ramshackle towns and tent cities spring up all the

**Hanging Rock races.**

Forest and Blackwood, and easy access from there to Daylesford (and on into the Goldfields region, see Ch 8). A 40min drive along the Hume Fwy from Melbourne takes you to Kilmore on the eastern rim of the region. The Lancefield Rd, is another option. It runs directly off the Tullamarine Fwy, giving perhaps the best access to the bulk of the wineries in the Sunbury-Lancefield corridor.

### By rail
Trains leave Spencer St Stn several times a day for Bendigo, stopping at Sunbury, Gisborne, Macedon, Woodend, Kyneton and Malmsbury. Buses connect at Woodend for Daylesford. However, not all trains stop at all stations on the Bendigo line, so buses from Woodend to Daylesford connect with only some Melbourne trains. A shuttle service operates between Daylesford and Hepburn Springs on weekdays. Train timetables can be obtained from V\Line. Ph: 13 22 32. The trip to Kyneton from Melbourne takes approximately 1hr. The trip to Daylesford takes 2hrs.

Railway buses leave from Spencer St Stn for Kilmore twice a day. Bookings are essential. Buses connect once a day at Sunbury Stn for Romsey and Lancefield. Reaching the far west of the region by public transport is difficult, but taxis can be hired at Bacchus Marsh (on the Ballarat train line) for Blackwood and the Lerderderg Gorge.

## Getting around

**Taxis and hire cars** are available in the larger towns. V/Line buses run from Daylesford to other centres in adjacent regions. Buses to Castlemaine, Bendigo and Ballarat leave from Little's Garage in Vincent St, Daylesford.

Several private companies offer small group tours out of Melbourne with specific destinations: the region's wineries, Mt Macedon's gardens, and the spa towns. Only one operates out of the region directly, and its passion for local history and culture is evident. **Macedon and Spa Country Tours,** Ph: (03) 5429 2333.

way from Blackwood to Daylesford in the west, to the provisioning towns like Kyneton, and Kilmore in the east. Many tiny towns that now have one pub once sported a dozen.

Mt Macedon's most distinctive attractions and famous gardens date from the 1870s when wealthy industrialists built their 'hill stations'. Daylesford was to emerge as a pre-eminent destination for honeymooners and jaded Melburnians seeking the benefits of bracing mountain air and the tonic of its different mineral waters.

## Getting there
### By road
There are 4 major routes into the region. The Calder Hwy is the most central, offering a number of alternative routes to places of interest. Branching off the Tullamarine Fwy, the Calder Hwy passes through Gisborne (with turn-offs to Macedon and Mt Macedon in the Black Forest), Woodend, Kyneton and Malmsbury. Once over the ranges, various routes can be taken to the spa towns of Daylesford and Hepburn Springs. Similarly, several picturesque routes can be taken in the direction of Lancefield and Kilmore, to the east.

The Western Fwy offers the most direct route to the Lerderderg State

# Festivals and events

### Hanging Rock Races

This fabled race, in the prettiest of locations, beside Hanging Rock, is run on New Years Day. Under sunny skies, typical at this time, what better way to start the year? Ph: (03) 5422 1866

### Lavender Harvest Festival

An intoxicating day's activities in high summer, on the 2nd weekend in Jan, the harvest takes place 5km out of Hepburn Springs at **Lavandula**, a refurbished Italian-style farmhouse and lavender farm. Not to be missed. Ph: (03) 5476 4393

### Hanging Rock Vintage and Class

Held on the 2nd Sun in Feb, this festival is a favourite both with vintage car enthusiasts and the uninitiated. With 1500 collectible vehicles on display, best car prizes and trophies, entertainment and BBQs available, it is an ideal family outing. Ph: 1800 244 711

### Harvest Picnic at Hanging Rock

Specialist producers and growers sell their wines, cheeses, sausages, breads, pastries and other foods in a gorgeous setting on the last weekend in Feb. Ph: (03) 9650 7655

### Hepburn Springs Swiss/Italian Festa

This festival celebrates the influences of the Swiss-Italian immigrants who worked as miners in the area and who later established farms around Hepburn Springs. A weekend of festivities at the end of May which include special exhibitions, a spaghetti sauce-making competition, wine-tasting, a masked ball and an eccentric street parade, mark this as fine midwinter madness.

### Sip'n Sup

Sip'n Sup, held the last Sun of Aug, is a celebration of new wine releases from **Sunbury**'s thriving vineyards. Six historic locations offer regional foods and entertainment. Venues are 5min drive apart and are serviced by a shuttle bus. Ph: (03) 9744 2291

### Kyneton Daffodil Festival and Arts Festival

Every spring Kyneton's roads, gardens and shops burst forth in a blaze of yellow. At the Showgrounds pavilion, the more subtle shades and varieties of rare narcissi are on display. These 10 days of events, commencing 1st weekend in Sept, include open gardens, an old-time ball, a

**The annual show**
A number of towns in the region hold annual agricultural shows. Check with visitor info centres for the dates of the **Kilmore**, **Daylesford** and **Melton** shows.

*Daffodils abound in Spring at Kyneton.*

**Mineral water: its health-giving constituents**

**Calcium:** makes strong bones

**Iron:** aids red blood cells

**Magnesium:** for nerves, muscles and kidneys

**Potassium:** for muscles

**Silica:** for skin, bone and hair

**Sulphate:** purifies the liver

**Sodium:** prevents stomach disorders

*Convent Gallery, Dalesford.*

street parade, children's day and window displays. The **Kyneton Antique and Collectables Fair** is held in conjunction with the Daffodil Festival at the Kyneton Town Hall. Ph: (03) 5432 3735; (03) 5422 3140

### Macedon Budburst Wine Celebration

Held on the last weekend of Oct, the Macedon wineries offer food and wine tasting to the sound of jazz. This festival specialises in 'wine dinners', which show the area's boutique wines off to best advantage. Ph: (03) 5427 2033

### The Great Australian Art Crawl

Initiated in 1997, Kyneton's Art Crawl is a quirky showcase for local artists and businesses, especially the Piper Street traders. Combining food and wine with art making and exhibiting, it is a fine sign of the region's cultural regeneration. Held bi-annually, late Oct. Ph: (03) 5422 3745

### Kyneton Agricultural Show

This traditional agricultural show held at the Kyneton Showgrounds revives more traditional 'old-time pleasures' with animal judging, agricultural displays, ring events, rides and side shows. Held on the 3rd weekend in Nov, it is one of several agricultural shows held in the region.

**Name that creek**

The very rich alluvial gold found at Blackwood came chiefly from the Lerderderg River and its tributaries, which had great names like Nuggety, Yankee, Dead Horse, Whipstick and Kangaroo Creeks.

Check with local info centres for the Kilmore and Daylesford shows.

## Main localities and towns

### Beveridge *Map 9 D4*

Only 30min outside Melbourne on the Hume Fwy, Beveridge is the site of the Kelly family's original farmhouse. Ned apparently lived there till 1864. Today it is closed to the public, a ruin awaiting restoration. But it can be viewed from the road. It is well worth turning off at

*Blackwood Mineral Springs.*

Beveridge to visit the surprisingly lovely bluestone tavern, the **Hunters Tryst**. Its tiny bar is warm and welcoming. Devonshire teas are served daily in the adjacent tearooms. Close by is the **Hampton Court Maze and Beveridge Birdworld** in Camerons Lane.

### Blackwood *Map 9 B4*

Blackwood was once home to 13 000 miners and their families. Today it is a sleepy hollow, tucked in close to the northern end of the Lerderderg Gorge SP. B&B and cabin lodging is available, and camping is permitted in several serviced and non-serviced areas. The local pub, the **Blackwood Hotel Motel**, once a staging post for Cobb & Co, exhibits the history of the town in sepia photographs on its pressed tin walls. With a fireplace that encourages friendly conversation, the pub itself is the seat of curious historical anecdotes.

Both Blackwood's mineral springs, discovered by Chinese miners, and the cemetery are worth visiting. Go to **Junction Old Wares** on the Greendale Rd for a glimpse of yesteryear. Check at the hotel for fishing and swimming spots along the **Lerderderg River**.

Blackwood is also a take-off point for bushwalks and 4WD treks through the rugged northern end of the **Lerderderg Gorge SP** (p.91). The river track that traverses the length of the park starts close to Golden Point Rd and is considered difficult after O'Brien's Crossing. There is car access, with panoramic views of the Gorge, to O'Brien's Crossing where there are picnic, fireplace and toilet facilities.

### Daylesford *Map 10*

The boom-time architecture of Daylesford gives the town an opulent feel, now reproduced in contemporary style in smart new cosmopolitan cafes and restaurants. But Daylesford is a mass of contradictions. It remains the provisioning centre for the local farming community, is

**Restaurant deserving of fame**

**Lake House, Daylesford** was judged Best Country Restaurant by American Express and best *Age Food Guide* gourmet retreat. It is famous for its elegant, contemporary cuisine and use of regional produce.
Ph: (03) 5348 3329

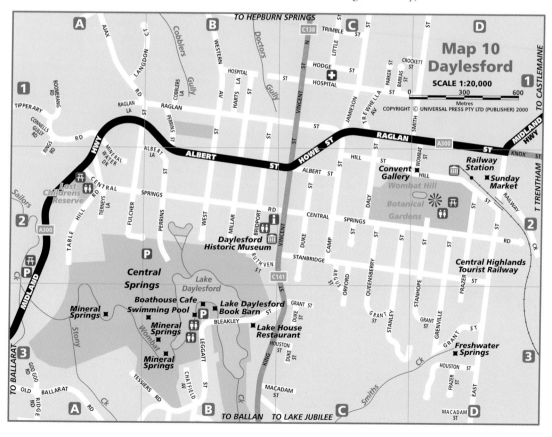

**Want to go green?**

Visit the region's mudbrick and rammed-earth houses and learn about permaculture, efficient energy sources and sustainable communities. **Green Living House Tours** are offered every Spring and Autumn. Ph: (03) 5470 5047

home to many city escapees looking for cheap land and housing, and is also the New Age centre of Victoria. Hippies, traditionals and cosmopolites each contribute a vital element to a regenerated Daylesford, a down-at-heels resort town only a decade or so ago.

Daylesford's mineral springs, together with **Hepburn Springs** 5km away, are the foundation of the local tourist industry. Since the town's heyday as a spa city in the 1920s, visitors have focused on the medicinal benefits of the waters. Today, a plethora of cultural, spiritual, recreational and commercial activities complement the spas and are helping to write a new chapter in the colourful history of this once frontier town.

Elements of Daylesford's pioneer past are curiously echoed in schemes like the town's 'LETS' program (a non-market bartering system), and those monuments to innovation and necessity, mudbrick houses, which dot the bush. The eyes of the hardworking Scots and Irish settlers would have popped, however, to see the alternative therapies on offer: iridology, yoga, aroma- and colour therapy, and endless varieties of massage. For details contact the Daylesford Tourist Info Centre.

**Vincent Street** offers an array of shops and opportunities for browsing and

*Boating on Lake Dalesford.*

grazing. Health food bakeries and excellent vegetarian cafes rub shoulders with the homemade chocolate shop **Sweet Decadence**, the intriguing **Avant Garden Bookshop**, as well as antique shops and small galleries. While the very popular Convent Gallery draws huge crowds, the smaller **Pantechnicon Gallery** on Vincent St offers an authentic view of local artists' and artisans' work. Craft and old wares shops also line **Albert St**.

**Convent Gallery** on Wombat Hill provides a glimpse of local history in this beautifully renovated Italianate building. Once home to the Presentation Sisters, it is now an exhibition space, with opulent displays of jewellery and decorative art for purchase. Open daily 10am-6pm. Ph: (03) 5348 3211

The **Daylesford Historical Museum** at 100 Vincent St, housed in the old School of Mines building, is a must for those who want to absorb the town's pioneer past. Learn about Daylesford's extensive mine system, the domestic life of the various ethnic communities, and the tragic tales that beset the town at different times in its growth. Open weekends, public and school holidays 1.30-4.30pm, or by appt.

**Daylesford Lake** is a pleasant walk from the centre of town. A ramble around its circumference takes about 40min and can be followed by tea at the **Boathouse Cafe**. Rowboats, canoes and pedal boats are available for hire. Swimming here is delightful. The renowned secondhand bookshop, **Lake Daylesford Book Barn**, a few metres away from the cafe, can distract for hours.

**Lake Jubilee**, 2km from the centre of Daylesford, also offers walks and boat hire, as well as swimming, fishing, picnic facilities and BBQs.

The easy to medium, short and longer bushwalks around Daylesford are a revelation. The **Tipperary Track**, for instance, runs beside the Coliban River and takes in various mineral springs and mining relics, through glistening eucalypt forest all the way to Hepburn Springs. BBQ and toilet facilities are available at many of the springs, but the sense of being in the heart of secluded bush is paramount. This track is suitable for family walks of various lengths. Pamphlets are available from the Daylesford Tourist Info Centre.

Another fun family outing is the steamtrain ride from Daylesford Stn to Musk or Bullarto. The **Central Highlands Tourist Railway** runs every Sun throughout the year. Ph: (03) 5348 3927. The station grounds are also home to the **Daylesford Community Market**, a quirky produce, craft and secondhand market. Open Sun 9am–3pm.

**Mount Franklin**, 10km north of Daylesford, offers commanding views from the summit lookout, short walks, an idyllic wooded picnic area, plus the thrill of knowing you are standing on an extinct volcano.

## Gisborne *Map 12 C3*

The last town before crossing the Macedon Ranges, Gisborne is now bypassed by the Calder Hwy. This pretty town offers picnic facilities by **Jacksons Ck** and light snacks at its gourmet delicatessen.

The colourful **Gisborne Outdoor Market** is held on the first Sun of the month, coinciding with the **Gisborne Vintage Machinery Society** miniature railway day. The society also runs a vintage engine rally and tractor pull in the Gisborne Steam Park on the third Sun in May. The **Skin Inn** on Main Rd sells Australian sheepskin products, as well as oilskin and moleskin products. Open daily.

The **Barringo Valley**, to the east, is reached by exiting from the Calder Hwy at Gisborne. This lovely approach to Mt Macedon and the ranges is a well-kept secret. This route takes in an idyllic picnic area before several turn-offs: to Cherokee, Macedon and Mt Macedon. The route to Cherokee, partly on dirt roads, is especially beautiful. The **Barringo Equestrian Centre** on Shannons Rd, the road to **Cherokee**, promises gorgeous rides through the mountains, even winter rides through the snow. Ph: (03) 5426 1778

*Hepburn Spa Resort.*

**Home of the brave?**
How did **Cherokee** get its name? Some say a Cherokee American lived here during the goldrush. Other say 2 Americans from Dakota saw a likeness in the area to their home state, land of the Cherokees.

## Hepburn Springs *Map 12 A2*

Hepburn Springs is Daylesford's 'little sister' town, though many would say it is the jewel in the crown. Only 5km from Daylesford, its **Hepburn Mineral Springs Reserve** and the refurbished **Hepburn Spa Resort** are huge tourist attractions. Old-style guest houses, as well as upmarket motels line the Hepburn Spa road, and on weekdays shuttle buses run several times a day from Daylesford. Most of the mineral springs in the region were discovered during mining excavation last century, and ironically were to give to the spa towns a more enduring prosperity than gold itself.

A map of the mineral springs of the whole Daylesford-Hepburn Springs area, available at the Daylesford Tourist Info Centre, outlines the constituents and medicinal properties of each available mineral water. Don't forget to take a cup, or bottles if you wish.

There are several short walks from the Hepburn Springs Reserve, which has picnic and BBQ facilities beside the many springs. Walks include the slightly longer trek to the **Blowhole**, which is on the **Tipperary Track**. During the winter months water thunders through this old stream diversion, another relic of the town's mining past.

The **Hepburn Spa Resort** is now a large modern complex in glass and steel, with outlooks onto Spring Creek and the

*Barringo Valley.*

*Lavender farm, Lavandula.*

Hepburn Springs Reserve. It offers part and full-day visits that include general access to its mineral springs pool, spa and relaxation lounge. Specific hydrotherapies and aerospa baths, sauna, flotation tank, massage and beauty therapies are all available. Open weekdays 10am–8pm and weekends 9am–8pm. Ph: (03) 5348 2034. A price list is available from the Daylesford Info Centre, and is well worth consulting before arriving at the resort.

On and off Main St several small-scale enterprises offer more individual moments. Local art works are displayed at the **Cosy Cafe**, and the **Old Billiard Hall Gallery** boasts not only the work of local artists and potters, but also an eccentric collection of secondhand artbooks, teapots, billy can canisters and bonsai. Open weekdays 12am–5pm.

The Swiss-Italian influence in Hepburn Springs is significant. The **Macaroni Factory** on Main Rd, built in 1859 by Giacomo and Pietro Lucini, has remained in the family and is now classified by the National Trust. Giacomo's granddaughter conducts tours over 2 weekends in Jan and Mar and during the Swiss-Italian Festa in May. Check at the Daylesford Tourist Info Centre for details.

The Newstead Rd out of Hepburn Springs passes through **Breakneck Gorge**, offering more rocky bushwalking tracks to

explore, and on to the region's famous lavender farm, **Lavandula**. With Mt Franklin as a distant backdrop, and rolling hills and pasturelands in the foreground, a prettier setting for fields of lavender and a Swiss-Italian-style farmhouse could not be found. The township of **Yandoit** close by is a jewel of undeveloped 19th century farmhouses.

### Kilmore *Map 9 D3*

Kilmore lies off the Hume Fwy on the old route to Sydney. A historic town, it retains something of the frontier atmosphere. The visitor can imagine horses tethered to hitching rails outside the bluestone pubs and stores that line its main street. Today there are good pubs and cafes, as well as a number of antique shops.

The Kilmore Info Centre provides a walking guide that highlights the various historic buildings. These include **Whitburgh Cottage**, the town-blacksmith's tiny home, open on Sun only, 2pm–4pm and the **Kilmore Gaol**, said to have periodically housed members of the Kelly family. The Gaol is open for tours of the cell block, but now also houses an impressive antique store and upmarket restaurant.

Kilmore holds several festivals throughout the year, including the **Celtic Festival** in Jun and the **Harness Pacing Cup** in Oct. It is a favourite location on the country racing circuit. Check with the visitor info centre for exact dates.

On the Lancefield road lie Kilmore's 2 cemeteries. These provide a wonderful insight into the locality's history, with generations of 'old colonists', as they described themselves, at rest in crumbling, sometimes elaborate tombs.

On the old Hume Hwy towards Pretty Sally is the wonderful oddity of **Victoria's Tramway Museum** on Union Lane. Open Sun, 10am–5pm, it is great place for a spot of family fun. Run by volunteers, mainly retired tram drivers and conductors ('connies'), it not only houses all sorts of dilapidated old trams but runs an antique tram along a section of an old railway line. No tram ride could be more beautiful, perched as this short

**Living it up**

For the opportunity to stay in one of Hepburn Spa's famed Swiss-Italian buildings, the **Villa Parma** on Main Rd offers pensione-style accommodation. Ph: (03) 5348 3512

run is against the backdrop of the Gt Dividing Range. Ph: (03) 4798 6035

## Kyneton *Map 12 B1*

Kyneton is a busy centre for the surrounding farming district and capital of the Macedon Ranges Shire. With its 19th century granite streets and bluestone architecture, its solid prosperity as an agricultural and trading town is evident. Originally opened up as a sheep run in 1837, and named after Kineton in Herefordshire, it became a thriving staging post for supplies to the gold diggings. It was to become known as the 'granary of the south'. The bluestone flour mills that grace the Calder Hwy nearby stand testament to this. The pasturelands of the Campaspe are Kyneton's economic strength and lend the district a gentle beauty.

**Piper St** is the heritage quarter of Kyneton. Fine wool is spun and sold at **Meskills**, and its beautiful knitted products are on display. Visitors are welcome to view the production process. Flour is still ground and bread baked at the **Old Steam Mill**, and wine pressing can be viewed and the local wines sampled at **Vincorp's Trio Station Winery**, a few doors further on. Shops selling secondhand books, old wares, antiques and plants make for pleasurable and informative browsing. The

proprietor of the **Kyneton Provender**, secondhand bookstore and deli, has a wealth of information about the region's Aboriginal history and local artistic community.

The **Kyneton Historical Museum**, also on Piper St, an imposing Georgian bluestone building, displays the typical domestic decor of the well-to-do colonial settler. By contrast, the 1840s timber cottage re-established in the grounds of the museum conjures up the rawer edge of early white settlement. Open daily 11am–4pm, school and public holidays. Ph: (03) 5422 1228. At **Kyneton Fine China** in Wedge St beautiful collector porcelain is made and sold to the public. Open weekdays, 9am–5pm. Ph: (03) 5422 3337

Get off the Hwy to discover Kyneton's outlying places of interest. **Mineral Springs** on the old Calder Hwy is an ideal picnic stopover, with period pagodas sheltering the springs, and children's play equipment. **Lauriston Reservoir** also offers picnic facilities and fishing. Travel east towards **Cobaw** to view a landscape reminiscent of the Yorkshire high country. **Bringalbit** is a romantic farmhouse and garden located in this wind-swept area. A luxury B&B, the gardens are open to the public, as is artist Allan Fox's studio. Ph: (03) 5423 7223

*Piper St, Kyneton.*

*Kyneton Museum.*

**Chainsaws or bust**
Ever seen a chainsaw sculpture? See the busty lady who greets travellers entering Kyneton from the north on the Calder Hwy. She was sculpted very loudly outside the local Safeway as part of the inaugural Great Australian Arts Crawl.

## Lancefield *Map 12 D2*

Lying on the plains in the east of the region, Lancefield, and Romsey to the south on the Lancefield Rd, give access to many of the region's wineries. **Monument Ck Herb Farm**, on Monument Rd, with picnic and toilet facilities, is also well worth a visit.

Lancefield's small township is dominated by the **Victorian Antique Centre**. A classic boom-time hotel of 50 rooms, it features 3 stories of furniture, decorative arts, clocks, motorcycles and jewellery from various periods. It also offers wine tasting of Cope-Williams wines and is home to Rusty's Restaurant. Open daily 10am–5pm, except Christmas day. Ph: (03) 5429 1666

The **Mt William Aboriginal Quarry** is accessible from Lancefield. Covering several acres, this site was prized for its greenstone, a superior material for stone axeheads, traded for 100s of kms around. This is a protected archeological site, managed by the Wurundjeri. Visits are by special arrangement only. Contact the Victoria Archaeological Survey. Ph:(03) 9690 5322

## Macedon *Map 12 C2*

Macedon sits at the base of Mt Macedon. Traditionally, it was the service centre for the grand houses on the hill. After the Ash Wednesday fires swept through the Macedon Ranges in 1983, some of the old 'upstairs/downstairs' divisions,

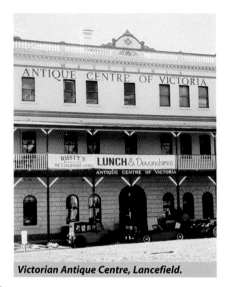

*Victorian Antique Centre, Lancefield.*

it is said, dissipated. This major natural disaster still shapes the memories and activities of people in the area.

The Anglican **Church of the Resurrection**, on the corner of Honour and Macedon Rds, epitomises the story of the Ash Wednesday fires. When two historic Anglican churches were lost in the fires, this single one was built in their stead, symbolically uniting the parishes of Macedon and Mt Macedon. It is a moving experience to visit this stunning, modern church and take in its design and works of art. Sun service: 9am. Ph: (03) 5428 4038

The **Macedon Walking Trail** *(Map 11)*, a substantial hike up Mt Macedon,

*Malmsbury viaduct.*

# Melton's tourist treats

Want to improve your odds when you take that flutter? How about riding with the champions? Or a hard canter through the Toolern Vale Hills? These and other adventures can be catered for by Melton Tourism and Leisure Services. In fact numerous exciting trips have been devised that incorporate stud farm visits, wine tastings at local vineyards and meals at award-winning restaurants. The **Stallions, Spatchcocks and Chardonnays** tour, speaks for itself. The 2-day **Ride with the Champions** tour includes riding instruction at the Hidden Valley Equestrian Centre, a parade of champion horses and tour of a leading stud farm, as well as excellent food and accommodation. Various half- and full-day trail rides leave from several farms in the area. Some of the organised tours require group bookings. Individual visits may be arranged by appt. Ph: (03) 9747 7390

At Melton's tourist precinct, **Warrensbrook Faire** in Rockbank, visitors will be astounded by the huge Dutch windmill that greets them on the Melton Hwy. The **Windmill Garden Estate** offers meals Thurs–Sun, and devonshire teas on weekends. A craft market is held here on the 2nd Sun of each month. Next door, the award-winning **Witchmont Winery** is open for cellar-door sales, while further up the road the **Gamekeeper's Secret** turns on traditional British fare, including an extensive selection of British and Irish beers and ales, steak and kidney pies and scotch eggs. St Patricks Day, a Robbie Burns commemoration and New Years Eve are all occasions to hold celebrations and unusual parties! Ph: (03) 9747 1000

commences at the Old Scout Camp in Macedon. A walking map is available from info centres, or the regional Parks Victoria office: Ph: (03) 5426 1866.

## Malmsbury *Map 12 B1*

The small town of Malmsbury, 10km from Kyneton on the Calder Hwy, was once a quarrying and provisioning town. Now it is a favourite stopover for cakes and coffee and a stroll or picnic beside the lake. The **Malmsbury Gardens** reveal a romantic Ferdinand von Mueller (Victoria's pre-eminent botanist) landscape and impressive five-arched railway viaduct classified by the National Trust. The **Mill Restaurant and Gallery**, which features local artists' work, offers a rare glimpse inside one of the region's 3-storey bluestone mills. Ph: (03) 5423 2267

Malmsbury's 'village green' market is held on the 2nd Sun of the month, and features rare iris, local country women's sponges and cream cakes (not to be missed), and other local produce.

## Melton *Map 9 C5*

Melton is a satellite city of Melbourne now bypassed by the Western Hwy. Once a staging post on the road to the Ballarat goldfields, it offers pleasant, modern shopping and other facilities. It now boasts extensive cycling paths along the Toolern and Little Blind Crks — maps are available from the Melton Civic Centre. Picnic facilities at the **Hannah Watts Park**, an oasis in the often parched western plains, are excellent. Connecting bike and walking paths link to Melton's historic homestead at the **Willows Historic Park**, open Wed, 9.30am–2pm and Sun, noon–4pm. Ph: (03) 9747 3333

The **Melton Waves Leisure Centre** was the first wave pool in Australia. It is a great attraction for kids. Open daily. Ph: (03) 9743 5311

Melton is at the centre of the region's bloodstock industry and has a long history as one of Melbourne's premier horse-breeding areas. The shire has 8 stud farms, including Birchwood Stud, Teppo

*Gamekeeper's Secret, Melton.*

*A beautiful home and garden at Mt Macedon.*

Park and the Independent Stallion Station and extensive eventing facilties. 'Equine tourism', including stud farm visits, has been a natural flow-on.

## Mt Macedon *Map 12 C2*

Gracious houses amid gorgeous gardens sit discreetly behind stone and iron fences. Mt Macedon has a hotel, a general store, several nurseries and a small antique shop, which indicates the pace and style of this classy nook. The **Mount Macedon Hotel** has a glorious garden, ideal for quaffing one of the local white wines on a hot summer's day.

Mt Macedon's most famous attractions are its gardens, some open to the public throughout the year, others in spring and autumn as part of open gardens scheme and special events, (p.92).

Within the **Macedon Regional Park** (p.91), there are endless opportunities for walking, picnicking, and sightseeing. From the summit of the imposing mountain, **Mt Macedon's Memorial Cross** presides over the surrounding country. The Cross is just a short walk from the carpark and picnic area. From there and **Major Mitchell's Lookout**, there are spectacular views stretching for miles towards the south and west.

Proud Alpine Ash are evident along the short track to the **Camels Hump**, although the scene is transformed when gnarled snow gums and alpine mosses greet the walker at its rocky outcrop. The **Eco-Tourism Walking Trail** (*Map 11*) close to **Sanatorium Lake** begins a half km further on, from the Lions Head Rd carpark, which has picnic, fireplace and toilet facilities. The best info boards in the region are to be found here, with concise Aboriginal and settler histories, as well as environmental information.

## Riddles Ck *Map 12 C2*

Dromkeen, the home of Australian children's literature, is on Main Rd, to the east of the Riddles Creek township. An ideal place for family

*Emu Bottom Homestead, Sunbury.*

outings, it also offers holiday program activities for children. Dromkeen runs special workshops, including 'meet-the-author/illustrator' sessions and various performances, and has a stunning collection of children's literature on display. There is a sculpture garden and teashop (open Sun only). Open weekdays 9am–5pm, Sun 12am–4pm. Ph: (03) 5428 6701

### Sunbury *Map 12 C3*
Named after the English town of Sunbury-on-Thames in Middlesex, Sunbury was settled soon after the arrival of John Pascoe Fawkner's party in Port Phillip in 1835. George Evans, a member of this party, was to take up land near Sunbury and name it Emu Bottom. The **Emu Bottom Homestead** has been preserved, but can be viewed only from the outside. The public is welcome to picnic on the lawns in this very pretty location, and Sunday lunch is available in the homestead's **Woolshed**. Bookings are essential. Ph: (03) 9744 1222

**Rupertswood**, an imposing mansion built some decades later, was home to the aristocratic Clarke family who took up huge tracts of land in the 1840s in the Sunbury-Bolinda area. Again, while this fine building is of great historical interest, access is limited. It is presently a college. Visits can be made on occasional open days or by appointment. Ph: (03) 9744 2467

Today Sunbury is a dormitory city for Melbourne and a centre of local economic activity. It also boasts its own Victoria University campus, which occupies the 19th century Sunbury Hospital complex, whose old **Boilerhouse** has been transformed into a community arts complex. For a program of exhibitions and performances, ph: (03) 9218 3330

The Sunbury Info Centre, located in Sunbury's quaint 19th century courthouse, is well stocked with material on local historical and nature walks and bicycle tracks around Sunbury, as well as extensive historical notes. Tea and coffee, and a cosy fire in the colder months, are free.

Sunbury's wineries are its most alluring attraction. The **Goona Warra** and **Craiglee** wineries, both on Sunbury Rd, are especially picturesque. Only 30min from Melbourne, half- and full-day car trips are quite possible, to some or all of Sunbury's 9 wineries (p.89).

### Trentham *Map 12 B2*
**Trentham Waterfall** is spectacular, especially during the wetter months. A 15min walk down the steep bank of the Coliban takes visitors to the soaking spray and crashing water, and on behind the

**The birth of the Ashes**
Lady Janet Clarke started a century of cricket rivalry in 1882 when she presented the captain of the English 11 with the ashes of a cricket bail at the oval beside Rupertswood.

# Macedon-Sunbury Wineries

The Macedon and Sunbury wineries are some of the closest to Melbourne. They also occupy some of the oldest viticultural sites in Victoria, many with wonderful bluestone farm buildings.

Vineyards were established here in the 1850s, and some operated for up to 60 years. Harsh economic times and disease led to the demise of the industry late in the 19th century.

Since the 1970s, a wine-growing renaissance has occurred. Old vineyards were replanted and new ones have been established.

Today this very welcoming boutique industry opens its cellar doors, and offers many other delights. Some wineries offer accommodation. Many also offer fine food.

The specialties of the Macedon Ranges — a cold-climate winegrowing region — are chardonnay, pinot noir and riesling. Sunbury experiences more maritime influences, and produces fuller-bodied, fuller-flavoured red and white wines.

*Cleveland Winery*

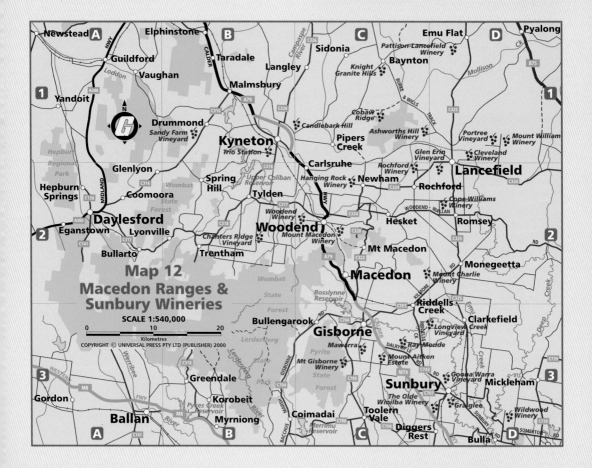

## Macedon ranges wineries

| NAME | ADDRESS | PHONE | OPEN |
|------|---------|-------|------|
| Ashworths Hill Winery | Ashworths Rd, Lancefield | (03) 5429 1689 | 10am–6pm daily |
| Candlebank Winery | Fordes Lane, Kyneton | (03) 9836 2712 | Some Suns, or by appt |
| Cleveland Winery | Off Shannons Rd, Lancefield | (03) 5429 1449 | 9am–5pm daily |
| Cobaw Ridge | Perc Boyers La, East Pastoria | (03) 5429 5428 | 10am–5pm weekends, or by appt |
| Cope Williams Winery | Glenfurn Rd, Romsey | (03) 5429 5428 | 11am–5pm daily |
| Eppalock Ridge | Metcalfe Pool Rd, Resedale | (03) 5425 3135 | 10am–6pm weekends |
| Glen Erin Vineyard | Woodend Rd, Lancefield | (03) 5429 1041 | 10am–late daily |
| Hanging Rock Winery | Jim Rd, Newham | (03) 5427 0542 | 10am–5pm daily |
| Knight Granite Hills | Burke and Wills Track, Bayton | (03) 5423 7264 | 10am–6pm Mon–Sat, 1pm–6pm Sun |
| Mount Aitken Estate | Calder Hwy, Gisbourne Sth | (03) 9744 6122 | 9am–5pm Mon–Fri, 10am–5pm weekends |
| Lancefield Wineries | Scrubby Camp Lane, Emu Flat | (03) 5429 1449 | By appt |
| Mount Macedon Winery | Bawden Rd, Mt Macedon | (03) 5427 2735 | 10am–5pm daily |
| Mount William Winery | Mt William Rd, Tantaraboo | (03) 5429 1595 | 11am–5pm weekends, or by appt |
| Portree Vineyard | 72 Main Rd, Lancefield | (030 5429 1422 | 10am–5pm daily |
| Rochford Wines | Lancefield-Woodend Rd | (03) 5429 1428 | By appt |
| Sandy Farm Vineyard and Winery | Sandy Farm Rd, Denver | (03) 5348 7610 | 11am–5pm weekends or by appt |
| Trio Station Winery | Piper St, Kyneton | (03) 5422 3034 | 10am–6pm daily |
| Woodend Winery | Mahoneys Rd, Woodend | (03) 5427 2183 | Weekends and public holidays |

## Sunbury wineries

| | | | |
|------|---------|-------|------|
| Craiglee | Sunbury Rd, Sunbury | (03) 9744 4489 | 11am–5pm Sun or by appt |
| Diggers Rest Vineyard | Old Vineyard Rd, Diggers Rest | (03) 9740 1660 | 10am–5pm weekends and public holidays |
| Goona Warra Vineyard | Sunbury Rd, Sunbury | (03) 9740 7766 | 10am–5pm daily |
| Longview Ck Vineyard | 150 Palmer Rd Sunbury | (03) 9744 1050 | 11am–5pm daily |
| Mount Charlie | Mt Charlie Rd, Riddells Creek | (03) 5428 6946 | Weekends by appt |
| Mount Gisborne Wines | Waterson Rd, Gisborne | (03) 5428 2834 | by appt |
| Olde Winilba Vineyard | 150 Vineyard Rd, Sunbury | (03) 9740 9703 | 10am–5pm weekends and public holidays or by appt |
| Ray-Monde Wines | 250 Dalrymple Rd, Sunbury | (03) 5427 2777 | Sun or by appt |
| Wildwood Vineyards | St Johns La, Bulla | (03) 9307 1118 | 10am–6pm daily |

## Melton wineries

| | | | |
|------|---------|-------|------|
| St Anne Winery | Western Fwy, Myrniong | (03) 5368 7209 | 9am–5pm weekdays, 10am–5pm weekends |
| Witchmount Estate | 557 Leakes Rd, Rockbank | (03) 9747 1155 | 11am–11.30pm Wed–Sun and 11am–4pm public hols |

**Hanging Rock.**

falls into a small cavern. On entering the park area there is a pleasant picnic area with BBQ facilities.

### Woodend *Map 12 C2*

Woodend lies on the far side of the ranges on the Calder Hwy, aptly named as it is at the woods end. After their arduous trip through the Black Forest, where thieves and bushrangers lay in wait, early settlers and diggers were pleased to reach the coffee houses, hotels and stores that quickly sprang up after gold was discovered further north. One of Caroline Chisholm's immigrant shelters was established here. The town developed around timber milling and farming in the lush lands on the northern face of the Macedon Ranges.

Today Woodend is a small, picturesque town. It has several fine coffee shops, a hotel, gift shops, and specialty shops. The **Woodend Craft Market**, on the 3rd Sun of each month is extensive, with locally made and grown plants, produce, crafts and food. Woodend offers the most direct route off the Calder Hwy to Daylesford, taking in Tylden and Trentham.

Woodend is also home to the **Insectarium of Victoria**, run by two enthusiastic entomologists, Bert and Amanda Caldusio. Ask the right questions and your knowledge of invertebrates will increase exponentially! The biggest yabbie in the world, a collection of gruesome

**Best coffee and cakes**

Betnick Guesthouse,
Woodend Convent
Gallery, Daylesford
Frangos and Frangos,
Vincent St, Daylesford
The Malmsbury Bakery
Sweet Excess, Kyneton
Wallwood, Woodend.

spiders, ant farms and cockroaches are just some of the attractions. Open 10am-4pm daily. Ph: (03) 5427 2222

Woodend's most famous attraction is **Hanging Rock**, 1km along the Romsey-Lancefield Rd. This brooding presence on the landscape is a geological oddity, and the source of considerable myth. While little is known about its significance in Aboriginal lore, it has taken on a mysterious air for generations of Victorians. Joan Linsday's story about the disappearance of three school girls at the turn of the century, and its adaptation for film in *Picnic at Hanging Rock* have been taken as fact. Few people can bring themselves to ignore this intriguing, completely fictional, tale. Numerous walks wend their way around and through the rock.

The **Hanging Rock Reserve** has picnic and BBQ facilities, and a cafe. Various activities, such as night walks and wagon rides are organised in the warmer months. Check with the Woodend Tourist Info Centre. Close by at **Bindara Farm and Nursery** in Goochs Lane, peacock and guinea fowl wander among the topiary gardens and orchards. Children will love the farm and native animals. Open weekends, 9am-5.30pm. Ph: (03) 5423 5237

## National Parks and State Forests

### Brimbank Park *Map 9 C5*

Brimbank Park near Keilor, lies 55m below the western plains where the Maribyrnong River has cut a natural amphitheatre. The rich river flats to the east of the river were market gardens until 1983. Native grasslands and red gums dominate here, and a great variety of birds can be viewed. There is an Australian Plant Trail to explore, and the Maribyrnong River Trail ends here. Cycling and walking are ideal pursuits. Canoeing and fishing are also popular.

There is an info centre here, BBQs, toilets and shelters. Ph: (03) 9336 3911.

### Gellibrand Hill Park *Map 9 C5*

Close to Melbourne Airport, and therefore rather noisy, Gellibrand Hill

Park provides easy walking over 645ha of grassy slopes and woodlands, to Gellibrand Hill. It is named after one of John Batman's Port Phillip Association partners present at the supposed treaty-signing between Batman and the 'Melbourne tribe'. Gellibrand Hill provides extensive views over the plains to Melbourne. The park's major features are its basalt tors and stands of the now rare river red gum along the Moonee Ponds Ck. Eight 'canoe trees' indicate the Aboriginal practice of cutting large oval pieces of timber for canoes, shields and shelters. Kangaroos are plentiful, while the rare, shy Eastern Bandicoot has a preservation area devoted to it. Open 8.30am–4.30pm, Jun–Aug. Ph: (03) 9390 1082

### Lerderderg Gorge SP *Map 12 B3*

By far the largest of the reserves in the region, the Lerderderg SP is the serious bushwalker's option. The terrain is rugged, and the park's interior remote. Short easy walks can be taken at either end of the gorge, from **Blackwood** in the north and **Mackenzies Flat** in the south, where there are picnic facilities. Medium and difficult walks snake along the spectacular weathered sandstone gorge. The park is home to several rare and endangered animal species, and is abundant with bird life. Keep an eye out for wedge-tail eagles.

While the main camping area is at **O'Briens Crossing**, bush camping is allowed throughout the park, as is 4WD along many old logging tracks. Walkers considering difficult day and overnight treks need to be fully prepared, and should consult Parks Victoria literature. 4WD enthusiasts should check for road closures during the winter months. Ph: (03) 5367 2922

### Macedon Regional Park *Map 12 C2*

Heavily wooded, with mountain ash and lush fern gullies, this park embraces the Mt Macedon summit, the Camels Hump – a volcanic protuberance – and the Sanatorium Lake area, as well as the lower, drier areas traversed by the Macedon Walking Trail near Macedon township (p.84). While bushwalkers are welcome, no camping is allowed. The round-trip along the Macedon Walking Trail takes approximately 7hrs. A walking map is available from the Macedon Regional Park office. Ph: (03) 5426 1866

### Organ Pipes NP *Map 9 C5*

This tiny national park is a gem. Its fantastic volcanic formations exude a quiet mystery; particularly interesting are the Organ Pipes and the Rosette Stone. This park has returned a small section of the dry western plains to its pre-settlement splendour. The coverage afforded by the indigenous habitat comes

**Six-legged cure**
The Insectarium of Victoria supplies quantities of ants from its extensive ant colonies to doctors working with cancer patients. Fancy a vegemite and ant sandwich? That's how they are made into medicine.

*Camels Hump — summit of Mt Macedon.*

**Organ Pipes National Park.**

as quite a contrast to those who consider the barrenness of the western plains landscape to be natural.

The park is home to rather tame rock wallabies, and the endangered legless lizard. The walk through the park takes approximately 1hr. Before walking, visitors may view the Organ Pipes slide show, which explains not only the formation of the organ pipes, but the fascinating history of the region's volcanic activity generally. Picnic facilities are available. Ph: (03) 9390 1082

### The Wombat SF *Map 12 B2*

This large state forest borders many of the region's towns and settlements. General recreational use is not, however, encouraged here, as hunting and 4WD are permitted. Access is possible at **Firth Park** near Bullengarook, where Joseph Firth built a home and processed gum leaves for eucalyptus oil distillation in the late 19th century. Walks into the bush, beyond Firth's home garden of exotic trees, lead to a disused sawmill. Various early settlement relics are displayed. This location is ideal for picnicking and camping is permitted.

## Gardens
### Mt Macedon

Mt Macedon's gardens are famous for their glorious mountain settings and colonial graciousness. Many have sweeping lawns and rare specimen

trees, as well as vivid displays of colour in spring and autumn. The gardens – planted 1870s-1890s – feature rhododendrons and hydrangeas, dogwoods in spring, and maples, beeches and oaks in autumn.

The **Forest Glade** on the Mt Macedon Rd is open daily, Sept-May, 10am-5pm. **Tanah-Merah**, meaning 'red earth' in Malay, features a unique Japanese maple walk, sweeping lawns and terraced slopes, and has fabulous views out to Mt Towrong. The work of established contemporary sculptors is exhibited in the garden in 2 shows, held each year, in spring and autumn. The garden and **Tower Gallery** is open Fri-Sun, Sept-June, 11am-4.30pm, or by appt. Ph: (03) 5426 4232

**Hascombe** is another of the Mt's celebrated hilltop glories, one of the few of the grand old gardens to completely escape the Ash Wednesday fires. Open on the 1st Fri of the month, 10am-4pm.

### Gardens across the region

**Bringalbit Garden** is a romantic farmhouse garden that features century-old trees and a willow-lined lake beside a 19th century bluestone farmhouse. Open daily. Ph: (03) 5423 7223

**Forget-Me-Not Cottage Garden and Nursery**, 7-9 Stanhope St, Daylesford is a small garden set around a timber cottage close to Wombat Hill. Colourful, aromatic flowers and herbs are the

**Flowering beauties**
Check *Australia's Open Garden Scheme Guide Book*, available at ABC Shops and newsagents for the Mt Macedon gardens open in spring and autumn. Also, Mt Macedon Horticultural Society, for special events. Ph: (03) 5426 2080/1274

specialty here. Open daily, except Wed, 10am–5pm. Ph: (03) 5348 3507

The **Garden of St Erth** is one of the most popular destinations for garden lovers in the region. Arranged around a small stone miner's cottage in rather inhospitable bush beside the rugged Lerderderg River, its delicately landscaped paths and garden settings offer many pleasant surprises. As well as its fine summer display of abundant daffodils and old-fashioned roses, it features lush herbaceous borders. Open daily, 10am–4pm. Closed Jun, Jul and Dec. Ph: (03) 5368 6514

Quite unlike other botanical gardens in the region, **Gisborne Botanical Gardens**, beside Jacksons Ck, is newly established, offering scope for unusual plantings and modern design. The town's strong relationship with its sister-city in New Zealand is shown here in the decision to specialise in New Zealand plants and to feature a sculpture of a Maori forest god.

The **Kyneton Botanical Gardens**, a quiet place to picnic close to the centre of a busy shopping precinct, are also of botanical interest. Baron Ferdinand von Mueller donated several specimens. The Chilean wine palm and Algerian oak are magnificent trees worthy of a visit in their own right. Von Mueller's

influence can be seen more clearly in the gently landscaped **Malmsbury Gardens**, bounded by the Coliban River.

From the **Wombat Hill Botanic Gardens** you can overlook Daylesford and, from the top of the memorial tower, the whole of the surrounding country. The tower offers magnificent views, especially at sunset. Designed (1870s) by William Sangster the gardens have many rare plantings, including linden, Chinese oak, Bhutan pine, Japanese cedar and crucifix trees. There is a fernery, a begonia house, with seasonal displays, and a gracious elm tree drive.

## Other attractions
### Nurseries

**Dicksonia Rare Plants** at 341 Mt Macedon Rd, Mt Macedon sells a wide range of rare conifers and unusual climbing and rock garden plants. Open 10am–5pm, closed Wed and Thurs. Ph: (03) 5426 3075. **Tristania Park Nursery**, in Honour Ave, is well known for its wide range of plants, including rare species. Ph: (03) 5426 1667. Also in Honour Ave, **Mountside Nursery** specialises in shrubs and trees. Ph: (03) 5426 1443

For rare bulbs, visit **The Bulb Shop**, located beside the Woodend clock tower on the Calder Hwy, open daily, 10am–5pm. **Pronks Bulb Farm** is open to

*View from Wombat Hill Botanic Gardens.*

**Norgates Plant Farm.**

blaze of colours as you round the bend on Old Blackwood Rd, near Barrys Reef. It offers bare-root stock at extremely reasonable prices. BYO gumboots in the wetter months. Open daily, 9am–5pm. Ph: (03) 5424 1777

**Acres Wild** in Woodend is one of the newer specialist nurseries, featuring indigenous trees of the Macedon Ranges, as well as local ground covers, ferns and grasses. Offering knowledge of the area's local natural history, it gives farmers and others the opportunity to re-establish pre-European settlement habitats. With a large display area and cafe planned, it is a pleasant and informative place to visit. Presently open Thurs–Sun, 10am–4pm, with plans to open daily. Ph: (03) 5427 2007

visitors for bulb sales daily, Jan–Apr, 8am–5pm and for viewing the glorious display of colour in Sept. There are BBQs and a picnic area, as well as a walk to Blue Mountain, which takes approx 1.5hrs to complete.

In the Barringo Valley on Ashbourne Rd, **Jack in the Green Nursery** specialises in primulas, while **Barringo Valley Nursery** offers a large display of fuschias under shade cloth. Open daily 9am–5pm, except Tues; closed in winter. Ph: (03) 5426 1565

**Norgates Plant Farm** is famous for its old-fashioned perennials. It is always a delight to come upon the farm's summer

## Recreational activities

### Action

For the action seeker the region offers a number of highlights. **4WD tracks** are accessible from Blackwood into the Lerderderg SF. Maps and info about road closures during winter are available from **Parks Victoria** at Bacchus Marsh. Ph (03) 5367 2922

**Harley Davidson Tours** are also available. Ph: (03) 5429 2292

At Sunbury Airfield **Ultra Light Flying Machines** offers trial instructional flights. Ph: (03) 9744 1305. **Transaero** offers general aviational instruction. Ph: (03) 9740 6277

## Fun for the young

- ★ Bindara Farm and Nursery (p.90)
- ★ Boating on Lake Daylesford (p.80)
- ★ Central Highlands Tourist Railway, Daylesford (p.81)
- ★ Dromkeen Holiday Programs (p.86)
- ★ Fishing, Lauriston Reservoir (p.95)
- ★ Hanging Rock bushwalking and wagon rides (p.90)
- ★ Horseriding in the Barringo Valley (p.95)

- ★ Insectarium of Victoria, Woodend (p.90)
- ★ Melton Waves Leisure Centre Pool (p.85)
- ★ Mineral springs, found throughout the region; kids can pump water endlessly
- ★ Tipperary Track, Daylesford (p.80)
- ★ Tramrides in the bush, Victoria's Tramway Museum (p.82)
- ★ Trentham Falls (p.87)

## Bushwalking

Easy to moderate bushwalks are accessible at Macedon and Mt Macedon along the **Macedon Ranges Walking Trail** (p.84), which takes in the shorter **Eco-Tourism Walking Trail** and Sanatorium Lake (p.86). Similarly, easy to moderate walks can be taken in the Wombat SF outside Daylesford, along the **Tipperary Walking Track** (p.80) and in parts of the Lerderderg Gorge SP. For experienced walkers the **Lerderderg Gorge** offers the most satisfying, remote bushwalking in the region (p.91).

The **Dry Diggings Track**, part of the Gt Dividing Trail, begins in Daylesford and takes in parts of the Goldfields Region, including Fryerstown and Castlemaine. This 55km track winds its way past relics from the region's gold mining past. A map is available from the Daylesford and Castlemaine Tourist Info Centres.

## Camping

Overnight bush camping is possible throughout the Lerderderg Gorge SP wherever the hard day's walk ends. O'Briens Crossing in the north of the forest near Blackwood is accessible by car and has fireplaces and toilet facilities.

Camping is permitted at Firth Park, and also at Mt Franklin but campers will have to take their own water. Caravan parks across the region offer cheap facilities for campers, for instance, at Lake Jubilee, Daylesford, Victoria Park on the Ballan Rd outside Daylesford, and at Hepburn Springs on Forest Ave.

## Cycling

Information on graded road cycling routes to and around the region is available from Sunbury Info Centre, as well as Bicycle Victoria. Ph: (03) 9328 3000. **Earth Active Tours** offers a group cycling tour of the Macedon and Hanging Rock area, departing daily, Mon–Fri, from the Victorian Arts Centre in Melbourne. Ph: (03) 9499 3802

Cycling is an ideal way to see Daylesford and its immediate surrounds, including Hepburn Springs. **Daylesford Bicycle Hire** is located in Vincent St. Ph: (03) 5348 1518

*Victoria's Tramway Museum.*

## Fishing

Stop at the Kyneton Visitor Info Centre for all you need to know about fishing in the region. While catching a trout is almost foolproof at **Tuki Trout Farm**, Smeaton, Ph: (03) 5345 6233, fishers can also try the Coliban, Lauriston and Malmsbury Reservoirs. Lakes, rivers and smaller streams are also listed in visitor info literature.

## Golf

The region boasts a number of beautifully situated golf courses, for instance, at Gisborne, Mt Macedon, Trentham and Woodend. Leaflets are available at tourist info centres.

## Horseriding

There are numerous opportunities for horseriding in the region. **Lancefield Bush Ride and Tucker** on Mt William Rd, Lancefield offers a 1-day option, unique tour and ride, as well as 3hr rides that include a break for tucker and billy tea. Ph:(03) 5429 1627

The **Barringo Valley Equestrian Centre** on Shannons Rd is located in idyllic surrounds on Mt Robertson in the Macedon Ranges. It specialises in small group rides of only 5-6, and beginners are welcome. Glorious 2hr rides to Cherokee are a favourite. Open daily, except Mon and Tues, with rides commencing approx 10am. Ph: (03) 5426 1778.

For trail rides in the Melton area that specialise in 'equine tourism' Ph: (03) 9747 7390.

*Flying at Sunbury.*

# Suggested tours – Map 13

## Weekend escape tour

**Distance**
285km return from
Melbourne CBD

**About this tour**
Be pampered. This 2–3
day tour is dedicated to
browsing, a little
indulgence and
relaxation. It includes
stopovers for some of
the region's best food
and wine, some
exceptional bookshops
and galleries, some
lovely rural retreats
and the ultimate in body
therapy, the Hepburn Spa
Resort. The complex offers
various services to suit your
bank balance. Choose from any
number of charming B&Bs in the
Macedon area for overnight
accommodation. Pond Cottage and
Bringilbit are certainly recommended.
For a really special meal, eat at Lake
House, Daylesford.

**Places of interest**

❶ Woodend township shops and coffee (p.90)

❷ Hanging Rock Winery (p.89)

❸ Piper St, Kyneton (p.83)

❹ Vincent St, Daylesford (p.80)

❺ Pantechnicon Gallery (p.80)

❻ Avant Garden Bookshop (p.80)

❼ Convent Gallery (p.80)

❽ Lake Daylesford (p.80)

❾ Book Barn (p.80)

❿ Hepburn Spa Resort (p.81)

⑪ Lavandula lavender farm (p.82)

⑫ Yandoit (p.82)

*Hanging Rock Winery.*

# Gardeners' tour

### Distance
150km return from Melbourne CBD

### About this tour
This tour takes visitors to some of Mt Macedon's legendary mountain gardens and nurseries, as well as several places of general interest. Other Mt Macedon gardens could be included, depending on season and special opening times. Check with the Woodend Info Centre. Ph: (03) 5427 2033. The gardens and nurseries listed here are open throughout the year, excepting Jul-Aug. Even these few, which are large gardens of considerable interest, represent quite a time-consuming ramble. The trip over the Mt could readily take you on to Hanging Rock on your way to Woodend township.

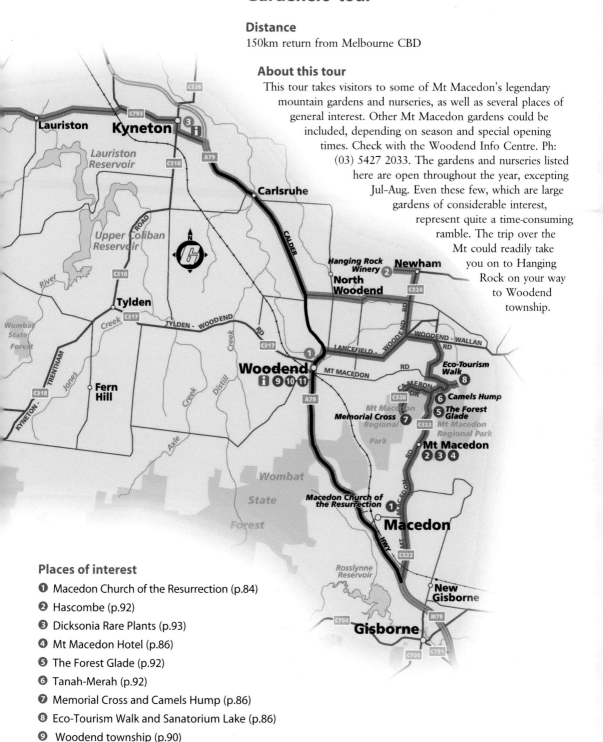

### Places of interest
❶ Macedon Church of the Resurrection (p.84)

❷ Hascombe (p.92)

❸ Dicksonia Rare Plants (p.93)

❹ Mt Macedon Hotel (p.86)

❺ The Forest Glade (p.92)

❻ Tanah-Merah (p.92)

❼ Memorial Cross and Camels Hump (p.86)

❽ Eco-Tourism Walk and Sanatorium Lake (p.86)

❾ Woodend township (p.90)

❿ The Bulb Shop (p.93)

⓫ Acres Wild (p.94)

Left: **Hot air balloon over the Yarra Valley.**
Right: **Koala, Healesville Sanctuary**

# Yarra Valley, Dandenongs and the Ranges

On a clear day in Melbourne, a purple-blue arm of mountains rises up at the edge of the eastern suburbs — a reminder of a natural get-away close at hand. Since the late 1800s this has been the destination for visitors seeking the good things in life.

From the Yarra Valley's plentiful harvest of wine and cheese, to the tempting tea rooms, galleries and gardens of the Dandenongs few guests can spend only 1 day. Most travellers spend a night or 3 at one of the region's charming B&Bs, insisting they need more time to fully explore the ribbons of road that wind their way through towering stands of mountain ash forest and ferns.

Here nature is its own therapy. In a region with 3 National Parks, Victoria's highest waterfalls and an endless web of cross country ski trails you can take your relaxation as you like it. Relaxation is the raison d'être at Warburton's 'hands on health' resort, where Vichy massage, aero baths and fragrant foams banish city stresses.

And who could forget Puffing Billy, the legendary steam train, or Healesville Sanctuary where Australia's best-loved animals can be seen so near. Memories unforgettable are just waiting to be made.

## ℹ Tourist information

**Dandenong Ranges and Knox Visitor Info Centre**
1211 Burwood Hwy
Ferntree Gully 3156
Ph: (03) 9758 7522
Freecall: 1 800 645 505

**Marysville Visitor Info Centre**
Burengeen Park
11 Murchison St, Marysville 3779
Ph: (03) 5963 4567

**Warburton Water Wheel and Visitor Centre**
3400 Warburton Hwy
Warburton 3799
Ph: (03) 5966 5996

**Yarra Valley Visitor Info Centre**
The Old Court House, Harker St,
Healesville 3777
Ph: (03) 5962 2600

**Websites**
www.dandenongranges.tourism.
  asn.au
www.mmtourism.com.au
www.yarraconf.com.au

## Must see, must do

* **Cross-country skiing, Lake Mountain** (p.115)
* **Grape Grazing Festival** (p.102)
* **Yarra Valley Wineries** (p.111)
* **Healesville Sanctuary** (p.107)
* **Puffing Billy Steam Railway** (p.103)
* **William Ricketts Sanctuary** (p.104)

## Radio stations

**Gold:** 104.3 FM
**Radio National:** 621 AM
**Today's Best Music**
**Fox:** 101.9 FM
**Triple J:** 107.5FM
**TT:** FM 101.1

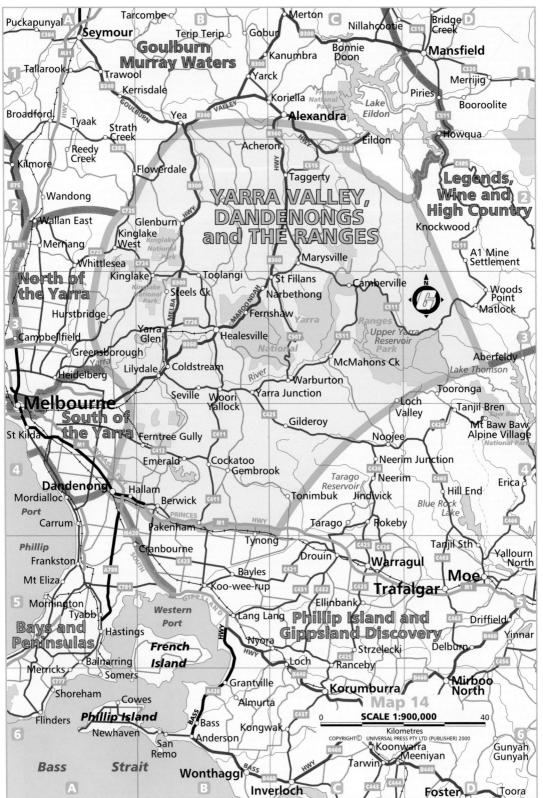

Map 14

SCALE 1:900,000

0          Kilometres          40

COPYRIGHT© UNIVERSAL PRESS PTY LTD (PUBLISHER) 2000

*Horseriding in the Dandenongs.*

**Bird calls**

One famous resident of the region is the **superb lyrebird**. This remarkable creature not only imitates animal calls, it has also been heard mimicking motorbikes, trains and car alarms.

## Natural features

The Yarra Valley, Dandenongs and The Ranges are substantially the result of one of the more dramatic acts in nature's theatre – volcanic eruption. In the south the Dandenongs rise at an average elevation of 500-600m up to the highest point, Mt Dandenong at 633m, and in the east the ranges form the foothills of the Victorian Alps.

Lava flows have not only fashioned and contoured ranges and peaks, they have also helped to create a climate conducive to growth. When prevailing westerly winds reach the natural barrier of the ranges they are forced to rise, cooling the air. Rain is the inevitable result. Flowers and plants flourish in rich volcanic soils that are well-watered with plentiful and regular rain. Blessed with these two vital ingredients (including 1000mm average annual rainfall) the Dandenongs not only boast 5 of The Great Gardens of Melbourne, they also support a myriad of nurseries, aboretums, and smaller gardens. Vineyards of the Yarra Valley, too, know the value of good dirt and seasonal weather: the proof is in the tasting.

In the north, Kinglake NP spreads across the slopes of the Gt Dividing Range. Here, as throughout the region, timber cutters took advantage of the plentiful trees. Today, those with foresight have reserved Kinglake, and sections of the Upper Yarra and Dandenongs as national parks to be enjoyed by future generations.

## History

Beauty and bounty have long been terms synonymous with the Yarra Valley, Dandenongs and the Ranges. To the Aboriginal people whose history in the territory spans 1000s of years, the lush and plentiful Dandenongs were known as *Corhanwarrabul*, meaning 'the creek of the kangaroo', though *Dandenong* itself is of Aboriginal origin, derived from 'banyenong' which means 'a burning' and 'the past'.

Soon after Melbourne's founding in 1835, white explorers recognised the natural mountain asset in the east. Eager pastoralists cleared runs and began grazing sheep and cattle, and as early as 1838 grape vines were planted in the Yarra Valley. Gold proved yet another incentive to head to the region and during the 1850s-1860s miners took their chances at Woods Point and Jericho goldfields in the Upper Yarra.

Timber was one of the region's most coveted assets and thousands of mountain ash trees were felled to construct bridges, piers and wharves in the city of Melbourne. At the turn of the century a narrow gauge rail line was built, eventually extending from Ringwood to

**Racing challenge**

Try racing Puffing Billy: in late Apr the **Great Train Race Fun Run** pits human muscle against railway steam. Ph: (03) 9754 6800

Gembrook, and industry boomed. By 1926 some 42 timber mills were operating in the Upper Yarra.

With the arrival of the railway (and new-fangled motor cars) it was suddenly possible for tourists to escape the city into the peace of the hills. Guest houses and gardens flourished as the region became Melbourne's most fashionable weekend destination. It is this tradition, and a respectful enjoyment of the forests, which continues to delight visitors today.

## Getting there
### By road

To get the best coverage of the region your own wheels are highly recommended. Main access is via the Maroondah Hwy to Lilydale, or via the Burwood Hwy to Upper Ferntree Gully. Brown gum leaf signs map out each tourist route by colour code: green for the Dandenongs, orange for the Yarra Valley, and blue for the Upper Yarra and Marysville.

### By rail

The Met's suburban trains run regularly to Lilydale, Upper Ferntree Gully and Belgrave. Ph: 13 16 38 for timetable and ticket info, plus details of connecting bus services covering towns further afield.

## Getting around
### By coach

Take a day trip from Melbourne to the region's major attractions: **Melbourne's Best Tours** (limit 21 passengers or less), Ph: (03) 9372 8111; **Great Sights**, Ph:

*Grape Grazing.*

(03) 9639 2211; **Gray Line**, Ph: (03) 9663 4455, **Australian Pacific Tours**, Ph: (03) 9663 1611; and **AAT Kings**, Ph: (03) 9663 3377. If the Valley's vineyards are your preferred destination you can also travel there and around by coach, van or mini bus with **Yarra Valley Winery Tours**. Ph: (03) 5962 3870

## Festivals and events
### Coldstream Country and Western Festival

A chance to let down your hair, kick up your heels or just sit back and enjoy 7hrs of non-stop country music from some of Australia's best performers. Food, drinks, amusement rides and stalls are also on offer. Held at the spacious **Coldstream Reserve**, South Gateway, Coldstream during mid Feb. Ph: (03) 9735 1622

### Grape Grazing, Yarra Valley Wineries

This is a celebration of life. Wine, food, music and glorious views encourage groups of friends, families and couples to visit the Yarra Valley wineries for this spirited event held over the 1st weekend in Mar. Ph: (03) 9761 8474

### Yarra Valley Expo, Yarra Glen

Showcasing the Yarra Valley, the expo's diversity appeals to a wide variety of interests: from organics, wine and gourmet food, to fashion parades, art and whipcracking. In addition to novelty events like pig races, there are stalls offering information on business and trade products and services. Mid May weekend, **Yarra Valley Racing Centre**, Yarra Glen. Ph: (03) 9730 1722

### Dandenong Ranges Winter Festival

A chance for residents of the southern hemisphere to sample a wintry Christmas. Traditional dinners, open fires, theatre, carols and other musical performances all create a season to be jolly from Jun–Aug. Freecall: 1 800 645 505

### Winterfest in Warburton

With its history in timber, Warburton is an appropriate host for this highly regarded 'wood-fest' held during the 1st 2 wks of July. Woodwork exhibitions and workshops are complemented by demonstrations from international woodworkers. Other workshops include needlecraft, photography and more. Ph: (03) 5966 5996

### Spring Floral Festival, Olinda

A daffodil display featuring more than 5000 blooms from around the world is the main attraction at the **National Rhododendron Gardens Hall** during Aug; Camellia Fortnight provides additional floral delights. A stunning welcome to spring. Admission fee. Ph: 13 19 63

### Tesselaar's Tulip Festival, Silvan

From mid Sept–mid Oct Tesselaar's Tulip Farm, 357 Monbulk Rd, awakens to a celebration of spring and all things Dutch. A riot of colourful tulips, daffodils and other spring flowers provide the setting for music, food and other festivities. Admission fee. Ph: (03) 9737 9811

### Puffing Billy Carols by Candlelight, Emerald

A traditional affair in an enchanted setting, the performance takes place on a weekend before Christmas. Carols are sung at **Emerald Park Lake** which can be reached by catching a magical ride on a 'Carol Train', departing from the Puffing Billy station, Belgrave or directly, by car. Ph: (03) 9754 6800

## Main localities and towns

This region can be divided up into 3 main areas: the Dandenongs, the Mystic Mts and Warburton Ranges, and the Yarra Valley area.

### Dandenongs

**Belgrave** *Map 17a*

Follow the Burwood Hwy from Upper Ferntree Gully and you'll soon reach Belgrave, best known and loved for its steam train. Take a ride on **Puffing Billy**, Australia's premier steam railway, and you'll travel through hushed majestic mountain ash, over timber trestle bridges, opening out to awesome valley views — this is the way to see the Dandenongs!

*Tesselar's Tulip Festival.*

Puffing Billy had its debut on 18 Dec 1900 when the rail route from Upper Ferntree Gully to Gembrook opened, making accessible previously remote land. In 1953 a landslide threatened to put an end to the train, but dedicated volunteers stepped in, restoring the line in stages.

Puffing Billy's schedule offers a variety of 1-way and return options. From the start of the line at Belgrave you can travel to Menzies Ck where the **Steam Museum** makes a noteworthy stop (open Sat-Sun and public holidays, 10.30am-4.30pm); continue to picturesque **Emerald Lake Park** for a picnic; or travel to the end of the line at Gembrook. Pamphlets available at the stations point out historical and scenic landmarks to look out for on the trip as well as attractions to visit at each destination. Boarding points are at the start of the line at Belgrave, at Menzies Ck, Emerald Lake or Gembrook. For a complete rail experience you can catch the suburban Belgrave train from Flinders St and walk the short distance from the Belgrave platform down to the Puffing Billy platform. Specialty trains include **The Luncheon** or **Afternoon Tea Specials** and **The Dinner Train.** Open daily. Ph: (03) 9754 6800. For fares and timetable 24-hr, Ph: 1 900 937 069 (35c per min).

At 62 Monbulk Rd, Belgrave is the **Sherbrooke Art Gallery**, chosen by the

**Classic tour**
Relive an era and tour the Dandenongs or Yarra Valley in stately 1951 Mark V Jaguars. Call **Pentillie Classic Jaguar Tours** for details. Ph: (03) 9844 4443

Sherbrooke Art Society back in 1973 as a suitable venue for displaying its works. Here you'll discover wonderful individual exhibitions of paintings, pottery, ceramics and jewellery. Most works are for sale. Open Tues–Sun, 10.30am–5pm. Ph: (03) 9754 4264

### Emerald *Map 14 B4*

The first settlement in the Dandenongs, Emerald today lures thousands of visitors to its utopian lakeside park. In 1867 Carl Alix Nobelius arrived in Australia and established in Emerald a nursery that by 1914 was one of the largest in the southern hemisphere (boasting 2 000 000 trees on 180ha). Although Nobelius Nursery no longer exists, **Emerald Lake Park** presently occupies part of the land. Few reserves rival the attractions on offer at the park: picture-perfect lake and footbridge, waterslides, aqua-bikes for hire, children's wading pool, picnic tables, BBQs, tearooms and walking trails. Maps for the walks are available at the kiosk. Admission fee per car. Not only is the park one of Puffing Billy's stopping points, you can also see the largest model railway this side of the equator. **Emerald Lake Model Railway** runs approx 35 model trains through its

*Rows of tulips, Tesselaars, Silvan.*

circuit of tracks. Open Tues–Sun, 11.30am–5.00pm. Ph: (03) 5968 3455

### Kalorama *Map 17*

High in the Dandenongs, where 5 ways intersect, Kalorama offers stunning views over Silvan Reservoir from a **lookout** located along the Mt Dandenong Tourist Rd. Also along the tourist road is **Five Ways Gallery** which features the work of notable Australian artists plus regular solo exhibitions. Open Sat–Thurs, 11am–5pm. Ph: (03) 9728 5975. Nearby, the 22ha **Kalorama Park** has walking tracks to explore. Pick up a pamphlet with maps of the walks at the visitor info centres.

### Mt Dandenong *Map 17a*

For a memorable view of Melbourne take the drive up Ridge Rd to the **Mt Dandenong Lookout**. From this 633m vantage it's an aspect of the city not to be missed. You can picnic here, or take Falls Rd, north of Mt Dandenong, and stop for lunch at **Olinda Falls Picnic Ground**.

Along the tourist road, north of Mt Dandenong, is **William Ricketts Sanctuary**. Set among the mountain ash, its fern gardens and trickling rock waterfalls are a natural gallery for kiln-

## Nursery Highlights

Inspired by nature's generous landscaping many visitors to the Dandenongs enthusiastically tour the nurseries searching for plants to create their own private Eden. Following is a sample of the many nurseries to visit, though watch out for many more signposts inviting you to browse or buy.

**Cloudehill Nursery**, Cnr Woolrich Rd and Olinda-Monbulk Rd. Open daily, 10am–5pm, Ph: (03) 9751 1009.

**Gardeners Gallery**, Cnr Mt Dandenong Tourist and Ridge Rds. Open daily, 10.30am–5pm, Ph: (03) 9751 2525.

**Kallista Corner Garden**, Mt Dandenong Tourist Rd Roundabout, Kallista. Open Tues–Sun, 9am–5pm, Ph: (03) 9755 1945.

**Karwarra Australian Plant Garden**, Mt Dandenong Tourist Rd, Kalorama. Open Tues–Fri, 10am–4pm, Sat–Sun, 1pm–4pm, Ph: (03) 9728 4256.

**National Rhododendron Gardens Nursery**, The Georgian Rd, Olinda. Open Mon–Sun, 10am–5pm, Ph: (03) 9751 1980.

**Tesselaars Bulbs**, 357 Monbulk Rd, Silvan. Open Mon–Fri, 8am–4.30pm, Sat–Sun, 10am–5pm, Ph: (03) 9737 9811.

**Yamina Rare Plants**, Moores Rd, Monbulk. Open Mon–Fri, 9am–4.30pm, Sat–Sun 1pm–4.30pm, Ph: (03) 9752 0035.

fired sculptures of Aboriginal figures, each crafted by the visionary William Ricketts (1899-1993). Ricketts' personal experience with the Aboriginal people of Central Australia influenced his particular reverence for life and his quest for oneness. Open daily, 10am-4.30pm. Ph: 13 19 63. For those affected by the message, Rickett's book *All Life is One* is available for purchase at the entrance.

### Olinda *Map 17a*

Spanish for 'Oh, most beautiful', Olinda is a town north of Sassafras on the Mt Dandenong Tourist Rd. Not only known for its beauty, the town also boasts a cluster of galleries and craft shops. Here you can be assured of finding the perfect gift, selecting from rustic Australian furniture, prints and paintings, glassware, jewellery, leatherwork and many more fine crafts. The town's most prominent feature, however, are its gardens: the **National Rhododendron Gardens, Cloudehill, R J Hamer Forest Arboretum** and **Pirianda** are exquisite to visit year round (p.114) – even the golf course is well-known for its scenery.

### Sassafras *Map 17a*

Following the Mt Dandenong Tourist Rd NE from Upper Ferntree Gully you soon reach Sassafras, a town synonymous with delightful diversions. One of the main attractions **Chudleigh Park of Sassafras** has a reputation for excellent devonshire and other teas and refreshments. Art, crafts and over 2ha of stunning gardens are also there to be enjoyed. Located at 6 Chudleigh Cres. Open Sat–Wed, 10.30am-5.30pm. Ph: (03) 9755 2320. Sassafras can keep you busy for hours exploring its shops and galleries filled with items ranging from Australian bushcraft and art, specialty teas and chocolates to country crafts and Indian antiques.

### *Mystic Mountains and the Warburton Ranges*
### Marysville *Map 14 C2*

Generations of town-weary travellers attest to a spirit of tranquillity lingering in the mystic mountains of Marysville. Once a stopover for miners en route to

*Sculpture, William Ricketts Sanctuary.*

goldfields at Woods Pt, the town was permanently settled in 1863 by John Steavenson and his wife Mary (for whom the -ville was named). Here B&Bs embody a long-standing tradition of gracious hospitality, which is just one reason honeymooners since the 1920s have chosen this destination for their nuptial retreat.

Wandering the main street is an ideal way to acquaint yourself with the town's charm. From the sherbet fountains at **Uncle Fred and Aunty Vals Old Fashioned Lolly Shop** to the lace and local crafts at the **Post Shop**, beautiful clay creations at **Country Touch Pottery** and tempting pastries at glorious smelling bakeries, time is quickly passed and well-spent.

Time is preserved, however, at the **Marysville Museum**. A replica of an English coach house, the museum is home to an impressive display of wheels: vintage, veteran and classic. Notable highlights among the wheeled vehicles and memorabilia that form the Sawyer Family Collection are a horse drawn fire-engine from the 1890s and a 1904 Romany Vardo horsedrawn caravan, both fascinating links in the evolutionary chain of transport. Guided tours available. Located

*Arcadia bed and breakfast, Olinda.*

### Tall stories

Victoria's tallest living tree can be found at the **Cumberland Memorial Scenic Reserve**, 20km east of Marysville. A mountain ash, the Big Tree is 84m high, the tallest of a group appropriately named 'The Tall Trees'.

just off Murchison St at 49 Darwin St. Open Wed-Sun and public holidays, 10am-4.30pm. Ph: (03) 5963 3777

To capture the area's renowned magical mood pay a visit to **Bruno's Art and Sculpture Gallery**. Fantasy and fun intertwine in a gallery and garden featuring more than 200 works, surprising in their beauty and variety. The gallery indoors and the garden outdoors make it a suitable stop regardless of the weather. Gallery and garden open Sat-Sun and public holidays, 10am-5pm; garden also open Mon-Fri, 10am-5pm. Ph: (03) 5963 3513

Nature still works the most enchanting magic. Turn onto Pack Rd off Murchison St then detour left along Falls Rd till you reach the well signposted **Steavenson Falls**. With a drop of 83m over 3 levels, these are Victoria's highest falls. And they are even more spectacular at night, lit up by power generated from a hydro-electric turbine. For an unforgettable forest tour do not miss **Lady Talbot Dr** which starts 500m east of the town's centre off the Marysville-Woods Pt Rd. Named after the wife of Sir Reginald Talbot, Governor of Victoria 1903-1908, the drive covers approx 46km and takes in lush fern gullies, perfect picnic spots and a host of waterfalls and walks. Stops of interest include **Phantom Falls, Keppel Falls Lookout,** an

***Bridge at Steavenson Falls.***

informative **Timber Production Walk** and a scenic view of Marysville. Note that sections of the drive are only accessible to 2WD vehicles in dry weather conditions. Pick up a copy of the DNRE *Marysville Forest Walks and Drives* pamphlet, available from the visitor info centre, for more detailed info on the Lady Talbot Dr plus 7 suggested walks ranging from the easy 1km **Beauty Spot Nature Trail** to the more challenging **Marysville Tour** covering 18km. **Lake Mountain,** 21km east of Marysville off Woods Pt Rd, is best known for cross-country skiing (p.115); however, it is also an excellent area for bushwalking.

Yet another adventure can be had following **The Beeches Rainforest Walk**. Approx 14km from Marysville on the Lady Talbot Dr, ancient moss-covered myrtle beech trees transform this secluded spot into a world of fantasy.

### Warburton Map 14 C3

Picture a friendly town nestled in a valley, a river running through it, an abundance of scenic walks with shady trees and plenty of fresh air – a vision of the perfect retreat. Such a vision describes perfectly the town of Warburton which for almost 100 yrs has been known as an ideal place to relax and unwind.

Since its opening in 1910, languishing Melburnians have come to the **Warburton Health Resort** for a stay of rejuvenation and pampering. Victoria's only fully residential health resort, it offers short-break stays and special lifestyle programs including stress management, weight management and women's health. Ph: (03) 5954 7000 or Freecall: 1800 64 4466. Casual visitors looking to unwind can enjoy a relaxing massage, mud bath, hot pack, or spa treatment with a range of options at the **Warburton Health Spa**, Donna Buang Rd. Bookings required. Open Sun-Fri, 8.30am-4.30pm. Ph: (03) 5954 7461

Stand and watch the **Warburton Water Wheel** in action and you'll soon be hypnotised by the rhythmic churning of the 6m diameter old-style wheel chosen for its role in the town's timber milling past. The wheel is the centrepiece for the visitor info centre located at 3400 Warburton Hwy. The centre also houses an **Interactive Display** that, for a small entry fee, provides an introduction to local history. It also houses a **Gallery Space** showcasing local art, and a **Woodfired Bakery** for the hungry. Open daily, 9am–5pm. Ph: (03) 5966 5996

**Tommy Finn's Trout Farm** on the Warburton Hwy offers the pleasure of fishing in stunning surrounds plus the guarantee of a well-stocked dam. Equipment can be hired if needed and BBQs and picnic facilities are also available. Open daily, 10am–5pm. Ph: (03) 5966 2054

One of the most effective and cheap ways to leave stress behind is to walk. Take a stroll along the **Yarra River** running through the town, along **The Centenary Trail** (mapped in pamphlets) or look out for the *Walks Around Warburton 1* and *2* brochures. **Mt Donna Buang** is Melbourne's closest snow 'playground', off Donna Buang Rd, north of Warburton. Known for its snowmen and tobogganing (p.113), there are also numerous lookouts and trails to enjoy throughout the year.

## Yarra Valley area
### Healesville *Map 14 C2, 15 C3*
Look on your map for the point marked 'nature, culture and fun' and you'll no doubt have discovered Healesville. There are many attractions in this small town, but undoubtedly the most notable is **Healesville Sanctuary** which was initially born of the vision of Sir Colin McKenzie, a noted Australian surgeon and one-time director of the National Museum. In 1929 McKenzie convinced the government to set aside as a reserve for native animals the park he had used in his study of Australian marsupials. Today that land is a haven for the world's largest collection of Australian wildlife. Walking tracks and boardwalks guide you through enclosures, aviaries and wetlands guaranteeing intimate encounters in the animals' natural habitat. The Tasmanian Devil exhibit, Animals of the Night, Frog Bog and World of Platypus prove ever-popular attractions while staff

*Sanctuary attendant with bird of prey.*

demonstrations, including snake shows and bird of prey flights are mesmerising. Because human visitors also require food, a bistro, kiosks, picnic tables and BBQs are available. Off Badger Ck Rd, open daily, 9am–5pm. Note that a number of exhibits are open restricted hours. Ph: (03) 5962 4022. www.zoo.org.au/hs

Appropriately located across the road from the sanctuary, **Galeena Beek Living Cultural Centre** traces the Aboriginal people's culture and relationship with the land. Compelling exhibits recount the history of the Coranderrk Aboriginal Stn, one of the most important stations in Victoria. A 230m outdoor trail provides a fascinating introduction to bush tucker and bush medicine and an authentic Aboriginal artifacts shop sells art, jewellery, and other crafts made by Victorian Aboriginal artists. Guided tours during summer months. At 22–24 Glen Eadie Ave. Open Wed–Sun, 10am–5pm. Ph: (03) 5962 1119

Though you may have lost yourself in a myriad of mazes, **Hedgend Maze**, 132 Albert Rd, offers the challenge of a giant hedge maze (complete with treasure hunt), adventurous mini-golf, rainbow maze, frisbee golf, a giant board for checkers (draughts), as well as dramatic (free) views of the Yarra Ranges. All activities are included in the admission price. BBQs, tearooms and picnic facilities available. Open 10am–dusk.

**Time walk**
Old tramlines from the timber days still lace much of the Warburton area. A 2-day, 36 km walk from Powelltown to Warburton follows old tramways along a **Walk into History** trail detailed in a pamphlet available from the visitor info centre.

Ph: (03) 5962 3636. Enjoy valley views on the **Yarra Valley Tourist Railway**. Departing from the Healesville Railway Stn, trolley trains cross Watts River, pass under Donovans Rd overbridge and travel through a historic tunnel at Tarrawarra Winery. Open Sun and public holidays, departing 11am, then every 30min till 4.30pm (weather permitting). Ph: (03) 5962 2220

Healesville's sweeping scenery and relaxed pace of life provide inspiration for many local artists. You can enjoy their handiwork and pick up a hand-crafted souvenir at various small local galleries including the **Healesville Art Gallery of Lapidary and Pottery**, 13 Nigel Crt, which features Australian opals among its varied collection. Open daily, 10am–5pm. Ph: (03) 5962 4147. Enjoy a coffee then peruse the art in the **Church Street Gallery and Cafe**, 4 Church St, Ph: (03) 5962 2117 or browse paintings by renowned Australian artists at **Tuscany Galleries**, adjacent the Maroondah

Reservoir on McKenzie Ave. Open Fri–Sun and public holidays, 10.30am–5pm. Ph: (03) 5962 5917

### Lilydale *Map 15 A3*

Since the late 1830s Lilydale has been a wine-growing region — the suburb even bears the name of vigneron Paul de Castella's wife. Today Lilydale is a doorway to the wine region of the Yarra Valley, offering attractions of its own worth visiting en route.

Opera diva Dame Nellie Melba retired to the Lilydale area after an internationally acclaimed career. At 33 Castella St, **The Museum of Lillydale** houses Australia's only permanent collection in tribute to her, including photographs, programs, clothing and other memorabilia. The museum also features historical detail on the local area plus temporary exhibits on a range of themes. Open Wed–Sun, 11am–4pm. Ph: (03) 9739 7230. Lilydale is also proud of its picturesque **Lillydale Lake**, an ideal stopping point to stretch your legs and enjoy the waterbirds and other wildlife. Picnic facilities and BBQs available.

### Toolangi *Map 14 B3*

Sixteen km north of Healesville the small town of Toolangi has a generous handful of attractions that make it a memorable spot on the map. C J Dennis evidently thought so. At 98 Kinglake Rd **The Singing Gardens of C J Dennis** are a memorial to the Australian poet and journalist best known for his book *The Sentimental Bloke*. From 1915-1935 (the year of his death), Dennis lived here at Arden. *The Singing Gardens*, his last published book, has provided a fitting name for the 2ha gardens and tearooms. Open Sat–Thurs, 10am–5pm, closed during Aug. Ph: (03) 5962 9282. To appreciate the work of another gifted artist visit **Toolangi Pottery** at 95 Kinglake Rd and marvel at David Williams' crystalline glazed pottery. Open daily, 10am–5pm. Ph: (03) 5962 9287

In this region of astonishing trees the **Toolangi Forest Discovery Centre** tells an important story — the story of the forest. Appearing in the bush like a

**Hedgend Maze.**

*Scenic road, Black Spur.*

**Black spur**

The stunning section of scenic road between Healesville and Marysville, Black Spur (Black's Spur), was so named because displaced Aboriginal people from northern Victoria took this route on their way to Coranderrk Stn near Healesville.

ground-level treehouse, the centre, on Kinglake Rd, explains the history and use of trees. Outside a **Sculpture Trail** continues the message with 9 sculptures from a 1996 International Sculpture Event, each made from materials found in the forest. While you're here, pick up a unique gift crafted from Australian timber. Open daily, 10am–5pm. Ph: (03) 5962 9314. The centre also has pamphlets on the 44km **Toolangi Black Range Forest Dve** (off Myers Ck Rd). Highlights along the way include the **Mt St Leonard lookout**; the 15min **Wirrawilla boardwalk** that winds its way through rainforest; watery enchantment at the **Murrindindi Cascades** and **Wilhelmina Falls**; and any number of appealing picnic areas.

Drive west from Toolangi on the Kinglake-Healesville Rd and you'll soon reach the lake-less town of Kinglake. Just before reaching the town, near **Kinglake NP** (p.113), there is a museum built from 13 569 bottles. At 8 Parkland Rd, **Kinglakes House of Bottles** and tearooms is open Sat–Thurs and public and school holidays, 10am–5pm. Ph: (03) 5786 1328

## Wandin and district *Map 15 B3*

Wandin and the surrounding region's rich volcanic soils are a point of pride for its residents – local lore tells of early settlers carrying handfuls of the earth in their pockets to show off to friends. During Nov and Dec, **Wandin Valley Farms** at 75 Wellington Rd (adjacent Mont De Lancey) offer a chance to sample some fruit of that earth: luscious cherries. From the sales centre you can also view the cherry grading production line. Open Nov–Dec, 2pm–6pm. Ph: (03) 5964 4669. **Warratina Lavender Farm**, on Quayle Rd, off the Warburton Hwy, offers fragrant proof of the soil's fertility. The farm sells lavender plants and products and has picnic facilities to encourage you to take your time enjoying the flowers and the view. Open Sat–Wed, 10am–4pm. Ph: (03) 5964 4650

Appreciation for a place is helped by an understanding of its past: at **Mont De Lancey** the Sebire's family home offers a personal glimpse into life of the period. Built in 1882, the house has been refurnished with much of its original fittings – look out for the main bed (itself a work of art) and the cherry pips used to warm it. Tour the reconstructed slab kitchen then for more insight into the pioneering past visit the museum which proudly recounts the district's cultural, sporting and farming life. The relocated chapel and Martha's tearooms make pleasant stops for rest and reflection. Located on Wellington Rd, off

**Fruit festa**

When the season is right take up the invitation to pick your own berry and stone fruits at any number of establishments around Wandin, Silvan and Seville.

**Produce of the
Yarra Valley Dairy.**

Warburton Hwy. Open Wed–Sun,
10am–5pm. Ph: (03) 5964 3855

### Yarra Valley *Map 15*

Driving into the Yarra Valley the 1st thing
you notice is the sweeping view out to
the ranges; the 2nd thing you notice is
the perfect lattice of vines. Wine has an
undisputed history in this region.
Grapevines were planted as early as the
1830s and the industry continued to
thrive till the turn of the century. Dairy
farming dominated for a time, but the era
of wine was born again in the 1960s.
Today the region boasts almost 2500ha
of vines, producing a diverse variety
including pinot noirs, chardonnays,
cabernet sauvignons and world-class
sparkling wines.

When settlers were first putting their
land to use, not everyone opted for vines.
In the 1850s the Bell family, immigrants
from Scotland, established **Gulf Stn** at

**View from the Green Point Room, Domaine
Chandon Winery.**

Yarra Glen to provide meat for the
goldminers. With an eye for opportunity
they continued to expand: Ayrshire dairy
cows were introduced once the railway

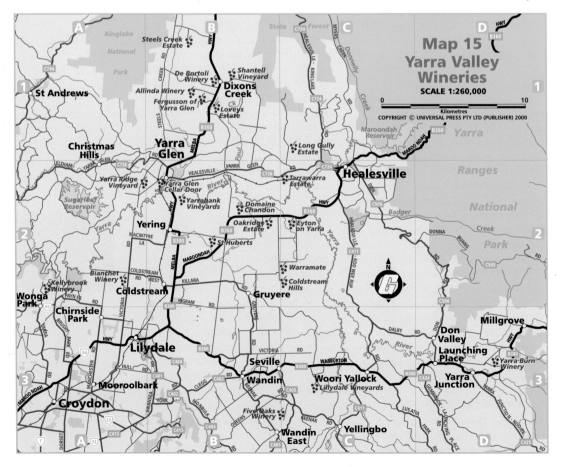

## Wineries of the Yarra Valley

| NAME | ADDRESS | PHONE | OPEN |
| --- | --- | --- | --- |
| **Allinda Winery** | 119 Lorimers La, Dixon Creek | Ph: (03) 5965 2467 | *11am–5pm, weekends and public hols* |
| **Bianchet Winery\*** | 187 Victoria Rd, Lilydale | Ph: (03) 9739 1779 | *10am–6pm daily* |
| **Brahams Creek** | Woods Point Rd, E Warburton | Ph: (03) 9560 0016 | *11am–5pm daily* |
| **Coldstream Hills** | 31 Maddens Ln, Coldstream | Ph: (03) 5964 9388 | *10am–5pm daily* |
| **De Bortoli Winery and Restaurant\*** | Pinnacle Ln, Dixon Ck | Ph: (03) 5965 2271 | *10am–5pm daily* |
| **Domaine Chandon** | 'Green Point' Maroondah Hwy, Coldstream | Ph: (03) 9739 1110 | *10.30am–4.30pm daily* |
| **Eyton on Yarra\*** | Cnr Maroondah Hwy and Hill Rd, Coldstream | Ph: (03) 5962 2119 | *10am–5pm daily* |
| **Fergusson of Yarra Glen\*** | Wills Rd, Yarra Glen | Ph: (03) 5965 2237 | *11am–5pm daily* |
| **Five Oaks Winery** | Aitken Rd, Seville | Ph: (03) 5964 3704 | *10am–5pm weekends and public hols* |
| **Gembrook Hill Vineyard** | 2km north of Gembrook on Launching Place Rd, Gembrook | Ph: (03) 5968 1622 | *By appointment only* |
| **Kellybrook Winery and Restaurant\*** | Fulford Rd, Wonga Pk | Ph: (03) 9722 1304 | *9am–6pm, Mon–Sat, 11am–6pm, Sun* |
| **Lillydale Vineyards\*** | 10 Davross Crt, Seville | Ph: (03) 5964 2016 | *11am–5pm daily* |
| **Long Gully Estate** | Long Gully Rd, Healesville | Ph: (03) 9807 4246 | *11am–5pm weekends and public hols* |
| **Loveys Estate and Restaurant\*** | 1548 Melba Hwy, Yarra Glen | Ph: (03) 5965 2422 | *12pm–5pm, Wed–Sun* |
| **Oakridge Estate** | 864 Maroondah Hwy, Coldstream | Ph: (03) 9739 1920 | *10am–5pm daily* |
| **Shantell Vineyard** | 1974 Melba Hwy, Dixons Ck | Ph: (03) 5965 2264 | *10.30am–5pm, Thur–Mon* |
| **St Huberts** | Cnr Maroondah Hwy and St Huberts Rd, Coldstream | Ph: (03) 9739 1118 | *9.30am–5pm, Mon–Fri, 10.30am–5.30pm, weekends and public hols* |
| **Steels Ck Estate** | 1 Sewell Rd, Steels Ck | Ph: (03) 5965 2448 | *10am–6pm weekends and public hols* |
| **Tarrawarra Vineyard** | Healesville Rd, Yarra Glen | Ph: (03) 5962 331 | *10.30am–4.30pm daily* |
| **Warramate** | 27 Maddens Ln, Gruyere | Ph: (03) 5964 9219 | *10am–6pm weekends and public hols* |
| **Yarra Burn Winery\*** | 60 Settlement Rd, Yarra Jctn | Ph: (03) 5967 1428 | *10am–6pm daily* |
| **Yarra Glen Vineyard** | Cellar Door, 19 Bell St, Yarra Glen | Ph: (03) 9730 1230 | *9.30am–4.30pm daily* |
| **Yarra Ridge Vineyard** | Glenview Rd, Yarra Glen | Ph: (03) 9730 1022 | *10am–5pm daily* |
| **Yering Station-Yarrabank Vineyards\*** | 38 Melba Hwy, Yarra Glen | Ph: (03) 9730 1107 | *9am–5pm, Mon–Fri, 10am–6pm, weekends* |

\* denotes restaurant facility

opened (as milk could then be supplied to Melbourne) and draught horses were bred to pull guns for the Indian army. A host of other farmyard animals were bred. During the past century only minor changes have been made, making Gulf Stn one of the most unique working farms to visit. Visitors can explore the solid timber slab buildings, household effects, farming implements, formal garden and of course, see the farm animals. Open Wed–Sun, 10am–4pm, Melba Hwy, Yarra Glen. Ph: (03) 9730 1286. Wine's perfect complement — cheese — is available for purchase at the renowned **Yarra Valley Dairy** boutique cheese factory, McMeikans Rd, Yering.

*Yarra Valley.*

Enjoy a taste of both at its on-site cafe.
Open Sun–Thurs, 10am–5pm, Fri–Sat,
10.30am–10pm. Ph: (03) 9739 0023

## National Parks and State Parks

### Cathedral Range SP *Map 14 C2*

Approximately 10km NW of Marysville,
Cathedral Range SP is a jagged 7km
ridge of upturned rock. Walks vary from
the easy 40min **Little River Track**, the
steeper 10min **Sth Jawbone Track**
(Sth and Nth Jawbone are popular with
experienced rockclimbers), to a wide
selection of difficult walks including
the 30min **Little Cathedral Peak Track**
and the very difficult, 30min **Wells
Cave Track**. Koalas are commonly
sighted in the park which is also home
to other wildlife including the lyrebird.
In springtime, the native orchids are
enchanting. Camping is permitted at
Neds Gully, Blackwood Flat, Cooks
Mill, Sugarloaf Saddle and the Farmyard.
Ph: 13 19 63

### Dandenong Ranges NP *Map 17a*

Declared in 1987, Dandenong Ranges NP
covers 3215 ha, incorporating 5 sections:
**Fern Tree Gully, Sherbrooke, Olinda,
Doongala** and **Mt Evelyn**. The world's
tallest flowering plant, the mountain ash
tree, is trademark of the park, along with

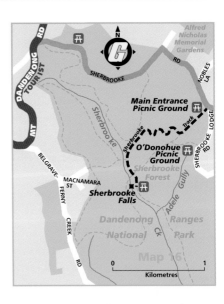

lush fern gullies and prolific wildlife.
Admission is charged in some sections.

The oldest area in the NP, Fern Tree
Gully occupies the SW area. Take the
3km **Living Bush Nature Walk** (1.5hr
loop) from the Lower Picnic Ground, cnr
Mt Dandenong Tourist Rd and Burwood
Hwy, to acquaint yourself with the
features of the forest, or the 5km **Kokoda
Trail** (2hrs) with its steep 1000 steps
dedicated to those who died on the
Kokoda Trail in Papua New Guinea
during WWII. From the One Tree Hill
picnic area, along the road of the same
name, you can take the 3.7km **One Tree
Hill trail** (1.5hr loop).

Covering 800ha in the southern
section, Sherbrooke is the largest part of
the NP and is known for its stunning
mountain ash forest and for its resident
superb lyrebird. A popular walk is
**Sherbrooke Falls** (1hr return, 2.4km),
accessible from either the main entrance
or O'Donohue Picnic Grounds, off
Sherbrooke Rd. Other trails range from
300m to 7.1km. The Olinda area of the
NP has several popular picnic reserves,
including **Olinda Falls Reserve, Valley
Picnic Ground** and **Eagles Nest Picnic
Ground**. A challenging walk for
experienced bushwalkers is on the 6.5km
**Valley Walk**. Mt Evelyn and Doongalla
areas are also laced with walking trails and
the **Doongalla Homestead and Stables
Site** is a fabulous setting for a picnic lunch.

*Beeches Walk, Sherbrooke Forest.*

### Kinglake NP *Map 14 B2*

Divided into 3 main sections (east, west and north), the 21 600ha Kinglake NP incorporates a diverse range of natural attractions. **Masons Falls** (west), **Mt Everard Track** (east) and **Wombelano Falls** (north) are popular destinations. Messmate forest, open grassy areas, rainforest and wet and dry forests host plentiful wildlife, in fact; it was here that David Attenborough, famous naturalist filmmaker, came to film the superb lyrebird in action. Caravan and camping facilities are at **The Gums** on the Kinglake-Glenburn Rd, including access for people with limited mobility. Bookings required. Ph: (03) 5786 5351

### Yarra Ranges NP *Map 14 C3*

Declared in 1995, the 76 000ha Yarra Ranges NP serves a special purpose — as a vast water catchment area for Melbourne's water supply. Though visitor access is restricted to preserve water quality, there are numerous breathtaking walks, waterfalls and picnic spots. Popular sites are **Mt Donna Buang, Keppels Falls, Lake Mountain** and **The Beeches**. Trademark to the NP are its mountain ash, lush ferns and temperate rainforest, and the park provides habitat for around 40 native mammals and 120 species of native birds. Camping is available at Upper Yarra Reservoir Parklands and at campsites at Warburton and Marysville. Bookings required. Ph: 13 19 63

## Parks and gardens

### Alfred Nicholas Gardens *Map 16*

The 13ha Alfred Nicholas Gardens, Sherbrooke Rd, Sherbrooke were once the idyllic backyard of a family famous for developing the pain relieving Aspro. Pack a picnic and enjoy a pain-free afternoon by the ornamental lake shaded by generous trees. Admission is charged. Open daily, 10am–5pm. Ph: (03) 9755 2912

### Cloudehill *Map 14 B4*

Set in the old Woolrich estate, Cloudehill complements its established gardens with contemporary planting and landscaping. Highlights include an Italian-styled Green

*Alfred Nicholas Gardens Sherbrooke.*

Gardens, an old Rose Walk and a Maple Court featuring 2 weeping Japanese maples imported from Yokohama in 1928. Open daily, 10am–5pm. Ph: (03) 9751 1009. Cnr Woolrich Rd, Olinda-Monbulk Rd.

### George Tindale Gardens *Map 17a*

Under a canopy of mountain ash trees the George Tindale Gardens are a pleasure to explore. Enchanting paths through flowering beds open up into graceful stretches of lawn. Colours are vibrant in every season and in winter the daphne is divine. At 33 Sherbrooke Rd, Sherbrooke. Open daily, 10am–5pm. Ph: (03) 9755 2912. Admission is charged.

### Karwarra *Map 17a*

Specialising in native Australian plants, Karwarra is particularly popular with overseas visitors. Set in 2ha surrounded by stunning views it is renowned for its banksia, boronia, grevillea and waratah and an 'unusual' Tasmanian plants section. Guided tours available. Located along the Mt Dandenong Tourist Rd, Kalorama. Admission is charged. Open

**Shy possum**

Yarra Ranges NP is host to Victoria's fauna emblem — the endangered **Leadbeaters possum**. Up until 1961 this shy possum was thought to be extinct.

**Tea time**

Eco Adventure Tours operate **Nature Walks with Billy Tea and Damper**, offering guided tours of the Maroondah Reservoir Park, Badger Weir, Donellys Weir and Silvan Reservoir Park and their natural environs, finishing off with campfire bread and a cuppa.

Ph: 13 19 63

*Tour of the National Rhododendron Gardens.*

Tues–Fri, 11am–4pm, Sat–Sun, 1pm–4pm.
Ph: (03) 9728 4256

### Maroondah Reservoir Park
### Map 15 C1

Approximately 3km from Healesville on McKenzie Ave is one of Melburnians' best-loved picnic spots: **Maroondah Reservoir Park**. Blending traditional early English landscaping with native trees and plants, the park features a Rose Stairway, historic valve house, bush tracks through stands of eucalypts and ample picnic and BBQ facilities. Open Mon–Fri, 8.30am–4pm, Sat–Sun, 8.30am–5pm; open till 8pm in Nov, and 9pm, Dec–Jan. Ph: 13 19 63

### National Rhododendron Gardens
### Map 17a

The National Rhododendron Gardens, The Georgian Rd, Olinda displays 40ha of alluring blooms: 15 000 rhododendrons, 12 000 azaleas, 3000 camellias and 250 000 daffodils, each in their season. Enjoy the entire gardens on a 3hr self-guided walk, or take a shorter route for a more relaxed visit. In spring the Garden Explorer provides a comfortable ride through the stunning colours. Open Mon–Sun, 10am–5pm. Ph: 9751 1980. Admission is charged Sept–Nov.

### Pirianda Gardens *Map 17a*

Terraced along the mountain slopes, the 11ha Pirianda Gardens are interlaced with walking paths to wander and enjoy the range of native and exotic vegetation. Discover native fern gullies, giant lilies and a plethora of resident birds. Hacketts Rd, off Olinda-Monbulk Rd. Open daily, 10am–5pm. Ph: (03) 9751 1980

### R J Hamer Aboretum *Map 17a*

Turn onto Woolrich Rd off the Olinda-Monbulk Rd to retreat into the shade of the R J Hamer Arboretum. More than 150 species of trees, both native and exotic cover 100ha of woodland. Walk the trails or picnic among the groves. Unforgettable in autumn. Open daily, 10am–5pm. Ph: (03) 9751 1980

### Silvan Reservoir Park *Map 15 B3*

On Stonyford Rd, Silvan off Lilydale-Monbulk Rd, Silvan Reservoir Park is as accessible as it is beautiful. Only 50km from Melbourne, the park is well-equipped with picnic and BBQ facilities and a playground for the kids. Walks range from 30mins–2½hr. Open daily, 8.30am–sunset. Ph: 13 19 63

## Other attractions

### Buxton Trout and Salmon Farm

On the Maroondah Hwy at Buxton is Victoria's oldest commercial trout hatchery — a fitting venue for a guaranteed catch of fresh rainbow trout or Atlantic salmon. BYO or hire equipment and bait or simply purchase fish product at their counter sales.

BBQ and picnic facilities. Open daily, 9am–5pm. Ph: (03) 5774 7370

**Great Dandenongs Treasure Hunt**
Prepare to embark on a day or more of discovery and adventure. Designed for 2 adults and 3 children, the award-winning Treasure Hunt pack includes: a map, clues to tour you round various venues in The Dandenongs, *Masquerading in the Rainforest* book and several admission tickets, including 4 family passes to various venues and 2 children's tickets to Puffing Billy. For around $30, the package is great value. Ph: (03) 9761 8055

## Recreational activities

### Air adventure
Take in the breathtaking Yarra Valley in all its morning glory on a champagne breakfast balloon ride. Although expensive, the view of the valley makes for a truly inspired diary entry. Contact **Global Ballooning**, Ph: 1 800 627 661, **Go Wild Ballooning**, Ph: (03) 9890 0339, or **Peregrine**, Ph: (03) 9662 2800

### Exploring
**All Trails**, based at 14 Maroondah Hwy, Lilydale run group bicycle tours and walks throughout the Yarra Valley, Marysville and towns of The Dandenongs. Trips range from 1–14 days. BYO wheels or use one of the bikes available for hire. Scrumptious home-baked meals are included in the cost. Bookings required. Ph: (03) 9735 5592. www.alltrails.com.au

Eco-Adventure Tours specialise in forest night walks, spotlighting the night life of wildlife in the Dandenongs and Yarra Valley. Night safaris in purpose-built vehicles are also available. Bookings required. Ph: (03) 5962 5115

### Horseriding
Just north of Healesville is the well-regarded **Black Spur Trail Riding Centre**. The Centre caters for beginners through to experts, offering 2hr rides around the Mt Dom Dom area, 3hr supper rides at dusk, a range of overnight rides camping under the stars and 7-day Heritage Horse

*Cross country skiers, Lake Mountain.*

**Feathered welcome**
Be prepared to share your picnic with hundreds of colourful feathered companions at **Grants Picnic Ground**, off Monbulk Rd, Kallista, famed for its friendly Crimson Rosellas.

trail rides. Maroondah Hwy, Narbethong (1km past the hotel). Ph: (03) 5963 7191

### Snow action
Less than 2hrs from Melbourne via Marysville, **Lake Mountain** is Victoria's premier cross-country skiing venue. More than 40km of trails are ranked from beginner to intermediate and advanced. Three toboggan runs also operate. Equipment can be hired on the mountain or from ski shops in Marysville and the Alpine Resorts Commission info centre on Lake Mountain is open daily during snow season from 6am–6.30pm. Ph: (03) 5963 3288. Tobogganing is also popular at **Mt Donna Buang**, north of Warburton. Toboggans are usually available for hire on the mountain or in Warburton. Contact the DNRE for snow reports and info. Ph: (03) 5964 7088

## Fun for the young
★ Black Spur Trail Riding Centre (p.115)
★ Emerald Lake Model Railway (p.104)
★ Great Dandenongs Treasure Hunt (p.115)
★ Healesville Sanctuary (p.107)
★ Hedgend Maze (p.107)
★ Puffing Billy (p.103)
★ Tobogganing, Lake Mountain or Mt Donna Buang (p.115)

# Suggested tours — Maps 17a and b

## Garden tour — Map 17a

### Approximate distance

110km return from Mlebourne CBD

*Rhododendron Gardens in Autumn.*

### About the tour

Although spring is the obvious season to take this tour, each of the gardens are planted for year-round enjoyment. From Belgrave take the tourist road to Kallista, stopping at Piranda gardens before setting out towards Sherbrooke and the stunning rhododendrons at Olinda. Stop at Mt Dandenong where you can consider a contrasting urban view from the Mt Dandenong lookout or be enchanted by sculptures in a garden sanctuary. Experience a distinctively Australian nursery at Karwiarra before returning home refreshed. No matter where you are on the tour there is sure to be a cafe, tearoom or hotel to amply cater to your appetite.

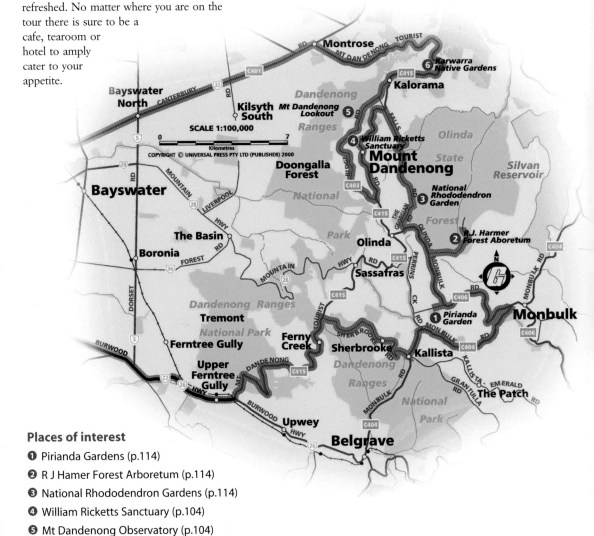

### Places of interest

❶ Pirianda Gardens (p.114)

❷ R J Hamer Forest Arboretum (p.114)

❸ National Rhododendron Gardens (p.114)

❹ William Ricketts Sanctuary (p.104)

❺ Mt Dandenong Observatory (p.104)

❻ Kawarra (p.113)

# Suggested tours
## Romantic escape — Map 17b

**Approximate distance**
210km return from Melbourne CBD

***Bruno's Sculpture Garden.***

**About the tour**
Share a weekend away discovering some of Victoria's most enchanting sights. The Yarra Valley offers plentiful wineries to wander, plus acclaimed restaurants where you can enjoy a relaxing lunch with a glass of the local vintage. Continue up through Healesville, taking in a gallery or 2 with coffee, then continue up the Maroondah Hwy, along the scenic Black Spur to Marysville. Enjoy a night in the B&B of your choice then drive the scenic Acheron Way to Warburton where you have time for a relaxing massage and spa. Head for home along the pleasant route through Wandin and Seville.

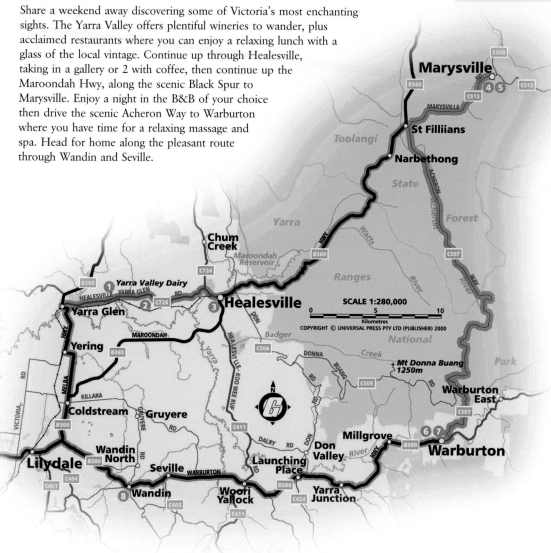

**Places of interest**

❶ Wineries of the Yarra Valley (p.111)

❷ Yarra Valley Dairy (p.111)

❸ Healesville galleries (p.108)

❹ Steavensons Falls, Marysville (p.106)

❺ Bruno's Art and Sculpture Gallery, Marysville (p.106)

❻ Warburton Health Spa (p.106)

❼ Stroll along the Yarra River, Warburton (p.107)

❽ Mont De Lancey Historic Home and Garden, Wandin (p.109)

Left: **Sorrento Bay.**
Right: **Brighton bathing boxes.**

# Bays and Peninsulas

**P**ort Phillip Bay is renowned for its gentle waters and hazy beauty. A vast area of sea, it laps suburban Melbourne as well as distant rural shores. Safe boating and swimming, relaxing beachcombing and family picnicking are ideal pursuits. On the Bellarine and Mornington Peninsulas wild ocean beaches are never far away. Dramatic rock and cliff formations, deep blue rockpools the size of swimming pools, and fabulous surf entice swimmers and surfers, walkers and hang gliders.

The region is also a warm and wonderful winter destination. The exuberant inner suburbs of Port Melbourne and St Kilda and prestigious middle suburbs like Brighton, have many cosmopolitan entertainments — markets, art cinema, cafes and restaurants. Williamstown, a short distance from Melbourne by ferry or by car and the Westgate Bridge, is a historic port town. The little known Werribee has many a fantastic tale to tell of early settlement, and some major tourist attractions. The hinterlands of the Bellarine and Mornington Peninsulas — the region's premier destinations — are brimming with energy in the arts, viticulture, food production and craft. Exceptional B&Bs, fine wineries and marvellous restaurants with wood fires and great views greet visitors in many beautiful locations.

## Must see, must do

★ **Arthurs Seat** (p.129)

★ **Coastal Art Trail** (p.137)

★ **Cycling on Pt Nepean** (p.144)

★ **Dolphin swimming tours** (p.144)

★ **Queenscliff township** (p.127)

★ **Red Hill Estate Winery** (p.133)

★ **Sorrento** (p.135)

★ **Werribee Mansion and Open Range Zoo** (p.138)

## Radio stations

**Geelong and Bellarine Peninsula**

**Bay FM:** 93.9 FM

**Geelong Radio:** 100.3 FM

**Tourist radio:** 88.00 FM

**Mornington Peninsula Visitor radio:** 87.6 FM

**3RPP:** 98.7 FM

**Top of the Bay**

**Southern FM:** 88.3FM

**Werribee and Pt Cook**

**WYN FM:** 88.9 FM

## ℹ Tourist information

**Geelong and Gt Ocean Rd Visitor Info Centre**
Stead Park, Princes Hwy, Geelong 3214
Ph: (03) 5275 5797

**Hobson Bay Visitor Info Centre**
Commonwealth Reserve, Nelson Place, Williamstown 3016
Ph: (03) 9397 3791

**Market Square Shopping Centre Visitor Info Centre**
Moorabool St, Geelong 3214
Ph: (03) 5222 6126

**National Wool Museum**
26 Moorabool St, Geelong 3220
Ph: (03) 5222 2900

**Peninsula Visitor Info Centre**
Nepean Hwy, Dromana 3936
Ph: (03) 5987 2817

**Werribee Tourism Association**
Ph: (03) 9741 9500/ (03) 9748 5094

**Western Port Info Centre,**
Western Port Marina Resort, Mullett St, Hastings 3915
Ph: (03) 5979 3699

**Websites**
www.greatoceanrd.org.au

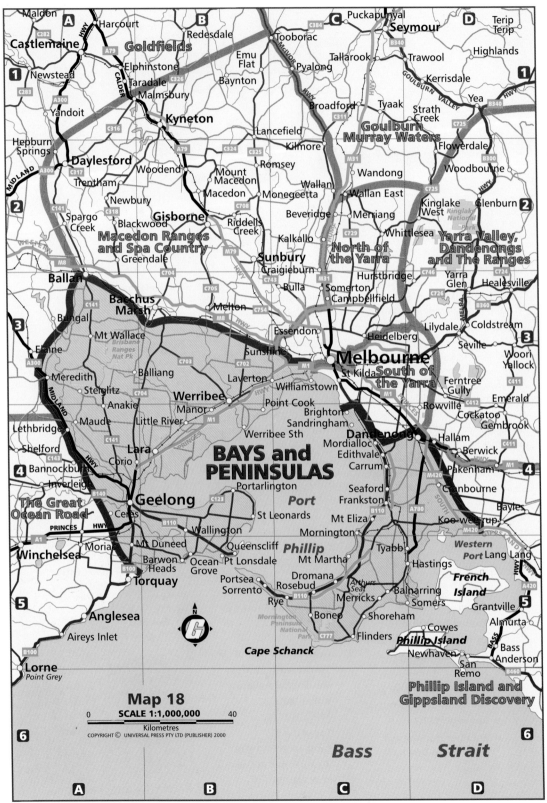

Map 18

SCALE 1:1,000,000

0 — 40
Kilometres

Bass Strait

*Geelong waterfront.*

**The safe flame**
Shell's oil refinery can be seen from the Princes Hwy just north of Geelong. Part of the refinery's safety system, an 80m flare burns day and night, combusting unwanted gases.

## Natural features

Port Phillip Bay was created 8000 years ago when the seas rose and the old course of the Yarra River was submerged – the Rip was once the head of the river. Today it is the treacherous entrance to the Bay where huge tidal flows must pass through a tiny opening. It also harbours hidden reefs and rockshelves, as many shipwrecks that litter the area attest. The Bay has a coastline of 264km, but its peninsulas cover many more kms of coastline, their spectacular ocean beaches confronting an unforgiving Bass Strait. To the south and east of Melbourne, the Bay's suburban beaches are extensive, occasionally punctuated with sandy cliff formations. To the west, industry has taken up the less spectacular beachfronts that were once prolific wetlands, remnants of which still remain.

Further west, the dry basalt plains of that region meet the Bay around Geelong, with the mysterious You Yangs close by. To the east, a vast sandbelt extends to Frankston. Several gentle escarpments embrace the Bay, at Frankston and Mount Martha, while Arthurs Seat, behind Dromana, is a spectacular 314m, harbouring a hilly rural hinterland. This hinterland adjoins Western Port Bay whose sandy beaches meet with mangrove wetlands around Hastings (p.130).

## History

Port Phillip Bay is the cradle of European settlement in Victoria, as it was once a spiritual home and plentiful food source for the Aborigines. The Woiworung and Wathaurong peoples first saw white people enter the bay in the *Lady Sullivan* in 1802. The first official European settlement was established soon after, in 1803, at Sullivans Bay, Sorrento. But this small township, made from convict hands, was soon disbanded due to an inadequate water supply.

In 1835, with settlement of the Port Phillip district, land was taken for sheep and cattle grazing. Melbourne and the bay area developed rapidly. Squatters took up richly productive land on the Bellarine Peninsula and around Geelong, a deep-sea port that once rivalled Melbourne as the location for the settlement's first city. Squatters soon took up land on the Mornington Peninsula too, and fishing villages came to dot the bay.

With the goldrush came the first of Melbourne's building booms and the need for lime. Lime burning around both sides of the bay saw the disappearance of much of the native vegetation to fire the kilns. In the 20th century, large-scale industrial development took place in the beachside suburbs west of Melbourne and north of Geelong, where petrochemical complexes are evident from the Hwy. Nevertheless,

**Watch out for powerful rips**
For an understanding of how the rip exerts its tremendous pull, visit the Queenscliff Maritime Museum which features a hydrographic model of the rip and its sea floor. (p.128)

*Sorrento-Queenscliff ferry.*

much of Port Phillip Bay and its peninsulas have remained remote and undeveloped.

## Getting there

### By road

Scenic waterfront roads ring the bay from Port Melbourne and St Kilda to Mordialloc, the Esplanade at St Kilda joining the spectacular Beach Rd, which dips in and out of the various picturesque bays. For Williamstown, cross the Yarra River via the Westgate Bridge.

For the Mornington Peninsula, take the Nepean Hwy to Frankston and from here either proceed along the Nepean Hwy and Peninsula Fwy, or take the Moorooduc Hwy. Turnoffs to the Peninsula hinterland — Red Hill and the vineyards — are marked, as are the several routes to Western Port locations. Some Western Port destinations, such as Hastings and Somers, may be better reached from Melbourne via the SE Arterial, which bypasses Dandenong.

For Werribee take the Princes Fwy to Laverton, turning at the Pt Cook exit. For Geelong and the Bellarine Peninsula, take the Princes Fwy.

### By tram

Trams travel to many suburban beaches, for example Sth Melbourne, Middle Park and St Kilda.

### By rail and coach

Met trains leave Flinders St Stn regularly for the several suburban beaches on the

**Get into the swim by tram**
Tram travel to the beach is a unique Melbourne experience. Catch the light rail at Flinders St Stn for a rollicking trip to the old St Kilda Stn, located in the heart of Fitzroy St, close to Acland St, or the tram from Swanston St to Sth Melbourne beach.

Sandringham line. Trains also leave here every 30min on the Frankston line, meeting the beach at Mordialloc and stopping at all of the beachside suburbs from Edithvale to Seaford. Met trains to Williamstown also leave regularly from Flinders St Stn.

Peninsula Bus Line coaches connect at Frankston for Portsea and all the towns between, as well as for the Mornington Peninsula hinterland, including Red Hill and the beaches and villages of Western Port. For Peninsula Bus Line, Ph: (03) 9786 7088

V/Line trains to Geelong leave from Spencer St Stn regularly and connect with buses to all the major towns on the Bellarine Peninsula.

The Met also offers the 'Round the Bay in a Day' package deal to V/Line Holiday Ticket holders. It covers the train journey to Frankston, coach to Sorrento, ferry to Queenscliff and coach and rail trip back to Spencer St via Geelong. Visitors can break their journey and stay overnight if they wish. Ph: 13 16 38

### Ferries

The *John Batman* carries passengers between St Kilda Pier and Williamstown on weekends. Ph: (03) 9682 9555

Ferries leave daily for Williamstown from Southbank.

The **Queenscliff-Sorrento Vehicular/ Passenger Ferry** departs daily, all year, at 2-hrly intervals, connecting the Mornington and Bellarine Peninsulas. Ph: (03) 5258 3244.

A passenger-only ferry stops at Sorrento, Portsea and Queenscliff. Ph: (03) 5984 1602

Ferries connect with trains at Stony Pt for French and Phillip Is. Ph: (03) 5978 5642

## Getting around

### By car

Cars can be rented on the Mornington Peninsula at Frankston, Mornington, Rosebud and Somerville, and at Geelong for the Bellarine Peninsula. Hire in Melbourne for the 'Top of the Bay'. Hire in Werribee or Hoppers Crossing for Werribee and Pt Cook.

Local taxi services operate in Frankston, Geelong and Werribee. The suburban bay area is accessible by taxi from Melbourne.

### By air

Several companies offer charter flights from Essendon and Moorabbin Airports. **Nationwide Air Charter**, Ph: (03) 9374 2100

### Tours

**Peninsula Discovery Tours**, with 20yrs experience on the Mornington Peninsula, offers relaxed and informative individual and small group tours. Ph: (03) 5984 0948. **Coastal View Tours** specialise in Mornington Peninsula winery tours. Ph: (03) 5988 9562. Tours from Geelong often take in the Gt Ocean Rd. Consult the Geelong and Gt Ocean Rd Visitor Info Centre.

### Bay cruises and charters

Check with visitor info centres for the many boat charter companies operating out of Geelong, Hastings, Sorrento or some of the suburban marinas, including Mordialloc and Sandringham.

## Festivals and events

### Sail Melbourne

Port Phillip Bay dances with myriad sails in early Jan during Sail Melbourne. Hosted by yacht clubs around the bay, it attracts local and interstate participants in championship races for all classes. Visitors can watch from various vantage points or charter a boat to watch from the waves. Ph: (03) 5986 0223

### Rip View Swim Classic

The Rip View Swim Classic is an open water race for all age groups leaving from the Pt Lonsdale front beach the first weekend in Jan. With Pt Nepean as backdrop and the treacherous rip close by, this is an exhilarating competition. Ph: (03) 5258 1257

### Skilled Bay Cycling Classic

On the 2nd weekend in Jan, the Skilled Bay Cycling Classic wends its way through various Bellarine Peninsula

towns, attracting top local and interstate riders. Ph: (03) 5244 2341

### Queenscliff Bluewater Challenge

Another open water swim, the Queenscliff Bluewater Challenge, including a 'Dash for Cash' competition, takes off from the Queenscliff Pier on the last Sun in Jan. Ph: (03) 5255 2741

### Geelong Waterfront Festival

On Australia Day, 26 Jan, the Geelong Waterfront Festival comes alive with a major regatta, a wooden boats festival, food, music, rides and fireworks. Ph: (03) 5225 1204

### Australian International Airshow

'Zoom Boom Grumble and Twist', reads the literature for the Australian International Airshow, held mid Feb every 2nd year at Avalon Airport. This hallmark event of the world aviation community attracts many 1000s of visitors. Ph: (03) 5282 4400

### Mornington Peninsula Extravaganza

With a street parade, music, fireworks, a fun run, a ceramics show and historical displays, the Mornington Peninsula

*National Celtic Folk Festival, Geelong.*

**Ewe owe it to yourself**
When in Geelong buy yourself some pure new wool! **Only Ewe**, Ph: (03) 5241 1243, and **Weaver to Ware**, Ph: (03) 5221 3247, sell premium wool fabrics and clothing.

**Ford Discovery Centre**

The waterfront precinct is home to Geelong's newest tourist attraction, the **Ford Discovery Centre**, on the corner of Gheringhap and Brougham Sts. Featuring a virtual assembly plant, its interactive displays draw visitors into the production process as the story of the Ford motor car unfolds. Open 6 days per week, 10am–5pm, closed Tues. Ph: (03) 5227 8700

Extravaganza is a great family event. It is held on the Hastings waterfront the last weekend in Feb. Ph: (03) 5979 3783

### Ocean Grove Cup

The Ocean Grove Cup Carnival is unique. Horses and jockeys battle it out in 6-8 races right beside the surf. While the carnival is held in early to mid Feb, exact dates depend on the tide. $5 entry, children free, or $45 a head for VIP treatment, including lunch and drinks in the marquee and entrance onto RAAF's Beach. Ph: (03) 5229 5824

### Sorrento Street Festival

The main street is closed for the day when the Sorrento Street Festival takes off on the last Sun in Mar, showcasing the region's fine foods and wines, as well as music and activities for children. Ph: (03) 5984 1762

### Peninsula Pinot Week

Peninsula Pinot Week is held in the last week in Mar at the end of the harvest. It celebrates the region's great love affair — pinot noir. Each vigneron prepares a special program of wine tasting, winemaker dinners, and musical and other events. Ph: (03) 5989 2377

### National Wool Week

Held over the last week in May, National Wool Week celebrates a key aspect of Geelong's identity. There are seminars

*Ocean Grove Cup, RAAF's Beach.*

and farm and family days at various locations, and special activities at Geelong's National Wool Museum. Ph: (03) 5229 5824

### Queens Birthday Wine Weekend

Another great Mornington Peninsula wine event, the Queens Birthday Wine Weekend, 2nd weekend in Jun, features a wine exhibition at the Mornington Peninsula Regional Gallery, and various activities at the region's wineries. Ph: (03) 5989 2377

### National Celtic Folk Festival

Also held over the Queens Birthday weekend, the National Celtic Folk Festival is an event that will immerse visitors in a living history and culture. Join the crowds on the Geelong Waterfront to participate in a feast of music, dance, traditional crafts, food and film. Ph: (03) 5222 5989

### Jazz on the Bay

Another mid-year festival is Jazz on the Bay, held in Jul in a variety of Geelong waterfront locations. Featuring traditional and modern jazz in cosy venues, this is a fine way to spend a wintry afternoon or two. Ph: (03) 5221 3247

### Mornington Tea-Tree Festival

Taking to Mornington's streets and parks in late Oct, the Tea-Tree Festival runs fishing competitions, a bush dance, sailing on the *Alma Doepel*, bazaars and many street entertainments. Ph: (03) 5974 2935

### International Seafood Fair

Geelong's International Seafood Fair is a mouth-watering must for all who travel on their stomachs. Held over the last weekend in Oct, visitors can taste and buy. There are trade and festival exhibitions, and cooking demonstrations. Geelong's fishing fleet is out in force on Corio Bay, as are visiting tall ships. Ph: (03) 9261 4500

### Queenscliff Music Festival

Held in Nov, the Queenscliff Music Festival is very suitably located in this

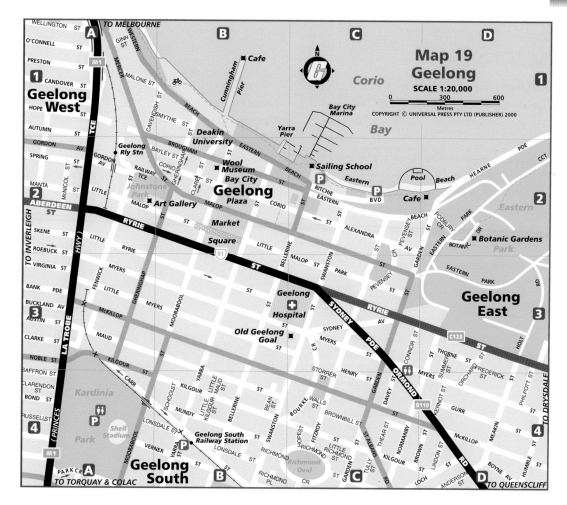

**Map 19 Geelong**
SCALE 1:20,000

relaxed seaside town. Performances take place in a variety of local venues. The feel is intimate; the music eclectic and inventive. Booking is essential. Ph: 1900 130 060

## Main towns and localities
### Geelong and the Bellarine Peninsula
#### Barwon Heads *Map 18 B5*
Barwon Heads is a sleepy little holiday town with a great jetty, some semi-derelict beachfront houses, as well as a more well-to-do area of tucked-away beach houses. The river meets the ocean here and the head of the river offers good coastal views. There is safe swimming and relaxed boating inland along the river and its extensive wetlands. **13th Beach** is a popular surf beach. From the Rip to Barwon Heads there are 11km of expansive surf beach.

### Geelong *Map 19*
Geelong is a major regional city and gateway to the Bellarine Peninsula and Gt Ocean Rd. It has a fascinating settler history and is today a lively hub of cultural and recreational activity. With many fine attractions itself, it is a prime place to stop and shop before proceeding to other holiday destinations.

Geelong's economic history is intimately connected with sheep farming and fine wool production. At the **National Wool Museum**, located in the Lascelles Woolstore in Moorabool St, visitors are treated to a high-quality multimedia presentation of Australian wool growing. You will see an operating loom which makes impressive patterned rugs for purchase. Open daily, 10am–5pm. Ph: (03) 5227 0701

**Crafts and tales**
The **Narana Aboriginal Craft and Cultural Interpretation Centre** on Grovedale Rd tells the story of Aboriginal life in the region and sells traditional and contemporary Aboriginal crafts. Ph: (03) 5241 5700

# SeaChange

Every Australian knows the *SeaChange* story, filmed on location at Barwon Heads. One of Australia's most popular TV shows, it has struck a nerve with the career-obsessed workaholics of the 1990s. Laura, a 40-something corporate lawyer, throws it all in when she finds out her husband has had an affair and is up on charges for some dubious scam. The apparently idyllic Pearl Bay needs a magistrate, so she impetuously buys a derelict house on the foreshore and struggles for several episodes to adjust to the mores of this salt-of-the-earth rural Australian town. The characters are all so fondly constructed that even though snobbery on Laura's part, meets small-town insularity, human generosity is found and good relationships develop. Best of all, Laura meets Diver Dan (now a pin-up boy for many Australian women). Various local scandals are eventually resolved, and, Hallelujah!, Laura and Dan finally get together. Unfortunately, Dan leaves town and in a second series, the quest for love, fulfilment and meaning continues!

**Summer fun**

**Coast Action** offers a great summer activities program. Canoe on Swan Bay, snorkel at Portarlington jetty, take a trip to Mud Is. Most activities are free. Ph: (03) 5226 4669

Geelong's massive bluestone and redbrick woolstores are located on the **Geelong Waterfront**, which has been redeveloped and enlivened with trendy beachfront cafes, a refurbished **Cunningham Pier**, cycling and walking paths, art deco seabaths at Eastern Beach, a fun play area for children and an extensive marina.

The city area boasts many fine old buildings, including civic buildings. A walking tour of historic Geelong is well worth doing. Pamphlets are available from the visitor info centre. The **Old Geelong Gaol** is open for inspection on weekends from 1pm-4pm. In Nth Geelong the **Naval and Maritime Museum** tells the story of the Port of Geelong, relishing the once heady days of sail and steamships. Open daily, except Tues and Thurs. Ph: (03) 5277 2260

The city centre is also the arts centre. Geelong's fine regional art gallery is in Little Malop St. Open Mon-Fri, 10am-6pm, weekends 1pm-5pm. The **Geelong Performing Arts Centre** and **Ford Centre** regularly stage works by the Geelong Symphony Orchestra and other local and touring music and theatre companies.

The other major area of interest is the **Barwon River** and surrounds. Shared walking and cycling paths wind their way through several kms of scenic parkland.

There are a number of themed walking tours outlined in pamphlets available from visitor info centres. The most extensive one, the '**Industrial Heritage Track**', is fascinating. **Barwon Valley Park** has an adventure playground and **Byalong Sanctuary**, on the north bank, is a lovely spot to picnic.

Various regattas are held on the Barwon River from early-late Mar, with the traditional **Head of the River** the last scheduled for the season. The *Barwon River Queen* offers 2hr river cruises at very reasonable rates. Ph: (03) 5254 3000

### Ocean Grove *Map 18 B5*

Ocean Grove is adjacent to Barwon Heads. It has clean surf beaches and is a vibrant little town, with good cafes and shopping. There are several nature reserves close by (p.140).

Other attractions include **A Maze 'N Things**, cnr Grubb Rd and Bellarine Hwy. In late Nov the Wallington Primary School hosts the **Wallington Strawberry Fair**, with 160 stalls offering a wide range of new season's produce and various strawberry-inspired delights. Ph: (03) 5250 1841

### Port Lonsdale *Map 24*

Port Lonsdale stands on one side of the Rip. From the lighthouse carpark, visitors can get impressive views of the big ships as they enter Port Phillip. Lighthouse tours can be booked through the Queenscliff Maritime Museum. Ph: (03) 5258 3440

A few wartime bunkers litter Port Lonsdale, and visitors will find a useful display board telling the William Buckley story (p.134).

Port Lonsdale front beach is ideal for small children – good swimming and snorkelling. The backbeach is exhilarating, but dangerous – observe the Surf Lifesaving Club flags. As Port Lonsdale is only a short distance from Queenscliff, visitors often make the trip from Queenscliff to Port Lonsdale, swim, potter around the rocks, watch the ships cross the Rip, and then retire to one of Pt Lonsdale's special cafes.

### Portarlington *Map 18 B4*

A busy holiday town in summer, once fishing port and mill town, Portarlington looks out across Corio Bay towards the You Yangs. It offers safe bay swimming and boating. The **Portarlington Mill**, a National Trust building (1850s), once processed grain for transport to Van Diemens Land. Archeological digs have revealed evidence of Aboriginal occupation as well as artefacts from early European settlement. The Mill is open Sun, 2pm–5pm, Sept to the Queen's Birthday as well as Wed and Sat, in Jan.

The historic township of **Drysdale** and a host of farms and wineries are close by. A pleasant afternoon can be spent tasting wine, visiting gardens and nurseries, and picking berries.

### Queenscliff *Map 20*

The view across the bay is glorious. This is especially so from **Nuns Beach**, off Henry St, where safe swimming in pristine waters is just perfect. From the **Queenscliff Pier** – a favourite fishing spot – visitors can watch the car and passenger ferries ply the waters on their way to Portsea and Sorrento (pp.134, 135).

Queenscliff is the jewel of the Bellarine Peninsula. A medium-sized town, it remains a sleepy hollow, despite its many grand buildings and active cultural life. It is a haunt of writers and fishermen; artists and gourmands.

**Gellibrand St**, hosting some gracious old hotels, faces out over the bay. **Miettas Queenscliff Hotel** is the premier luxury hotel, famous for its formal dining and National Trust building. The **Ozone Hotel** is another grand location. Inside its comfortable lounge the story of the wreck of the *Ozone* is graphically told in period photographs. Fish and chips from the **Trident**, eaten under the giant cypress trees in Gellibrand Park, is a favourite of families in the area.

**Hesse St** is the main shopping centre. Despite its several fine galleries, an impressive secondhand bookstore, memorable gift and memorabilia shops,

*Miettass Queenscliff Hotel.*

**Concerts and great views**
**Spray Farm**, a historic vineyard, puts on a celebrated program of open-air concerts every summer, Jan–Feb. Glorious views across Corio Bay provide an ideal setting.
Ph: 1900 937 020

**Step back in time**
Locate the site of Geelong's yellow hangman's gibbet. Discover the bluestone pier forged by convicts' hands. Find our about 'Curly Annie'. For a different kind of guided tour try **A Tale of Time Tours**. Ph: 0419 544 402

**Hoot scooting**
For a bit of a hoot, you can't beat the **Queenscliff Scooter Challenge**, a race from Queenscliff to Port Lonsdale, mid Aug. Ph: (03) 5258 1377

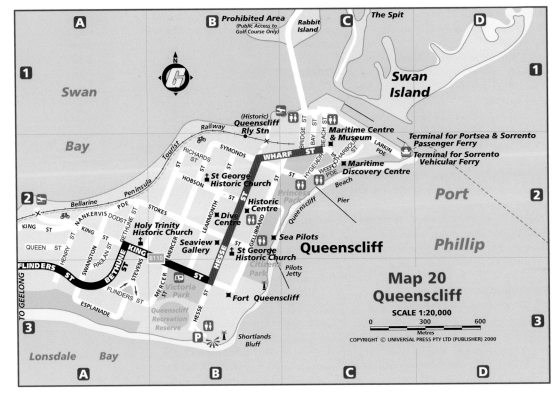

Map 20
Queenscliff

SCALE 1:20,000

0      300      600
Metres
COPYRIGHT © UNIVERSAL PRESS PTY LTD (PUBLISHER) 2000

and fine food establishments, it retains a relaxed, even sedate air.

Fort Queenscliff, built in 1853 at the height of the Crimean War, runs a limited number of tours. Weekends 1pm and 3pm; public and school holidays, 11am, 1pm and 3pm. Ph: (03) 5258 0730

The Queenscliff Maritime Museum gives visitors a graphic picture of life beside the turbulent sea. Visitors can see a Couta boat under construction, learn about Port Phillip's pilot boats, and locate the historic shipwrecks around Port Phillip. Open Sat-Sun, 1.30pm-4.30pm

Arthurs Seat chairlift.

and public and school holidays, 10.30am–4.30pm. Ph: (03) 5258 3440

A great favourite with children and adults alike, the **Bellarine Peninsula Railway** takes steamtrain journeys around Swan Bay, a low reedy bay with prolific bird life, to Drysdale. The round trip takes 1hr 45min. For the timetable, Ph: 1900 931 452.

## *Mornington Peninsula*
### Arthurs Seat *Map 22 A2*

This glorious 314m peak is named after a mountain near Edinburgh, Scotland. Take an exhilarating ride on the famous **Arthurs Seat Chairlift** – from the peak or from the base of the mountain, 1-way or round trip. Open daily Mon–Fri, 11am–5pm, Sat 11am–5.30pm, Sun 11am–6pm, Sept–May. Open weekends, school and public holidays throughout the year.

**Arthurs Seat Reserve**, located at the summit, is a scenic picnic spot. There are BBQs and undercover picnic tables, as well as other amenities. The **Peak Restaurant** serves meals and coffee from an expansive deck overlooking a garden and vineyards. Several walking tracks leave from **Arthurs Seat Reserve** (p.141) and the peaceful **Seawinds Gardens** (p.143) is a short distance away.

Close by in Purves Rd, the **Arthurs Seat Maze**, is a very popular attraction. It has a series of theme gardens, a small hedge maze, the ingenious Maize Maze, at its peak in Feb, and a bush setting with chainsaw sculptures and maze puzzles for children. Open daily, 10am–6pm. Ph: (03) 5981 8449

The **Pine Ridge Car and Folk Museum**, on Purves Rd, displays vintage cars and motoring memorabilia. Open daily, 10am–5pm, all year, except Aug.

The countryside of **Main Ridge** and **Red Hill**, to the south and west of the summit, is exquisite. Rolling green hills dotted with orchards, vineyards and small farms, give onto magnificent views of both Port Phillip Bay and Western Port Bay. The **Red Hill Community Market** is a much-loved excursion for Melburnians. Open 7am–1pm, 1st Sat of the month, Sept–May.

*Cape Schanck Lightstation.*

There are also many interesting small galleries in this vicinity, including **Noels Gallery and Artists Cafe**, Ph: (03) 5989 2538 and the **Marion Rosetzky Gallery**, which specialises in icon-like hand-painted tiles, Ph: (03) 5989 2557. Both are on the Mornington-Flinders Rd and open most days.

### Cape Schanck *Map 18 B5*

Cape Schanck lies within the **Mornington Peninsula NP** (p.141) and is the Peninsula's southern-most tip. It divides the quieter back beaches of Flinders, Pt Leo and Shoreham from the wilder ones which lie along the fabulous section of coast from Gunnamatta to Pt Nepean. A spectacular stairway and boardwalk clings to the side of Cape Schanck, guiding visitors to Pulpit Rock, jutting out into Bass Strait.

A 140-yr-old limestone lighthouse sits beside the dramatic Cape Schanck headland and is classified by the National Trust. The **Cape Schanck Lightstation and Museum** has accommodation available. Ph: (03) 9568 6411. There is a kiosk, picnic and BBQ facilities for day visitors. Open daily, 10am–5pm. Ph: (03) 5988 6184

**Mornington Peninsula's top monthly markets**
**Balnarring Emu Plains**, 3rd Sat, Nov–May
**Moorooduc Coolstores**, 1st Sun, all year
**Mornington Craft**, 2nd Sun, all year
**Red Hill Community**, 1st Sat, Sept–May
**Sorrento Craft**, 4th Sat, Sept–May

*Western Port Marina, Hastings.*

### Flinders *Map 18 C5*

Flinders is a handsome settlement with many big houses tucked away on old farm properties. The township is small but has several good eating places and B&Bs. Its front beach lies at the base of a dramatic drop, where **Flinders Pier** juts out into the protected waters of Western Port Bay, an ideal spot for fishing. **Flinders Back Beach** is a spectacular cliff-rimmed ocean beach, close to the **Blowhole**.

### Frankston *Map 18 C4*

This busy regional city is a major shopping centre and gateway to the Mornington Peninsula. Its wide sandy beaches are sheltered and safe, and ideal for surfboarding. Frankston boasts dozens of eating places, pubs, bookshops, a cinema complex and several galleries.

### Hastings *Map 18 D5*

Hastings is Western Port's largest town. The Bass Strait oilfields pump their crude oil here, where it is refined and transported out through Hastings deep-water harbour. Long Is, off Hastings, is the location of a huge BHP steelworks. Visitors can look out to the mangrove-clad northern part of the bay from **Hastings Foreshore Reserve** and jetty. Extensive walking and cycling paths wind around the foreshore area.

The **Western Port Marina** offers the range of boating facilities and services,

including charter hire, sailing and navigational instruction, and boating and fishing equipment for sale. This is one of the largest marinas in Australia. Visitors can poke around the floating pontoons and relax at one of its cafes or take lunch at the **Marina Hotel**, a resort-style complex. Unique accommodation is available on board *Xanadu*, Australia's only floating hotel.

Close by at **Crib Pt**, the Australian Navy opens its doors at *HMAS Cerberus*. Visitors may drive through the base and its gardens and view the exhibits of the *HMAS Cerberus* **Museum**. Open weekends 10am–noon; 1.30pm–5pm. Ph: (03) 5950 7011

### Mornington *Map 18 C4*

Fishing village and market town, the old Mornington was sometimes likened to the pretty seaside villages of southern England. Retaining a good deal of this quality, it is today also a lively cosmopolitan centre. **Main St** and its environs have been pleasantly redesigned with pedestrians in mind. The many historic buildings house sidewalk cafes, gift, antiques, book and boating shops.

The **Mornington Regional Gallery** is a must for visitors wishing to feel the cultural pulse of the region. Purpose-built to house its 'works on paper' collection, it curates special exhibitions and welcomes touring exhibitions of note across the full range of visual art forms. Check for the gallery's lively program of events. Open Tues-Fri, 10am-4.30pm, weekends and holidays, noon-4.30pm.

Despite Mornington's suburban expansion, its beaches are unspoilt. Each little bay or cove has a distinct character. **Mothers Beach**, backed by Mornington's famous red cliffs, is the closest beach to the township, on the north side of **Schnapper Pt**. There is the added interest here of a busy pier where Mornington's fishing fleet, yacht club, and boatshed kiosk are located. Facilities include toilets and picnic tables.

Above the beach at **Mornington Park** children can have great fun in an imaginative adventure playground. There are various amenities here too, including picnic tables under the park's shady cypress trees. Elegant coffee houses and galleries sit opposite.

Good swimming beaches north and south of Schnapper Pt abound, including **Canadian Bay** beach, made famous in the film of Neville Shute's *On the Beach*. **Fossil Beach** which lies on the border with Mount Martha, is, as its name suggests, of geological interest.

### Mount Martha *Map 22 B1*

On the Nepean Hwy, **Briars Historic Park** is a very pleasant surprise. The historic homestead looks out over wetland and woodland settings with extensive walking tracks. In the homestead, a collection of Napoleonic artefacts is expertly displayed. The collection was donated by Dame Mabel Brooks, and is a legacy marking the odd historical coincidence of Alexander Balcombe, her grandfather and one-time owner of the Briars, befriending Napolean on St Helena, the Atlantic island to which

**Take care in the surf!** Gunnamatta is considered one of the most dangerous beaches on the peninsula. Its Surf Lifesaving Club has rescued over 3000 people since 1966.

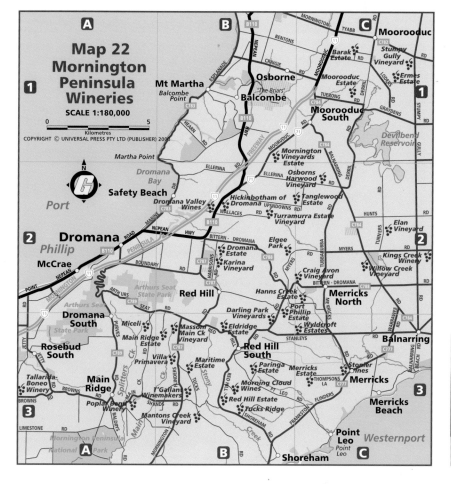

*Mornington Vineyards.*

# Wineries

## Geelong and Bellarine Peninsula

| NAME | MAP 24 ADDRESS | PHONE | OPEN |
|------|------|------|------|
| Asher Vineyard | 360 Goldsworthy Rd, Lovely Banks | (03) 5276 1365 | Noon–5pm weekends and public holidays or by appt |
| Idyll Winery | 265 Ballan Rd, Moorabool | (03) 5276 1280 | 10am–5pm Tues–Sun and public holidays |
| Innisfail Vineyard | Cross St, Batesford | (03) 5276 1258 | By appt |
| Kilgour Estate | 85 McAdams La, Bellarine | (03) 5251 2223 | 10.30am–5.30pm Tues–Sun in summer; Fri–Sun in winter |
| Mt Anakie Estate | 130 Staughton Vale Rd, Anakie | (03) 5284 1405 | 11am–5pm daily |
| Mt Duneed Winery | 70 Feehan's Rd, Mount Duneed | (03) 5264 1281 | 11am–5pm weekends and public holidays |
| Prince Albert Vineyard | 100 Lemins Rd, Waurn Ponds | (03) 5241 8091 | By appt |
| Scotchmans Hill | 190 Scotchmans Rd, Drysdale | (03) 5251 3176 | 10.30am–4.30pm daily |
| Staughton Vale Vineyard | Cnr Ballan and Staughton Vale Rds, Anakie | (03) 52841477 | 10am–5pm, Fri–Mon or by appt |
| The Minya Vineyard and Winery | Minya Lane, Connewarre | (03) 5264 1397 | 10am–5pm weekends and public holidays, Christmas–Easter or by appt |
| Waybourne Winery | 60 Lemins Rd, Waurn Ponds | (03) 5241 8477 | By appt |

## Mornington Peninsula

| NAME | MAP 22 ADDRESS | PHONE | OPEN |
|------|------|------|------|
| Barak Estate | Lot 4 Barak Rd, Moorooduc | (03) 5978 8439 | 11am–5pm Wed and public holidays |
| Craig Avon Vineyard | Craig Avon Lane, Merricks Nth | (03)5989 7465 | noon–5pm weekends, public holidays and daily in Jan |
| Darling Park Vineyards | Red Hill Rd, Red Hill | (03) 5989 2324 | 11am–5pm weekends and public holidays, daily in Jan |
| Dromana Estate | Cnr Bittern and Dromana Rds, Dromana | (03) 5987 3800 | 11am–4pm daily |
| Elan Vineyard | 17 Turners Rd, Bittern | (03) 5983 1858 | First weekend of each month or by appt |
| Eldridge Estate | Red Hill Rd, Red Hill | (03) 59892644 | Noon–5pm weekends and school holidays |
| Elgee Park | Junction Rd, Merricks Nth | (03) 5989 7338 | By appt only |

*Kilgour Estate.*

*Winery dining.*

## Mornington Peninsula (cont.)

| NAME | MAP 22 ADDRESS | PHONE | OPEN |
|---|---|---|---|
| **Ermes Estate** | Godings Rd, Moorooduc | (03) 5978 8376 | *11am–5pm weekends and public hols* |
| **Hanns Creek Estate** | 26 Kentucky Rd, Merricks Nth | (03) 5989 7266 | *11am–5pm daily* |
| **Hickinbotham of Dromana** | Nepean Hwy near Wallaces Rd, Dromana | (03) 5981 0355 | *11am–6pm weekends and most weekdays* |
| **Karina Vineyard** | Harrisons Rd, Dromana | (03) 5981 0137 | *11am–5pm weekends and daily in Jan* |
| **King's Creek Winery** | 237 Myers Rd, Bittern | (03) 5983 2102 | *11am–5pm weekends and public hols* |
| **Main Ridge Estate** | William Rd, Red Hill | (03) 59892686 | *12noon–4pm week days, 12noon–5pm weekends* |
| **Maritime Estate** | Tucks Rd, Red Hill | (03) 5989 2735 | *11am–5pm, 27 Dec–26 Jan* |
| **Massoni Main Ck Vineyard** | Mornington-Flinders Rd, Red Hill | (03) 5989 2352 | *By appt only* |
| **Merricks Estate** | Thompsons Lane, Merricks | (03) 5989 8416 | *First weekend in the month, each weekend in Jan and public hols weekends. Phone for times* |
| **Miceli** | 9230 Main Ck Rd, Main Ridge | (03) 5989 2755 | *Noon–5pm 1st weekend of the month and every weekend in Jan* |
| **Moorooduc Estate** | 501 Derril Rd, Moorooduc | (03) 5978 8585 /9696 4130 | *Noon–5pm 1st weekend of each month, each weekend in Jan* |
| **Mornington Vineyards Estate** | Moorooduc Rd, Moorooduc Sth | (03) 5974 2097 | *11am–5pm weekends and public hols* |
| **Osborns Vineyard** | Ellerina Rd, Merricks Nth | (03) 5989 7417 | *By appt only* |
| **Paringa Estate** | 44 Paringa Rd, Red Hill Sth | (030 5989 2669 | *Noon–5pm weekdays (excluding Tues), 11am–5pm weekends* |
| **Poplar Bend Winery** | Main Ck Rd, Main Ridge | (03) 5989 6046 | *10am–5pm Sat, 11am–5pm Sun or by appt* |
| **Port Phillip Estate** | 261 Red Hill Rd, Red Hill | (03) 5989 2708 | *Noon–5pm weekends, public hols and late Dec–mid Jan* |
| **Red Hill Estate** | 53 Red Hill-Shoreham Rd, Red Hill Sth | (03) 5989 2838 | *1pm–5pm daily* |
| **Ryland River** | Main Ck Rd, Main Ridge | (03) 5989 6098 | *10am–5pm Mon, weekends and public hols or by appt* |
| **Stonier** | 362 Frankston–Flinders Rd, Merricks | (03) 5989 8300 | *Noon–5pm daily* |
| **Stumpy Gully Vineyard** | 1247 Stumpy Gully Rd, Moorooduc | (03) 5978 8429 | *11am–5pm 1st weekend of the month* |
| **Tallarida – Boneo Winery** | 1400 Browns Rd, Sth Rosebud | (03) 5988 6208 | *Noon–5pm weekends and public hols* |
| **Tanglewood Estate** | Bulldog Creek, Merricks Nth | (03) 5974 3325 | *Noon–5pm daily* |
| **T'Gallant** | Mornington–Flinders Rd, Main Ridge | (03) 5989 6565 | *10am–5pm daily* |
| **Tucks Ridge** | 37 Red Hill-Shoreham Rd[SK4], Red Hill | (03) 5989 8660 | *Noon–5pm daily* |
| **Turramurra Estate Vineyard** | Wallaces Rd, Dromana | (03) 5987 1146 | *Noon–5pm 1st weekend of the month or by appt* |
| **Villa Primavera** | Mornington-Flinders Rd, Red Hill | (03) 5989 2129 | *From 10am–5pm, weekends and public hols and daily Boxing Day-Australia Day* |
| **Willow Ck Vineyard** | 166 Balnarring Rd, Merricks Nth | (03) 5989 7448 | *10am–5pm daily* |
| **Wyldcroft Estates** | 98 Stanleys Rd, Red Hill Sth | (03) 5989 2646 | *10am–5pm weekends and public hols* |

*Portsea.*

he was banished in 1815. Open daily, 9am–5pm. The homestead is open daily, 11am–4pm. Ph: (03) 5974 3686

Mount Martha's **beaches** are considered some of the prettiest on the peninsula. The bayside road from Mornington to Mount Martha and **Safety Beach** is a most appealing alternative to the Peninsula Fwy.

*McCrae Homestead.*

### Moorooduc *Map 22 C1*

Inland from Mornington, the Moorooduc corridor is a pretty rural area. The **Moorooduc Coolstores**, have been refurbished to house galleries, restaurants and shops, including the **Moorooduc**

**Rock Candy and Humbug Factory**. The coolstores are also the location of **Studio City, the Australian Museum of Modern Media**, cnr Eramosa Rd and Moorooduc Hwy, last resting place of Rolf Harris's wobble board and Ossie Ostrich's feathers. It's great fun, as well as a serious archive. Open daily, 10am–5pm. Ph: (03) 5978 8766

### Portsea *Map 18 B5*

Home to the rich and famous, the Portsea front beaches are wall-to-wall with mansions. Visitors to the area will enjoy the **Portsea Pier**, a favourite of scuba-diving instructors, and can swim in the

# The William Buckley story

William Buckley was one of 307 convicts sent to Sullivans Bay near Sorrento in 1803. They were to be the brawn behind Lieutenant–Governor Collins' attempt to establish Victoria's first official settlement. When the settlement failed due to lack of availability of fresh water, Collins decamped to Van Diemen's land, where the infamous convict prison, Port Arthur, was established. Buckley, however, had escaped into the bush with 19 other convicts some months before. Some were recaptured. Others vanished without trace.

To John Batman's great surprise some 30 yrs

later, a strange figure approached his men at Indented Head near Geelong. Buckley could barely make himself understood. He had lived for those 30 yrs with the Wathaurong people, adopting their language and customs. He was known as 'Murrangurk', and was thought to be a reincarnation of an Aborignal man. Buckley was eventually pardoned by Governor Phillips in 1835. He died in Hobart in 1856.

For a poetic account of Buckley's experiences, try Queenscliff poet Barry Hill's evocative *Ghosting William Buckley*.

peaceful coves that are reached at various points along the Nepean Hwy. A few cafes and icecream shops cater for quite large crowds in peak season. The **Portsea Hotel**, with a generous beer garden adjacent to the beach, is an institution!

**Portsea Back Beach** is breathtaking. Fabulous views extend in all directions. Swimming and surfing are exceptional, but the beach has dangerous rips. It is patrolled by the Portsea Surf Lifesaving Club throughout summer. A short drive away, visitors can explore the extraordinary rock formations and pleasant rockpools at **London Bridge**.

### Pt Leo *Map 22 C3*

Pt Leo and **Shoreham** are popular surf beaches on Western Port Bay. Looking out to Phillip Is, and rimmed by farming land, this is a very picturesque area. Shoreham's pine trees offer an idyllic spot for beachside picnics.

### Rosebud to Rye *Map 24*

A fishing village in the 1950s, **Rosebud** is now a thriving summer holiday destination. Thousands of campers descend on the public camping grounds and foreshore in Jan. The long sweep of white sandy beach from Dromana and McCrae all the way to Rye is protected by extensive sand bars.

Rosebud has an extensive shopping strip and large cinema complex. Various seaside entertainments dot the foreshore during peak season. The **Wittingslow Carnival** is a summer favourite. **Rye** is the first of the bayside townships to also have an ocean back beach.

In McCrae, the **McCrae Homestead** offers a unique insight into the European history of the Mornington Peninsula. Home to Georgiana McCrae and her family from the 1840s, this simple whitewashed building breathes pioneer history. Georgiana is famous for her courage as pioneer wife and mother; her diaries documenting early settler life. Open daily, noon–4.30pm. Ph: (03) 5986 5688

### Sorrento *Map 21*

Sorrento is a glamorous location. A busy destination, it has upmarket shopping and eating establishments along its main street, many housed in Sorrento's famous limestone buildings. Located on a sharp rise, the towers of Sorrento's classic 19th century hotels protrude above Norfolk pines. The town offers some very classy accommodation.

During high season, Sorrento is a hub of activity, with hotels abuzz with guests, al fresco dining, a busy cinema, and bathing well into the evening. From its wide front beach there are magnificent views across the bay towards Arthurs Seat; from the spectacular natural amphitheatre of its back beach, stirring views of the turbulent Bass Strait.

Swim or picnic at Sorrento front beach, next door to the Sorrento Pier. It is here that the **Queenscliff-Sorrento Car and Passenger Ferry**, as well as the many charter tours, depart. Sorrento's famous 'swim with the dolphins' and seal watch tours leave from the pier (p.144). **Sorrento Park** is situated on the hill overlooking the pier, beside the Peninsula Rescue helipad.

At the back beach there are tearooms and various amenities. A children's sea pool means that even small children can enjoy this ocean beach. Beautiful rockpools — many big enough to swim in — are revealed at low tide. Visitors can take walking paths along the coast in either direction. The walk to **Coppins Lookout** is spectacular.

A historic town walk — maps available from visitor info centres — takes in

*Historic Sorrento village.*

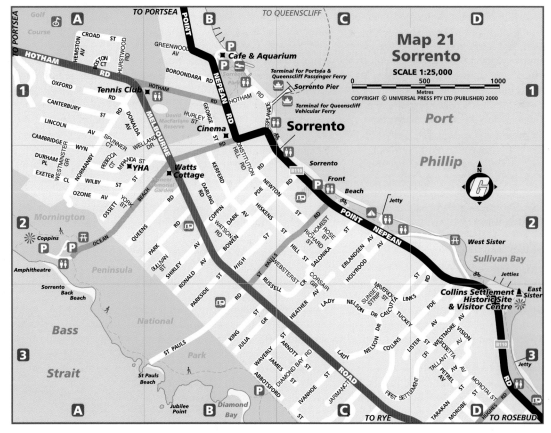

**Map 21 Sorrento**

SCALE 1:25,000

0    500    1000

Metres

COPYRIGHT © UNIVERSAL PRESS PTY LTD (PUBLISHER) 2000

Sorrento's many fine buildings and gardens, as well as its intriguing cemetery. The **Sorrento Museum**, one of Victoria's top 8, displays memorabilia and artefacts from the peninsula's pioneering period. The **Early Settlers Graves** at Sullivans Bay mark the site of Victoria's first official settlement.

**Sorrento Pier.**

## Somers Map 18 D5

South of Hastings on Western Port Bay, Somers is one of several sandy bay beaches that look out to Phillip Is. Merricks and Balnarring beaches are similarly gentle bay beaches, ideal for family outings.

**Coolart**, in Somers, is Western Port's most visited attraction. The property was taken up as a cattle run in the 1840s. The mansion dates from later in the century when the Grimwade family owned it. Coolart is a fully restored National Trust property, with expansive gardens and wetlands. Regular concerts are held here during summer. There are bird hides and short walking tracks around the lake and across the sand dunes. Open daily, 10am–5pm. Ph: (03) 5983 1333

## Top of the Bay

Melbourne's sandy southern suburban beaches extend from Port Melbourne through St Kilda all the way to Seaford. Port Melbourne and St Kilda offer a cosmopolitan backdrop to the highly accessible and popular beaches of Port and South Melbourne, Albert Park, St Kilda and Elwood. As well as being great places for swimming in summer, these beaches are popular for their walking, cycling and rollerblading paths. Shopping centres, cafes, restaurants, markets and various entertainments are close by. **St Kilda Pier**, a heritage-listed Victorian beauty, and **Acland St** are not to be missed.

### Beaumaris *Map 18 C4*

**Ricketts Pt**, where Beach Rd drops down to sea level and the waters lap gently, was once a favourite location of the Heidelberg School painters who worked at these sites over a 100 years ago. This spot is popular with families. The **Ricketts Pt Tea House** is nestled on the beach among the ancient banksias, and serves lunches and afternoon teas. There are picnic tables, BBQs and toilets close by.

This is a good launching point for the **Coastal Art Trail**, which features stories and reproductions of works by Heidelberg School painters and other notable Australian artists. Art Trail maps are available free at the tea house.

At **Keys St**, further along Beach Rd are a number of cafes and restaurants. **Keiffers Shellfish and Boat Hire** is signposted. Keiffers' runs a mussel farm and sells direct to the public. The **Beaumaris** and **Mentone Hotels** are both fine buildings restored to their former glory, offering modern menus and great views.

### Brighton *Map 18*

Brighton is an exclusive residential area with two upmarket shopping centres – in Bay and Church Sts. There is the arthouse cinema, **Brighton Bay Cinema**, 294 Bay St, and good hotels and cafes in both shopping centres. A drive through Brighton's leafy avenues will reveal palatial residences and several fine churches, such as **John Knox Uniting Church**, cnr North Rd and New St. The lush **Kamensburgh Gardens**, 102 North Rd, and **Billilla**, 26 Halifax St are a delight and open to the public.

**St Kilda Pier.**

Brighton's beaches range from those tucked away, behind the houses and apartments that abut the bay directly, to more frequented beaches like Middle Brighton, accessible by train. **Middle Brighton Beach** sports the much photographed Brighton bathing boxes. A sea baths and spa, change rooms for swimmers, picnic tables and BBQs are located close by. Several fine old hotels along Beach Rd have been converted into gaming houses, open for lunches and evening meals.

### Edithvale to Seaford *Map 18 C4*

The fine sandy beaches from Mordialloc to Chelsea are perfect for relaxed family outings. They abut private housing, but there are car and pedestrian access points along the way, with picnic and toilet facilities.

If you prefer a more natural setting, it is well worth travelling a little further, to **Seaford**. For nearly 1km before Frankston natural vegetation and small dunes shelter this beach, where the swimming is glorious. Many locals fish from the pier.

### Mordialloc *Map 18 C4*

A quite spectacular, open beach is to be found on either side of Mordialloc Ck, behind a busy Nepean Hwy. At **Peter Scullin Reserve**, the attractive **Windows**

**Bird watching?**
On the breakwater beside St Kilda Pier a colony of fairy penguins has established itself. The penguins are notoriously hard to spot, but you can try, early in the morning or at dusk.

**South base stone**
One of 2 blocks of granite located in a small reserve between the Princes Hwy and the railway line west of Hoppers Crossing railway crossing forms the baseline from which the entire state of Victoria was surveyed.

**Coastal Art Trail**
Two of the paintings featured on this trail can be viewed at the Nat Gallery of Vic: Tom Roberts' *The Slumbering Sea, Mentone*, 1887 and George Conder's *Ricketts Pt*, 1890.

**by the Bay** restaurant and kiosk look out towards the silhouette of Ricketts Pt. There are picnic and BBQ facilities, undercover picnic tables and toilets, and a playground. The pier beside **Mordialloc Ck** makes for a pleasant walk, as does the creek itself. It winds back to Pompei's boatyard, where the fishermen clean their catch and moor their boats.

## Sandringham *Map 18 C4*

Sandringham is one of the prettiest suburban beaches, with high cliffs and fine sandy coves looking south to the picturesque **Red Bluff**. The beaches from **Hampton** to **Black Rock** are more secluded than those closer to Melbourne. Coastal walking tracks join these beaches, winding their way through tea-tree and banksia groves. Carparks along Beach Rd provide beach access.

**Half Moon Bay** also offers secluded swimming, close to the partly submerged wreck of the *HVS Ceberus*. At **Picnic Pt** a pier and marina associated with the Sandringham Yacht Club, provide a pleasant diversion. The **Sailboard HQ and Kiosk** is also tucked away here. You can hire sailboarding equipment and have lessons; novices welcome. Ph: 1800 355 045

*Mansion at Werribee Park.*

Sandringham, Hampton and Black Rock beaches are all close to train stations which are situated in pleasant village shopping centres. Sandringham is especially convivial. Visitors can explore several small streets fanning out from the station. The small **Without Pier Gallery**, 27 Bay Rd, features exhibitions of Australian art. **Trackside Cafe**, 94 Station St, is a modest cafe with newspapers to read and simple, scrumptious lunches.

## Werribee *Map 18 B3*

Werribee is a quick trip from Melbourne over the Westgate Bridge. Visitors can exit the Princes Fwy at Laverton and follow the **Bay West Trail** as marked. It travels south to Pt Cook and South Werribee, ending with the area's major attractions, the Mansion at Werribee Park and the Open Range Zoo. Visitors can also exit the fwy directly at Werribee.

Werribee was once a premier sheep-growing area. Hundreds of thousands of hectares of land were owned by the Chirnside family from the 1840s till late in the century. The **Mansion at Werribee Park** was their spectacular home. Splendidly restored, it features many fine rooms with period decor, as well as the original farmhouse, a formal garden with sweeping lawns, a parterre garden and a most unusual little grotto beside the lake. The historical commentary provided by audio headsets is first class.

Visitors can take a leisurely ramble over the 140ha property, including the **Riverine** area close to the Werribee River, or catch the trolley car for an additional cost. Werribee Park and Mansion are open daily, 10am–4.45pm during daylight saving; on weekends and school holidays, 10am–3.45pm at other times of the year.

Next door, the **National Equestrian Centre**, is a hive of activity. Polo matches are held on the Chirnsides' original polo field. The centre caters for all equestrian activities, including the 3 Olympic events, showjumping, dressage and eventing. Visitors are welcome to view events. Ph: (03) 9741 7672. The **State Rose Garden** (p.000) shares a common carpark with Werribee Park. Opening times as for Werribee Park. Admission is free.

A few minutes away the **Open Range Zoo** has turned Melbourne's western plains into an African savannah. Safari-style bus tours take visitors up close to rhinoceros, giraffe, zebra and other plains animals like the endangered adax and the beautiful scimitar oryx. It is best to book safari tours in advance. Ph: (03) 9731 9600

Close by are the fabulous red **K Road Cliffs** of the Werribee River. A lovely river valley, dotted with grazing sheep and embracing **Werribee Park Golf Course** stretches away towards the distant You Yangs.

From the beach at **South Werribee**, visitors can enjoy an uninterrupted panorama – from the Melbourne skyline to Portarlington on the Bellarine Peninsula. Boating and fishing from the jetty are popular pastimes.

The **RAAF Museum** at Point Cook is certainly a must-see. Expertly curated audiovisual displays of the RAAF's history, since its inception in WWI, sit beside huge hangars housing an array of restored RAAF aircraft. Visitors can view the restoration process and watch many of these fabulous flying machines in the air. Check for special airfield events. Ph: (03) 9256 1300. The museum is open Tues-Fri, 10am-3pm, weekends and public holidays, 10am-5pm.

Right next door to the RAAF Museum several attractions are gathered together within the **Pt Cook Coastal Park**. There is a sheltered picnic ground with various amenities. Open daily, 8am-5pm, and 8am-8pm during daylight saving. Free admission. The **Pt Cook Homestead**, built by Thomas Chirnside in 1857, offers another opportunity to glimpse the colonial lifestyle. Open weekends and school holidays, 10am-5pm. Ph: (03) 9395 1293. The **Cheetham Wetlands** and **Wetlands Viewing Tower** are fascinating (p.142).

## Williamstown *Map 18 C3*

Only 15min from the centre of Melbourne, Williamstown retains many of the unique qualities of a 19th century port village.

**Nelson Place**, opposite **Commonwealth Reserve** and **Gem Pier**, is a row of brick and bluestone buildings, housing,

*Open Range Zoo, Werribee.*

interesting shops and fashionable eateries that look out across the bay to Melbourne's western skyline. Coffee and cakes, or fish and chips at an outside table are ideal ways to experience Williamstown.

Gem Pier was at the hub of Melbourne's port life before the construction of the Coode Canal, which allowed shipping and loading to be done further up the Yarra River. The grand **Old Customs House**, a National Trust building (Williamstown has many) bears witness to this history. Today it is an extensive gallery and gift shop, sitting beside the tasteful dockside **Pelicans Landing Hotel** and an extensive marina.

Ferries from St Kilda and Southgate arrive and depart at Gem Pier. So do the sailing ships *Alma Doepel* and *Enterprize* at certain times of the year. The Corvette class minesweeper, the HMAS Castlemaine, built at Williamstown, is now a museum. Open to the public on weekends.

Commonwealth Reserve hosts the excellent **Williamstown Craft Market** on the 3rd Sun of the month. Many Melburnians make the trip by ferry. Beyond the reserve, extensive cycling and walking trails snake along the bay and river, past rusting boatsheds and the Newport Power Station and ending at **Stony Ck Backwash** beneath the magnificent **Westgate Bridge**. For tours of the Newport Power Station, Ph: (03) 9749 1244.

*Scienceworks.*

**Scienceworks**, located close by in Spotswood, is a terrific science and technology museum, especially for kids. There are permanent and visiting exhibitions, with an emphasis on interactive technology and educational fun. The imaginative holiday programs are well worth a look. Ph: (03) 9392 4800

At the **Spotswood Pumping Station**, refurbished as part of the museum, the incredible story of the engineering feats associated with Melbourne's sewage system, is told.

A state of the art **Planetarium** has recently opened. Day and night-time shows, lasting 40min, are a fascinating way to explore the heavens. Ph: (03) 9252 2358

## National Parks, Parks and Reserves

### Geelong and Bellarine Peninsula

**Brisbane Ranges NP** *Map 18 A3*

These ranges are rugged and remote, with steep rocky ridges and deep gullies. They are Victoria's richest wildflower habitat, at their peak Sept-Nov. This exciting park offers great bushwalking and camping. There are short walks, and a 3-day trek, on high-quality tracks through the **Anakie Gorge** and to the **Outlook**. Picnic areas at Stony Creek and Anakie Gorge have fireplaces (BYO wood), toilets and tables. Campsites at

Boar Gully need to be booked. Ph: (03) 5284 1230

**Lake Connewarre State Game Reserve and Reedy Lake** *Map 24*

Part of the Barwon River system as it flows out to Barwon Heads, this park is renowned for birdwatching. Egrets, terns, godwits and sandpipers are just some of the birds to be found here. Try not to visit during duck-shooting season, Mar-Jun. Access via Grimsmeade La and Moolap Stn Rd. Maps are available. Ph: (03) 5226 4667

**Ocean Grove Nature Reserve** *Map 24*

A very active 'friends' group maintains this reserve, which features the only remaining example of unaltered woodland on the Bellarine Peninsula. Native fauna, including the red-necked wallaby and an abundance of birds, frequent the reserve. The reserve's info centre — open weekends — provides walking notes. The reserve is open daily.

**Serendip Sanctuary** *Map 18 A4*

Once a wildlife research station monitoring threatened bird populations and breeding brolga, bustards and magpie geese, Serendip, at Lara, continues as a research and educational facility. Here you have the rare opportunity to learn about and experience the distinctive western plains environment. This extensive woodland and wetlands sanctuary has numerous enclosures, aviaries and display areas. Remember, on very hot days the western plains are forbidding, and in drought conditions, the wetlands shrink significantly. Ph: (03) 5282 2570

**You Yangs Regional Park** *Map 18 B4*

The You Yangs emerge dramatically out of the western plains near Lara at Little River. The granite peaks can be seen from Melbourne and around the bay. You can visit several Aboriginal rock wells on **Big Rock** and there are 4 marked walking tracks, including to the summit of Flinders Peak. The **Gt Circle Dve** rings the park and directs visitors to

*Pt Nepean.*

most of the park's features. There are
BBQs, picnic tables and toilets.

### Mornington Peninsula
### Arthurs Seat Pk *Map 22 A2*

This imposing setting offers fabulous
views of the full breadth of Port Phillip
Bay and the full length of the Mornington
Peninsula as it tapers off to Pt Nepean.
The park is in several scattered pieces on
the slopes of Arthurs Seat.

Wild cherries, fern gullies and
waterfalls are a feature of walks on its
southern slopes. The **Kings Falls Circuit
Track** is an easy 40min walk accessed at
Waterfall Gully Rd. The **Two Bays
Walking Track**, a 25km walk, leaves from
Seawinds Botanical Garden and connects

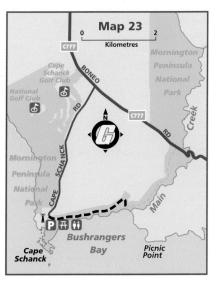

to Bushrangers Bay near Cape Schanck.
You can take a 3km section of the walk
from Seawinds to King Falls. No camping
is allowed in the park.

### Devilbend Reserve *Map 22 C1*

This patch of bush is not as ominous as
it sounds. It has shady picnic areas, and
good facilities, including fireplaces
supplied with wood, overlooking
Devilbend Reservoir.

### Mornington Peninsula NP
### *Map 21 A2, 24*

The **Mornington Peninsula NP** extends
from **Pt Nepean** to **Cape Schanck** along
the Bass Strait coast, and from here along
**Bushrangers Bay** into the hinterland area
known as **Greens Bush**. A further short
stretch of coast near Flinders, which takes
in the infamous Blowhole, is also part of
the NP. These 27kms of walking track
along the back beach cliffs are the most
spectacular in the Bays and Peninsulas
region.

The **Pt Nepean** section of the park,
closed to the public until 1988, is
accessible from Portsea. Facilities here
include a Parks Victoria info centre,
BBQs, picnic tables and toilets. The 19th
century **Quarantine Stn**, whose heart-
rending stories of displacement and
sickness are recounted, is also accessed
here. Bike hire is available the 4th
weekend of each month at the entrance
to the park. There are superb views of
the bay and Bass Strait from the viewing

**Know your flora
and fauna**
*Mornington Peninsula
Birds* and *Mornington
Peninsula Local Plant*s
are illustrated
pamphlets that will
help identify local flora
and fauna. Free from
the Peninsula Visitor
Info Centre in Dromana.

platforms that dot the roadway to the fortifications at the point. A fascinating network of underground military installations, with excellent audiovisual explanations of Pt Nepean's history, await visitors. Ph: (03) 5984 4276

**Cape Schanck**'s rugged basalt formation, set against coastal heathland and banksia forest, is an exciting part of the Mornington Peninsula NP. The Lightstation, (p.129), open to the public, is well worth a visit. Amenities available.

Two spectacular walks start from Cape Schanck. Taking 1hr each way, the **Bushrangers Bay** walk is an easy trek on a well-marked track. The **Fingal Coastal Circuit Walk** (1hr) includes a steep descent to Fingal beach. Walkers can proceed to **Gunnamatta** along the beach, but only at low tide. Gunnamatta is a wild lonely beach. While it is famed for its surfing conditions, it is also treacherous.

**Greens Bush** is the largest remnant of natural bushland on the peninsula, retaining varied vegetation – from banksia and grass tree forests to fern gullies – and native fauna. Highfield, with several marked walking tracks, is a good area for viewing the Mornington Peninsula's largest concentration of eastern grey kangaroos.

### Mt Martha Park *Map 22 B1, 24*

This 54ha reserve on the Mt – with exceptional views of Port Phillip Bay – is a mix of grassy woodland, forest habitats and coastal heathland. There are marked walks, including one to the lookout platform, which is also accessible via Bradford Rd. The picnic area has BBQs, tables and toilets.

### Pines Flora and Fauna Reserve
*Map 18 C4*

The Eureka Flag was raised here in the 1970s by local people in defiance of a proposal to sand mine the last remaining area of remnant bushland in the fast growing suburbs of Frankston. Located only 3km from Frankston, this 108ha reserve is a haven for bandicoots, swamp wallabies, echidnas, many native birds and plants. A network of tracks cut through the reserve, but there are no facilities.

### *Top of the Bay*
### Cheetham Wetlands *Map 18 C4*

These protected wetlands are a collection of lagoons and saltmarsh in the Pt Cook Coastal Park area, close to the site of an old saltworks. The many ponds attract large numbers of local and migratory birds. In Jul-Nov many travel up to 10 000km from Siberia and Japan to feed and roost in these wetlands. A fabulous tower and viewing platform, designed as a public artwork, gives expansive views of this special habitat and across the bay.

## Gardens
### *Geelong and Bellarine Peninsula*
### Barrabool Maze and Gardens
*Map 18 B4*

Ten minutes west of Geelong in the rolling Barrabool Hills, this Mediterranean-style garden and cypress hedge maze, is a pleasant distraction en route to the beach. Good tea room too. Open daily, 10am-5pm. Ph: (03) 5249 1250

### Barwon Grange and The Heights
*Map 18 B5*

Barwon Grange (1855) is a gracious Victorian home and garden on the banks of the Barwon River. Huge old peppercorn trees, monterey cyprus and moreton bay figs grace gently sloping lawns. Open Wed and weekends, 11am-4.30pm, in Fernleigh St, Newtown.

*Views End, Bellarine.*

*Ashcombe Maze.*

The Heights, established in the 1850s, was redesigned in the 1930s. Various small outhouses, including a dovecote and bluestone gardener's cottage, give this garden an especially picturesque quality.

### Geelong Botanical Gardens *Map 19 D2*

This is a classic 19th century botanical garden, with magnificent tree plantings dating from that period. Listed by the National Trust, it has many rare trees, including the largest gingko biloba in Australia, a mighty old Qld kauri and copper beech and giant redwoods. There is also a fern glade, rhododendron walk and pelargonium collection. Open weekdays, 7.30am–5pm, Sat–Sun, during daylight.

### Views End *Map 18 B4*

Views End in Scotchmans Rd, Portarlington is a pleasant country garden with colourful cottage garden plantings and lovely views of the bay and You Yangs. Open daily, 10am–4pm, Oct–Apr. Ph (03) 5253 1695

## *Mornington Peninsula*
### Ashcombe Maze *Map 18 C5*

Ashcombe Maze, on the Red Hill-Shoreham Rd, Shoreham, is a classic, long-established hedge maze with over 1km of intriguing pathways, leading to water features and deftly positioned sculptures. The Rose Maze, some 1200 roses densely planted for near year-round colour and perfume, is a lovely romantic whimsy. Open daily, 10am–5pm.

### Herronswood Gardens *Map 22 A2*

Herronswood is a stunning gothic revival home, classified by the National Trust. It is set in a 2ha garden, landscaped to take full advantage of glorious bay vistas, located as it is part-way up Arthurs Seat. The present owners, Penny and Clive Blazey, also manage the Garden of St Erth at Blackwood.

Herronswood's herbaceous borders experiment with unusual colour combinations and plantings of rare stock. Unimproved flowers and heirloom vegetables are a specialty. Delicious light luncheons are served in a charming adobe thatched cottage. Open Mon–Fri, 10am–4pm. Check for Herronswood's spring and summer festivals, and special open-house days. Ph: (03) 5987 1877

### Seawinds Botanic Gardens *Map 22 A2*

Seawinds Gardens seems to be suspended between sea and sky. Pretty paths and terraces lead the visitor through relaxed plantings of European and native trees and shrubs. Several sculptures by William Ricketts are featured. Sweeping lawns make for an ideal picnic spot where there

**Hive of activity**
The **Diggers Club**, famous for its mail-order seed and good-gardening programs, works out of Herronswood. Behind the scenes, a hive of activity takes place around telephones and computer screens to service its 1000s of members.

are electric BBQs and other facilities.
Gates to the carpark open at 10am daily.

## Recreational activities

### Birdwatching
Popular birdwatching locations include
Briars Historic Park, Cape Schanck, Swan
Bay, Coolart, Pt Cook Coastal Park,
Serendip Sanctuary and Lake Connewarre.

### Bushwalking
Check with visitor info centres for maps
and walking notes, and check NPs (p.140).

### Camping
Camping on the foreshores of the
Mornington and Bellarine Peninsulas is
popular and cheap. There are public
foreshore campsites from Rosebud to
Sorrento, and on several of the Western
Port beaches. Pt Leo is one of the few
ocean beach camping grounds. On the
Bellarine Peninsula, there is camping beside
Lonsdale Bay and at Barwon Heads. In
summer these may be booked out, so
check in advance with local info centres.

For the dedicated bushwalker-camper,
there is the 3-day walk through the
challenging Brisbane Ranges (p.140).
Ph: (03) 5284 1230

### Cycling
Shared cycling, walking and rollerblading
paths snake around large stretches of the
'Top of the Bay'. From Port Melbourne
to Black Rock, tracks wind past beachside
shopping centres and markets, kiosks and
cafes and through tea-tree and banksia
foreshore areas.

In the west, good cycling paths are to
be found at Williamstown, with great
views of the Melbourne skyline and
Westgate Bridge.

Excellent pamphlets, available from
the Geelong visitor info centre, outline
cycling routes around the Geelong,
Barwon River and Bellarine Peninsula
areas. For something out-of-the-way, try
the off-road bicycle path from the North
Shore to Limeburners Bay and Hovells
Reservoir. The best cycling on the hilly
Mornington Peninsula is to found in the
NP at Pt Nepean. Check with Parks
Victoria at Pt Nepean for the dates of

**Dolphin swim, Polperro.**

bicycle-only days for the best possible
conditions (p.141).

Mopeds are also available in some
locations. **Geelong and Bellarine Mopeds**
offer daily and hourly rates and leave
from Queenscliff. Ph: (03) 5258 4796.
For the Mornington Peninsula, phone
**Rent-a-Moped**. Ph: (03) 5983 2466

### Dolphin swims and seal watching
Swim with the bay's bottle-nose dolphins.
It's a favourite; a great privilege and
terrific fun. Several operators promise
environmentally sensitive tours. **Polperro
Dolphin Swims**, leaving Sorrento Pier, is
a highly respected, award-winning eco-
tourism company. Ph: (03) 5988 8437

Seal colonies also abound in Port
Phillip Bay, especially around the 'Fort',
Mud Is and Hovel Light. The *Jillian* takes
1/2-day tours, weather permitting to these
locations. Ph: (03) 5988 9638

### Fishing
Fish at any number of suburban and
country jetties and piers, such as Kerford
Rd pier in Middle Park or Seaford pier.
Flinders Pier and the historic Queenscliff
pier are popular locations, far from the
madding crowd. Portsea and Pt Lonsdale
back beaches are ideal for surf fishing.

For deep-sea fishing, put your own
craft in at any of the numerous boat
launches around the bay, or charter a boat.
**Proline Fishing Charters**, specialists with

**Ply the skies**
For another exciting
activity, try hot air
ballooning at 3000ft
over Geelong and the
Bellarine Peninsula.
After your pre-dawn
start, take breakfast at
the **Wharf Shed Cafe**
on Eastern Beach. Ph:
(03) 9890 0339

over 150 years of family tradition on Port Phillip, leave from Sorrento pier. Ph: 015 846 279. At Hastings, **The Kooga** is recommended for fishing in Western Port Bay. Ph: 0417 590 553

## Golf

The brochure *Melbourne's Golf Coast* — available at the Peninsula Visitor Info Centre — describes the 'sand belt' golf courses located around the Top of the Bay and on Mornington Peninsula. **Sandringham Golf Links** is one of Melbourne's best public golf courses. **Flinders Golf Club** and **Mornington Country Golf Club** have magnificent coastal views. Ask at the Geelong visitor info centre for the Geelong and Bellarine Peninsula golf guide.

*Surfing, Sorrento.*

## Horseriding

Specialty rides of Mornington Peninsula include ocean beach rides and rides to wineries. **Gunnamatta Trail Rides** are highly recommended. Ph: 1800 801 003. On the Bellarine Peninsula, **Koombahla Park Equestrian Centre** on Wallington Rd offers professional riding instruction as well as pleasure rides. Ph: (03) 5255 1020

## Paragliding

The cliffs at Flinders and Portsea back beaches are ideal for hang-gliding and paragliding. The **Melbourne Paragliding Centre** runs accredited courses. Ph: (03) 9770 2400

## Sailing

For a tall ships sailing experience, board the **Alma Doepel Sailing Ship**, which sets sail from various locations during summer. Ph: (03) 9646 5211

The **Yachtmaster Sailing School**, operating from Brighton and Hastings, teaches bay and ocean sailing, and navigation. For Brighton, Ph: (03) 9592 6672; Hastings, Ph: (03) 5995 7155.

The **Vicsail Sailing School**, operates from the Royal Geelong Yacht Club Marina, Eastern Beach. Ph: (03) 5223 2733

## Scuba diving

Several companies operate from the Mornington Peninsula. They teach the rudiments of diving, supply equipment and ferry divers to the many fascinating dive sites. Especially popular are the 19th century shipwreck sites around the Rip. Check at visitor info centres for dive locations and regulations regarding spearfishing.

## Surfing

The learn-to-surf classes on Sorrento back beach are a joy to behold. **Sorrento Surf School** takes all ages. Ph: (03) 5988 6143

At Pt Leo, the **East Coast Surf School** offers a similar service. Ph: (03) 5989 2198

# Fun for the young

★ Arthurs Seat Chairlift (p.129)

★ Bellarine Peninsula Railway (p.129)

★ Surfing at Sorrento back beach (p.145)

★ Fishing at Flinders pier (p.144)

★ Horseriding on Gunnamatta beach (p.145)

★ Moorooduc Rock Candy and Humbug Factory (p.134)

★ Open Range Zoo (p.139)

★ RAAF Museum (p.139)

★ *HMAS Castlemaine* (p.139)

★ Scienceworks and Planetarium (p.140)

# Suggested tours – Map 24

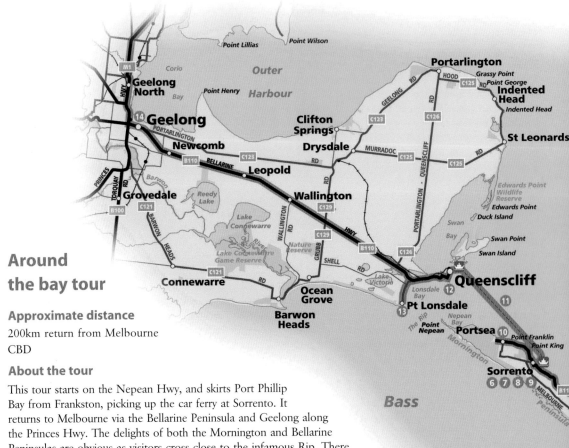

## Around the bay tour

### Approximate distance

200km return from Melbourne CBD

### About the tour

This tour starts on the Nepean Hwy, and skirts Port Phillip Bay from Frankston, picking up the car ferry at Sorrento. It returns to Melbourne via the Bellarine Peninsula and Geelong along the Princes Hwy. The delights of both the Mornington and Bellarine Peninsulas are obvious as visitors cross close to the infamous Rip. There are spectacular views of Port Phillip Bay and the peninsulas at many points. Places of historical interest, impressive gardens and the attractions of rural hinterlands are readily accessed.

Stop for coffee or luncheon at Schnapper Pt, Herronswood's Thatched Cottage, or one of Sorrento's many trendy cafes, perhaps Stringer's Store. The trip is best taken over 3 days, which allows 1 overnight stay in Sorrento and 1 in Queenscliff. The trip can quite comfortably be done over 2 days if some itinerary items are dropped. It is advisable to pre-book the car ferry in summer.

## Places of interest

❶ **Schnapper Pt, Mornington** (p.131)

❷ **Beachside route to Mount Martha** (p.134)

❸ **Arthurs Seat summit and chairlift** (p.129)

❹ **Herronswood Garden; McCrae Homestead** (p.135)

❺ **Rye Pier** (p.135)

❻ **Early settlers' graves, Sullivans Bay** (p.136)

❼ **Sorrento township** (p.135)

❽ **Sorrento back beach** (p.135)

❾ **Portsea** (p.134)

❿ **Polperro Dolphin Swim** (p.144)

⓫ **Queenscliff-Sorrento Car Ferry, Sorrento Pier** (p.135)

⓬ **Queenscliff township** (p.127)

⓭ **Pt Lonsdale Rip View** (p.126)

⓮ **Geelong waterfront and Eastern Beach** (p.126)

*Red Hill Estate.*

# Wine and day tour

## Approximate distance
150km return from Melbourne CBD

## About the tour
The Mornington Peninsula is renowned for its vineyards and wineries. Six very different wineries are suggested here for cellardoor tastings. (The tour also takes in 2 galleries, close to the selected wineries.) Conditions on the peninsula are likened to those of the Burgundy region in France, where the pinot noir grape thrives. Pinot is the peninsula's true love affair, but a number of other wines are produced here too. At Dromana Estate, for instance, Gary Crittenden is successfully experimenting with Italian varieties.

For lunch, Red Hill Estate offers an a la carte menu with one of the best views on the Mornington Peninsula. For a more earthy, but very stylish lunch, T'Gallant's rustic La Baracca is highly recommended. Log fires burn in both restaurants during winter. A tasting fee of $2 applies in most wineries, but is refunded on purchase.

## Places of interest
❶ **Mornington Vineyards Estate** (p.133)
❷ **Hickinbotham of Dromana** (p.133)
❸ **Dromana Estate** (p.132)
❹ **Noels Gallery** (p.129)
❺ **T'Gallant** (p.133)
❻ **Red Hill Estate** (p.133)
❼ **The Barn — Country Art and Craft Centre** (p.129)
❽ **Willow Creek Vineyard** (p.133)

Left: **Norman Bay,
Wilsons Promontory**.
Right: **Penguin
Parade.**

# Phillip Island
## and Gippsland
# Discovery

**B**ushwalking on Wilsons Promontory, surfing at Cape Woolamai, snow skiing at Mt Baw Baw, dinosaur hunting at Inverloch, touring the Grand Ridge Road – what a fabulous array of activities on offer. To the north of the region, the Gt Dividing Range is home to summer and winter alpine experiences. To the south, the wilderness coast stretches from Phillip Is to Wilsons Promontory and beyond. In between, lush countryside supports Australia's premier dairy industry, which is also the source of mouth-watering gourmet food production. Along the Princes Hwy the mighty chimney stacks of the Latrobe Valley mark the location of Australia's largest brown coal deposits and various industrial tourism opportunities.

This region surely rates as one of Victoria's most spectacular, yet also one of the state's least explored and appreciated. Phillip Is receives large numbers of tourists who enjoy its many tourist attractions. Its Penguin Parade is Victoria's number one tourist destination for overseas visitors. But anyone limiting their travels to this western-most part of the region will miss an abundance of less developed and, if desired, rugged and remote locations. This region is unique for the number and variety of its national and state parks, and the many small nature reserves dedicated to conservation and active recreational pursuits.

## Tourist information

**Central Gippsland Visitor Info Centre**
8 Foster St, Sale 3850
Ph: (03) 5144 1108
Freecall: 1800 637 060

**Foster Tourist Info**
Stockyard Gallery, Pioneer St
Foster 3960
Ph: (03) 5682 1125

**Sth Gippsland Visitor Info Centre**
Cnr Sth Gippsland Hwy and
Silkstone Rd, Korumburra 3950
Ph: (03) 5655 2233
Toll Free: 1800 630 704

**Phillip Is Info Centre**
Phillip Is Tourist Rd, Newhaven 3925
Ph: (03) 5956 7447
Toll Free 1300 366 422

**Gippsland Country Tourism Info Centre**
Shop 1, Southside Central
Princes Hwy, Traralgon 3844
Ph: (03) 5174 3199
Toll Free: 1800 621 409

**Wilsons Promontory National Park**
Park Office and Visitors Centre
Tidal River 3960
Ph: 1800 350 552

**Websites**
http://www.phillipisland.net.au
http://www.sgsc.vic.gov.au

## Must see, must do

★ **Coal Creek Historical Village** (p.164)
★ **Grand Ridge Rd** (p.166)
★ **Penguin Parade** (p.159)
★ **Tarra Bulga NP** (p.170)
★ **Walhalla township** (p.157)
★ **Wilsons Promontory** (p.172)

## Radio stations

**Gippsland FM:** 104.7 FM
**3GG:** 531 AM
**3GIFM:** 100.7 FM
**3MFM:** 88.1 FM
**3TR:** 1242 AM
**Phillip Island tourist information:** 87.6 FM

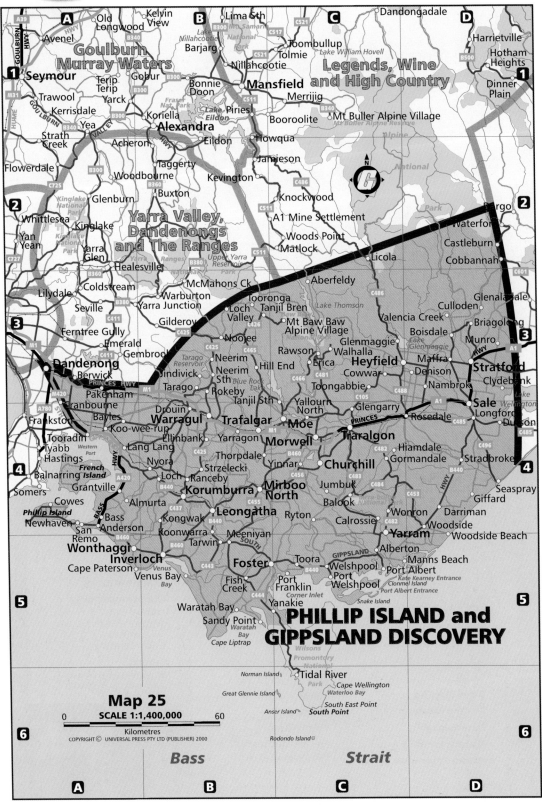

Map 25

SCALE 1:1,400,000

0    60

Kilometres

COPYRIGHT © UNIVERSAL PRESS PTY LTD (PUBLISHER) 2000

# PHILLIP ISLAND and
# GIPPSLAND DISCOVERY

*Bass*    *Strait*

## Natural features

In the west of the region, Westernport Bay and its two main islands, French Is and Phillip Is, together with a vast area of drained swampland to the north of the bay, lie within the Westernport sunkland. This area was once connected to Tasmania, submerged with the end of the last Ice Age around 15 000 years ago.

Interspersed along the coast from Kilcunda to Waratah Bay are rolling sand dunes, rugged cliffs and intertidal rock shelves, as well as more pastoral scenes associated with extensive estuaries and wetlands like those at Inverloch. Wilsons Promontory, in the east, is the southern-most tip of the Australian continent and remains a pristine wilderness area. A huge volcanic outcrop connected to the mainland by Yanakie Isthmus, the Promontory harbours the shallow waters of Corner Inlet and many mangrove-clad fishing villages to its north.

The region is cut through by the Latrobe Valley. A huge deposit of brown coal formed here over millions of years, the result of rich layers of plant matter being carbonised. To the north, the Gt Dividing Range reaches altitudes of over 1500m. The high country supports sub-alpine eucalypt forests, rising to alpine heathlands and snow gum forests. Marking the sub-region of Sth Gippsland, the Strzelecki Ranges — once the Gt Southern Forest — extend over 100km,

*Strezlecki Ranges.*

rising to quite rugged terrain in the east. For the most part, the Strzeleckis are a vivid green patchwork pastureland of interweaving hills. Only small remnants of the once magnificent cool temperate rainforests remain.

## History

European sealers arrived on the south coast around 1803, beginning the 1st displacement of the Victorian Aborigines – the Kurnai, to the east of Tarwin Lower, and the Bunurong, who occupied the coastal area from Inverloch to Melbourne. George Bass, with 6 crew, had navigated the coast from Botany Bay to Westernport in 1798 to prove the existence of a strait separating the mainland from Van Dieman's Land. Soon sealers, whalers, traders and tin miners were plying the waters of Bass Strait 40 years before permanent settlements of any size were established.

The Westernport swamps made settlement east from Melbourne virtually impossible. Gippsland was initially opened up from the NE, with the trailblazing explorations of Angus McMillan in 1839 and Sir Paul Edmund de Strzelecki in 1840. McMillan established cattle runs as he came, reaching Port Albert — which was to become an important trading link — in the south. Strzelecki made an arduous journey through the length of the Gt Southern Forest.

*Whale Rock, Wilson's Promontory.*

**Life-saving wildlife**
Strzelecki and his party are said to have survived their arduous journey through the Gt Southern Forest by eating raw koala. The weather too damp to be able to light fires, Tarra their Aboriginal guide (after whom the Tarra Bulga NP is named), suggested this life-saving dish.

The draining of the swamps, the arrival of the railway, and the clearing of the Gt Southern Forest in the late 19th century transformed Gippsland into a highly productive pastoral and coal producing region.

## Getting there

### By road

The Sth Gippsland Hwy, which branches off from Melbourne's SE Arterial, heads deep into Sth Gippsland through major dairying centres to the coast and Wilsons Promontory. The Bass Hwy branches off from the Sth Gippsland Hwy to Phillip Is and the townships of Wonthaggi and Inverloch.

The Princes Hwy traverses Central Gippsland, taking in the major dairying centres of Drouin and Warragul and the cities and towns of the Latrobe Valley. The Gt Dividing Range lies north and the Strzeleckis lie to the south.

### By rail and coach

Trains leave daily from Spencer St Stn for Central Gippsland, with some services terminating at Warragul and others terminating at Traralgon and Sale. Connecting coaches leave for towns in the north, including Heyfield and Maffra. **Greyhound Pioneer** operates an evening coach through Central Gippsland.

V/Line coaches also leave Spencer St and Dandenong Stns daily for Phillip Is and Sth Gippsland. The Phillip Is coach takes the Bass Hwy, with stops including San Remo, Cowes, Wonthaggi and Inverloch. The coach to Sth Gippsland follows the Sth Gippsland Hwy through Korumburra and Leongatha to Foster and Fish Creek, terminating at Yarram. Ph: (03) 13 22 32

Backpackers and others can catch the postie run to Tidal River, Wilsons Promontory on Mon, Wed and Fri from the Foster Backpack Hostel at 17 Pioneer St, Foster. Ph: (03) 5682 2614

### By ferry

The **Inter-island Ferry Service** runs regular services all year connecting Stony Pt on the Mornington Peninsula (with connections from Frankston Stn) to Cowes on Phillip Is. Ph: (03) 9585 5730. Ferries also leave Stony Pt for French Is. Ph: (03) 5978 5642

### By air

Several airlines fly from Melbourne and interstate to the Latrobe Regional Airport.

## Getting around

**Latrobe Valley Bus Lines** operates a service between Moe, Morwell, Churchill and Traralgon. Ph: (03) 5134 2055. Town bus services operate in the region's large centres. Hire cars are also available.

For visitors to Phillip Is, **Bay Connections** offers various cruises from Cowes and San Remo, including seal-watching and French Is tours. Ph: (03) 5678 5642. Car rental is available at **Island Car Rentals**, Ph: (03) 5956 6696. Harley Davidson tours, with **Island Rides and Tours**, are another way to see the island. Ph: (03) 5956 9551. Scenic flights with **Phillip Island Air**, Ph: (03) 5956 7316, and helicopter rides, leaving from the **Seal Rock Sea Life Centre**, are particularly exciting. Freecall: 1300 367 325

For Sth Gippsland, **Surefoot Explorations** runs a number of intriguing farm, bush, star-gazing and dinosaur tours. Ph: (03) 5952 1533. The **Koonwarra Education Environment Centre**'s farm tours, geared to the region's environment-friendly agri-development, including the region's burgeoning gourmet food industry, are unique. Ph: (03) 5664 2361

*Exploring Wilsons Promontory.*

On the SE coast, leaving from Port Welshpool, the **Prom Adventurer** offers day trips by boat exploring the isolated beaches of Wilsons Promontory. Ph: (03) 5682 2633. **Wilsons Promontory Tours** offers personalised tours of the 'Prom Coast' and eastern Strzeleckis. Ph: (03) 5681 2260

For mountain tours, visitors cannot go past **Mountain Top Experience**, which takes exciting 4WD expeditions, including passenger and tag-along tours. Vehicle hire is also available. Ph: (03) 5134 6876

## Festivals and events

### Leongatha Food and Wine Festival

The Leongatha Food and Wine Festival, held on the 1st Fri in Jan, will whet your appetite for Sth Gippsland's bountiful gourmet produce. Taste wines, cheeses, meats, seafood, bush tucker and organic produce at Memorial Hall in the town's centre. Ph: 1800 630 704

### Cowes Classic Biathlon

Need to take off those kilos you put on at Leongatha? Enter, or perhaps just come to watch, the Cowes Classic Biathlon. Held 3rd Sun in Jan, entrants swim 500m from the beach around the jetty and run 5km through the streets of Cowes. The sister event, the **San Remo Channel Challenge**, is held on the 3rd Sun of Feb. Ph: (03) 595 67311

### Strzelecki Ranges Festival

The Strzelecki Ranges Festival runs for 1 wk at Mirboo Nth from the 1st Sat in Feb. Commencing with the annual agricultural show, a full program of music, historical and environmental activities follows, concluding with a country market. Mirboo Nth's boutique Grand Ridge Brewery sponsors a home-brewing competition unique in Australia. Ph: (03) 5664 8239

### Sth Gippsland Golf Classic

The Sth Gippsland Golf Classic is a must. Held in the 2nd week of Feb, over 100 clubs participate in over 180 games a day on courses all the way from Korumburra to Yarram. Ph: (03) 5688 1315

*King of the Mountain Race.*

### Festival in the Forest

In the mountain ash forests of the Gt Dividing Range, the cries of the currawongs compete with the hoots of happy festival goers at the Festival in the Forest on the 2nd weekend in Feb. The big event is the festival's mountain horse race. The 3km track, with good viewing positions, cuts through gullies and mountain streams in the Loch Valley. Visitors can camp for the weekend, or come for the day. Ph: (03) 5628 9511

### Bunyip Country Music Festival

Country music fans don't have to travel to Tamworth to hear their heroes. The Bunyip Country Music Festival, held in the Bunyip Reserve on the last Sun in Feb, is only 1hr from Melbourne. This laid-back affair features Australian stars from the country music circuit, as well as local wannabes. Ph: (03) 5629 5388

### Toora Festival

Labour Day weekend in Mar sees the Toora Festival — a quirky country festival, in a pretty coastal town north of Wilsons Promontory. Apart from its music, food and children's entertainments, it features the King of the Mountain Race — locals race to the top of the mountain carrying sacks of powdered milk. Ph: (03) 5688 1264

**Precautions for drivers and walkers**
- Watch out for logging trucks on forest roads.
- In winter, you are obliged to carry car chains.
- As weather changes can be dramatic, carry warm clothing and make sure someone else knows where you are going.

*Leongatha Food and Wine Festival.*

### Churchill Is Autumn Festival

The Churchill Is Autumn Festival is held in the grounds of the Churchill Is Homestead, accessible from Phillip Is, on the Sun and Mon of Labour Day weekend in Mar. This 19th century farm puts on its full heritage garb, with blacksmithing, woodworking, spinning and whip-cracking demonstrations, sheepdog trials, horse and cart rides, clowns, and egg and spoon races. Ph: (03) 5956 8300

### Inverloch Jazz Festival

The Inverloch Jazz Festival runs from Fri night through to Mon on Labour Day weekend in Mar. Fifty bands play popular jazz with a mixture of free and paid-for events. On Mon — a free concert on the beach behind Wyeth Park. Ph: (03) 5674 2706

### Powerscourt Harvest Festival

One of Gippsland's major food and wine events, the Powerscourt Harvest Festival in Maffra attracts over 5000 people to its weekend of gourmandising, music and fun. Five stages are set up for a wide variety of musical events. The festival is held on the 2nd weekend in Mar and showcases the region's produce (eel included). Ph: (03) 5147 1897

### Stony Ck Cup

The Stony Ck Cup shows country racing at its most picturesque. Meeting at the Stony Ck racecourse on Labour Day weekend in Mar, families can relax with a picnic in the shade of a gum tree. Ph: (03) 5664 0099

### Tarwin Lower Riverfest

The beautiful Tarwin River hosts this community festival, also held over Labour Day Weekend in Mar. A kayak regatta takes place on Sat, with boat cruises, bands, a children's carnival and arts and crafts events throughout the weekend. Ph: (03) 5663 5383

### Thorpdale Potato Festival,

The Thorpdale Potato Festival, held on Labour Day in Mar at Thorpdale Reserve, celebrates the potato harvest and attracts 1000s of people. Photographic and cooking competitions feature the potato; the Thorpdale iron men race with a sack of potatoes on their back; there is a potato picking competition; kids get to bowl potatoes; and everyone can have a baked potato for lunch! Ph: (03) 5634 6341. The **Koo-We-Rup Potato Festival** takes place later in the month, with its own mix of quirky events. Ph: (03) 5997 1265

### The World's Longest Lunch

Visitors can sit down to The World's Longest Lunch in Gippsland's gourmet deli country near Warragul. Each Mar this decadent foodie event takes place as part of Melbourne's Food and Wine Festival. Award-winning meats and cheeses, berries and cream, pies and breads, and an array of indigenous foods are the basis of each year's exceptional menu. Ph: (03) 5174 3199

### Moe Jazz Festival

The Moe Jazz Festival is another favourite of jazz lovers. Held on Easter weekend in Apr, over a 100 musicians play in local venues. Ph: (03) 5127 1839

### Lang Lang Rodeo

Another Easter event is the well-known Lang Lang Rodeo, held on Easter Mon in Apr. With 'cowboys' riding the broncos, traditional sideshows and circus events, it's a classic. Ph: (03) 5997 5396

*Motorcycle Grand Prix.*

### Maffra Scotfest

Maffra Scotfest highlights the Scottish pioneer heritage of the Maffra area. This highland festival, held each Apr, features pipe and brass bands, massed bands, a mini tattoo, clan tents, highland Scottish dancing, and the grand Caledonian Ball. Ph: (03) 5144 5308

### Australian 500cc Motorcycle Grand Prix

Get revved up at the Australian 500cc Motorcycle Grand Prix, at the Phillip Is Racing Circuit, staged on the 1st weekend in Oct. This event attracts 30 000–50 000 people and accommodation on the island is rapidly booked out. Ph: (03) 5952 2710

### Koonwarra Country Fair

Held on the 3rd weekend in Nov, the Koonwarra Country Fair is not to be missed. The wonderful Koonwarra General Store has inspired a country gourmet culture in this little borough. Eat, drink and be very chirpy as you watch street theatre and visit the unique native flower show, environment education centre and local farms. Ph: (03) 5664 2285

### New Year's Eve Festival

To round off the year, in the midst of its busy summer season, Cowes throws a big street party. Its New Year's Eve Festival sees in the New Year with music and entertainment. Children are catered for with an early fireworks display at 9pm.

## Main towns and localities
### Central and West Gippsland
#### Heyfield Map 25 C3

Originally Hayfield, after its fields of corn, Heyfield is now a timber town, producing kiln-dried hardwoods. It is located on the Licola road, heading north into the Gt Dividing Range. From Heyfield visitors can gain access to remote mountain locations, some of which are suitable for cross-country skiing. At **Lake Glenmaggie**, 11km north, visitors can camp, fish and go boating. Beautiful picnic spots are to be found all along the **Macalister River** north to Licola.

**Maffra.**

### Maffra Map 25 D3

Soldiers returning from the Peninsula Wars in Spain and Portugal are said to have named Maffra after a Portuguese town. This is at odds with the overwhelmingly Scottish flavour of the area. Angus McMillan passed through the area in 1841, establishing cattle runs for John Macalister, a wealthy NSW pastoralist. Maffra was originally an outpost of the Boisdale Run, named after a remote New Hebrides island. Maffra's Scottish heritage is celebrated at its annual **Scotfest** (p.155). **Bushy Park Reserve** is the site of the original Angus MacMillan homestead, which is now at the Gippsland Heritage Park in Moe. **Boisdale House**, made of 300 000 hand-made bricks, still stands overlooking the Avon River.

Close by, the **Wa-de Lock Vineyards** are open weekdays for cellar door sales and tastings, 10am–5pm, Ph: (03) 5147 3244, while the highly respected **Pino Deriu Gemstone and Mineral Collection** is on display in Johnson St. It is open daily, except Wed, 10am–5pm. Ph: (03) 5141 1811

### Moe Map 25 C4

Moe lies at the entrance to the Latrobe Valley, close to the Yallourn open cut mine and power station. Tours can be arranged through **PowerWorks** in Morwell. Ph: (03) 5135 3415. Moe is also the turnoff point for Walhalla and Blue Rock Lake, and other mountain locations on the signposted **Mountain Rivers Trail**.

**Abundant coal stores**
The Latrobe Valley produces up to 60 million tonnes of brown coal a year. Yallourn near Moe and Hazelwood in Morwell produce 50 000 tonnes a day each, while Loy Yang near Traralgon produces up to 90 000 tonnes a day.

## Farmgate sales

**Asparagus:** 300 Railway Rd, Koo-Wee-Rup
**Blueberries:** Ameys Track, Foster
**Cheese:** Top Paddock Cheeses, Bena
**Venison:** Inverloch-Tarwin Rd, Inverloch
**Herbs:** Thompson Ave, Cowes
**Berries:** Yilleen Organic Berry Farm, Hallston

**Gippsland Heritage Park**, located in the centre of Moe, provides affordable family entertainment. A historical theme park recreating a 19th rural community, there are working displays of various trades and crafts, horse-drawn rides, period shops and devonshire teas.

### Morwell *Map 25 C4*

The vast, gentle Latrobe Valley stretches out along the Princes Hwy, its vistas dramatically interrupted by billowing plumes of steam from huge chimneys, and by the gaping holes which are its open cut mines. In Morwell the Hazelwood mine and power station are clearly visible from the Hwy. Originally on the supply route to the eastern goldfields, Morwell developed as a pastoral and timber-milling centre. Today, the 2nd largest town in Gippsland, it produces up to 50 000 tonnes of coal a day.

All you ever wanted to know about generating-capacity and the engineering feats associated with open cut mining is explained at **PowerWorks**, open 7 days a week, 9am–5pm. This high-tech, interactive museum is located on site, with regular tours of the mine and power station. Twilight tours, which include a meal with fabulous night-time views are a great way to get the feel of the valley. Ph: (03) 5135 3415

### Neerim Sth *Map 25 B3*

Just over 1hr from Melbourne, the country around Neerim Sth feels a little like Switzerland with its lush mountain pastures. Perhaps this is why the gourmet deli trail has so many stops here. An often snow-capped Mt Baw Baw and the Gt Dividing Range provide a magnificent backdrop.

The town itself is neat and prosperous, with two small galleries well worth visiting. The **Serigraph Gallery**, open Fri, Sat and Sun, 10.30am–4.30pm, or by appt, exhibits exquisite screen prints, ceramics, glass and timber ware. Ph: (03) 5628 1519. **Gippsland Picture Framers** across the road exhibits original, traditional works in oils and water colours. Neerim Sth is also known for its wood-fired bakery.

A short distance north of the town, the famed **Tarago River Cheese Co** offers visitors the chance to sample its award-winning 'Shadows of Blue', brie and farmhouse cheeses. Cheese-making can be viewed by the public at specified times. Milking is at 4pm daily. Ph: (03) 5628 1528. The **Ada Valley Winery** close by will complement any cheeses purchased with a locally grown vintage. Open weekends and public holidays, 10am–6pm. Ph: (03) 5623 1342

From Neerim Sth, it is short but spectacular drive to **Jindivick**, with its smokehouse and lovely **Jindivick Gardens** (p.173). The **Tarago Reservoir** lies a short distance out from Neerim Sth on the Jindivick Rd. A haven for various water birds, with short walks marked around the reservoir, it is a very pleasant picnic site. It has wet weather shelters, toilets and fireplaces, with wood provided. Open daily, 8.30am–8pm, 8.30am–6pm winter.

### Noojee *Map 25 B3*

A small timber town, Noojee is the last port of call before the road to Mt Baw Baw. Stock up with provisions well before you get here — possibly at Neerim Sth — as the town has only a couple of shops and a pub to cater for travellers. On weekends, the **Outpost Inn**, tucked away from the main road, is open for meals. Its associated 'Toolshed' — announcing 'Ammo on sale here' — offers bar meals at night. Noojee's municipal camping and picnic ground beside the Latrobe River is

*Serigraph Gallery, Neerim South.*

**Wetlands, Sale.**

**Gippsland Art Gallery, Sale.**

pleasantly located and has good facilities, free. There are BBQs, tables under cover, toilets and showers.

The **Alpine Trout Farm**, 2km west of Noojee on the Mt Baw Baw Tourist Rd, offers fishing and trout sales. Open daily, 9am–5pm. Close by, Noojee's impressive 102m **Trestle Bridge** is a reminder of the role played by the early railways in servicing such remote logging towns. There is a picnic area and short walks on walking tracks.

From Noojee, various drives into the Gt Dividing Range are possible. **Toorongo Falls Scenic Reserve** is reached via an unsealed road off the Baw Baw Rd. Camping is allowed in the reserve, which features an 1800m walking track that takes in both the Toorongo and Amphitheatre Falls set in lush mountain ash forest. The reserve has fireplaces and toilets. To the east of Noojee, via the Yarra Junction-Noojee Rd, visitors will find the protected **Ada River Tree**, a spectacular giant mountain ash.

### Sale *Map 25 D4*

It is astounding to think that Sale was a thriving port in the late 19th century, connected via the Thompson River to the Gippsland Lakes and thus to the open sea. The 'Port of Sale' remains a local placename, but the channel that once carried the regular steamboat run to Melbourne is no longer viable. This area

incorporates the town's **Lake Guthridge** and the **Sale Common**, which have boardwalks and bird hides.

The city boasts many 19th century buildings, two cathedrals, several fine old schools and Australia's southern-most RAAF base, home to the aerobatics team, the Roulettes.

The **Gippsland Art Gallery, Sale**, located in the Sale Civic Centre, is a sophisticated regional gallery showing visiting exhibitions and promoting the work of regional artists and craftspeople. It is open daily except public hols, 10am–5pm. Ph: (03) 5142 3372. Anamieke Mein's *Wall of Fame*, a series of brass plaques depicting the early pioneers, is permanently located in the foyer of the shire offices. Several of her well-known embroidered works are on permanent display in the gallery.

Several long road tours commence in Sale. The **Bataluk Cultural Trail** into East Gippsland passes through various sites of importance in local Aboriginal history. Sale is a major point of contact with the High Country in the north and with the Gippsland Lakes to the east.

### Traralgon *Map 25 C4*

Traralgon is the Latrobe Valley's largest town and designated regional growth centre, with excellent shopping, a good selection of restaurants and accommodation, as well as a large regional library and leisure complex. **Victory Park**, adjacent to the Traralgon Creek, has a lovely rotunda and picnic area.

Traralgon is home to the valley's newest power stations, Loy Yang A and B, and to the state's largest unmined deposit of brown coal. A drive out to the **Loy Yang Open Cut** and **Power Station** provides awe-inspiring views from the viewing area beside the cavernous open cut. Information boards tell the history of the plant.

### Walhalla *Map 25 C3*

Gold was discovered here in 1862. In the 1880s 5000 people lived in Walhalla, working large and small mines scattered through the mountains at makeshift villages like 'Povery Point' and 'Maiden

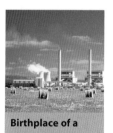

**Birthplace of a prizewinner**
Traralgon is the birthplace of Nobel Prize winner Sir Frank Macfarlane Burnett. Born in 1899, he became one of the world's leading virologists. He died in 1985.

*Hillside Cemetary.*

Town'. In 1900, with a population of 3000, Walhalla was still one of Gippsland's largest towns. Today, it is a quiet mountain retreat and heritage town.

There are many reminders of Walhalla's rough and ready past. Photographs of frontier life adorn the walls of the local pub, a friendly place to stop and chat. The **Walhalla Museum**, with a variety of displays, is open daily, 10.30am–4pm, except Tues and Thurs. While most of Walhalla's many timber buildings were moved out when the town declined, the **Fire Station**, **Band Rotunda** and several old stores remain. The **Hillside Cemetery**, perched on the rim of the steep valley in which Walhalla is nestled, is a reminder of the hardships endured by pioneers, especially women and children.

The **Long Tunnel Gold Mine** gives a vivid indication of the size of Walhalla's mining operations. Visitors are ushered into a huge cavern — the machinery chamber — where the mine's steam-power requirements were generated. The mine is open for tours on weekends, school and public holidays, from 11am, Oct–Easter; 1.30pm Easter–Aug. Ph: (03) 5165 6242

Reconstruction of the steam train line to Walhalla has been the passion of many hardworking local volunteers. You can take a 40min return trip up the Stringers Ck Gorge on the **Walhalla Goldfields Railway** from Thomson to the Happy Ck picnic area. With the steepest curves of any railway constructed in Victoria, this is a very exciting run. For times ph: (03) 9513 3969

Numerous walks around Walhalla include the interstate **Alpine Walking Track** which ends at Walhalla. A walking guide for this area is available from the general store. Ph: (03) 5165 6227. Walhalla is an ideal place for a stopover, being adjacent to many beauty spots in the Baw Baw area, including the towns of **Erica** and **Rawson**. Swimming and picnic spots abound — on the Thomson River south of Walhalla and at Blue Rock Lake on the Tanjil River.

## Warragul *Map 25 B4*

Warragul is a large regional city in the heart of dairying country. It is a lively retail centre, with fine buildings and civic areas. The Warragul swimming pool is located beside Civic Park, behind the Baw Baw Shire offices and Warragul Arts Centre.

The **Flamin' Bull Bush Tucker Restaurant** in Mason St offers a highly original gastronomic experience. The Flamin' Bull employs local Koories in various training schemes, including indigenous food preparation. Kangaroo, emu and yabbie feature on the menu, along with emu egg quiche, wattle-seed coffee and rosella flower muffins. Caving tours also leave from the Flamin' Bull. Aboriginal guides take small groups to the Labertouche Caves where participants learn about the Kurnai and Kulin peoples — the bush tucker they ate and much more. Ph: (03) 5623 2377

Something quite different is the **Darnum Musical Village**, 8km east of Warragul. Housed in several restored 19th century buildings is a lifetime's collection of fine instruments including a piano said to have been Chopin's favourite. Visitors can see instruments being repaired by expert craftsmen and are welcome to handle them. Ph: (03) 5627 8235

### Yarragon *Map 25 B4*

Yarragon village is a good spot to break your drive down the Princes Hwy. It offers a collection of food, craft and specialty shops. The **Mouton Noir** has gifts and a wide range of craft materials of natural fibres and fabrics. **Candleberry Country** also specialises in country crafts. The **Gippsland Food and Wine Tea Rooms** is done up in period style. Besides its usual fare, it offers its 'Big Breakfast' from 7.30am–10am.

## Phillip Island

George Bass charted the waters of Westernport Bay in 1898, naming the island after Captain Arthur Phillip, commander of the First Fleet. In 1826 Victoria's earliest settlement was briefly established at Corinella. The island was only really opened up after land was offered for selection in 1869. Since the 1890s, with the commencement of ferries from Stony Pt, it has been a favourite summer holiday destination.

Today Phillip Is is Victoria's premier international tourist destination. The Penguin Parade attracts over 500 000 visitors a year, and the population swells from 6000 to 40 000 during summer. The island boasts major attractions, foreshore hotels, restaurants, holiday flats and B&Bs. In summer, there is a busy, festive air.

### Bass *Map 25 A4*

At Bass, on the Sth Gippsland Hwy just before the turn-off to Phillip Is, **Wildlife Wonderland** attracts large numbers of tourists to its native animal enclosures, white shark display and indoor trout fishing. Large glass cases allow visitors to view Gippsland's giant worms in their muddy habitat, although they are often sleeping! Open daily, 9.30am–5.30pm. Ph: (03) 5678 2222

### Cowes *Map 26 B1*

Cowes is the island's main town, with shopping facilities, cinemas, eating houses, and other entertainments. Ferries and bay cruises take off from this location on the north of the island facing the Mornington Peninsula. The sandy safety beaches are ideal for leisurely swimming. Strolling out onto the jetty, visitors will see French Is to the right and Stony Pt to the left.

Cowes is also the turn-off point to the **Penguin Parade** and the lookout to the **Nobbies** and **Seal Rocks**. Every evening, the fairy penguins emerge from the ocean to waddle up the beach to their nests and are seen from a specially-constructed viewing area. Access to the Penguin Parade is strictly controlled, and bookings are essential in peak season. The visitor centre, which has interactive displays, a cafe and giftshop

*Cowes.*

**Yarragon.**

*The Nobbies.*

*Pyramid Rock.*

is open daily from 10am–dusk. Ph: (03) 5956 8300

The **Seal Life Centre** is also open daily from 10am. Tourists can take a simulated voyage on Bass's open whale boat and view a video relay of the seal colony. Cost: $15 per adult, $35 family. Ph: 1300 367 325. There are spectacular walks around the point from the Nobbies to the **Blowhole** and **Pyramid Rock**.

Touring in this SW corner of the island, travellers will find the **Phillip**

**Island Winery**, open daily, 10am–8pm from Jan–Mar, and the **Woolshed**, serving wholesome farmhouse grills and selling high quality woollen products. Open daily from noon–dusk. **A Maze 'N Things**, featuring mind-teasing optical illusions will entertain the children on non-beach days. Open daily, 9am–6pm.

At the **Koala Conservation Centre** visitors walk at tree-top level on specially-constructed boardwalks to maximise viewing. Open daily, 10am–7pm. Phillip Is Nature Park, the body which coordinates the island's various nature activities, offers a terrific range of summer activities — campfire nights, special event walks and family bike tours. Ph: (03) 5956 8300 for a program.

Phillip Island's famous ocean beaches are located in the south-east of the island. **Smiths Beach** and **Woolamai Beach** are especially popular. At Woolamai marked tracks lead past shearwater rookeries and various natural formations to Cape Woolamai. Lifesavers patrol both these beaches during summer.

The **Phillip Is Grand Prix Circuit Info Centre,** is located close by at the Grand Prix Circuit (p.155). Open daily, 10am–7pm.

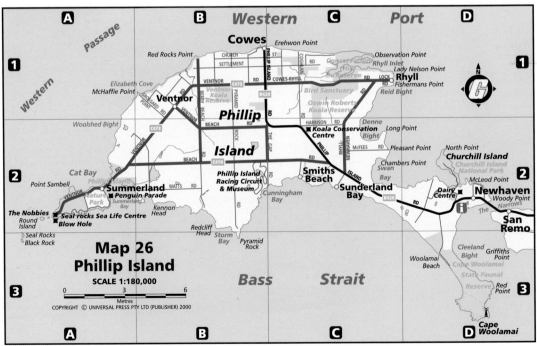

**Map 26**
**Phillip Island**

SCALE 1:180,000

0    3    6
Metres

COPYRIGHT © UNIVERSAL PRESS PTY LTD (PUBLISHER) 2000

*Penguin Parade.*

### Newhaven *Map 26 D2*

Newhaven lies just across the bridge from San Remo on the mainland. Campers arrive here in droves to enjoy the clear waters of the San Remo Channel. The **Richard Graydon Park** has BBQs, toilets and a playground. Close to the **Big Flower Farm** (p.173) is the **Australian Dairy Centre**, with historical displays and cheese sales.

The turn-off to **Churchill Is** is here also. An historic homestead and garden are at the centre of this lovely conservation property. Drivers are met by highland cattle and clydesdales wandering freely outside the homestead fence. A walk takes visitors around the island, past the site of a vegetable garden sown by explorers in 1801 and to various observation points. Open daily, 10am–5pm, King tides excepted. Ph: (03) 5956 7214

### Rhyll *Map 26 D1*

At the northern edge of the island, Rhyll is a quiet boating and fishing location. You can hire boats and fishing gear, and there is an all-tide boat ramp. Several marked walks leave from Rhyll Inlet, a swampy area, including a 45min walk which takes in Conservation Hill — good for viewing the abundant bird life.

### San Remo *Map 26 D2*

San Remo, joined to the island by San Remo Bridge, is a commercial fishing port. Fish and chips from the **San Remo**

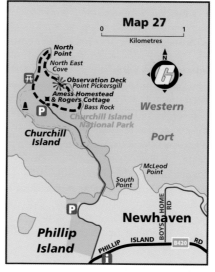

**Fishing Co-op** are a must. The pelicans are fed daily in summer at 11.30am beside the jetty. Swimming and boating from San Remo are popular. A new addition to San Remo is the **Vietnam Museum**, open daily, 9.30am–4pm. Ph: (03) 5678 5728

The **George Bass Coastal Walk** from Kilcunda to Punchbowl is a spectacular walk along Bass Strait. It is accessed from the Phillip Is Tourist Rd, 3km from San Remo.

### *Sth Gippsland*
### Fish Ck *Map 25 B5*

Fish Ck is a quaint little town, with a bookshop, antiques, bric-a-brac, fuel and a

**Wildlife research — you can help**
If you spot a koala during your stay in Sth Gippsland, the Conservation Society wants to know about it. Record the time, place and activities of the koala, its size and any markings, and then phone to record your sighting. Ph: (03) 5674 3072

**A giant awakes**

Don't miss the Foster Nth Lookout on the Sth Gippsland Hwy. On a clear day, it affords the best possible view of Wilsons Promontory. Like a sleepy giant, it appears to rise out of the primordial swamps and into the glistening seas.

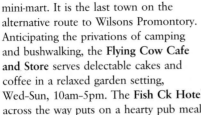

mini-mart. It is the last town on the alternative route to Wilsons Promontory. Anticipating the privations of camping and bushwalking, the **Flying Cow Cafe and Store** serves delectable cakes and coffee in a relaxed garden setting, Wed–Sun, 10am–5pm. The **Fish Ck Hotel** across the way puts on a hearty pub meal.

Several artisans' studios are located close by. **Battery Creek Glassworks**, 5km out of Fish Ck on the road to Yanakie, is the studio of Allan Crynes, whose work is represented in various collections, including the National Gallery of Victoria. Open most days, 10am–4pm. Ph: (03) 5683 2488. The **Stefani Hilltop Gallery**, a fine art gallery, specialises in traditional land and seascapes. It occupies 4 rooms in a historic homestead on a working dairy farm, open Wed–Sun, 10.30am–5pm. Ph: (03) 5683 2377

### Foster *Map 25 B5*

The last town before Wilsons Promontory on the Sth Gippsland Hwy, Foster is prosperous and friendly. A goldmining town from the 1870s–1930s, it now services the local dairy industry and is a centre for eco-tourism along the 'Prom Coast'. Consult the Foster Visitor Info Centre for boating, fishing, bushwalking and diving tours and charters on and around Wilsons Promontory, or the Sth Gippsland Visitor Info Centre, Freecall: 1800 630 704

A small stream runs beside Foster's main street through **Pearl Park**, where

picnic tables and toilets are set among shady tree ferns. Across the road, the **Stockyard Gallery** shows high quality visiting exhibitions and is well worth a visit. Open Thurs–Sat, 10am–4pm, Sun, 1pm–4pm, and school and public holidays, 10am–4pm. Adjacent to the gallery, the **Foster Historical Museum**, open Sun, 11am–4pm tells the story of Foster's gold and pioneering past.

Many scenic drives can be taken from Foster into the eastern Strzeleckis. The round trip to **Turtons Ck Falls** via Ameys Track takes about 1hr, passing through superb tree fern gullies. Other scenic drives branch off from Toora, 14km east of Foster. At **Grassy Spur** picnic area, close to Ameys Track, a swimming hole fed by an icy creek is a terrific spot to take a summer's dip. Maps are available from the visitor info centre.

At the **Franklin River Reserve** on the Sth Gippsland Hwy the local Land Care group has established an Information and Educational Rotunda. It outlines an extensive network of koala corridors, including the reserve's own koala walk. There are BBQs, toilets and picnic facilities. Further west again, **Agnes Falls** is spectacular. A scenic drive taking in township of Toora, Agnes Falls and Port Welshpool is signposted on the Hwy.

Beaches south of Foster on **Waratah Bay** and **Shallow Inlet** — at Sandy Pt, Waratah Bay township and Walkerville — offer magnificent views of the promontory and Bass Strait. They are quite isolated, and have few facilities. The conditions on Shallow Inlet are ideal for sailboarding. Sandy Pt and Waratah Bay township have glorious surf beaches, while Walkerville is of considerable historical interest, being the site of lime kilns dating from the 1840s. Boats can be launched from the beach here, where there are picnic tables, toilets and BBQs.

### French Is *Map 25 A4*

Until quite recently, French Is, if known at all, was known for its prison farm. Access was restricted and the island played 'second cousin' to the glamorous Phillip Is, with its surf beaches and tourist attractions. But it is precisely this

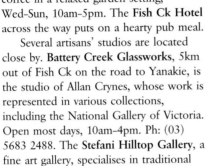

*Fish Creek.*

*Post office, Foster.*

diminutive status that attracts those who now visit it. It is ideal terrain for family bike riding. It also introduces visitors to the pleasures of the wetlands and mud flats. The French Is NP lies to the north of the island (p.170). **French Is Transport** will pick visitors up at Tankerton Jetty and drop them off at camping, bushwalking, sketching, photography, cycling and bird watching locations as arranged. Booking is essential. Ph: (03) 5980 1241. There are few facilities – only 1 general store, and visitors are advised to take their own drinking water.

French **Eco-Tours** offer tours of the island. Ph: (03) 5980 1210. Their tours include **McLeod Prison Farm**, with overnight accommodation on site. Ph: (03) 5678 0155

*Walkerville.*

### Inverloch *Map 25 A5*

A small settlement was established at Inverloch in the 1840s as a port for transporting timber from the north and supplying the early pioneers. Inverloch is named after Loch Inver in Scotland; Andersons inlet after Inverloch's European 'discoverer', Samuel Anderson.

The shallow waters of the inlet are ideal for children's swimming, windsurfing and boating, while the ocean beach has good surf and fine coastal views. Inverloch is both wild and pastoral, depending on where you stand. The township is large and quite suburban, its numbers swelling dramatically during the summer holiday period.

There is an extensive public camping area along the inlet shoreline to the east of the township. The foreshore area close to the mouth of the inlet has picnic facilities and toilets. Further to the west, car parks give access to the surf.

Beach walks of varying length are possible. It takes approx. 5hr to walk to Cape Paterson one way. The view along the coast to Cape Woolamai is spectacular. To see the estuarine side of Inverloch, visitors can take the 1hr **Screw Ck Nature Walk**, which commences at the Eastern Area Camping Ground. It passes through dunes and saltmarsh, offering an intimate view of a wetlands area. Keep an eye out

for the royal spoonbill. A short drive to **Maher's Landing**, also east of the township, has good bird watching and fine views across Andersons Inlet.

Inverloch's **Bunurong Environment Centre** is a must. Run by the Sth Gippsland Conservation Society, it carries extensive information on Sth Gippsland's natural history, including Inverloch's famous 'Dinosaur Dreaming' dig site. It sells nature posters, games and books, houses a fascinating shell collection, and coordinates holiday programs, including 'possum prowls', 'rockpool rambles' and guided walks for adults. It is open Thurs–Sun and daily during school and public holidays, 10am–4pm. Ph: (03) 5674 3738

*Windsurfing, Inverloch.*

### Koonwarra *Map 25 B4*

Don't miss the **Koonwarra General Store**, open 7 days, 7.30am–5.30pm. This store, post office and gourmet café sells delicious fare made from locally grown produce and is at the centre of the area's thriving local culture, including the Koonwarra Country Festival held in Nov (p.000). Koonwarra has a pottery and is home to the **Koonwarra Environment Education Centre**, which runs school holiday camps for children and organises a variety of land care, exotic animal and other farm tours. Ph (03) 566 42361

**Day trips**
*Beach and Bush Day Trips,* available at the Bunurong Environment Centre for $6, is an invaluable guide to walks and scenic drives from the western to the eastern Strzeleckis, and along the coast from Kilcunda to Wilsons Promontory.

# Dinosaur Dreaming

The Dinosaur Dreaming dig, located in the Bunurong Marine Park, is run by the Monash University Science Centre. Paleontologists commenced their work here in 1988, and have recovered the fossilised teeth and bones of numerous dinosaur species. The site is a 4m cross-section of the original flood plain that was home to these dinosaurs of the Cretaceous period, some 115 million years ago. No full skeleton has yet been discovered, but many of the Inverloch fossils are helping to reformulate scientific thinking on the evolution and extinction of the dinosaurs.

For example, a pair of lower jaws belonging to a very large crocodile-like amphibian called a *labyrinthodont* show how an animal group thought to have disappeared with the Jurassic period survived for tens of millions of years in Inverloch's ancient rivers. Inverloch's most famous find has been the 'Inverloch mammal', or *Austribosphenos nyktos*. This rat-like creature has led scientists to question theories about the origins of placental mammals. A big achievement for such a little creature!

The **Lyrebird Hill Winery and Guesthouse** on Inverloch Rd is open for cellar door sales on weekends and public holidays, 10am–5pm, while **Terrima Deer Farm** on Caithness Rd sells venison. Ph: (03) 5664 2368

The **South Gippsland Rail Trail**, along the old Sth Gippsland railway line, is open from Leongatha to Koonwarra, with plans to open all the way to Yarram. The walk from Leongatha to Koonwarra takes 2hrs and ends at the Koonwarra Store.

## Korumburra *Map 25 B4*

Korumburra is a prosperous town set in the western Strzelecki Ranges servicing the local dairy industry. Count Strzelecki passed this way in 1841 towards the end of his harrowing journey. A cairn just outside the town on the road to Warragul marks the site. Originally opened up for cattle grazing, Korumburra was built around the discovery of black coal in the 1870s. The town's last mine closed in 1958.

Sth Gippsland's premier tourist attraction, the **Coal Ck Historical Village**, celebrates its mining history. Located in a steep gully that was once a busy mining site, the village is a living recreation of a miner's town. Blacksmithing, spinning, bootmaking, printing, and wood joining are all on display. A recreated 1880s dairy farm has recently been added. The very pleasant setting beside Coal Ck and several small lakes can be explored on foot or aboard the bush tramway. BBQ and picnic facilities are available. Open daily, 10am–4.30pm. Ph: (03) 5655 1811

Korumburra is also the point of departure for the recently reopened **Sth Gippsland Railway**. For a very reasonable fare, travellers can board the old steam

*Lyrebird Hill winery.*

train to Leongatha. Leaving from Korumburra's impressive Edwardian station, both day and evening runs during summer carry passengers through up to 80km of glorious Strzelecki country. Ph: (03) 5658 1111

Trips into the Strzeleckis north of Korumburra are very rewarding. The road to **Arawata**, returning to Leongatha is especially beautiful. The **Quilters' Barn** at Arawata is a must for quilters and crafts people of any kind. Located on a remote farm, deep in an emerald-green valley, it offers a unique experience for everyone. Open Tues-Sat, 10am-4pm, Ph: (03) 5659 8271

Also in this vicinity is the **Gooseneck Pottery** at Kardella, which operates one of the largest wood-fired kilns in Australia. Open weekends and most weekdays, 11am-4pm. Ph: (03) 5655 2405. Kardella is also a bush tucker growing area. Warrigal greens, wattle seed and indigenous mints and peppers are some of the local produce. Farm visits can be arranged through the Koonwarra Environment Education Centre (p.163).

The environs of Korumburra also offer a number of gourmet delights. The road trip to the award-winning **Top Paddock Cheeses** in Fitzgeralds Rd, Bena,

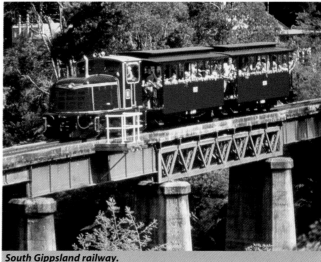

*South Gippsland railway.*

is another scenic route. It is open for door sales Mon-Fri, 10am-4pm and Sun, noon-4pm. Ph: (03) 5657 2291 **Paradise Enough Winery** lies half-way between Korumburra and Inverloch. Take the road to Kongwak, another delightful hamlet. Open weekends and holidays, 12am-5pm. Ph: (03) 5657 4241

### Leongatha *Map 25 B4*

Like Korumburra, Leongatha is a prosperous dairy town. The Leongatha

**The cream trail**
Cows — mainly jerseys and friesians — are everywhere, dotting the hills, on their way to the milking sheds. Slow down at roadside 'Cattle Crossing' signs, and trace the cow tracks that ridge the hillsides.

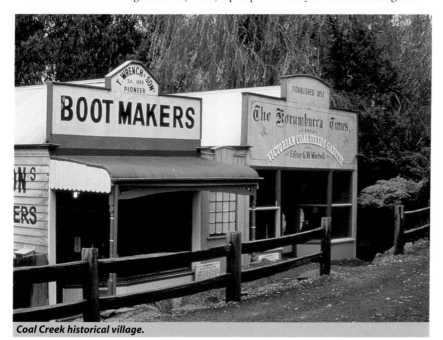

*Coal Creek historical village.*

**Take home a pack or two**

Sample packs from the Grand Ridge Brewery include the bitter ale 'Gippsland Gold', with lyrebird insignia — an ideal gift or memento, with an authentic regional flavour.

Butter and Cheese factory is testament to the highly productive land that feeds it. Watch out for all those milk tankers!

The township has a pleasant shopping area, and several fine old public buildings. **Leongatha Gallery** is housed in an imposing 19th century building. Although small, the gallery sells a range of quality country crafts. Open Mon–Fri, 10am–5pm. Almost next door, the Mechanics Institute is home to the **Historical Society Museum**, open Thurs–Fri, noon–4pm, or by appt. Ph: (03) 5662 3492

Agri-tourism and value-added home paddock food production is at the heart of Leongatha's regional economic development plan. Make sure you get a copy of *Taste, Trek and Travel: A Food Lover's Guide to South Gippsland*, available from info centres and the Sth Gippsland Shire offices in Leongatha. As well as listing the region's food producers and farm gate sales, it explains the Home Paddock Coop Project's hope 'to flush out those legendary country cooks whose wonderful recipes [usually] go no further than the family and the local fete'.

Leongatha makes up the 'triangle' between Korumburra and Mirboo North. Almost any road north will provide scenic views and many places of interest. **Lancey Lookout** and the road to **Marden** are recommended, as is a visit to the small town of **Stony Ck**. The **Firelight Museum** on Leongatha Nth Rd exhibits antique lamps dating back to the 1880s and a large collection of antique firearms. Devonshire teas are served and there are BBQ and picnic facilities. Open weekends and school holidays, 10am–5pm.

### Loch *Map 25 B4*
Loch lies in the undulating Bass Valley hills, the 1st town after the Sth Gippsland Hwy branches away from the coast. Its antique shops and tearooms make it a pleasant place to break the drive. The **Weemala Alpaca Gardens**, 1km west of Loch, sells fine alpaca products, by appt. Ph: (03) 5659 4365. **Mudlark Pottery Gallery** on Poowong Rd exhibits fine ceramics, also appt only. Ph: (03) 5659 2292

**Henry's Creek Sanctuary** is Loch's special secret. Gordon and Joan Henry have constructed a 4km fox- and cat-proof fence around 40.5ha of virgin messmate forest. The University of Melbourne is working here to catalogue the many bird species — some very rare — of this remnant of the Bass Hills habitat. The Henrys offer B&B, including an overnight sleep-out in the bird observatory. By appt only. Ph: (03) 5659 0139

### Mirboo Nth *Map 25 C4*
Mirboo Nth is one of the northern gateways into Sth Gippsland. Sitting on 'top' of the Strzelecki Ranges, it is an ideal place from which to venture into these wonderful hills, east and west along the **Grand Ridge Rd**. For a short drive with panoramic views, drive to **Dickies Hill Reserve** and return along the Grand Ridge Rd.

The town and its immediate locality offer many enjoyable activities. BBQs and picnic facilities are available at both **Baromi Pk** and the baths in **Baths Rd Reserve**. The swimming pool is located near an original spring in a natural bush setting. The reserve has 2km of easy walking tracks through fern gullies and bushland.

*Good'Evans Emu farm.*

**Port Albert.**

The **Grand Ridge Brewery** is an ideal place to break a trip, whether walking or driving. Particularly enjoyable on a hot day, its several boutique beers can be enjoyed over a meal, or by themselves. The proprietors are happy to inform visitors on the art of brewing — it's also possible to see beer production in process.

Approximately 3km north of Mirboo Nth, the **Lyrebird Forest Walk** wends its way through the Strzeleckis. Locals recommend a torch-lit walk at night along the 5km of marked track for spotting the reserve's shy inhabitants. **Hallston Bush** and **Mt Worth SP** (p.170) are also within easy driving distance from Mirboo Nth. The township is located on the **Mirboo Nth to Boolarra Rail Trail**. Commencing at the Grand Ridge Brewery, it follows the Little Morwell River for 13km, ending at the historic 'Old Pub' café bar in Boolarra. Dogs are allowed on this walk.

At **Good'Evans Emu Farm** 1.5km west along the Grand Ridge Rd, visitors can see emu chicks, and be convinced of the healing power of emu oil. Once used by Aborigines, this natural source of vitamins E and A is available in various cosmetic and therapeutic forms. Ph: (03) 5668 1656

## Port Albert *Map 25 C5*

Port Albert is a charming fishing village situated on Corner Inlet. It looks out over a vast marine and wetlands area and the northern peaks of Wilsons Promontory. Port Albert was settled soon after the shipwreck of the *Clonmel* in 1841, survivors returning to Sydney with stories of its commercial potential. It was to become a gateway to Gippsland, a major port trading in timber and cattle, as well as shipping gold from Walhalla and Omeo later in the century.

A dozen or more quaint Georgian-style buildings from the 1850s–70s are listed by the National Trust. Each bears a plaque explaining its original use. Exhibits at the **Port Albert Maritime Museum** confirm Port Albert as one of Victoria's most important 19th century seaports. It houses the canon of the *Clonmel*, one of its lifeboats and many seafaring instruments and oddities. Open on weekends, school and public holidays, 10.30am–4.30pm or by appt. Ph: (03) 5183 2206. The **Warren Curry Gallery** opposite occupies a beautifully restored colonial building, and exhibits original oil paintings.

On a calm day take a stroll around the township, propping on one of the historic timber jetties and eat fish and

**Myth or excuse?**
The story of 'lost white woman', supposedly shipwrecked and held captive by the Kurnai near Port Albert, appears in many tourist brochures. Historians now see the tale as a possible excuse for the pursuit of local Aborigines.

chips from the fishermen's coop, looking out to Wilsons Promontory. For the more energetic, there is a 4hr walk along **Seabank Walk** from Stockyard Point to the old port area.

### Tarwin Lower *Map 25 B5*

The Tarwin River meanders through the lush lowlands of the Tarwin estuary, beef cattle grazing in this picturesque setting as you look west towards Andersons Inlet. Fishing platforms dot the river. One is nicely located on the main road directly opposite Tarwin Lower's colonial, be-palmed pub, the **Riverview Hotel**.

    **Venus Bay**, 1km away, is frequented for its surfing and fishing. Extending from Pt Smythe in the west to Cape Liptrap in the east, it is a remote bay, with few facilities in the winter months. It is patrolled during summer.

### Tooradin *Map 25 A4*

A small fishing village, the tide races in past Tooradin's wooden jetties and under the Sth Gippsland Hwy bridge to a small backwater. Tooradin sits among mangroves in the upper reaches of Westernport Bay, and is a favourite spot for pelicans. There are picnic tables, a walking bridge and an historic fisherman's cottage, open on weekends in summer school and public holidays, 9am-6pm; winter weekends, 11am-5pm. Closed August. When the tide is in, many people fish here. When it's out, there's plenty of mud.

    Interesting sites to be found along the Hwy include **Harewood House**, a 19th

century homestead, open to the public Sun, 10am-5pm; the **Harewood Airfield**, which offers joy rides over Westernport Bay, sells fresh crayfish flown in from Tasmania. (Look for the refrigerated van!)

    The **Koo-Wee-Rup Swamp Observation Tower** on the Hwy is well worth a climb, providing fine views over the Westernport sunkland out to the bay. Noticeboards tell the story of the draining of the swamps in the late 19th century.

    Further along the Hwy, the historic **Warrook Cattle Farm**, established in the 1880s, is a popular tourist farm. Farm demonstrations include shearing and hand milking. Kangaroo feeding and hayrides are a favourite with overseas visitors. Ph: 613 5997 1321

    Part of the Shire of Cardinia, this western part of the region is linked north and east to a number of small towns in and out of the Gippsland region by the tourist route **Bunyip Byways**. It is named after a creature of the swamplands, said to have been a spirit in local Aboriginal lore. The route is occasionally marked on the Hwy as it crosses to various places off the beaten track.

### Wonthaggi *Map 25 A5*

Wonthaggi's 1st permanent buildings were established in 1910, with the opening of its famous coalmine. It is a friendly town servicing a healthy dairy industry. This is a good centre for shopping before taking off to the various coastal towns nearby. The **Taberner Hotel**, adorned with the jawbones of a whale washed up on a local beach in 1923, serves excellent seafood.

    **Harmers Haven**, which marks one end of the Bunurong Marine Park (p.169), is reached via a turn off not far from the centre of the township. Similarly, the road to **Cape Patterson** – a family holiday destination within the Marine Park – and the scenic coastal route to Inverloch, are signposted in Wonthaggi. Surfing, rockpooling, fishing and beach walks are all close at hand.

    Wonthaggi's favourite tourist attraction is the **State Coal Mine**. Run in part as a community project, largely by the sons and daughters of old miners, it

*Warrook Cattle Farm, Tooradin.*

*Eilean Donan Garden.*

is a delight and an education to visit. Well-informed guides take visitors deep into the earth along sections of what were once 100s of km of working mine. Children love the ride in the coal train, and can meet the last surviving pit pony in the fields above. Underground tours are run daily from 10am–3.30pm. Ph: (03) 5672 3053

### Yarram *Map 25 C5*

Yarram is a lovely old town – the last before the Tarra Bulga NP, if coming from the south. Once a swamp the Aborigines knew as Yarram Yarram – meaning plenty of water – it was a prosperous market town in the heyday of the Sth Gippsland ports. Get your provisions here if you are heading into the eastern Strzelecki Ranges.

Visit the enchanting **Tarra Valley** to the NW. This is a beautiful drive beside the Tarra River, past the **Eilean Donan Garden** (p.173), and on towards the Tarra Bulga NP (p.170). Trail rides and gypsy wagon holidays are favourite ways to travel through the eastern Strzeleckis. **Fernholme Caravan Park** is located deep in the forest on the Tarra Valley Rd. It offers idyllic camping and log cabin accommodation at very inexpensive rates. Ph: (03) 5186 1283

Many other scenic drives can be made from Yarram, for example, to **Hiawatha** and the picnic ground at the **Minnie Ha Ha Falls.**

## National Parks and Reserves

### Baldhills Wetland Reserve *Map 25 B5*

This small reserve associated with the Tarwin Estuary is one of the last remnants of the Sth Gippsland wetlands. Over 100 bird species, and native mammals, reptiles and frogs, live in this swampy haven. There is a walking track, incorporating a boardwalk, and a bird hide. A list of the birds observable at Bald Hills is available from Bunurong Environment Centre in Inverloch.

### Baw Baw NP *Map 25 C5*

Incorporating a large area of the Baw Baw Plateau in the southern alps, this NP is home to the Baw Baw village and ski resort. The village is connected along a marked trail to Mt St Gwinear, which is linked by road to Erica. Tobogganning at the Mt St Gwinear carpark is a favourite with children.

From Noojee, a long drive over unsealed roads to the Baw Baw village passes through beautiful fern gullies. The park incorporates alpine areas with grassy snow plains and gnarled snow gums. Wildflowers are a feature of the snow plains in spring and summer.

Baw Baw village is largely deserted in spring and summer.

### Bunurong Marine Pk *Map 25*

This unique park, devoted to the marine environment, is famed for its underwater

*Country perennials.*

*Skiing, Baw Baw NP.*

and a wondrous assembly of rare birds, including waders, plentiful pelican and the less-seen sea eagle. The island's koalas abound as do its long-nosed potoroos.

Access to this very sparsely populated island – ideal for cycling and walking – is by ferry. Camping is permitted but there are few facilities.

### Morwell NP *Map 29*

This small NP is a delight, especially so close to the industrial heartland of the Latrobe Valley. It features remnant vegetation of the Gt Southern Forest. The park is best known for its 40 species of native orchid. A self-guided tour starting at the Kerry Rd picnic area takes about 1hr. There are picnic facilities here and tables at Lyndons Clearing. No camping is permitted.

### Mt Worth SP *Map 29*

Timber cutting and grazing razed the mountain ash and fern gullies which once flourished in this area of the western Strzelecki Ranges. Today, a program of indigenous reforestation is underway, and birds and animals are returning. Along Moonlight Ck original stands of indigenous vegetation give some insight into the landscape prior to European contact. Walkers should keep an eye out for platypus and water rats, as well as swamp wallabies. Several walks are marked. Toilets, picnic and BBQ facilities are available.

### Tarra-bulga NP *Map 25 C4*

Situated in the eastern Strzelecki Ranges, Tarra Bulga NP can be reached via Traralgon, from the coast via Yarram, or as the last port of call along the Grand Ridge Rd. This remnant of the Gt Southern Forest is a precious reminder of the glorious cool temperate rainforest that once stretched across the region. Its spectacular tree ferns, mountain ash and ancient myrtle beeches are best seen by walking along the few easy walking tracks – clearly marked at the 2 picnic areas – and by car, along the narrow, winding road beside the Tarra River.

The Bulga picnic ground gives walking access to Corrigan's suspension

landscapes. Stretching from Harmers Haven in the west to near Inverloch in the east, it extends from the high water mark 1km out to sea. Take the children rockpooling at Inverloch or Cape Paterson, or snorkel in the rockpools and learn about the myriad life-forms of the intertidal rockshelf. Angling, diving, beachcombing along secluded beaches, swimming and boating are all possible within the park.

### Corner Inlet Marine Coastal Pk *Map 28 B2*

What is commonly referred to as the Corner Inlet Pk actually comprises two parks. To the east of Corner Inlet NP lies the Nooramunga Marine and Coastal Pk, which takes in Snake Is and the coast from Port Welshpool to Port Albert. The parks are divided by a commercial sea channel.

Listed as wetlands of international significance under the Ramsar Convention, they are well known for excellent fishing, boating and birdwatching. They are home to over 10 000 black swans and the many migratory birds which make their way south in the northern winter. The park also protects wild populations of hog deer, an introduced species, which is now threatened with extinction in Asia.

### French Is NP *Map 25 A4*

Situated at the northern end of French Island, the NP protects heathlands and open woodlands, sea grass meadows and the white mangroves that ring the island. The park boasts 580 indigenous plant species, including more than 100 orchids,

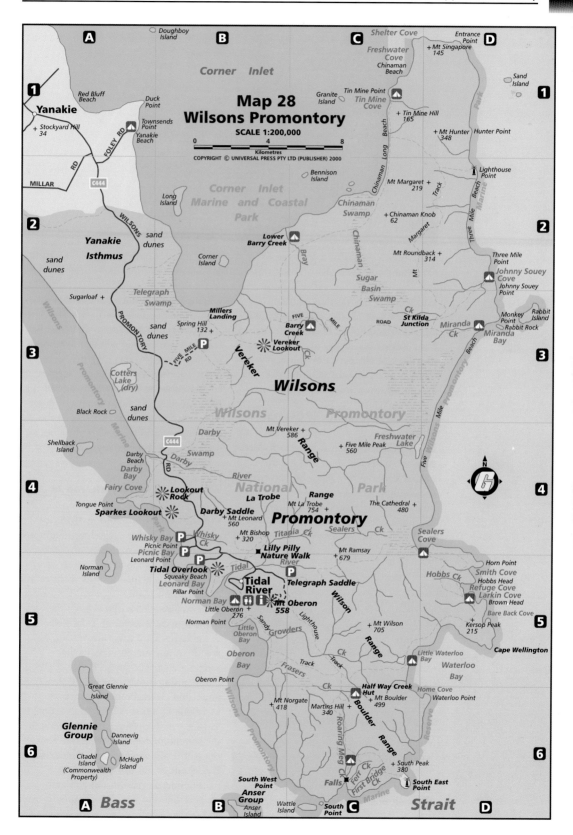

Map 28
Wilsons Promontory
SCALE 1:200,000

0   4   8
Kilometres
COPYRIGHT © UNIVERSAL PRESS PTY LTD (PUBLISHER) 2000

*Tarra Bulga NP.*

bridge and is the location of the Rainforest Info Centre. Open only on weekends and during holidays, this centre has a wonderful display of photographs that dramatically depict the pioneer struggle to subdue the rainforest, as well as information about walking tracks.

### Venus Bay-Waratah Bay Coastal Pk *Map 25 B5*

This park takes in the Pt Smythe Reserve at its western-most end. The point, named after the brothers who surveyed the coastline in the early 1840s, is a large sand spit. Over 10 000 years it has helped to form Andersons Inlet. The reserve is reached by road via Tarwin Lower. Easy

walking tracks through banksia and myrtle lead to the point.

The magnificent sweep of Venus Bay ends at Cape Liptrap where a lighthouse stands sentinel over an area rich in the history of shipwrecks. The beach from Cape Liptrap to Walkerville is one of the most scenic walks along the south coast, with Wilsons Promontory rising in the east, and steep cliffs, boulder beaches and, close to Waratah Bay, fern gullies and wet heathlands.

### Wilsons Promontory NP *Map 28*

Wilsons Promontory NP is one of Victoria's oldest, reserved in 1898. It is also one of Victoria's best loved and most spectacular. The remoteness of its coves and beaches, its mountain ranges, creeks and rivers has helped to preserve it as a natural wonderland.

Thousands of campers pitch their tents or occupy cabins at Tidal River during school holidays. But visitors can readily escape the business of the camping area. The broad sweep of Norman Bay is only ever lightly populated. Several other beaches are accessible by car or a short walk from Tidal River. The short but steep walk to the summit of Mt Oberon, which looks out to the glittering granite islands of Bass Strait, is not to be missed.

On longer walks, south and east, walkers will find deserted pristine forests and perfect beaches. Some are suitable for

*Boulders, tidal river, Wilsons Promontory.*

family treks. Sealers Cove is a memorable favourite. The walk to the lighthouse is another that will leave indelible images. Overnight accommodation at the lighthouse can be booked at Tidal River. During holidays, Parks Victoria rangers run educational programs, and an outdoor cinema operates.

## Gardens
### Central Gippsland
The **Bon Accord Garden** in Dawson St, Sale is one of Sale's oldest heritage properties, now run as a luxury B&B. This small formal garden is open daily during daylight hours. A garden plan with botanical names is available at the main house. Ph: (03) 5144 5555

The **Morwell Centenary Rose Garden**, displays more than 2000 roses in 80 beds. This 2ha public garden, at its best in Nov, is located at the western end of Morwell in Commercial Rd.

### Mountain gardens
The **Clover Patch Garden** on Brandy Ck Rd in Rokeby is an informal cottage garden in a picturesque setting beside the Tarago River. Open by appt. Ph: (03) 5626 8510

Wenseley Farm on Laings Rd Nayook, near Neerim Sth, is home to **Country Farm Perennials Garden and Nursery**. This farmhouse garden specialises in perfumed roses and rare bulbs. The nursery issues an extensive catalogue, holds a spring perennial sale in Nov, and runs various activities for gardeners. Open daily, Mon-Fri, 9am-4pm, Sat-Sun, 10am-5pm. Ph: (03) 5628 4202

Close by on the Gourmet Deli Trail (p.176), the **Jindivick Gardens and Tearooms** look out over the steep valleys towards Tarago. Once a dairy farm, the garden covers 4ha and is elaborately landscaped on several tiers, including a croquet lawn. Open Sat-Sun and public holidays, 10am-4pm, or by appt. Ph: (03) 5628 5319

The **Rawson Mountain Farm Nursery** has landscaped gardens around several large dams, lovely dry stone walls and panoramic views of the Gt Dividing Range. A magnificent arbour of over

**Bon Accord, Sale.**

1000 roses is a delight to see in Nov and Dec. Open Thurs-Mon and public hols, 10am-5pm. Ph: (03) 5165 3601

### Phillip Is
The **Big Flower Farm**, a member of the Maxiflora group of companies, is a high-tech flower factory specialising in gerbera. Sixty thousand flowers, in all their vibrant colour, are grown in a 1ha greenhouse. Tours of the greehouse leave every 30min, daily 10am-5pm. Ph: (03) 5956 6777

### Sth Gippsland
**Brown's Native Wildflower Garden** at 340 One Chain Rd Kardella, boasts the one of the largest collection of grevilleas in Australia. Ph: (03) 5659 8219

The **Eilean Donan Garden**, situated in the Tarra Valley, is associated with a heritage homestead available for holiday rental. Open by appt. An enchanting garden, it features century-old trees, including magnificent magnolias, maples and liquid ambers. Ph: (03) 5182 6165

At the **Rewah Native Plant Farm**, the Rathgens have replanted their 4th generation farm with over 40 000 local trees and restocked the river with native fish. Their nursery and agro-forestry demonstration areas can be visited by appt. Ph: (03) 5686 2315

## Recreational activities
### 4WD
Several 4WD clubs operate in the region, including the Latrobe Valley 4WD Club at

*Rafting.*

Morwell, Ph: (03) 5174 9997; Gippsland 4WD Club in Warragul, Ph: (03) 5625 2326. For 4WD tours, contact **Mountain Top Experience**. Ph: (03) 5134 6876

### Camping and bushwalking

Camping and bushwalking are a major feature of this region. The range of NPs and SFs in this region is truly remarkable (p.169) and these provide some of the best walks and most beautiful camping locations — in the alps, beside the coast, on the promontory. The Sth Gippsland rail trails are another popular option for walking.

Boat-based camping is a special treat on Wilsons Promontory. Check with the Wilsons Promontory Park Office and Visitor Centre (p.149) for suitable locations, or take a charter from Port Welshpool.

### Canoeing and rafting

The Thomson River downstream from the Thomson Dam offers especially exciting whitewater rafting and canoeing. For other mountain rafting and canoeing locations, check with the Gippsland Country Tourist Info Centre. The many inlets of the south coast offer more relaxed canoeing, from Inverloch and Tarwin Lower, to Sandy Pt and Shallow Inlet.

### Fishing

Boat fishing from Rhyll, Inverloch, Port Welshpool and Port Albert are all likely to be very productive. Fishing in Westernport Bay on charter with the

*Fishing.*

**Phillip Island Fishing Centre** promises bags of shark, snapper and scale fish. Ph: 015 339 177. Surf fishing is a favourite pastime along the south coast at many locations, for example, Cape Paterson and Harmers Haven, Venus Bay and Seaspray.

River fishing on the meandering Tarwin River at Tarwin Lower is a relaxed, meditative experience. For mountain river fishing, ask at the general store at Rawson, Walhalla or Heyfield. The Thompson, Tyers and Aberfeldie Rivers are all recommended. Blue Rock Lake near Moe and Lake Glenmaggie have good stocks of trout and redfin.

### Horseriding

For the eastern Strzeleckis, and rides beside the sea at Sandy Pt, contact **Waitara Trail Rides**. Ph: (03) 5686 259. In the emerald green of the western Strzeleckis, north of Korumburra, **Halston Trail Riders** offer rides and weekend stays. Ph: (03) 5668 5287. **Mountain Saddle Safaris** is renowned for its 1-day trail ride from Erica to Walhalla in the Gt Dividing Range. Bookings essential. Ph: (03) 516 3365

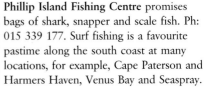

# Fun for the young

- ★ A Maze 'N Things (p.160)
- ★ Bush walks, Wilsons Promontory (p.172)
- ★ Coal Creek Historical Village (p.164)
- ★ Cycling on French Island (p.163)
- ★ Dinosaur Dreaming archeological dig at Inverloch (p.164)
- ★ Horseriding with Mountain Saddle Safaris (p.174)
- ★ Phillip Island's 'front' beaches (p.159)
- ★ Sailing at Inverloch (p.162)
- ★ Tobogganning at Mt St Gwinear (p.175)
- ★ Wonthaggi State Coal Mine (p.168)

## Gippsland Wineries

| NAME | MAP 25  ADDRESS | PHONE | OPEN |
|---|---|---|---|
| The Gurdies Winery | St Helier Rd, The Gurdies | (03) 5997 6208 | 10am–5pm daily |
| Phillip Island Vineyard and Winery | Berrys Beach Rd, Phillip Is | (03) 5956 8465 | Nov–Mar 11am–7pm daily, Apr–Oct 11am–5pm |
| Bass Valley Estate Wines | St Helier Rd, Loch | (03) 5659 6306 | 10am–6pm daily |
| Kongwak Hills Winery | Korumburra-Kongwak Rd, Kongwak | (03) 5657 3267 | 10am–5pm weekends and public hols |
| Paradise Enough Vineyards | Stewarts Rd, Kongwak | (03 5657 4241 | Noon–5pm weekends and hols |
| Djinta Djinta Winery | 10 Stevens Rd, Kardella Sth | (03) 5658 1163 | 10am–6pm weekends and public hols |
| Lyrebird Hill Winery and Guesthouse | Inverloch Rd, Koonwarra | (03) 5664 3204 | 10am–5pm weekends and public hols |
| Tarwin Ridge Wines | Wintles Rd, Leongatha Sth | (03) 5664 3211 | 11am–6pm most weekends and public hols, phone to check. |
| Windy Ridge Winery | Fish Creek Rd, Foster | (03) 5682 2035 | 10am–5pm most holiday weekends, phone to check |
| Jinks Creek Winery | Tonimbuk Rd, Tonimbuk | (03) 5629 8502 | By appt |
| Ada River Vineyard | Main Neerim Rd, Neerim Sth | (03) 5628 1221 | 10am–6pm weekends and public hols |
| Wild Dog Winery | Warragul-Korumburra Rd, Warragul | (03) 5623 1117 | 9am–5pm daily |
| Coalville Vineyard | Moe South Rd, Moe | (03) 5127 4229 | 10am–5pm daily |
| Narkoojee Vineyard | Francis Rd, Glengarry | (03) 5192 4257 | Most days, 9am–5pm, phone first |
| Wa-de-lock Vineyard | Stratford Rd, Maffra | (03) 5147 3244 | Fri–Mon, 10am–5pm |

## Snow skiing

Mt Baw Baw alpine village, located in the Baw Baw NP (p.169) is Melbourne's most accessible ski resort. Downhill skiing is catered for by 8 ski tows on 7 easy, 9 hard and 5 difficult slopes. While experienced skiers frequent Mt Baw Baw, it is also an ideal location for learners and families. Cross-country skiing is also a highlight, with good trails to Mt St Gwinear. For snow reports, Ph: (03) 5265 3481. For less travelled tracks, try cross-country skiing around Mt Tamboritha and Mt Skene near Heyfield, Jun–Sept.

*Wild Dog Winery.*

## Surf and sail

On Phillip Is, Woolamai's famous Bass Strait waves are powered by the Roaring 40s. This is one of Victoria's premier surf beaches. Excellent surfing for experienced surfers is also to be found in more remote locations – Venus Bay and Waratah Bay.

Sandy Pt, south of Foster, is renowned for windsurfing. Sea kayaking is another way to experience the south coast. Mal Cowell, an experienced instructor, takes families and individuals in small groups. Ph: (03) 5966 5110

The **Sth Gippsland Yacht Club** in Inverloch runs training days for adults and youth, as well as races, on specified days in summer. Ph: (03) 5674 1797. **Lake Wellington**, south of Sale, also boasts fine sailing conditions at Marley Pt. Phone the **Lake Wellington Yacht Club** on (03) 5149 8257. At **Lake Glenmaggie**, on the Macalister River near Heyfield, both sailing and waterskiing are popular.

# Suggested tours — Map 29

## Gourmet deli tour

### Distance

190km return from Melbourne CBD

### About the tour

This route takes visitors into lush pastureland heading towards the Baw Baw plateau. Snow-capped mountains are sometimes visible into spring, when this area and its various gourmet destinations really come to life. Cheese and wine, wonderful smoked meats, trout and indigenous cuisine are all represented in this round trip, which leaves the Princes Hwy at Robin Hood and rejoins it at Warragul. The breathtaking scenery of the Tarago Valley is a fabulous backdrop to local food production and other cultural delights like those represented in the Serigraph and Gippsland Fine Art galleries.

### Places of interest

❶ **Jindivick Smokehouse** (p.156)

❷ **Jindivick Gardens and Tearooms** (p.156)

❸ **Serigraph Gallery and Gippsland Fine Art Gallery, Neerim South** (p.156)

❹ **Tarago River Cheese Co.** (p.156)

❺ **Tarago Reservoir roadside lookout** (p.156)

❻ **Ada River Winery** (p.156)

❼ **Country Farm Perennials Nursery** (p.173)

❽ **Alpine Trout Farm** (p.157)

❾ **Toorongo Falls Scenic Reserve** (p.157)

❿ **Clover Patch Garden, Rokeby** (p.173)

⓫ **Flamin' Bull Bush Tucker Restaurant, Warragul** (p.158)

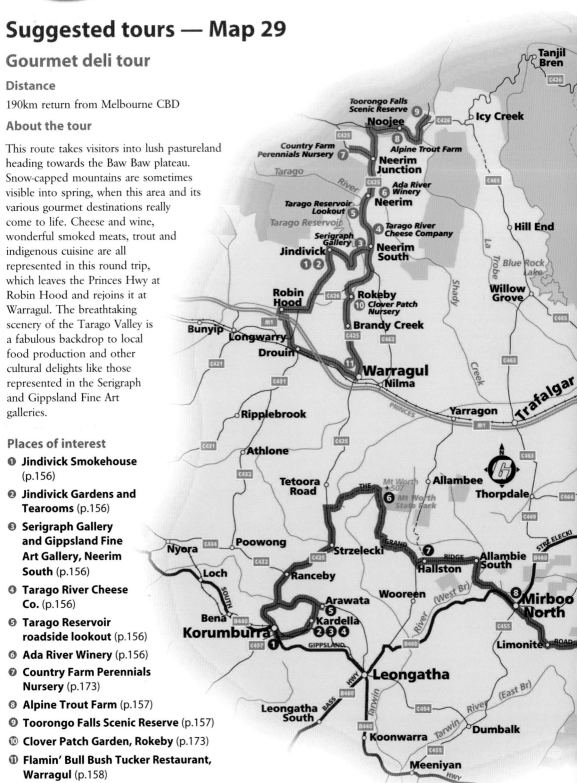

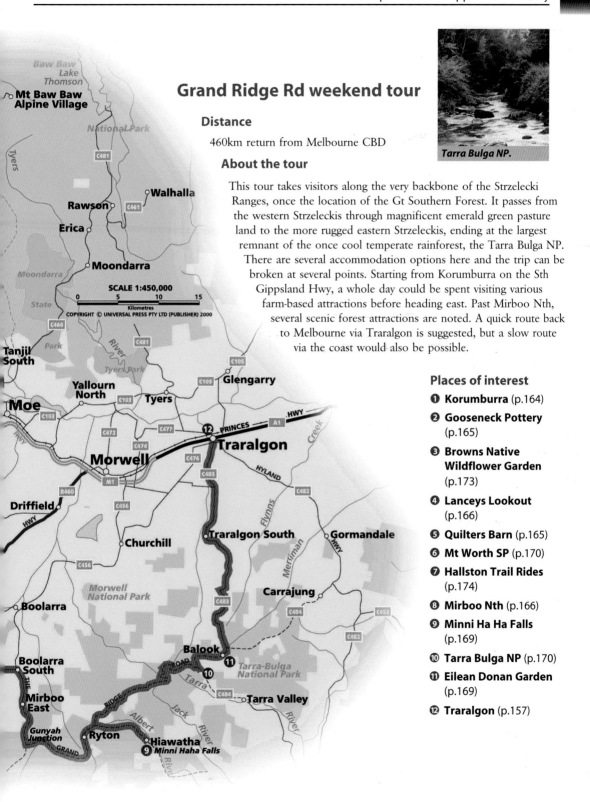

*Tarra Bulga NP.*

# Grand Ridge Rd weekend tour

## Distance

460km return from Melbourne CBD

## About the tour

This tour takes visitors along the very backbone of the Strzelecki Ranges, once the location of the Gt Southern Forest. It passes from the western Strzeleckis through magnificent emerald green pasture land to the more rugged eastern Strzeleckis, ending at the largest remnant of the once cool temperate rainforest, the Tarra Bulga NP. There are several accommodation options here and the trip can be broken at several points. Starting from Korumburra on the Sth Gippsland Hwy, a whole day could be spent visiting various farm-based attractions before heading east. Past Mirboo Nth, several scenic forest attractions are noted. A quick route back to Melbourne via Traralgon is suggested, but a slow route via the coast would also be possible.

## Places of interest

❶ **Korumburra** (p.164)

❷ **Gooseneck Pottery** (p.165)

❸ **Browns Native Wildflower Garden** (p.173)

❹ **Lanceys Lookout** (p.166)

❺ **Quilters Barn** (p.165)

❻ **Mt Worth SP** (p.170)

❼ **Hallston Trail Rides** (p.174)

❽ **Mirboo Nth** (p.166)

❾ **Minni Ha Ha Falls** (p.169)

❿ **Tarra Bulga NP** (p.170)

⓫ **Eilean Donan Garden** (p.169)

⓬ **Traralgon** (p.157)

*Left: **Sovereign Hill**.*
*Right: **Maldon** steam train.*

# The Goldfields

**W**hen gold was unearthed in 1851 near present-day Warrandyte (on the Upper Yarra River) a flood of eager prospectors headed to the goldfields, impatient for the fortunes to be found. Tent cities sprang up overnight and though some faded to an echo when the gold ran out, others, built on firm foundations (and rich veins of gold), grew into stately centres of culture.

From the thriving cities of Ballarat, Bendigo and Stawell, to the old-world charm of Maldon, Maryborough and spirited Castlemaine, the region's present bounty is as rich and rewarding as its gold hauls of the past.

Discovery now includes much more than precious metal (though prospecting could prove your luckiest trip). Art galleries, gardens, wineries and wildlife attract just as many visitors as those intent on recapturing the heady 'gold' era. World-renowned and awarded, Ballarat's Sovereign Hill is the region's historic centrepiece — a living museum where the goldfields have been brought back to life.

Kids too can mimic those times armed with ink and quill in an 1850s classroom, go 10-pin bowling like their ancestors, measure their length against dragons Sun Loong and Old Loong, or make friends with a dingo pup — the action appeals to all ages.

## Tourist information

**Ararat Visitor Info Centre**
Railway Station
High St, Ararat 3377
Ph: (03) 5352 2096

**Pyrenees Visitor Info Centre**
122 High St, Avoca 3467
Ph: (03) 5465 3767
www.pyrenees.vic.gov.au

**Ballarat Visitor Info Centre**
39 Sturt St, Ballarat 3350
Ph: (03) 5320 5741
www.ballarat.com.au

**Bendigo Visitor Info Centre**
51–67 Old Post-Office, Pall Mall, Bendigo 3550
Ph: (03) 5444 4445

**Castlemaine Visitor Info Centre**
Market Building, Mostyn St
Castlemaine 3450
Ph: (03) 5470 6200

**Maldon Visitor Info Centre**
High St, Maldon 3463
Ph: (03) 5475 2569

**Maryborough Central Goldfields Visitor Info Centre**
Railway Station,
Maryborough 3465
Ph: (03) 5460 4511

## Must see, must do

★ **Buda Historic Home and Garden, Castlemaine** (p.191)

★ **Golden Dragon Museum, Bendigo** (p.189)

★ **Maldon Steam Train** (p.194)

★ **Seppelt Great Western Winery** (p.193)

★ **Sovereign Hill, Ballarat** (p.185)

## Radio stations

**Ballarat**
**3BA:** FM 103.1
**POWER:** FM 102.3

**Bendigo**
**3BO:** FM 93.5
**3CV:** AM 1071

**Stawell**
**3WM:** AM 1080

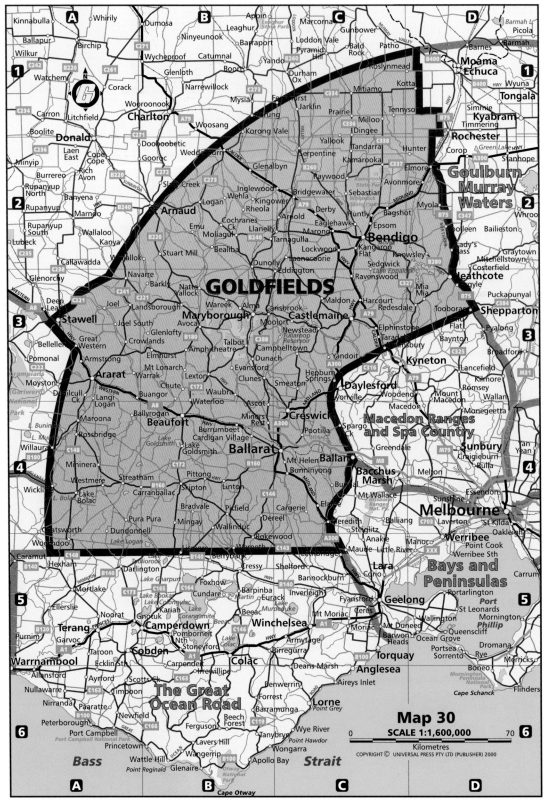

**GOLDFIELDS**

Map 30

SCALE 1:1,600,000

0          70

Kilometres

COPYRIGHT © UNIVERSAL PRESS PTY LTD (PUBLISHER) 2000

*Scenic Goldfields countryside.*

## Natural features

The tranquil countryside of the Goldfields now contrasts with the dramatic erupting volcanoes that once shaped much of the region. Between 7500–57000 years ago lava flows disrupted and buried streams, filled valleys and blanketed plains. This natural event was to have great significance on several goldfields, including Ballarat, where mining companies were formed to blast through the basalt (hardened lava) to access the gold ore.

Volcanic cones persist today as features in the landscape — Mts Buninyong and Warrenheip near Ballarat, Mt Tarrengower near Maldon and Mt Alexander near Castlemaine are all distinctive geological remnants.

To the west of the region, the Gt Dividing Range rises in granite peaks and plateaus — Mt Cole (899m), Mt Buangor (989m) and Mt Langi Ghiran (950m) are embedded in state parks boasting waterfalls, abundant wildlife and inspiring views of the farming district around. The Pyrenees Ranges to the north offer their own scenic interlude.

## History

A long and vibrant history enjoyed by the Aboriginal peoples of the Djadjawurrung, Djab Wurrung and Wadawurung language groups was abruptly disrupted, initially by the intrusion of European pastoralists and then by the goldrushes with their characteristic overturning of the land and social upheaval.

In 1836 Major Thomas Mitchell passed through the NW of the region, detouring from a planned trip along the Murray River after glimpsing country 'too inviting to be left behind us unexplored'. His reports helped encourage many of the pastoralists who took up short-term licenses there under the 'squatting' system. But the period of pastoral dominance was soon to be challenged.

The first reported gold discovery in Victoria was made as early as 1840, but its pursuit wasn't sanctioned or publicised until 1851 when £200 was offered for a successfully proven find. A Melbourne publican announced his discovery on 5 July 1851 (his was at Warrandyte on the Yarra Lucky Strike River). Shortly thereafter, richer discoveries were made in the west. James Esmond's find at Clunes in July 1851 was quickly followed by claims at Buninyong, Ballarat and Mt Alexander. Melbourne was soon deserted — in late 1851, 20 000 of its then 25 000 population up and left for the Mt Alexander diggings. Itinerant diggers moved from one lucky (or unlucky) strike to the next. In this environment of struggle and determination in 1857 the Eureka Stockade erupted as a crisis point in a fight against a mining license (see p.186). It was a brief battle that had widespread influence on the flavour and development of democracy in Victoria.

In the early days gold was found in stream beds and in gravel near the ground's surface but by late 1850s most

**Local lore**
When pastoralist Yuille asked an Aboriginal woman the name of the local swamp she is said to have replied 'wendaaree' — meaning 'go away' … The name stuck: that swamp is now Ballarat's beautiful **Lake Wendouree**.

*Ballarat's begonias.*

of this had been depleted. Gold was now to be found in deep quartz reefs or underground leads that required specialised equipment and capital. Mining companies formed and many miners became salaried employees. Trades and services continued to grow, supporting the surrounding agricultural districts and providing a sound base for the economic stability that continues today.

## Getting there

### By road

Gateways to the Goldfields are via the Western and Calder Hwys from the south, or the Calder and Northern Hwys from the north. Once there, take the well-signposted **Goldfields Tourist Route** circumnavigating the region, which travels through Ballarat, Ararat, Gt Western, Stawell, Avoca, Maldon, Maryborough, Bendigo, Castlemaine and Creswick. Detours to some smaller centres are well-rewarded, both for the scenery en-route and the attractions once you arrive.

### By rail

V/Line, Victoria's public country train/coach service, offers daily departures to west and NW Victoria. Trains travel regularly to Ballarat and a connecting coach takes the route to Stawell several times a day. Trains to Bendigo depart approximately every 2 hrs, making smaller stops along the way. Reservations are recommended. Ph: 132 232 for timetable and ticketing.

## Getting around

### By coach

Day trips to the region's main attractions are run by the major tour operators including: **Australian Pacific Tours**, Ph: (03) 9663 1611; **Gray Line**, Ph: (03) 9663 4455; **AAT Kings**, Ph: (03) 9663 3377; **Great Sights**, Ph: (03) 9639 2211 or for group tours taking less than 21 passengers, try **Melbourne's Best Tours**, Ph: (03) 9372 8111

### By double-decker bus

The London Bus Company runs daily **City Circle Heritage Tours** around Ballarat and Bendigo. The service provides a full tour of the town's major attractions along with informative commentary. Departures start at 9.30am from Sovereign Hill, Ballarat, and 10am from the Central Deborah Gold Mine, Bendigo. Ph: 0500 544 169

## Festivals and events

### Ballarat Begonia Festival

**Ballarat**'s begonias are a stunning centrepiece for the festival generally held Feb/Mar. A colourful parade, floral carpet, fireworks on the lake and local entertainment make this a great summer event. Ph: (03) 5320 7444

**Recommended reading**
For a comprehensive guide to local happenings, pick up a copy of *Victoria's Fantastic Festivals and Fun Events* by J Wadsworth and B Richardson.

*Pyrenees Winery picnic.*

*Ararat's stately town hall.*

### Bendigo Easter Festival

Renowned for the awakening of the dragons during the Easter Monday parade in Apr, the festival attracts 1000s to its events and entertainment which are often based around a theme to capture the best of **Bendigo**. Ph: (03) 5444 4445

### Maldon Easter Fair

An open-air combined church service, street dancing, concerts and a scone bake competition are just some of the events enjoyed at **Maldon** during Easter, in Apr. Ph: (03) 5475 1363

### Stawell Easter Gift Carnival

Worldwide attention is focused on the richest foot-race in the world. It's the annual embodiment of 125 years of athletics, as Olympians and locals mingle at the historic Stawell track each Easter. Ph: (03) 5358 2314

### Castlemaine Biennial State Arts Festival

Over 10 days during late Apr–early May in odd-numbered years this is regarded as one of Victoria's best celebrations of theatre, visual arts, music and dance. The event reinforces **Castlemaine**'s reputation for excellence in the arts. Ph: (03) 5472 3733

### Ballarat Grand National Eistedford of Australia

Acclaimed Australia-wide, the competitions attract thousands to Ballarat during mid Aug–late Oct. Content is delightfully varied and diverse – from elocution, opera and rock to calisthenics, dance, and more. The venue is the beautifully restored **Her Majesty's Theatre** on Lydiard St. Ph: (03) 5332 1054

### Maryborough Golden Wattle Festival

Held from mid Sep–early Oct the highlights of this festival include Australian gumleaf playing and bird call championships, art shows, a twilight parade, possum prowl, fairs and music. Ph: (03) 5460 4511

### Ararat Golden Gateway Festival

This annual 10-day fiesta in Oct, features gold digs, concerts, dancing, sports, markets, parades and a colourful carnival. At venues around Ararat. Ph: (03) 5352 2096

### Maldon Folk Festival

A tradition since 1974 this festival of music provides a spirited weekend in the country during the last weekend in Oct. Ph: (03) 5475 2166

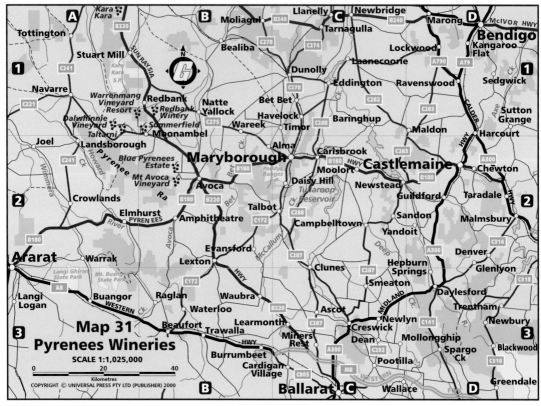

### Castlemaine Biennial Garden Festival

An 'open-house' of the town's prized gardens is held in the 1st week of Nov during odd-numbered years. Guided wildflower walks, gardening tips and workshops, theatre and art exhibits delight both green-thumbs and novices. Ph: (03) 5472 2086

### Pyrenees Vignerons Petanque Festival

For the uninitiated this is the perfect time to learn the game — either watching the tournament or joining the clinic taught by Australian Petanque champions. Art exhibits, cemetery tours, and plenty of wine and food make this a great weekend in late Nov. Ph: (03) 5465 3193

## Main localities and towns
### Ararat Map 30 A3

Ararat was named in 1841 by squatter H S Wills who recalled the Biblical story of Noah in making the choice: 'for like the Ark, we rested there...'. However, the

recorded founding of the city was in 1857 when a group of 700 Chinese discovered one of Victoria's richest alluvial leads while en route to the Ballarat goldfields. The group had been forced to trek overland from Robe, South Australia to avoid a head-tax on Chinese immigrants which was collected at Victorian ports. The **Gum San Cultural Chinese Museum** is located on the Western Hwy toward Adelaide, just past the town's centre. The

**A good drop**
Hunt out **Cathcart Ridge Estate and Montara Winery**, 2 local Ararat vineyards that offer daily tastings at their cellar doors.

*Redbank Winery.*

## Wineries of the Pyrenees

| NAME | MAP 31 ADDRESS | PHONE | OPEN |
|---|---|---|---|
| **Blue Pyrenees Estate** | Vinoca Rd, Avoca | Ph: (03) 5465 3202 | *10am–4.30pm, Mon–Fri, 10am–5pm, Sat–Sun* |
| **Dalwhinnie Vineyard** | Taltarni Rd, Moonambel | Ph: (03) 5467 2388 | *10am–5pm daily* |
| **Kara Kara** | Sunraysia Hwy, 10km south of St Arnaud | Ph: (03) 5496 3294 | *10am–6pm daily* |
| **Mt Avoca Vineyard** | Moates Ln, Avoca | Ph: (03) 5465 3282 | *9am–5pm, Mon–Fri, 10am–5pm, weekends and public hols* |
| **Redbank Winery** | Sunraysia Hwy, Redbank | Ph: (03) 5467 7255 | *9am–5pm, Mon–Sat, 10am–5pm Sun* |
| **Summerfield** | Main Rd, Moonambel | Ph: (03) 5467 2264 | *9am–6pm, Mon–Sat, 10am–6pm Sun* |
| **Taltarni** | Taltarni Rd, off Avoca-Stawell Rd | Ph: (03) 5467 2218 | *10am–5pm daily* |
| **Warrenmang Vineyard Resort** | Mountain Ck Rd, Moonambel | Ph: (03) 5467 2233 | *10am–5pm daily* |

museum highlights the goldminers' journey from China to Ararat, life on the goldfields and the growth of Ararat to its present size as a well-established centre for the surrounding farming districts.

Collections abound in Ararat. **Langi Morgala Museum** at 48 Queen St houses relics of local mining and agricultural history and, more importantly, the Mooney collection of Aboriginal artefacts. Open Sat-Sun, 1pm–4pm. Ph: (03) 5352 4858 or (03) 5352 2541. Capitalising on its agricultural influences the **Ararat Art Gallery** in Vincent St focuses on contemporary work in textiles and fibres. Open Mon-Fri, 11am–4pm, Sun and public holidays, 12–4pm, Sat and school holidays, 12–4pm. Ph: (03) 5352 2836

An institution for the criminally insane for more than 100 years, **J Ward**, on Gridlestone St, has a difficult history to tell. Curiously, graves of the 3 men hanged at the gaol never have a cover of frost, even in the freeze of winter (most likely a natural phenomenon due to the quicklime the bodies were buried with). Open for tours Mon-Sat, 11am, Sun, public and school holidays, 11am–3pm. Night tours by appt. Ph: (03) 5352 3621

### Avoca and the Pyrenees Ranges
**Map 30 B3, 31 B2**
At the junction of the Sunraysia and Pyrenees Hwys, Avoca is a friendly township proudly bordering a wine-rich region of stunning natural beauty. Named after the French Pyrenees, the ranges at times appear hazy blue, a phenomenon known as Raleigh's effect, which is caused by sunlight mingling with eucalyptus oil from the trees. Favourite picnic spots in the Pyrenees include the signposted **Waterfalls** and **Governors Lookout**.

Nestled in the foothills of the ranges are a cluster of vineyards and wineries, each offering notable wines and attractions. **Blue Pyrenees Estate** has an art display, restaurant and petanque (a popular game at many of the wineries); **Warrenmang** is renowned for its award-winning restaurant and accommodation featuring views out over the vines; and in season, *Taltarni* displays welcoming beds of Fidelio red roses.

### Ballarat *Map 32*
Gold fever was the catalyst for this grand and historically vocal township. Here the cry 'Eureka' came to mean much more than the shout of discovery: it became a by-word for Australian civil uprising – a turning point for the nation. Located 110km NW of Melbourne, history is just one of Ballarat's many attractions.

No trip to the goldfields region would be complete without visiting **Sovereign Hill** and the **Gold Museum**. The historical theme park offers the best insight into life of the period. You can pan for gold, peer into miners' huts, sample boiled lollies or tour the underground mine. The Empire

**Three-in-one**
**The Welcome Pass** available from Sovereign Hill, the Gold Museum and Eureka Stockade is a 2-day pass that offers admission to all 3 attractions at a discounted rate.
Ph: (03) 5331 1944

*Sturt Street, Ballarat.*

Bowling Saloon and the Red Hills National School are popular with children of all ages. Staff dressed in period costume stage mini-dramas in the streets, while blacksmiths, potters and other crafts people work their trades; their wares are available for sale as souvenirs. Open daily, 10am–5pm. Ph: (03) 5331 1944. The **Gold Museum**, located across the road, adds detail to the historical account through interactive exhibits and displays. Open daily, 9.30–5.20pm. Ph: (03) 5331 1944

At night, the drama of the Eureka Stockade unfolds as a spectacular sound and light show played across the 25ha of Sovereign Hill. **Blood on the Southern Cross** plays Mon–Sat. Bookings essential. Ph: (03) 5333 5777

Also located on the grounds, the **Sovereign Hill Lodge** complements the

## Eureka Stockade

In 1854 easy gold was scarce and life was a struggle for many of the miners. Enforced collection of a license fee (tax while not having political representation) was an intolerable burden, particularly when claims weren't yielding gold. Arrogant collections by police were resented as were other injustices. In Ballarat, hotel owner James Bentley was found not guilty of murder — by a magistrate who was also his business partner. Miners rioted and burnt down his hotel, initiating a retrial which convicted Bentley; however, the rioting miners were also imprisoned, leading to widespread animosity.

In this climate the Ballarat Reform League was formed and demands were made for abolition of the license fee, the right to vote and the opportunity to buy land. At a mass meeting on 29 Nov, hundreds of miners burned their licenses then began building a stockade at Eureka to fight for these rights.

On 3 Dec, just before dawn, well-armed government troops and police attacked 150 diggers in their make-shift stockade. At least 25 miners and 4 troopers were killed in a battle that lasted less than 20min. Although the miners were defeated, the public rallied behind the cause and the diggers aims were eventually realised. One of the leaders, Peter Lalor, was eventually elected to the Victorian Parliament.

experience offering uniquely situated accommodation, ranging from motel units to bunk style rooms. Ph: (03) 5333 3409

Less than 5min from Sovereign Hill is the **Eureka Stockade Centre**. Appropriately located on Eureka St, at the site of the 1854 rebellion, the centre recounts the battle in multi-media equipped galleries. A tranquil Contemplation Space encourages reflection on the significance of the event. Open daily, 9am–5pm. Ph: (03) 5333 1854. Offering a different voice in the retelling is 'The Women of Eureka'. It is one of the more notable exhibits of the Eureka Museum, housed in the National Trust classified **Montrose**

*Blood on the Southern Cross.*

Map 32
Ballarat
SCALE 1:25,000

0    400    800
Metres
COPYRIGHT © UNIVERSAL PRESS PTY LTD (PUBLISHER) 2000

*Mining Exchange, Ballarat.*

Cottage. At 111 Eureka St it was the first bluestone miner's cottage to be built on the goldfields; crafts and souvenirs are available. Open daily, 9am–5pm. Ph: (03) 5332 2554

Directly off Ballarat's main thoroughfare, **Lydiard St** is renowned for its majestic Victorian architecture. A walk along this historic street takes you past **Her Majesty's Theatre, Craig's Royal Hotel**, the **Post Office, The Mining Exchange** and the **Ballarat Railway Station**. At 40 Lydiard St the **Ballarat Fine Art Gallery** is home to the original Eureka Flag and sketches drawn on the Eureka battlefield by Canadian miner Charles Alphonse Doudiet. The collection includes works by S T Gill, Eugene Von Guerard, Sir Sidney Nolan, Tom Roberts and the Lindsay family. It is not to be missed. Open daily, 10.30am–5.30pm. Ph: (03) 5331 5622

Ballarat's picturesque **Lake Wendouree** is a popular spot for walks, picnics and BBQs. During the 1956 Olympics it was the venue for rowing, kayaking and canoeing events and remains a training ground for athletes – including local Olympian Steve Monaghetti. On the western shore is an excellent **community-built playground, paddlesteamers** *Begonia Princess* and *Golden City*, a **tram** travelling part of the foreshore and a **Tramways Museum**. Across the road are the **Botanic Gardens** (p.197). Every Sun from Jan–Apr, the gardens are the venue for **Arts in the Park** – with performances

of contemporary, classical, folk, Celtic and other music in this delightful setting. Also located in the gardens is the cottage of poet **Adam Lindsay Gordon**, stocking a unique range of creative crafts and gifts. Open daily, 10am–4pm, Sat-Sun and public holidays, Oct-Apr; 10am–4pm, May-Sep. Ph: (03) 5320 5643

Don't miss a hands-on introduction to Australian wildlife at the **Ballarat Wildlife Park**. Meet koalas, wallabies, emus and other native animals, or see crocodiles handled by an experienced keeper. Photo shoots with koalas, wombats or kangaroos are part of the fun. Guided tours 11am. Located 5min from Sovereign Hill, cnr York and Fussell Sts. Open daily, 9am–5pm. Picnic and BBQ facilities. Ph: (03) 5333 5933.

Comfortably located in an Aussie woolshed, the **Ballarat Exhibition and Entertainment Centre** features a different range of Australian animals. The woolshed includes ram parades, sheep-dog demonstrations, a farmyard animal nursery and a 3D display of the legend of Waltzing Matilda. Open daily, 9.30-5.30pm. Ph: (03) 5334 7877

Other attractions to look out for are **Ballarat's Aviation Museum** at the airport on Sunraysia Hwy, open weekends and public holidays,1pm–5pm; and **Kryal Castle**, a medieval castle on the Western Hwy toward Melbourne, open daily 9.30am–5pm, Ph: (03) 5334 7388

### Bendigo *Map 30 C2*

Dressed like an aristocrat in its Victorian-era architecture, Bendigo's city speaks of a prominence undiminished by time. Discovery of gold at Ravenswood in 1851 brought thousands to the Sandhurst diggings (as Bendigo was then known) to pocket a share from its 'carpet' of alluvial gold. By the 1860s mining methods changed as mining companies dug deep into quartz reefs building a labyrinth of tunnels beneath the town.

The opulent **Alexandra Fountain**, located above the diverted Bendigo Ck, is a fitting introduction to Bendigo's era of grandeur. Located at Charing Cross, at the heart of Bendigo, it is only a nugget's throw from the historic **Post Office**,

*Sacred Heart Cathedral, Bendigo.*

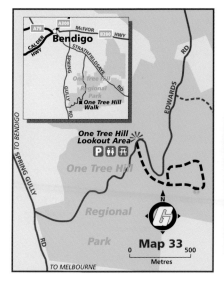

*Shamrock Hotel, Bendigo.*

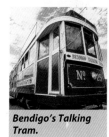

*Bendigo's Talking Tram.*

housing the Bendigo Tourist Information Centre and its **Interpretive Centre**. The Centre provides an interactive introduction to the history and attractions of the town and offers a variety of suggested walking tours, including *Significant Gold Sites* and *Beautiful Buildings*. The adjacent **Law Courts** continue the architectural tour, which must also include the **Shamrock Hotel**, the **Town Hall** on Hargreaves St and the towering English Gothic design **Sacred Heart Cathedral**.

Try a different view of Bendigo — from 61m underground! **Central Deborah Gold Mine** on Violet St features surface exhibits on mining and mine machinery, but its main attraction is a 70min underground tour. Wearing a hard-hat fitted with lights, you take a cage elevator down 30 storeys into the daily working environment of a miner. Open daily, 9.00am–5.15pm. Ph: (03) 5443 8322. Enjoy informative commentary in comfort on the **Vintage Talking Tram Tour**, which leaves from the Central Deborah Mine, travelling through the city and out to the **Tram Museum**.

Though the allure of gold brought Chinese miners to many of the goldfields, nowhere is their contribution better seen than in Bendigo. Step into the **Golden Dragon Museum**, at 5-11 Bridge St and

*Chinese Joss House.*

**Nature trail**

Pick up a copy of the brochure *Bendigo Naturally* from the visitor info centre and explore local wilderness on foot — the Burke and Wills campsite, Kamarooka SP, One Tree Hill (Map 34) and an old 'Eucy' (eucalyptus oil) distillery are some of the highlights.

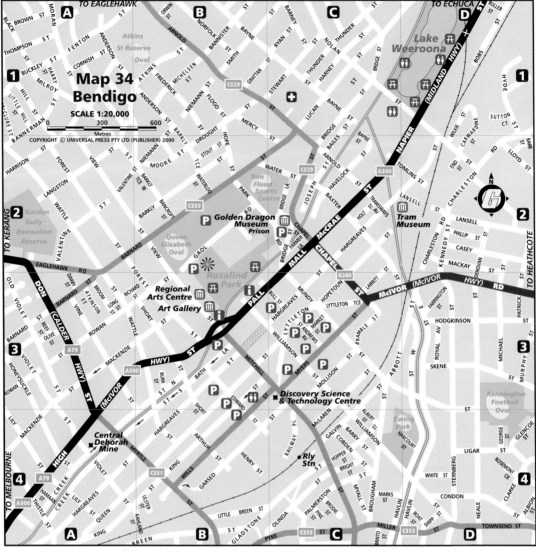

**Historic treat**

For an old-time taste sensation try **Castlemaine Rock** — the boiled lolly made according to an 1853 goldfields recipe.

meet Sun Loong, the world's longest imperial dragon (over 100m) and Old Loong, the dragons 'awakened' during the annual Bendigo Easter Fair. Exhibits provide an appreciation for the goldfields experience of the Chinese and the rich heritage of the nation's culture. An idyllic setting for serene reflection, the **Classical Chinese Gardens**, and **Guan Yin Temple** at the front of the museum are well worth a visit. Open daily, 9.30am–5pm daily. Ph: (03) 5441 5044. The **Chinese Joss House** at Finn St, Emu Point is the original temple built on the goldfields during the 1860s. It is the only one remaining of 4 joss houses built during

the goldrush and is both a place of worship and a museum. Open daily, 10am–5pm; 10am–4pm Winter. Ph: (03) 5442 1685

**View St**, Bendigo's well-regarded Arts Precinct, is a street of galleries and cafes housed in beautiful Victorian-era buildings. Its showpiece is the **Bendigo Art Gallery** — a substantial regional collection of works from Australia and Europe including such artists as Arthur Streeton, Margaret Preston, Patricia Piccinni and Robert Jacks. Open daily, 9am–5pm. Ph: (03) 5443 4991

Bendigo is great fun for kids. At the **Discovery Science and Technology**

**Centre** at 7 Railway Place they can hear their own blood, change their face, create laser art or leave their head on a platter. Open daily, 10am–5pm. Ph: (03) 5444 4400. Or for cooler fun, try the **Bendigo Ice Skating Stadium** at Hattam St, Golden Square. Open daily, 9.30am–11.45am, 1.30pm–4pm. Ph: (03) 5441 3000. At cnr Strickland and Rohs Rds there is double the action: **Round Australia Mini-golf** and **Protrack Indoor Go-Karts**, Tue–Thurs, 12pm–10pm, Fri 12pm–12am, Sat 10am–12am, Sun, 10am–6pm. Ph: (03) 5441 7046

Bendigo's unexpected lucky find was clay. Scottish potter George Duncan Guthrie recognised wealth in the earth, though not the gold he'd sought. He established his pottery in 1858 on what is now the Midland Highway, **Epsom**. The **Bendigo Pottery Tourist Complex** is one of the best regarded working potteries in Australia. You can inspect the large range of tableware for sale, stroll into an old kiln or purchase some clay for your own handiwork. Time is well spent in the nursery and garden pot centre, Potters Cafe and in the range of potters' studios. For car enthusiasts the **Bendigo Car Museum** is also located in the complex. Open daily, 9am–5pm. Ph: (03) 5448 4404

*Castlemaine.*

## Castlemaine *Map 31 C2*

Another town to flourish through 1850s gold, Castlemaine yields much more than precious metal. This soulful country town is haven for the muse, boasting galleries, resident artists – both past and present – and a bounty of book and antique shops.

Castlemaine's tradition of art and craftsmanship is at its best at the **Buda Historic Home and Garden**. Located at 42 Hunter St, this Victorian colonial home displays the lifestyle and art of the Leviny family who lived there from 1863–1981. Examples of their embroidery,

*Castlemaine Art Gallery.*

**Kid's delight**
The **Clunes Milk Bar** at 59 Fraser St boasts the biggest ice-creams in Victoria. You be the judge!

*Main street, Clunes.*

woodcarving, painting, photography, enamelling, metal work and jewellery decorate the rooms. The 1.8ha gardens are a rare example of 19th and 20th century landscaping and are exquisite in springtime. Open daily, 9am–5pm. Ph: (03) 5472 1032. The plant nursery, cafe and gift shop specialising in locally produced gifts are also worth a visit.

Noted for its excellent collection of Australian art, the **Castlemaine Art Gallery**, at 12 Lyttleton St, boasts works by Frederick McCubbin, Tom Roberts, Russell Drysdale and Wendy Stavrianos, among other early and contemporary artists. As you wander through the diverse collection, look for the charming portrait of the Queen Mother as a young woman. Downstairs, the **Historical Museum** offers an excellent introduction to the history and development of the town, including its Aboriginal heritage and the goldrush. Open daily, 10am–5pm. Ph: (03) 5472 2292

Art is not only showcased, it is also for sale at many of the studio galleries around the town. Stop in at the old convent school at 40-42 Campbell St and visit resident artist **Brian Nunan**, Ph: (03) 5470 6724, world-renowned glassblower Richard Morrell, 139-143 Mostyn St, Ph: (03) 5470 6800, or visit **Herons Gallery**, cnr Lytttleton and Hargraves Sts, featuring works by other

*Creswick.*

Central Goldfields artists. Open Sat-Sun, 11am–5pm. Ph: (03) 5472 1030

The photographic record of Castlemaine often includes views from the **Burke and Wills Monument** on Wills St (Burke, one of the 2 ill-fated explorers, served as superintendent of police in Castlemaine) and from the **Old Castlemaine Gaol** on Bowden St. The Gaol began in 1851 as 5 log huts to lock up the goldfields' unruly, but evolved into the impenetrable fortress preserved today. It offers not only a sobering reminder of prison life of the past, it is also a unique place to spend the night, sleeping in one of the refurnished cells. The Governor's Restaurant, Mess Hall and Dungeon Kitchen ensure you are well fed, whatever your length of stay. Tours and accommodation subject to availability. Ph: (03) 5470 5097

To gain an appreciation of life on the Mt Alexander Diggings (as Castlemaine was then known) you can purchase a **Diggings Passport**. Primarily available from the visitor info centre, Forest Ck Gold Mine and the Chewton Town Hall, the Passport entitles you to a tour through **Forest Creek Gold Mine** and an informative booklet providing historical commentary on other sites to visit including **Pennyweight Flat Children's Cemetery**, **Garfield Waterwheel** and **Herons Reef Gold Diggings**. If you don't have time for the full 'tour' it is still worth stopping at any of the listed sites.

## Clunes *Map 31 C3*

Clunes, Victoria's first gold town, has retained much of the character of that time of contrasts – in its stately buildings built from wealth and its cottages reflecting different fortunes. It is worth stopping in at **The Town Hall** and **Court House** to gain a sense of Clunes' influential past. For another historic excursion visit the **Bottle Museum** on Talbot Rd. It boasts the largest collection of bottles in the southern hemisphere and is shared by the visitor info centre and conveniently located tea rooms. Open daily, 10am–5pm. Ph: (03) 5345 3896. An important feature in Clunes is its creek. Shaded by 100yr-old trees you can take a

Creek **Walk** out to the site of the **Port Philip Mine** which in its day crushed more than 1 275 000 tonnes of quartz, yielding almost 500 000oz of gold.

### Creswick *Map 31 C3*

Creswick has a welcoming wide main street and shops brimmed with shady verandahs. During the frenzy of the goldrush the town was home to more than 25 000 miners; today, with a population of around 3000, Creswick has settled into a more relaxed and easy pace.

Creswick's attractions include the natural and the cultivated. St Georges Lake, Eaton Dam and Slaty Ck picnic area are all contained within the **Creswick RP**. Visitors enjoy fishing, gold panning, canoeing and walks through the bush (only on main tracks – mine shafts in the area are deep). **Creswick Nursery** and the **Landcare Centre** are also part of the park and are worth a visit. A few km from the nursery, further along the Midland Hwy (toward Daylesford) **The Tangled Maze and Nursery**, features a living maze constructed from thousands of plants. The maze complex also has mini golf, a plant nursery, cafe and picnic area. Open daily, 10am–5.30pm, Sept to mid-July. Ph: (03) 5345 2847

Also east on the Midland Hwy **World of Dinosaurs** offers the unexpected – 18 life-sized dinosaurs in a bush-setting. A wildlife park and playground, BBQs and picnic area make this a favoured family destination. Open daily, 9.30am–5pm. Ph: (03) 5345 2676

Mining history was made here, albeit tragically: in 1882 22 miners died when water flooded the No. 2 shaft of the Australasian Mine. An investigation into the disaster led to a review of mine safety practices (or the lack thereof), resulting in the improvement of conditions. A display has been erected on the site, 1.5km north on Clunes Rd; a **Monument** to the miners can be found in the Crewsick Cemetery. To learn more of the history of the town visit the **Creswick Historic Museum**, located in the Old Town Hall at 68 Albert St. Open Sun and public holidays, 1.30pm–4.30pm. Ph: (03) 5345 2892. Walking tours of the town are available from the Creswick Newsagency and from the visitor info centre near the post office (adjacent the playground).

### Great Western *Map 30 A3*

The birth of Victoria's vineyards was helped by gold miners who hailed from countries that enjoyed a tradition of wine making and drinking. The region around Great Western was quickly recognised as having great potential and as early as 1863 Jeanne Pierre Trouette planted vines.

**Seppelt Great Western Winery** offers excellent cellar door sales and tasting, but its unique feature is 'The Drives', a 3km series of cellar tunnels dug by goldminers in the 1860s and 70s. Guided tours Mon-Sat, 10.30am, 1.30pm and 3pm. Sun during school and public holiday weekends. Open Mon-Sun, 10am–5pm. Ph: (03) 5361 2222. BBQs and views of the vines make it a pleasant lunch spot, or stop at one of the eateries in town. **Best's Wines 'Concongella'** also has picnic facilities and offers self-guided tours plus wine tasting in a slab-timber hut. Open Mon-Fri 9am–5pm, Sat, 10am–5pm, Sun, 11am–4pm during school and public holidays. Ph: (03) 5356 2250

**Garden Gully Wines** is the youngest of the wineries, planted by Seppelt's approximately 40 yrs ago. Open Mon-Fri 12–5pm, Sat-Sun, 10am–5pm,

*Great Western vines.*

*Wine tasting, Best's Wines.*

*Historic Maldon.*

school and public holidays 10am–6pm.
Ph: (03) 5356 2400

### Harcourt *Map 31 D1*

An enchanting valley 29km south of
Bendigo on the Calder Hwy, Harcourt is
Victoria's premier apple growing region.
Sample fruit at the roadside stalls or visit
the **Harcourt Cidery** for a taste of locally
made apple and pear cider. Sparkling, still,
sweet or dry cider make tempting liquid
souvenirs. Open Tue–Sat, 9.30am–5.30pm,
public and school holidays. Vineyards,
**Harcourt Valley**, open daily, 11am–6pm,
Ph: (03) 5474 2223. **Mt Alexander**, open
daily, 10am–5pm. Ph: (03) 5474 2262; and
**Blackjack**, open Sat–Sun and public
holidays, 1pm–5pm, Ph: (03) 5474 2355
also make pleasant wine and cider stops
and are signposted on the drive.
**Skydancers Orchid and Butterfly Gardens,**
cnr Midland Hwy and Blackjack Rd,
Harcourt features butterflies, as its name
suggests, plus a restaurant, and an orchid
and native plant nursery. Open Mon–Wed,
10am–5pm; Thurs–Sun during Aug–July.
The restaurant is open for dinner by appt.
Ph: (03) 5474 2468

### Maldon *Map 31 D1*

In 1966 Maldon's contribution to
Australia's historical record was officially
recognised: it was declared the nation's
first 'notable town' by the National Trust.
This distinction ensures the preservation
of its past for enjoyment in the present.

And Maldon has a past: once known as
the Tarrengower Goldfields this town
yielded 59 530kg (60 tonnes) of gold in
73 years of mining from 1853 to 1926.
Most of the 20 000 miners who
descended in the first years of the rush
moved on, but those who remained
established a charming country town.

Year round, the verandah-lined **Main
St** provides shelter and shade to explore
shops filled with delightful wares –
antiques, lace, books, toys and crafts,
Scottish treats, and lollies for the sweet-
toothed.

Aspects of Victorian and Edwardian
architecture are to be admired throughout
Maldon. Notably, the Royal Hotel and
Royal Theatre, c.1860, have been restored
and now operate as the **Royal Theatre
Cafe and Gallery**. Other sites of interest
include the 24m high **Bee Hive Chimney**
and the **Maldon Post Office** once home
to Henry Handel Richardson, author of
*The Getting of Wisdom*. A 'Historic
Town Walk' pamphlet is available from
the visitor info centre in High St. Many
of the main street eateries also offer tales
of the past along with their excellent
menus. Join Clydesdales **Terry & Tangles**
for a horse-drawn carriage ride around
town. Picnic bookings available. Open
Sat–Sun and holidays. Ph: (03) 5475 2182

Just 2.7km south of Maldon **Carmans
Tunnel** offers 25min candlelight tours of
a 570m mining tunnel which preserves
samples of mining techniques used during
its operation by the Great International
Quartz Mining Company NL. Open
Sat–Sun, public and school holidays
1.30pm–4pm. Ph: (03) 5475 2667. A
favourite with the children and train
enthusiasts is a **steam locomotive** ride
through the picturesque Muckleford
Forest. The return trip departs from
Maldon Stn, Sun and public holidays
11.30am, 1pm and 2.30pm, Wed,
11.30am and 1pm. The service also
operates daily from Boxing Day through
mid-Jan. Ph: (03) 5475 2966

Other attractions in and around
Maldon include **Maldon Museum** on
High St, housing relics from the gold
mining days, open daily, 1.30–4pm, Ph:
(03) 5475 1027; **Porcupine Township**, a

**Scenic detour**

Detour to stretch your
legs at the **Oak Forest**
at the base of Mt
Alexander, Harcourt
planted by nostalgic
settlers to remind them
of 'home', or continue
up to the Mt Alexander
lookout for sweeping
views of the valley.

*Maldon's steam locomotive.*

re-creation of an 1850s alluvial mining town plus motel and cottages, located cnr Bendigo and Allans Rds, open daily, 10am-5pm, Ph: (03) 5475 1000; and the **Maldon Yabby Farm**, offering line and bait for yabby fishing, plus a range of yabby delicacies. Picnic and BBQ facilities available. Open daily, 10am-5pm. Ph: (03) 5475 1086. Phone ahead to check availability as yabbies hibernate.

Enjoy great views and walks at **Mt Tarrengower**, **Anzac Hill** and in the **Nuggety Ranges**, all signposted from the centre of Maldon.

### Maryborough *Map 31 B2*

Mark Twain once quipped that Maryborough was a railway station with a town attached. And this is definitely a **railway station** worth stopping at. The foundations for this impressive building were laid back in 1890 and the spirit of its glorious past lingers in the antiques and collectibles inside. Visitor info, art gallery, cafe and resident harpist create a welcoming mood for browsing or buying. Open daily, 10am-6pm. Ph: (03) 5461 4683. An antiques and collectibles market is held on the platform 4 times a year.

### Moliagul, Tarnagulla and Dunolly *Map 31 B1, C1, C1*

Known as the Golden Triangle for its astonishing yield of nuggets (339 found here as against 38 found in Ballarat), Moliagul, Tarnagulla and Dunolly are places to reflect on the history of the area. Now resembling a ghost town, Moliagul was once the centre of attention. On 6 Feb 1869 the Welcome Stranger nugget was found here by John Deeson and Richard Oates, 2 diggers who only a week before their lucky strike had been refused credit on a bag of flour. Weighing in at 65kg it was the world's largest gold nugget and had to be cut in pieces to fit on the scales at Dunolly. The vital spot is marked by a **memorial stone**. Dunolly's **Goldfields Historical Museum** on Broadway proudly displays the anvil on which the nugget was split, along with other relics from the glory days of mining. Open Sun and public holidays, 1.30pm-5pm. During the rushes

*Maryborough's grand railway station.*

a variety of travelling performers entertained the diggers at goldfields theatres and next door to Tarnagulla's **Victoria Hotel** (1853) is a theatre that hosted vaudeville shows until the early 1930s. This town's major gold find was Poverty Reef, discovered in 1962 which is today marked by a **memorial** near the Methodist Church.

### Smythesdale *Map 30 B4*

Smythesdale's **Court House**, **Cell Block** and **Court House Hotel** remind travellers of the trail of small towns touched by the goldrush. Today Smythesdale is best known for the **Yellowglen Winery**, named after the gold mine sunk where vines now grow. Only 20min from Ballarat along the Glenelg Hwy it is open for cellar door tasting and sales Mon-Fri 10am-5pm, Sat-Sun, 11am-5pm. Ph: (03) 5342 8617

### Stawell *Map 30 A3*

Speed was important in the early days of the goldrush as thousands competed in the race for 'easy' surface gold. Speed is still important here: every Easter Monday the town is host to Australia's richest footrace, the **Stawell Gift**, run at Central Park since 1878. Discover the history and excitement of this much-acclaimed event at the **Hall of Fame** located in Main St, opposite the Railway Hotel. Open Mon-Fri, 10am-4pm. Ph:(03) 5358 1326. After wandering the streets to sample

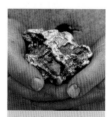

**Fossicker's find**

At 90 Broadway, Dunolly, Finders Prospecting Supplies can fit you with the right gold-seeking equipment and arrange tuition if needed. Ph: (03) 5468 1333

*Mining marked bushland.*

some of the fine architecture at the **Post Office**, **Town Hall** and **Court House** it is worth driving up Scenic Rd to **Pioneer's Lookout** to view the town framed by the alluring arm of the Grampians. On the way you pass the working **Magdala Gold Mine** and, although not open to the public, the glimpse offered hints at the amount of effort invested in what is presently one of Victoria's richest working gold mines.

You don't have to be in France to see the Eiffel Tower or in Egypt to see the Great Pyramid. On London Rd, **Casper's World in Miniature** has replicas of these and other landmarks of different cultures along with push-button audio commentary. Picnic and BBQs available. Open daily, 9am-6pm. Tel: (03) 5358 1877

Bunjil the Creator, a figure significant to the spiritual life of Aborigines of SE Australia, is depicted in Aboriginal art painted on rock at **Bunjil's Shelter**, 11km south of Stawell off the Pomonal Rd. Discovered in 1957 this is considered one of Victoria's most significant Aboriginal art sites.

### Talbot *Map 31 B2*

Turn off at Talbot and explore its narrow, winding streets. Once populated by 30 000 tent-dwelling miners, its historic buildings help to recreate a sense of its more permanent past — **St Michaels Church of**

**England**, the **Post Office, Public Library, Town Hall** and **Court House** all suggest a purposeful community. Thirsty miners once stopped in for a drink at the **Bull and Mouth Hotel** which was built in 1858 from local basalt. It is now a well-known country restaurant offering accommodation. Ph: (03) 5463 2325. **Talbot Museum** in Camp St houses local artefacts, documents and photographs. Open the 1st and 3rd Sun afternoon of each month.

## State parks, regional parks and state forests

### Langi Ghiran SP *Map 31 A3*

Travel 20km west from Mt Buangor on the Western Hwy to a SP distinctive for its rugged granite peaks, open woodlands and delightful springtime wildflowers. Car-based camping is available at the picnic area at the end of Kartuk Rd; remote camping is permitted in the more mountainous areas. A short walk from the picnic area takes you to a historic reservoir built from local granite blocks; allow a full day for the climb to the summit of Mt Langi Ghiran. 'Langi Ghiran' is the Aboriginal name for the yellow-tailed black cockatoo which is one of the many inhabitants to watch out for. **Mt Langi Ghiran Winery** is conveniently located on Vine Rd at the base of the SP. Open Mon-Fri, 9am-5pm, Sat-Sun,

12–5pm. BBQs and picnic facilities.
Ph: (03) 5354 3207

### Mt Buangor SP and Mt Cole SF *Map 31 A2*

Only 60km west of Ballarat along the Western Hwy, Mt Buangor SP and adjoining Mt Cole SF offer an abundance of natural diversions. Scenic walks take in shaded gullies supporting thriving tree ferns, waterfalls, eucalypt forests and wildlife – including more than 130 species of birds. An easy **Waterfalls Nature Walk** connects the Ferntree and Middle Ck picnic and camping areas while the **Cave Walking Track** starting from Middle Ck picnic area offers a challenge to those looking for a more strenuous trek. Other walks, picnic and camping areas are scattered throughout the SP and SF. Some logging occurs in the SF: as you drive be alert to logging trucks or other heavy vehicles.

### Paddy's Ranges SP and Maryborough RP *Map 31 B2*

Located south of Maryborough, the parks feature both the natural and the historic: relics from the goldmining era can be seen in box-ironbark forests full of wildlife. There are 2 small bush camping areas in the north and west, plenty of walking tracks, and an area set aside for gold fossicking and detecting. More than 230 species of wildflower have been recorded in the park and are at their best during spring.

## Parks and gardens

### Alexandra Gardens *Map 30 A3*

Located on Vincent St in Ararat these pretty regional gardens are popular for both recreation and reflection. An aptly named Orchid Glass House is enchanting to visit from May–Dec, though other features of the park are a walk-in fernery and waterfall, a bridge-linked Japanese island, plus convenient playground, BBQ and picnic facilities.

### Ballarat Botanic Gardens *Map 32 A1*

Planted in 1858, Ballarat's Botanic Gardens enclose 40ha of immaculately ordered beauty. Here you can recline under mature and magnificent trees, tour the season's blooms in the landmark glasshouse, ponder the *Flight from Pompeii* in an elegant statuary, or admire Australia's roll call of Prime Ministers in an avenue of artfully crafted bronze busts.

### Castlemaine Botanic Gardens *Map 31 C2*

Castlemaine is one of the many botanic gardens of Victoria to boast the creative handiwork of Baron Ferdinand von Mueller. The government botanist and director of Melbourne's Royal Botanic Gardens, von Mueller contributed to the design of the gardens located on Downes Rd. They were planted in the 1860s and feature one of Victoria's oldest cultivated trees – an English oak planted in 1867 by His Royal Highness Prince Alfred.

### Rosalind Park and Cascades *Map 34 B3*

At the centre of the city of Bendigo, Rosalind Park was once the site of a goldrush era government camp, but in 1861 it was set aside for recreational purposes. A stroll through the peaceful park offers encounters with some typical attractions such as a fernery, conservatory, stunning seasonal flower beds and ornate bridges, but there are some atypical features including a lookout tower for sighting the city and the Cascades, a restored late 1800s water feature complete with ornate fountain pools.

*Botanic Gardens statuary, Ballarat.*

## Other attractions

### Dingo Farm *Map 31 D2*

Was the dingo an assassin of evil spirits in the Dreamtime? If this question intrigues you and you would like to learn more about a much-discussed Australian animal then it is definitely worth visiting the Dingo Farm at **Chewton**, just outside of Castlemaine. Loved by kids (who get to see and touch one of the 100 dingoes) the farm has been widely publicised and acclaimed. Open daily, 9am-5pm. Ph: (03) 5470 5711. The drive there is a tour in itself, passing through scrubby bushland marked by alluvial mining.

### Dry Diggings Walk *Map 35*

From **Daylesford** through to **Castlemaine** remnants of goldrush towns and relics from the mines are silent monuments in the bush. The Dry Diggings Walk brochure is available for a reasonable cost and features a map and commentary to guide you through this historic mining landscape. The 55km walk is mapped to take 3 days if the entire trail is followed and possible camping sites are noted. Available from regional visitor info centres.

### Sedgwicks Camel Farm *Map 31 D1*

Camel rides in the bush bring people to Sedgwicks Camel Farm on Sutton Grange Rd, approximately 20km south of Bendigo at **Sedgwick**. In fine weather you can take a 30 min ride or enjoy

*Common sight at Chewton's Dingo Farm.*

BBQ tea on a sunset trek (though bookings are recommended Nov-Mar). For those seeking a more adventurous excursion overnight treks are also offered. Open Thurs-Mon, school and public holidays, 10am-5pm, 1 Sep-31 May. Ph: (03) 5439 6367

### Tuki Trout Farm *Map 31 C3*

A leisure fishing spot for the expert or the novice, Tuki Trout Farm has ponds stocked with rainbow trout ready for catching. Equipment is available for hire and basic instruction can be given if needed. All fish caught is paid for by the kilo and can be taken home clean and packed, or cooked and served in the restaurant on site. Located at Stoney Rises, **Smeaton**. Open daily, 11am-6pm. Ph: (03) 5345 6233. Cottage accommodation is also available.

## Recreational activities

### Cycling

Gentle inclines and picturesque countryside attract many cyclists to the Goldfields. Five well-developed routes are mapped in Tourism Victoria's *Goldfields* brochure; however, it is recommended that local visitor info centres be contacted for travel times, distances, difficulty levels and details of bike hire. Contact Bicycle Victoria for more information. Ph: 1 800 639 634.

### Water sports

Lakes and reservoirs throughout the region offer some excellent opportunities

*Camel kisses, Sedgwicks Camel farm.*

# Fun for the young

★ Ballarat Wildlife Park (p.188)
★ Bendigo Ice Skating Stadium (p.191)
★ Dingo Farm, Chewton (p.198)
★ Discovery Science and Technology Centre, Bendigo (p.190)
★ Pro-track Indoor Go-Karts and 'Round Australia' Mini Golf, Bendigo (p.191)
★ Sovereign Hill, Ballarat (p.185)
★ Steam locomotive ride, Maldon (p.194)
★ World of Dinosaurs Park, Creswick (p.193)

*Casting a line.*

*Wildlife Park, Ballarat.*

for boating, water skiing, fishing, swimming and camping.

- Lake Eppalock, 30km south-east of Bendigo via McIvor Hwy is popular for yachting, speed and ski boat racing, swimming and fishing. Facilities include camping sites, caravan parks, and public boat ramps.
- Lake Cairn Curran, 12km south of Maldon
- Lake Burrumbeet, 15km west of Ballarat via the Western Hwy.
- Lake Learmonth, 20km NW of Ballarat via the Sunraysia Hwy is notably home to the regional water ski club, although it is also popular for fishing and other boating.
- Green Hill Lake, 4.5km east of Ararat via the Western Hwy is a venue for perch, trout and yellow belly fishing, canoe trails through wetland flora, plus all the main water sports.

## Camping and bushwalking

The main camping and bushwalking spots in the Goldfields region are:

- Creswick Regional Park (p.193)
- Langi Ghiran SP (p.196)
- Mt Buangor SP and Mt Cole SF (p.197)
- Paddys Ranges SP and Maryborough RP (p.197)
- Pyrenees Ranges (p.185)
- Whipstick State Park, north of Bendigo.

Contact Parks Victoria on 131 963 for more information regarding facilities and maps.

## Prospecting

Although the miners of the past tried to be thorough, they didn't discover all of the gold. Prospecting equipment is available for hire throughout the region, and although metal-detectors are popular there are some who prefer traditional methods like panning. The relevant visitor info centres can advise on equipment hire, prospecting guidelines and restrictions.

*Panning for gold, Sovereign Hill.*

# Suggested tours – Map 35

## Weekend escape tour

### Approximate distance
510km return from Melbourne CBD.

### About the tour
Retreat into the country to relax and unwind. This route offers beautiful lakes, stunning gardens, wineries and wilderness. Ballarat has a large range of accommodation available, or for a special weekend, spend the night at the Warrenmang Winery near Avoca. Take as much time as needed and enjoy the scenery as you drive.

### Places of interest

❶ **Botanic Gardens, Ballarat** (p.197)

❷ **Lydiard St, Ballarat** (p.188)

❸ **The Pyrenees Wineries** (p.185)

❹ **Warrenmang Vineyard Resort** (p.185)

❺ **Ararat** (p.184)

❻ **Mt Langi Ghiran Vineyard** (p.196)

❼ **Mt Buangor SP** (p.197)

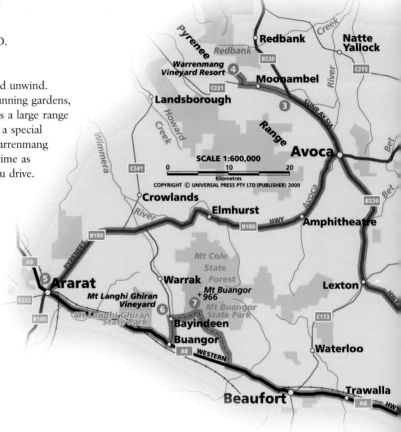

*Botanic Gardens, Ballarat.*

# Arts and antiques tour

## Approximate distance
430km return from Melbourne CBD

## About the tour
For those with a penchant for art, crafts, antiques and collectibles, this tour offers a good full day of browsing. Creswick, Clunes and Talbot showcase an interesting array of local crafts and collections and no antiques trip could miss the Maryborough Railway Stn Complex.

Castlemaine and Maldon will keep you occupied for hours and the return route takes in a spa country highlight at Daylesford.

## Places of interest
❶ **Springmount Pottery, Midland Hwy, Creswick** (p. 193)

❷ **Bottle Museum, Clunes** (p.192)

❸ **Talbot** (p.196)

❹ **Maryborough Railway Station** (p.195)

❺ **High St, Maldon** (p.194)

❻ **Buda Historic Home and Garden, Castlemaine** (p.191)

❼ **Castlemaine Art Gallery** (p.192) **and artist studios** (p.192)

❽ **Daylesford** (p.79)

*Beautiful Buda Garden, Castlemaine.*

Left: **Paddlesteamer,
Echuca.**
Right: **Michelton
Winery.**

# Goulburn-Murray Waters

Travelling north from Melbourne it's best to navigate, not by the stars, but by water. Goulburn-Murray Waters is a region routed along the natural flow of the Goulburn and Murray Rivers. Its meandering path takes in tranquil lakes, massive weirs, wineries, fertile farmland, spectacular river red gums and some unexpected sights, including army tanks, alpacas, cacti and gold era ghost towns.

There is fabulous fishing — silver perch, trout, yellowbelly, redfin, Murray Cod and yabbies are just a few of the items on the angler's menu. Water sports are another specialty: in this region you can swim, waterski, sail, commandeer a houseboat or learn to paddle your own canoe.

The rivers' most impressive watercraft, however, are its river boats. Once Australia's largest inland port, dramatised memorably in the mini-series *All the Rivers Run*, Echuca is today home to the world's largest collection of authentic paddlesteamers. You can not only see one of these stately vessels churning its way along the mighty Murray, you can also travel aboard — or even spend a night adrift. The historic port precinct recaptures the era, through faithful restoration rather than recreation, providing a memorable experience of a trade and time pivotal in Australia's past.

## Tourist information

**Echuca-Moama Visitor Info Centre**
Heygarth St, Echuca 3564
Ph: (03) 5480 7555
Freecall 1 800 804 446
www.echucamoama.com

**Eildon Visitor Info Centre**
Library Building, Main St, Eildon 3713
Ph: (03) 5774 2909

**Euroa Visitor Info Centre**
25 Kirkland Ave, Euroa 3666
Ph: (03) 5794 2647
Freecall 1 800 444 647

**Greater Shepparton Visitor Info Centre**
534 Wyndam St, Shepparton 3630
Ph: (03) 5831 4400
Freecall 1 800 808 839

**Nagambie Lakes Visitor Info Centre**
145 High St, Nagambie 3608
Ph: (03) 5794 2647
Freecall 1 800 444 647

**Seymour Visitor Info Centre**
Old Court House, Emily St, Seymour 3660
Ph: (03) 5799 0233

## Must see, must do

- ★ **Ardmona Kids Town, Shepparton** (p.216)
- ★ **Barmah State Forest** (p.216)
- ★ **Port of Echuca** (p.207)
- ★ **Chateau Tahbilk and Mitchelton Wineries, Nagambie** (p.211)
- ★ **RAAC Memorial and Tank Museum, Puckapunya** (p.218)

## Radio stations

**Deniliquin:** FM 102.5
**Echuca-Moama**
**EM:** FM 104
**Greater Shepparton**
**3SR:** 93.5
**Community radio:** FM 98.5
**Sun:** FM 96.9

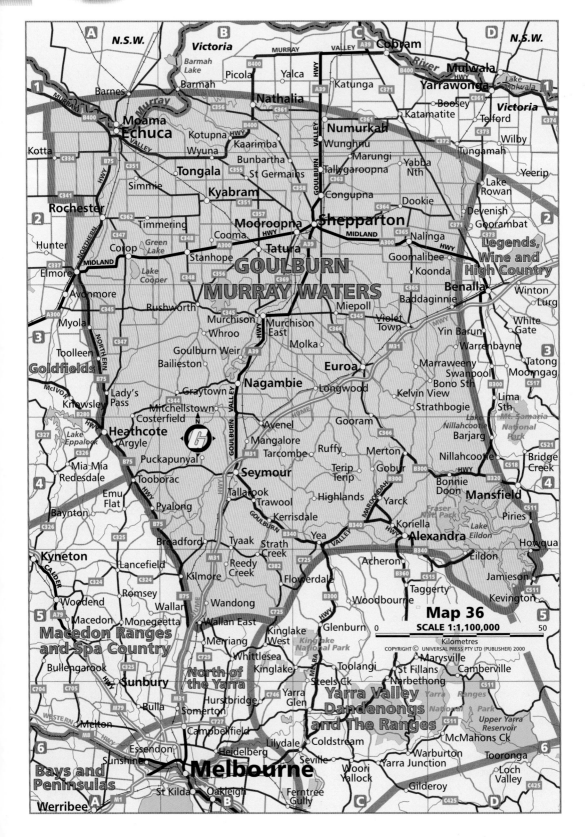

**Map 36**
SCALE 1:1,100,000
Kilometres

*Houseboat on Lake Eildon.*

**Meeting point**
Echuca' is an Aboriginal word meaning 'meeting of the waters' — appropriate since it is here that the Goulburn and Campaspe Rivers meet up with the mighty Murray.

## Natural features

Goulburn-Murray Waters is defined by its rivers and lakes. The first boundary-marker begins just north of Melbourne, on the shores of Lake Eildon, a built lake with a 3 500 000 megalitre storage capacity. From there the trail winds northward, following the Goulburn River through Alexandra, Seymour, Nagambie and Shepparton till it joins the mighty Murray River at Echuca. Labelled Australia's 'greatest' river, the Murray originates in the rugged mountains near Mt Kosciusko and travels 2756km to the sea, to Encounter Bay in Sth Australia.

Irrigation has also made its mark on the landscape. Networks of irrigation channels service 1000s of hectares of farmland: orchards, market gardens, dairy, grain, sheep and beef farms prosper in the sunny weather — a climate perfect, too, for the vineyards along the Goulburn River.

## History

Goulburn-Murray waters were first inhabited by Aboriginal peoples — canoes were carved from the trunks of trees along the river and those marks can still be seen today. Reports from Mitchell's expedition in 1836 brought the overlanders with stock from Sydney and squatters from Port Phillip, an influx that overturned the original inhabitants' pattern of life.

Echuca-Moama had their early beginnings as stock crossing points. In 1845 ex-convict James Maiden set up a punt on the NSW side of the Murray, and Maiden's Punt grew to be Moama. In 1853 another former convict, James Hopwood, established an inn and punt on the Victorian side, at present-day Echuca.

After the gold era passed, the demand for wool, grain, and red gum timber brought about the birth of the riverboat era, as remote farms and mills delivered their produce via the waterways. Business boomed once the Melbourne rail line reached Echuca (1864), which grew to be Australia's largest inland port, but once the railway line extended along the Murray, the river trade ended, though its heritage is well-preserved at Echuca.

In 1877–1881 a devastating drought hit northern Victoria. An Act passed in

*Paddlesteamer, Murray River, Echuca.*

*Seymour Alternative farming Expo.*

1886 authorised the building of major projects and in 1887 work began on Australia's first national irrigation storage, the Goulburn Weir. As irrigation expanded, predictability of water supply finally brought stability and prosperity to what is today a rich agricultural region.

## Getting there
### By road
Driving the Goulburn-Murray region the roads range from well-constructed highways to smaller, scenic country roads. From Melbourne, the Hume Hwy reaches the towns to the east, the Goulburn Valley Hwy travels up through the centre, and the Northern Hwy covers the western limits of the region, up to Echuca.

### By rail
V/Line trains depart daily from Melbourne's Spencer St Stn to Shepparton and connecting coaches travel to Echuca and the surrounding region. The Melbourne-Albury train also departs daily, making stops at Seymour and Euroa. Ph: 13 22 32. However, if Echuca is your direct destination **Dysons Coaches** depart Spencer St Stn daily. Ph: (03) 5482 2576 or 13 22 32

## Getting around
### By coach
Several companies run 1-day sightseeing trips to Echuca. Try **Great Sights**, Wed and Sun, Ph: (03) 9639 2211; **Gray Line**, Wed and Sun, Ph: (03) 9663 4455; **Australian Pacific Tours**, Wed and Sat, Ph: (03) 9663 1611; and **AAT Kings**, Wed and Sat, Ph: (03) 9663 3377. Inquire at the **Victorian Visitor Info Centre** for details of extended tours. Ph: (03) 9658 9955

## Festivals and events
### Seymour Alternative Farming Expo
Informative and entertaining, this 3-day farming expo showcases a world of alternatives ranging from organics and exotic animals, to natural fibres and mudbricks. At Kings Park, Tallarook St, **Seymour** during the 3rd week of Feb. Ph: (03) 5799 1211

### 3SR Shepparton Arts Festival
**Shepparton** is transformed into a hub of music, performance and visual arts for 10 days during mid Mar. Opera under the stars, fireworks, world music, musicals, theatre, wine and food guarantee an exciting time. Ph: (03) 5822 1959

### Taste of Tatura Wine and Food Festival
Stop in at Mactier Park, Hogan St, **Tatura** and enjoy a day sampling the region's finest food and wines. Set in a pleasant park environment, musicians add to the festive mood. Held in early Mar. Ph: (03) 5824 1003

### Birralee Goulburn Valley Children's Festival
A celebration of the creativity and imagination of children aged up to 12 years. Storytelling, crafts, fantasy and creative play areas, theatre, sport and special events make this a memorable outing for both children and their families. Held at Queen's Gardens, Wyndham St, **Shepparton** during mid Mar. Ph: (03) 5831 4400

### Port of Echuca Heritage Steam Festival
Formerly known as the Rich River Festival, this steam extravaganza held in **Echuca** during mid Oct awakens the past

with its range of river activities including the blessing of the fleet, land and water-based steam displays, river pageant and street parade. Ph: (03) 5482 4248

### Belstack Strawberry Fair

Kialla West's premier harvest is toasted with a day of fun devoted to the fruit. Strawberries feature throughout the day along with food, wine and jazz. Held early Nov at **Belstack Tourism Complex and Strawberry Farm** (p.217). Ph: (03) 5823 1324

## Main localities and towns

### Alexandra *Map 36 C4*

Originally known as Red Gate Diggings, Alexandra was transformed into a thriving timber town when milling began in the Rubicon Forest. To facilitate the transport of timber from bush sawmills back to the town, a steam railway system was built. At the **Timber Tramway** and **Museum** the era is recaptured in photos, displays and memorabilia. Several working locomotives are located on site at the old railway station, Station St. Open 2nd Sun each month, 10am–4pm, or by appt. Ph: (03) 5772 2392

### Echuca-Moama *Map 37, 38*

A wide snaking trail of swirling water, river red gums overhanging, a paddle-steamer churning round the nearest bend – life along the Murray is one of unhurried ease. But pause a moment to hear a riverboat's shrill whistle and you'll soon be swept into imagining the glory days when this river was king.

Twin towns along the banks of the Murray, Echuca is proudly part of Victoria and Moama equally proud to rest in NSW. While both share points of common history, each town offers a different range of rewarding attractions. To orient yourself to the river and its fascinating heritage, start at the **Port of Echuca**, along the Murray Esplanade.

For entry to 3 of the main historical venues, purchase a passport at the **Star Hotel** (1867), where after inspecting the paddle-steamer gallery you can escape out through an underground tunnel once used by illicit drinkers avoiding the police. The

admission price also provides entry to the **Echuca Wharf** (1865) which in its hey-day was almost 1km long (almost 5 times its current length). There are plenty of steam-powered things to see, an audiovisual presentation on life on the riverboats, plus the chance to board the moored paddle-steamers *Pevensey* and *Adelaide*. 'Our boats' pamphlet, available from the visitor info centre contains the vital statistics of the region's riverboats and barges. The final destination included in the price is the **Bridge Hotel** (1858). Built by Echuca's founding father, Henry Hopwood, the hotel has a historic gallery upstairs and a restaurant downstairs. In 1863 Hopwood wrote his own review of the place: 'As this is already known to be the best hotel out of Melbourne, further comment is unnecessary'. Open daily, 9am–5pm. Ph: (03) 5482 4248

Now it's time to take to the river: a visit to Echuca-Moama must include a trip down the Murray aboard one of its 'ladies'. Paddle-steamers depart from the Port with cruises ranging from 1hr trips, to lunch and dinner cruises or even overnight journeys. Book at the boarding agents: *MV Mary Anne*, 607 High St, Ph: (03) 5480 2200; *PS Canberra*, Murray Esplanade, Ph: (03) 5482 2711; *PS Pride of the Murray*, 57 Murray Esplanade, Ph: (03) 5482 5244; and *Emmylou* paddlesteamer, which offers 1 or 2 night passages, 57 Murray Esplanade, Ph: (03) 5480 2237.

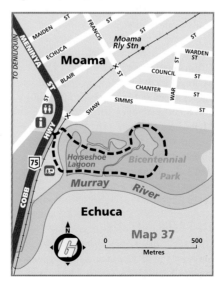

Moama

Moama Rly Stn

Echuca

Horseshoe Lagoon

Bicentennial Park

Murray River

Map 37

0 — 500
Metres

*Motor heaven, Echuca's Holden Museum.*

There is a real sense of history walking the unsealed road around the Port precinct – you can even tour in one of **Echuca Cobb & Co**'s horse drawn carriages (the pick-up point is along the Esplanade). Local lore has it that clouds of dust from racing horses were once common in High St, though the carriage ride today takes a more leisurely pace. Learn about a different sort of horsepower and an Australian icon touring the **National Holden Motor Museum**, 7-11 Warren St, which recounts the historical journey of makes and models through film footage, photos, sport memorabilia and more than 40 restored cars. Souvenirs are on sale for the devoted. Open daily 9am–5pm, Ph: (03) 5480 2033

Located in the old police station and lock-up buildings (1867), **Echuca Historical Society Museum** at 1 Dickson St broadens the account of the river history and local heritage through photos, charts and early records. Open daily, 11am–3pm. Ph: (03) 5482 4225

If you haven't yet noticed the beauty of river red gum timber, stop in at the **Red Gum Works** on the Esplanade where you can see woodturners masterfully crafting recycled and aged timber into works of art using traditional equipment. Their handiwork is available for sale. Open daily, 9am–5pm. Admission free. Discover the entertainment of a bygone era at **Sharps Magic Movie House and**

**Penny Arcade** nearby. Test your strength or have your fortune told on one of the 30 restored penny arcade machines, or watch archival film footage of Australian short films plus such classics as Laurel and Hardy. Entry ticket is valid all day. Open daily, 9am–5pm, Ph: (03) 5482 2361. The pioneering Henry Hopwood can be seen along with wax sculptures of other notables (including British royalty, Australian prime ministers, American presidents, horrible monsters and Madame Tussaud) at the **World in Wax Museum** at 630 High St. Open daily, 9am–5pm. Ph: (03) 5482 3630

The Murray River is home to an array of usual and unusual marine residents that are well-represented at the **Murray River Aquarium**, 640 High St. Encounter Murray pythons, fish, yabbies, shrimps, leeches and the unforgettable 'Ossie', the massive 9.1kg Murray cod. Learn how and why some species disappeared. Open daily, 9.30am–4.30pm, Ph: (03) 5480 7388. Children love the **Echuca Farm Yard** where they can pet rabbits, ducks, chooks, lambs and a barn full of other cute creatures. Located along the Murray Esplanade. Open daily, 9am–5pm. Ph: (03) 5480 7334. For some more challenging entertainment, visit **Oz Maze and Tea Rooms**, cnr Sturt and Anstruther Sts. True to its name, this labyrinth leads you around a map of Australia, where answers to questions must be resolved

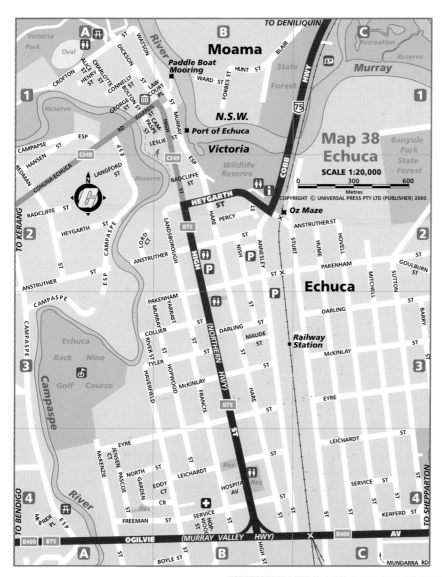

along the way. Early morning visits are advisable on hot days. Open daily, 10am–4pm. Ph: (03) 5480 2220

If you feel the need for speed head to **Silverstone Go-Karts** at Bremner Crt, Moama, which has a Grand Prix go-kart track, video games and BBQ facilities. Open Mon-Fri, 1.30pm–6pm, Sat-Sun, 10am–6.30pm, Ph: (03) 5482 6611. For enthusiasts of a different sort the **Echuca Gem Club** has its collection housed in the Echuca Railway Station, Sturt St, including a special display of gems that change colour under ultraviolet light. Jewellery and specimens are available for sale. Open Sat, 1pm–4pm, Sun,

*Penny Arcade, Echuca.*

public and school holidays 11am–4pm. Ph: (03) 5482 4642

A good drop can not only be purchased from the **Port of Call** historic cellar-door outlet in Radcliffe St, Echuca (open daily, 9am–5pm, Sun from 9.30am) and from **Murray Esplanade Cellars** in the old customs house, Port of Echuca (open daily, 9am–5pm), there is also a local vineyard to visit. **St Annes Vineyards**, cnr Perricoota Rd and 24 La, Moama, offers tastings from grapes grown in the Perricoota District, one of the country's newest wine regions. Open daily, 9am–5pm. Ph: (03) 5480 0099

No mention of Moama could fail to include one of its most popular attractions, the **Rich River Golf and Country Club** at 24 La, Moama. In addition to its scenic and highly regarded golf course, the club also has accommodation. Freecall: 1 800 035 634. www.richriver.com.au. Another recreational feature is the **Moama Bowling Club** at 6 Shaw St which boasts 5 international standard bowling greens, indoor bowls, darts, billiards, gaming facilities and dining. Ph: (03) 5480 9777

Before or after golf or bowls you could stop in at the **Moama Up Country Market**, stocked with local crafts, plants and edible fare. Held at the Kerrabee Soundshell Reserve, just over the bridge, from 8.30am–2pm, 2nd and 5th Sat each month.

*Hot air balooning, Tatura.*

River history can also be found only 25min east of Echuca. Take the Murray Valley Hwy to Kerang and turn off to **Torrumbarry Weir**, 5km past the town of Torrumbarry. The historic weir and its interpretive centre tell the story of the evolution of the control of water flow. Fascinating incidents recounted include a strike called during construction of the old weir that was caused by throwing a tomato. Open daily, 9am–4pm, Ph: (03) 5480 7555. The Weir is situated in the stunning **Gunbower State Forest**, an ideal place for walks or fishing.

## Eildon *Map 36 D5*

In the 1950s when workers on the Eildon Dam project needed a place to stay, Eildon proved the closest site for a town. Today it is still regarded as a base for visiting Lake Eildon — somewhere campers can stock up on supplies and where the less adventurous can find a bed for the night. Take a short drive from Eildon out along the top of the dam's **retaining wall** and marvel at the awesome view from the **lookout** point on the far side.

Six km SW of Eildon on the Goulburn Valley Hwy is **Snobs Creek Discovery Centre**. Run by the Department of Natural Resources and Environment, the trout farm and hatchery breeds fish for release into Victoria's inland waters. A video, displays and an aquarium filled with fish provide plenty of interesting info, though hand-feeding is a highlight for the kids. Open daily, 10am–4.30pm. Ph: (03) 5774 2208

## Euroa *Map 36 C3*

Only 1½hrs from Melbourne, Euroa is a town tinged with history. Among its best known founders is Eliza Forlonge who held Seven Cks station with her 2 sons. She pioneered merino flocks in Victoria using expertise gained in Germany in the mid-1820s. Euroa also knew the exploits of the Kelly gang: on 9 Dec 1878 they broke into a sheep farm, Faithful Ck Station, forced the manager to write a cheque drawn on the Bank of Euroa and, with this in-hand, gained access to the bank and their monies. Today the town is much more peaceful, proud of its woolgrowing traditions, its highly regarded horse-breeding stud farms, and its country lifestyle.

At the **Farmers Arms Museum**, 25 Kirkland Ave, you can see first-hand some of the pieces of the past, including costumes, quilts, farm equipment and machinery. Visitor info is available here Fri-Mon, 1pm-4pm, but for museum appts phone (03) 5795 2010. An impressive array of yarns and locally made bush clothing are logical specialties of the town; however, those who enjoy browsing antiquarian books should also make sure they stop in at **Euroa Fine Books**, 5 Binney St. Open daily, irregular hours. Ph: (03) 5795 1405

**Strathbogie Ranges** are well within reach for those visitors looking for wilderness, signposted via the town of Strathbogie. Picturesque **Polly McQuinns Reservoir** is en route, on Falls Gap Rd, NW of the town.

*Kangaroo reclining at Kyabram Fauna Park.*

### Kyabram *Map 36 B2*

In a region known for its dairying, fruit-growing and canning Kyabram's unexpected specialty is its wildlife. **Kyabram Fauna Park** offers up-close encounters with Australian animals in a natural bush setting to suit both animals and visitors. Wander through the 32ha wetlands — the territory of the waterbirds, where a viewing tower makes bird spotting easy. As you amble around the owl and flight aviaries, dingo and koala houses, you may also run into some of the free-roaming residents including kangaroos, wallabies and emus. Pass the open reptile enclosure on a sunny day and the Aussie expression 'flat out like a lizard' becomes suddenly meaningful. Facilities in the park include picnic areas, BBQs, kiosk and a nearby playground. Open daily, 9.30am-5.30pm. Ph: (03) 5852 2883

Located in the grounds of the Fauna Park is the **Historic Hazelman Cottage** (1867). Theodore Hazelman was born in France in 1847, and travelled to the USA as a cabin boy where he fought in the American Civil War, before moving on to Australia during the 1860s. With his wife, Elizabeth Blunt, and their 13 children, they ran a wheat and dairy farm. Today you can wander around their cottage, and explore the sheds and outhouse, sensing a little of the family's life from the historic furnishings and tools.

### Nagambie *Map 36 B3*

Situated on the eastern shores of **Lake Nagambie** the town's biggest attractions are watersports and wine, which means a visit to Nagambie can be adventurous and active or idyllic and relaxed, depending on your preference. The lake, which is fed by the Goulburn River, was formed when the Goulburn Weir was constructed in 1887. Waterskiing, fishing, canoeing, sailing, swimming and rowing are but a few of the popular pastimes enjoyed by visitors.

The Goulburn Weir is just one of Nagambie's historic attractions. A visit to the **Nagambie Folk Museum**, 344 High St, will help you uncover more of the town's early days. Memorabilia ranges from costumes and coins to farming implements and carriages. Open Sun, 2pm-4.30pm.

Wineries have flourished in the region's moderately warm climate, and include several of Victoria's most notable vineyards. Approximately 8km SW off the Goulburn Valley Hwy **Chateau Tahbilk** has a full-flavoured sense of history — here there are plantings of gnarled vines dating back to the 1860s, some of the oldest in the world. A self-guided tour of the dusty cellars is informative, though the highlight would have to be the tasting. Picnic areas available. Open Mon-Sat, 9am-5pm,

**Winery tour**

Journey aboard **Goulburn River Cruises** and you can visit both Chateau Tahbilk and Mitchelton Wines in casual comfort, enjoying a light lunch or evening meal.

Ph: (03) 5794 2877

**Random House.**

from the Waranga Reservoir and Campaspe Weir. **Random House** (1852) at 22 Bridge Rd is a stately example of how the town's wealthy once lived. This impressive homestead is now a restaurant, tearooms, guesthouse and museum. Open Sun 10am–4.30pm, Wed–Fri for tours by appt. Ph: (03) 5484 1792

One of Rochester's eminent past citizens is cycling hero, Sir Hubert Opperman, better known by his nickname 'Oppy'. Details of his impressive career and other memorabilia can be seen at the **'Oppy' Museum**, located at the railway station. Open Mon–Fri, 9am–5pm, Sat, 10am–12pm. Ph: (03) 5484 1860

### Rushworth *Map 36 B3*

Gold fever brought Rushworth to life back in the 1850s, when this former stopover between the Bendigo and Beechworth goldfields showed its own rich vein. Or, in this case, when local Aboriginal people showed some diggers to gold deposits at Main Gully. Once the alluvial gold was depleted, deep lead mining began in 1872. After the gold rush died down, timber became the natural resource to be mined – forests in the area supported 7 sawmills.

Today **High St** bears testimony to the past periods of wealth. Stroll this National Trust classified street and enjoy the charming architecture, including **St Pauls Anglican Church** (1869), the **Criterion Hotel** (1856), the old **Chronicle Newspaper Office** (1880s) and the **Rushworth Courthouse** (1870s). High Street's central plantation strip is a pleasant place for a picnic or BBQ – its distinctive Victorian era **band rotunda** (1888) provides shade on a sunny day. A **Historical Museum** in the old Mechanics Institute, High St, offers another foray into Rushworth's heritage. Open Sun, 2pm–5pm.

In the state forest, 7km south of Rushworth, is a dusty ghost town where the marks of the gold mining days can still be seen. **Whroo Historic Reserve** (pronounced 'roo') is a study in relics – old mine shafts, puddling machines, and the 25m open-cut **Balaclava mine** which is open for inspection via a walkway.

Sun 11am–5pm, Ph: (03) 5794 2555. For a study in contrasts, **Mitchelton Wines** is located close by, also signposted off the Hwy. Its progressive architecture includes a trademark arrow-shaped look out tower. In addition to its tastings and underground cellars toured by appt, an art gallery and restaurant make this a destination not to be missed. BBQs and picnic facilities. Open daily, 10am–5pm. Ph: (03) 5794 2710

Other notable wineries in the region include: **David Traeger Wines**, 139 High St, Nagambie. Open 10am–5pm daily. Ph: (03) 5794 2514; **Longleat Winery**, Old Weir Rd, Murchison (2km south of the town). Open Mon–Sat, 9am–5pm, Sun 10am–5pm. Ph: (03) 5826 2294; **Twelve Acres** at Bailieston, 16km NW of Nagambie on the Nagambie-Rushworth Rd. Open Thurs–Mon, 10am–6pm (weekends only during Jul). Ph: (03) 5794 2020; and **Plunketts Winery**, cnr Hume Hwy and Lambing Gully Rd, Avenel. Open daily, 11am–5pm, Ph: (03) 5796 2150

### Rochester *Map 36 A2*

South of Echuca on the Northern Hwy, Rochester sits on the banks of the Campaspe, a river named by Major Mitchell in 1838, after one of Alexander the Great's courtesans. During the 1880s irrigation brought stability to the region's farms and today almost 76 000ha of land are under irrigation, supplied by canals

# Rochester's Cycling Hero

From humble beginnings as a rider with the telegraph office, Sir Hubert Opperman (1904–1996), son of a Rochester butcher, achieved fame as a world champion cyclist holding more than 100 distance cycling records. One of his most extraordinary victories was the 1928 Bol D'or race in France where he overcame sabotage — filed bike chains, that inevitably snapped — to claim the world record on a borrowed bike from 10 laps behind. In addition to his celebrated cycling career, Oppy was later a distinguished Federal politician. He died at the age of 91yrs while pedalling his exercise bike at home.

Although the town once supported a school, church and library, the only current reminder of its citizens are the 340 graves in the National Trust classified **Whroo Cemetery**. Follow the signposts to the **Ngurai-illam-wurrung Aboriginal rock well,** or walk some of the trails through the reserve. Whroo has picnic and BBQ facilities and limited camping, though contact the Dept Of Natural Resources and Environment (DNRE) for suitability of camping conditions. Ph: (03) 5856 1434

If you are looking for a place to fish, water-ski or picnic, try the voluminous **Waranga Reservoir**, 6km north of Rushworth on the road to Tatura.

### Seymour *Map 36 B4*
In 1857 explorers Hume and Hovell traversed the Goulburn River at a 'New Crossing Place', replacing Mitchellstown as the preferred crossing on the route between Sydney and Melbourne. That place is today known as Seymour.

Host to an annual **Alternative Farming Expo** (p.206), it is not surprising that one of Seymour's main attractions is the **Capalba Park Alpacas and Tourist Farm**. Children are particularly enchanted by these unusual woolly creatures, though the monkeys, alligators and emus are also popular. Alpaca yarn and products are available for sale. Located on Kobyboyn Rd, 15min east of Seymour. Open daily, 10am–4pm. Ph (03) 5799 1688

For those on the winery trail, **Somerset Crossing Vineyard**, cnr Emily St and the old Hume Hwy, Seymour, is well

worth visiting. Open for tastings Fri-Sun and public holidays, 10am–5pm. Ph: (03) 5792 2445. Its restaurant is open for lunch Wed-Sun, and for dinner Wed-Sat, bookings preferred. Or take advantage of the pleasant picnic area. Continue along the road to Northwood where you'll find **Hankin Estate**, situated at 2 Johnsons La. Cellar door open weekends and public holidays, 10am–5pm. Facilities include BBQ and picnic area. Ph: (03) 5792 2396. **Haywards Winery**, Hall Ln, Seymour, is not irrigated and offers intensely flavoured wines. Open daily, Mon-Sat, 9am–5pm, Sun, 10am–5pm. Ph: (03) 5792 3050

### Shepparton *Map 39*
Undeniably the 'fruit-ful' centre of the region, Shepparton provides a taste of the best of the local harvest along with some surprising diversions into history and art.

From the town's early beginnings water has played a leading role. In 1850 McGuire's punt and inn were built as a crossing point along the Goulburn River, establishing a landmark and focal point for a fledgling town. In the peak of the steam days, and when river levels were high enough, paddle steamers travelled all the way to Shepparton along the river from Echuca. In 1912 irrigation technology transformed the district as Goulburn-Murray waters unlocked the potential of thousands of acres of farmland. Today Greater Shepparton is known as the food bowl of Victoria.

Start your travels tracing local history at the **Shepparton City Historical**

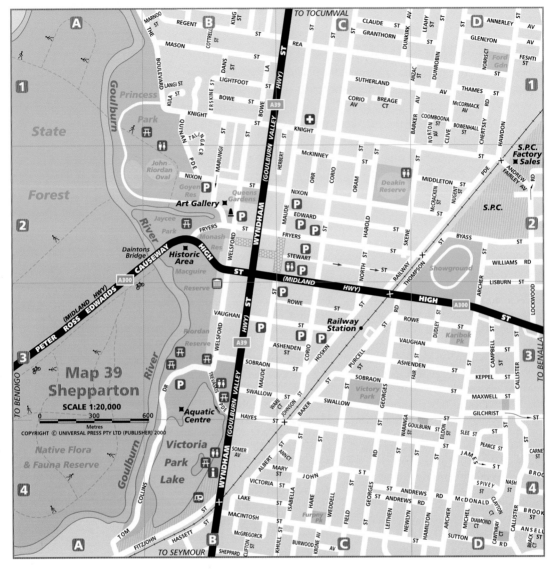

**Museum,** cnr High and Welsford Sts. Fascinating exhibits recount the pioneering days, including the history of the paddle-steamers and Shepparton Preserving Company. Hundreds of artefacts fill in the details of how daily life was once lived. Watch out for the huge post office clock which still keeps time after 100 yrs of service. Open Sun, 1pm-4pm or by request (inquire at the visitor info centre). The true record of the region would be incomplete without visiting the **Aboriginal Keeping Place** on Parkside Dve which tells the earlier story of the local Aboriginal people. Contemporary artefacts, including hand-

carved emu eggs are available for sale. Open daily, 9am-4pm. Ph: (03) 5831 1020

**Shepparton Art Gallery**'s diverse collection of ceramic art makes it a distinctive and important regional gallery. Works range from pieces titled *Sacrificial Platter for Royal Engagement* to a *Trivia Tea Time Table*. Paintings by notable Australian artists including Arthur Boyd, Frederick McCubbin, Margaret Preston and Arthur Streeton are also on display, and a separate gallery is used for travelling exhibitions. Located at the Civic Centre, Welford St. Open Tues-Fri, 10am-5pm, Sat-Sun, 2pm-5pm. Admission free on Fri. Ph: (03) 5832 9861.

*SPC Cannery, Shepparton.*

Visit the galleries and workshops of some of the many local potters.

For an overview of the town and a chance to stretch your legs try climbing 29m to the observation deck on the 77m **telecommunications tower** located in the Maude St Mall. Open daily, 9am–5pm. **Victoria Park Lake** on Wyndham St is

# Factory sales

If you can find some spare room in your car boot, back seat, or backpack it is worth taking advantage of the genuine bargains to be found at the local factory outlets. From soups and fruit to wood stoves and yarn there is reason enough to make a day trip from the city to stock up.

**Ardmona Foods Limited**
Canned and packaged fruit
McLennan Street, Mooroopna
*Open Mon–Fri, 8.30am–5pm,*
*Sat–Sun, 9am–4pm*
Ph: (03) 5825 2444

**Australian Country Spinners**
Knitting yarns
65 Lockwood Rd, Shepparton
*Open Tues–Thurs, 9.30am–noon, 12.30pm– 3.30pm*
Ph: (03) 5821 4522

**Campbell's Soups**
Canned food, confectionery, frozen meals,
Spring Valley juices and gift packs
Lemnos Rd, Lemnos
*Open Mon–Fri, 8am–4.30pm,*
*Sat, 9am–noon*
Ph: (03) 5833 3507

**Furphy's Foundry Pty Ltd**
Cast iron goods, camp ovens, fire grates,
wood heaters etc
Drummond Rd, Shepparton
*Open Mon–Fri, 10am–4pm*
Ph: (03) 5831 2777

**Southern Cross Health Foods**
Health food lines
Huggard Dve, Mooroopna
*Open Mon–Fri, 10am–4.30pm*
Ph: (03) 5825 3421

**SPC Ltd**
Canned foods, condiments, confectionery and jams
Andrew Fairley Ave, Shepparton
*Open Mon–Fri, 8.30am–4.30pm, Sat–Sun, 9am–5pm*
*Factory catwalk tours are available weekdays from*
*Jan–early Apr. Book at SPC.*
Ph: (03) 5833 3777

*Ardmona Kids Town.*

just one of the landmarks visible from the tower. Popular for passive watersports, picnics and BBQs, its lakeside cafe also makes it a pleasant stop for morning or afternoon tea.

Along the Midland Hwy between Shepparton and Mooroopna is a rainbow-coloured adventure playground guaranteed to brighten every child's day. **Ardmona Kids Town** has giant slides (sensibly shaded from the sun), Australia's longest monkey bars, a super-sized sandpit, swings of every shape and size and more. Kids' kiosk, BBQ and picnic facilities are available or take advantage of the a la carte restaurant located on site. Parents are catered for too — the quaint craft shop is stocked with an impressive display of local wares. Admission is free, though gold coin donations are appreciated. Ph: (03) 5831 4213

Just south of Shepparton along the Goulburn Valley Hwy, **Emerald Bank Heritage Farm**, offers a glimpse into farming life from the 1930s. Highlights include hand milking, an animal nursery, and Clydesdale and bullock team demonstrations. Open daily. Ph: (03) 5823 2500

### Tatura *Map 36 B2*

Travel back in time to the outbreak of WWII and the region between Tatura Murchison and Rushworth hosts some special residents — though not by their own choice. WWII internment camps were established here and throughout Australia, to confine 'enemy aliens' — Germans, Italians and Japanese already living in the country — and later, to hold prisoners of war (POWs). The internees story is richly retold at the **Tatura Irrigation and Wartime Camps Museum**, located cnr Ross and Hogan Sts. A video, aptly titled 'Collar the Lot', provides a 30min history; more of the story is recounted through photos, record books and memorabilia. The museum also houses items from the history of the area, including a section on the development of the region's irrigation systems. Open Sat-Sun and public holidays, 2pm-4pm, or by appt. Ph: (03) 5824 1084

Approximately 3km west of Tatura, signposted off the Midland Hwy, is the **German Military Cemetery**. In 1958 the German government established this place as a burial ground for German internees and POWs who died in Australia during WWI and WWII. Bodies of 250 civilians and soldiers were exhumed from cemeteries around the nation and transferred to this site. Adjacent the Murchison cemetery is the **Italian War Memorial and chapel** — paying tribute to 130 POWs relocated for burial here in 1961.

## National and State Parks

### Barmah SP and SF *Map 36 B1*

Approximately 30min NW of Echuca via Moama is the closest entrance to Victoria's largest river red gum forest and a wetland of international ecological importance. Situated on the Murray River flood plain, large sections of the Barmah SP (7900ha) and Barmah SF (21 600ha) are often underwater, creating a rich breeding environment for a complex web of creatures, including around 206 species of birds.

Walking tracks starting from the **Dharnya Centre** on Sandridge Rd, range from a 1.5km **Yamyabuc Discovery Trail** to a 4km **Lakes Loop Track**. The **Centre** has cultural info on the park's Aboriginal heritage, its recreational activities and ecology. Open daily 10.30am-4pm,

Ph: (03) 5869 3302. You can also pick up maps and details on the 5hr **Budgee Creek Canoe Trail**, walking tracks and info on accessibility of roads (flooding can often cause closures). A camping area is located at **Barmah Lakes**, and though remote camping is possible along the Murray riverfront it is important not to camp under river red gum trees as they have been known to drop their branches. Fishing and boating are other popular pastimes (pp.218, 219).

### Lake Eildon NP *Map 36 D4*
When the Goulburn and Delatite Rivers were flooded in the early 1950s to form Lake Eildon, the surrounding land, once cleared for gold and grazing, was able to regrow its native vegetation. Eventually 26 670ha of this land, the combination of Fraser NP and Eildon SP, were declared a NP. Today it is host to a range of wildlife including kangaroos, echidnas, wombats, kookaburras and wedge-tailed eagles, though the park's distinctive attraction is its lake. Camping is available at the **Fraser Camping Ground**, 17km north of Alexandra (sites and self-contained cabins and facilities) and at the **Jerusalem Ck** camping area (sites, fireplaces and toilets), only 10km from the town of Eildon. Permits are required. Ph: (03) 5772 1963. Remote camping, accessible by boat or on foot is available at **Taylors**

Ck, **Mountaineer Inlet** and **Coopers Pt**. Popular activities include fishing, boating, 4WD, bushwalking, swimming and, in some seasons, hunting.

## Other attractions

### Belstack Tourism Complex and Strawberry Farm *Map 36 C2*
Ten km south of Shepparton, at 80 Bennetts Rd, Kialla West, Belstack is known for its fabulous seasonal fruit, miniature golf, and its evening theatre restaurant featuring bushrangers, pirates and mystery nights. Open daily, Sep-end Apr; Sat-Sun, May-Aug, 9am-5pm. Theatre bookings required. Ph: (03) 5823 1324

### Campaspe Run *Map 40*
Located at Railway Place, Northern Hwy, Elmore the Campaspe Run, **HV McKay Rural Discovery Centre** provides an introduction to the agricultural heritage common to much of the region. Attractions include shearing demonstrations, interactive displays, video commentary and farm animals. Open daily, 10am-5pm. Ph: (03) 5432 6646

### Fields Cactus and Succulent Gardens *Map 36 A1*
Head 20km south from Echuca on the road to Rochester, turn right and drive a further 20km on the road to Tennyson

*Lake Eildon.*

**Watery wonderland**
For an excellent introduction to the Barmah SP and its wildlife, take a 2hr **Kingfisher Wetland Cruise**, Mon/Wed/Thurs/Sun 12.30pm. Bookings essential. Ph: (03) 5869 3399

and you'll soon reach an oasis of cacti. Set in more than a hectare of natural garden **Fields Cactus and Succulent Gardens** has 2000 varieties of cacti and succulents, some more than 80yrs old. Peak season to see flowering is Nov–Feb. Open daily for tours at 10.30am and 2pm or by appt. Aloe vera products and cacti are available for sale. Ph: (03) 5874 5271

### Golden Cow *Map 36 B2*

Perhaps the best place to learn about the origins of milk is in Tongala, the heart of dairy country. At the Golden Cow, located cnr Henderson and Finlay Rds, a day in the life of both dairy cow and farmer is brought to life, through an educational video and interactive displays, mini farm and tours of the dairy. A genuine highlight and calcium boost is the huge milkshake available from the cafe. Milking times are 11am, 2pm and 3.30pm, though arrive 30 min before for the full tour. Open daily, 10am–5pm. Ph: (03) 5859 1100

### Puckapunyal Army Base *Map 36 A4*

Only 18km west of Seymour, Puckapunyal Army Base is a community with a difference. Set in peaceful countryside, the traffic signs here warn that tanks and troops might be crossing. Located on the base is the well-regarded **RAAC Memorial and Army Tank Museum**. Indoor displays and outdoor undercover exhibits offer a comprehensive record, from the heritage of the Light Horsemen through to the mechanised counterparts used in present-day conflicts. More than 70 armoured vehicles are on site, plus photos, newspaper clippings, weapons and memorabilia. BBQs and picnic area are available and the convenience facilities are clearly marked 'Tankies' and 'Tankettes' to avoid confusion. Models, books and other army paraphernalia are available for sale at the entrance. Open daily, 10am–4pm. Ph: (03) 5735 7285

## Recreational activities

### Air adventure

Hot-air balloon flights are popular throughout the Goulburn-Murray region. **Balloon Flights Vic Pty Ltd**, Meades La, Euroa, show you a serene view of countryside not easily forgotten and provide a hearty champagne breakfast on landing. Ph: (03) 5798 5417. **Blue Skies Ballooning**, Echuca, take a delightful journey above the Murray valley, followed by breakfast at the historic Port. Ph: (03) 5480 0222

For a more comprehensive view of the Murray River, Barmah Forest and Torrumbarry Weir fly in a small plane with **Echuca Aviation**, based at the Echuca airport, Kyabram Rd. Ph: (03) 5480 7599. Or for a quick rush of adrenaline try a tandem skydive from 10 000–12 000ft. Experience 50sec freefall strapped to an instructor with **Melbourne City Skydivers**, Kettels Rd, Kirwins Bridge, via Nagambie. Ph: (03) 9537 2545 (Melbourne) or Ph: (03) 5794 2626 (Kirwins Bridge)

### Fishing

Sunshine, rivers and plenty of fish make the Goulburn-Murray a promising region for anglers. Although you can fish the Murray River for free, an Amateur Fishing License is required for most inland waters (if you are over 16yrs of age). An AFL is available from the DNRE, Kmart, fishing-tackle shops and visitor info centres. The area's most common catches include silver perch, trout, yellowbelly, redfin, and if you're lucky Murray cod. Contact the DNRE for a copy of their *Victorian Recreational Fishing Regulations Guide* which contains regulations and limits, tips, and even a fish identification section. Ph: (03) 9412 4011

**Fishing on the Murray River.**

# Fun for the young

* Ardmona Kids Town,
  Shepparton (p.216)
* Capalba Park Alpacas and Tourist
  Farm, Seymour (p.213)
* Echuca Farm Yard (p.208)
* Golden Cow, Tongala (p.218)
* Gondwana Canoe Hire,
  Barmah (p.219)

* Kyabram Fauna Park,
  Kyabram (p.211)
* Murray River Aquarium,
  Echuca (p.208)
* Oz Maze, Echuca (p.208)
* Silverstone Go-Karts, Moama (p.209)
* Waterskiing on the Murray River,
  Echuca (p.219)

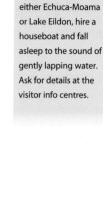

**On the water**

For a unique stay in either Echuca-Moama or Lake Eildon, hire a houseboat and fall asleep to the sound of gently lapping water. Ask for details at the visitor info centres.

*Waterskiing, Lake Eildon.*

## Horseriding

A few of the region's many rides include the scenic trails around the Murray and Barmah SFs. Contact **Billabong Trail Rides**, cnr Sturt and Anstruther Sts, Echuca, Ph: (03) 5480 1222 (AH) or 018 507 828; or **Firedust Horse Riding**, Victoria St, Moama, Ph: (03) 5482 5314.

## Watersports

The Goulburn-Murray region is a great place for watersports. Following are some of the local watersports specialists, though ask at the relevant visitor info centre for a full range of contacts:

* **Brett Sands Water Ski Resort**
  Echuca, Ph: (03) 5482 1851.
  Waterskiing for the whole family.
* **Canoes on the Goulburn**
  Shepparton, Ph: (03) 5852 2736.
  Phone to arrange canoeing on the
  Goulburn River and Victoria Lake.

* **Echuca Boat and Canoe Hire**
  Victoria Park Boat Ramp, Echuca,
  Ph: (03) 5480 6208. Motor boats,
  canoes, kayaks, gas BBQ pontoon,
  boats for up to 10 people. Trips from
  1hr to 2wks.
* **Gondwana Canoe Hire**
  Lot 25, Moira Lakes Rd, Barmah,
  Ph: (03) 5869 3347. Canoes available
  for 1hr to 3 or more days.
* **Lake Eildon Holiday Boats**
  Eildon Rd, Ph: (03) 5774 2107.
  Speed boats and houseboats for hire.
* **Nagambie Lakes Rowing and
  Canoeing Centre**
  Ph: (03) 5794 2444. Boat hire for
  novices and experts.
* **Ski Darrens School**
  95 Murray Dve, Echuca,
  Ph: (03) 5480 2666. Tuition from an
  AWSA accredited coach in
  waterskiing (including wakeboards,
  slalom and barefoot skiing).

# Suggested tours – Map 40

## Heritage trail

### Approximate distance
540km return from Melbourne CBD

### About the tour
One fascinating approach to history is to visit the sites to see and experience past incidents and eras. This tour takes in a number of chapters — from war internment camps and champion cyclists to golden ghost towns and the paddlesteamers. Take the Goulburn Valley Hwy, to Shepparton turning off at Tatura, then head to Echuca where it is advisable to stay at least 1 night, if not 3. Follow the Northern Hwy to Rochester then turn off to Rushworth and take a snapshot of yourself at the Balaclava Mine at Whroo. The return trip offers pleasant scenery to contemplate your discoveries.

### Places of interest
❶ **Shepparton City Historical Museum** (p.213)
❷ **Tatura Irrigation and Wartime Camps Museum** (p.216)
❸ **Port of Echuca** (p.207)
❹ **Rochester** (p.212)
❺ **Campaspe Run, H V McKay Rural Discovery Centre** (p.217)
❻ **High St, Rushworth** (p.212)
❼ **Whroo Historic Reserve** (p.212)

*Houseboat on the Murray River, Echuca.*

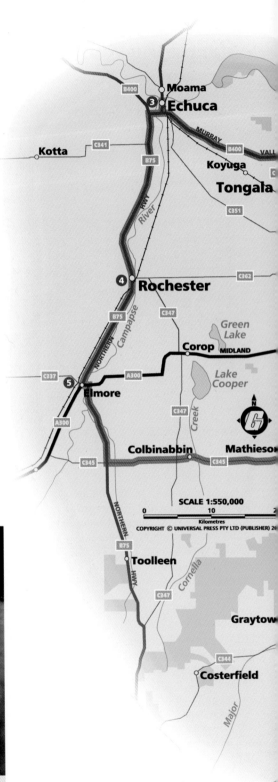

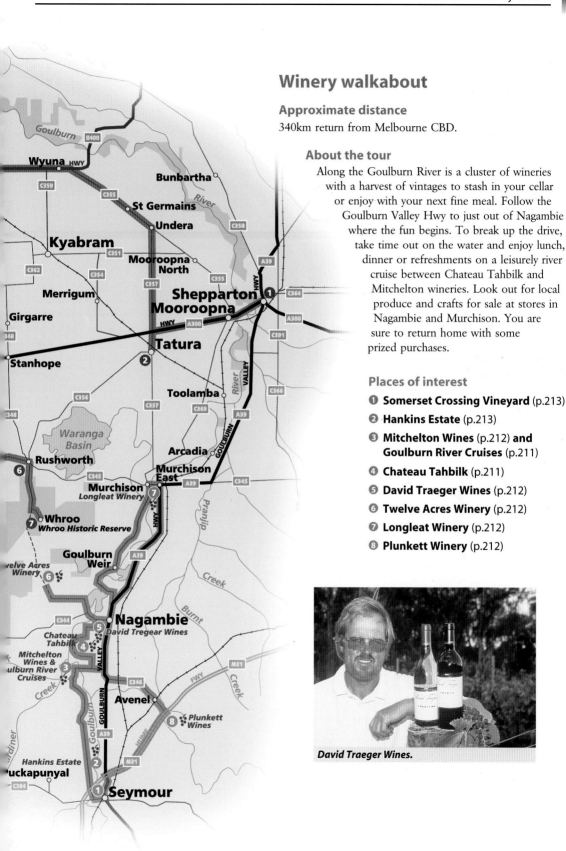

# Winery walkabout

## Approximate distance
340km return from Melbourne CBD.

### About the tour
Along the Goulburn River is a cluster of wineries with a harvest of vintages to stash in your cellar or enjoy with your next fine meal. Follow the Goulburn Valley Hwy to just out of Nagambie where the fun begins. To break up the drive, take time out on the water and enjoy lunch, dinner or refreshments on a leisurely river cruise between Chateau Tahbilk and Mitchelton wineries. Look out for local produce and crafts for sale at stores in Nagambie and Murchison. You are sure to return home with some prized purchases.

### Places of interest
1. **Somerset Crossing Vineyard** (p.213)
2. **Hankins Estate** (p.213)
3. **Mitchelton Wines** (p.212) **and Goulburn River Cruises** (p.211)
4. **Chateau Tahbilk** (p.211)
5. **David Traeger Wines** (p.212)
6. **Twelve Acres Winery** (p.212)
7. **Longleat Winery** (p.212)
8. **Plunkett Winery** (p.212)

*David Traeger Wines.*

Left: **The Balconies.**
Right: **Aboriginal rock painting.**

# The Grampians

Rising out of the flat plains of western Victoria the Grampians etched and rigid ranges bear witness to ages of uplift and weathering, to seasons and cycles past and to bountiful ecosystems sheltered in its shadows.

Today you can enter into this world to discover and explore its limitless beauty — from delicate wildflowers (including 18 species unique to the NP), to soaring peregrine falcons and panoramic mountain-top views. Spend the night in a tent pitched under the stars, hire a caravan or choose from a range of local motels, log cabins, youth hostels, B&Bs and even host farms.

Throughout your stay the Grampians' secrets will surprise you. More than 80% of Victoria's Aboriginal art sites are found here, each offering insight into the lives of the local Aboriginal people of Gariwerd (Grampians' traditional name), a heritage proudly celebrated at Brambuk Aboriginal Cultural Centre. Much is also revealed by touring: there are plenty of trails to hike, back roads to drive, routes to traverse 2-wheeled or 4-legged — there are even cliffs to climb with an experienced instructor. You can spend much more than a week here choosing your own memorable adventure.

## ℹ Tourist information

**Grampians National Park Visitor Centre**
Grampians Tourist Rd,
Halls Gap 3381
Ph: (03) 5356 4381
http://www.parks.vic.gov.au

**Halls Gap Visitor Info Centre**
Grampians Rd,
Halls Gap 3381
Ph: (03) 5358 2314

**Hamilton Visitor Info Centre**
Lonsdale St,
Hamilton 3300
Ph: (03) 5572 3746

**Stawell and Grampians Visitor Info Centre**
50–52 Western Hwy,
Stawell 3380
Ph: (03) 5358 2314

## Must see, must do

★ **Aboriginal Art Tour** (p.228)
★ **Brambuk Aboriginal Cultural Centre** (p.227)
★ **MacKenzie Falls** (p.231)
★ **The Pinnacle** (p.230)
★ **Zumstein** (p.231)

## Radio stations

**Hamilton 3HA:** 98.1 FM
**Horsham:** 98.5 FM
**Stawell 3WM:** 1080 AM
**Hint :** Take along a cassette player or CD player to use when signals are interrupted by the Ranges.

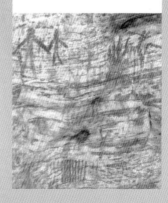

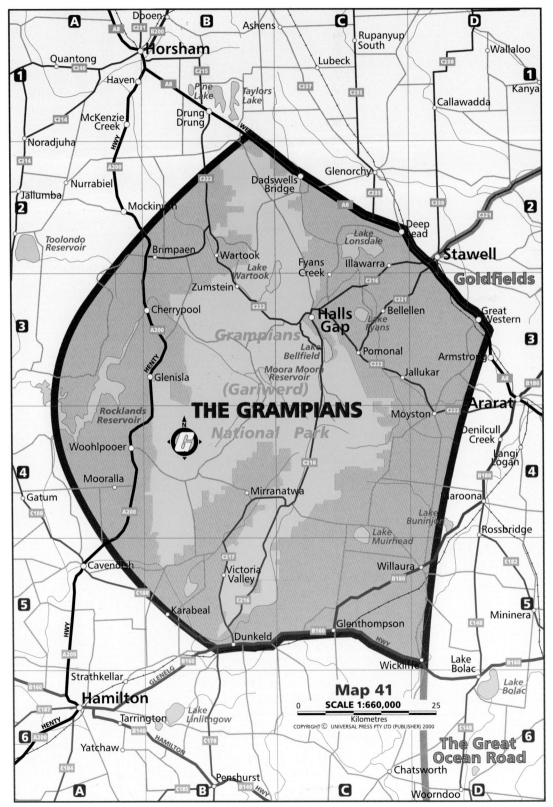

**THE GRAMPIANS**

National Park

*Grampians*

*(Gariwerd)*

Map 41

SCALE 1:660,000

0         25

Kilometres

COPYRIGHT © UNIVERSAL PRESS PTY LTD (PUBLISHER) 2000

## Natural features

The Grampians' distinctive sandstone formations – which comprise the western edge of the Gt Dividing Range – are grouped into 4 main ranges: Mt Difficult (north), Mount William (east), Serra (south) and Victoria (west). One of the state's largest national parks, the Grampians covers 167 000ha, stretching 100km north to south and 50km east to west.

Communities of plants flourish throughout the Grampians – approx. one third of Victoria's indigenous flora is here, including 19 unique species. Plentiful vegetation provides habitats for a population of wildlife that reads like a record book: 35 native species of mammals, over 200 species of birds, 27 of reptiles, and endangered species including the squirrel glider.

To ensure the preservation of the park and its inhabitants:

- do not pick wildflowers or other plants
- do not bring pets into the park (escaped pets become feral pests)
- do stay on marked walking tracks
- do observe fire restrictions
- do remember all native animals and birds are protected
- do take your rubbish home with you

## History

Gariwerd's original custodians were the people of the Djab Wurrung and Jardwadjali Aboriginal tribes. Campfire charcoal dated by archaeologists has established that the people's history here spans more than 5000 yrs, though dating of the earliest samples of Aboriginal art suggests activity as far back as 22 500 yrs ago.

In July 1836 Major Thomas Mitchell, the surveyor-general of NSW, saw a 'truly grand' range of mountains which he promptly named the Grampians, after a range familiar to him in Scotland. Mitchell's glowing reports of western Victoria attracted eager pastoralists; however, within 20 yrs of European settlement, the Aboriginal population was reduced by over 90% through disease, dispossession and massacres.

Rich in natural resources, the Grampians soon supported a variety of industries and services. From the late 1870s pipelines were constructed to supply water to Stawell and later, 3 reservoirs were built. Timber mills and timber tramways operated from the 1870s, mainly in Victoria Valley and at the borders of the ranges, but few establishments survived the bushfires of January 1939.

The earth also yielded mineral wealth: Mount William Goldfield was Victoria's last goldrush site, attracting prospectors from 1900–1902 and in late 1800s Heatherlie quarry supplied sandstone for such notable buildings as Melbourne's Parliament House and Town Hall.

Holiday-makers escaped to the Grampians as early as 1868. Walking trails and tourist roads were built through the 1900s. In 1984 the Grampians were declared a NP officially acknowledging the area as a heritage worth preserving for future generations.

## Getting there

### By road

The Grampians NP is 260km from Melbourne. Access is from the Western Hwy at Ararat, Stawell or Horsham. Alternatively, the southern entrance is accessed from the Glenelg Hwy at Dunkeld. This southern route from Melbourne provides a breathtaking view of the mountain range for the 50km before reaching Dunkeld. Western parts of the park are reached via the Henty Hwy.

**Floral emblem**
In your travels keep a watchful eye for the pink bell-shaped bloom of Victoria's floral emblem — **common heath** (*Epacris impressa*). It flowers spring and winter in the Grampians.

*The Grampians.*

*Dirt track to Dunkeld.*

Ph: (03) 5358 4677. The **Grampians Bushwalking Company's** 4WD Nature Tours take a maximum of 6 passengers on ½- or 1-day or specialised trips including waterfalls, wildflowers and wild nature, classic Grampians highlights, early bird sunrise tour and mountain sunset tour. Bookings at the Grampians Central Booking Office, Main St Newsagency, Halls Gap. Ph: (03) 5356 4654. Refreshments are provided on most tours – details with each operator.

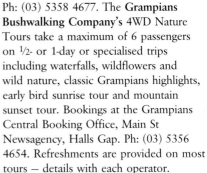

### By rail

V/Line trains or coaches depart daily from Spencer St Stn, Melbourne to Stawell, and a connecting bus service travels the rest of the way to Halls Gap. Travel time is approx 4hrs one-way. V/Line also services Dunkeld. Ph: 13 22 32

## Getting around

Sealed roads within the park are the Grampians Tourist Rd from Dunkeld to Halls Gap, the Mt Victory Rd to Wartook, and the Silverband Rd through the Wonderland ranges. All other roads are unsealed, and though usually accessible to conventional 2WD vehicles it is important to observe any barriers or signs indicating road closures. You can inquire at the NP visitor centre for specific restrictions. 4WDs and trail bikes can use any roads open to the public but must not be driven off-road.

Several operators provide excellent orientation and discovery tours of the NP including **Grampians NP Tours** who offer ¾- and 1-day trips in luxury all-terrain coaches visiting secluded parts of the park and providing local knowledge of pioneer history, wildflowers and wildlife, waterfalls and Aboriginal art sites. Ph: (03) 5356 6221. **Grampians Australia–Wide Adventures** provide ½- and 1-day tours, overnight trips or weekend campouts travelling in a 4WD off-road vehicle. Options include scenic tours, historical tours, twilight tours or the destination of your choice.

## Festivals and events

### Halls Gap Jazz Festival

Lovers of jazz are invited to a 3-day event where good music, good company and good food abound. Beginning as a reunion for traditional jazz musicians, this mid-Feb festival has evolved into a dynamic event with performances playing at various venues around **Halls Gap**. Street parade, impromptu singalongs and workshops are among the highlights.

### Grampians Outdoor Drama

Witness the intrigue and drama of Shakespeare's *King Lear* performed outdoors in one of nature's theatres, **Halls Gap** at Easter time (coinciding with the Stawell Easter Gift, p.183). Ph: (03) 5358 2314

### Grampians Gourmet Weekend

Escape the city to a celebration of food and wine featuring the best of the region's restaurants and vineyards. Held under a huge marquee at the **Halls Gap oval** over a weekend in early May, the festivities include tastings, waiter races, music and other entertainment. Ph: (03) 5358 2314

### Halls Gap Festival of Flowers

Discover an extraordinary array of scents, colours and blooms in this tribute to the floral bounty of the Grampians. Exhibited 4 days during mid-Oct in the **Halls Gap community hall**, wildflowers can be seen in replicas of their natural environments, including heathland, woodland, wetland, fern gullies, and sub-alpine settings. Native orchids are a highlight. Ph: (03) 5356 4437

**Picnic places**
If you are looking for a spot to unpack your picnic basket, try any one of the following: **Central**: Halls Gap Main St, Zumstein, MacKenzie Falls, Lake Bellfield; **North**: Golton Gorge, Mt Zero; **West**: Buandik, Lake Wartook, Wannon Ck.

### *Dunkeld Picnic Races*

Each Nov, in the shadow of Mt Sturgeon, 1000s attend the picnic races at the most stunning race track in the country. As if the scenery is not enough, the friendly party atmosphere — and of course the races — ensure this race meeting has become almost as famous as that other race held in Nov. Ph: (03) 5572 3746

## Main localities and towns

### Dunkeld *Map 41 B5*

Originally known as Mt Sturgeon, after the nearby peak named by Major Mitchell in 1936, this friendly township was later renamed 'Dunkeld' by nostalgic Scottish settlers who likened their location to a town near the Scottish Grampians. Dunkeld, in the foothills at the southern edge of the park, provides a convenient starting point for exploring the walking trails to Mt Sturgeon (593m) and Mt Abrupt (829m) and for discovering some of the local history of a region acclaimed for its superfine wool.

In the old bluestone church at the cnr of Templeton and Wills Sts you'll find one of the most welcoming excursions into local history. Although small, the **Dunkeld Historical Society Museum** is well laid out and well thought out, presenting displays including Aboriginal artefacts, a replica of Major Mitchell's uniform, plus a stump claimed to have been engraved by the explorer, a history of the Australian flag, and exhibits on the local wool industry. Open Sun and public holidays, 1pm–5pm or by appt. Ph: (03) 5577 2213

### Halls Gap *Map 42 B2*

Base camp for exploring the Grampians, Halls Gap is a charming valley-nestled village that was named after C B Hall, the first European to encounter its bushland in 1841. Today visitors stock up on supplies at the town's small but convenient shopping strip or enjoy a casual coffee at one of the local eateries. Others simply take stock of life, awed by the ranges rising to heights of 600m.

Approximately 2.5km south of the town centre is the best place to begin any trip. The **Grampians NP Visitor Centre**,

*Brambuk Aboriginal Cultural Centre.*

signposted off the Tourist Rd, provides an interactive orientation to the park's history, geology, geography and wildlife, plus ideas about where to walk, what routes to take and whether access is even possible in the wetter months. Camping and fishing permits are issued here, maps, books and gifts are available for purchase, and rangers are on-hand to provide sound advice. An excellent short film is shown hourly, offering an overview of the park before your exploration begins. Open daily, 9am–5pm. Ph: (03) 5356 4381

Follow the landscaped trail from the back of the NP building down to the **Brambuk Aboriginal Cultural Centre**. Run by 5 Koorie communities from SW Victoria, the centre offers an introduction

*Aerial view of Halls Gap.*

**Handiwork**
Hand-stencilled rock art at Manja shelter was created by spattering a mouthful of red ochre over and around a hand rested against the rock wall.

to the culture, heritage and experience of the Aboriginal people through exhibits, art, performances and displays. An excellent array of souvenirs is available for purchase at the art, craft and gift shop and the bush tucker cafe offers some unique refreshment. The centre's award-winning architecture is itself a participatory affair, as a pamphlet explains: 'The building ... represents the myths and legends of our area. You are free to interpret it as you wish'. Dance performances and other demonstrations are held throughout the year (often during peak holiday periods), though a regular feature is the **Gariwerd Dreaming Theatre** that runs a multimedia presentation of the ancestral creation stories of Gariwerd. A fee is charged for the theatre and performances. Open daily, 10am–5pm. Ph: (03) 5356 4452. The centre also organises and runs **Aboriginal Art Tours** to the main art shelters, departing most days at 2.15pm. Bookings 24hrs in advance.

A short drive from town, along the Pomonal Rd, is the **Halls Gap Wildlife Park and Zoo**. The 8ha park hosts a diverse range of native and exotic animals including red deer, kangaroos, ostriches

and monkeys. BBQs and playground are located on site. Open Wed–Mon, 10am–5pm. Ph: (03) 5356 4668. Nearby is **Jinchilla**, home of horse-drawn wagons that can be hired for a short ride or for a camping holiday. Ph: (03) 5356 4330. Also located east of Halls Gap on the Pomonal Rd is a venue of the vintage variety. **The Gap Vineyard** boasts as a backdrop the Mt Williams Range; cellar-door tasting and sales and a small but impressive gallery of prints and other works of art. Recently acquired by Mt Langi Ghiran Vineyards, their range of wines consists of not only estate grown, but also selections of Mt Langi Ghiran and Four Sisters wines. Open Wed–Sun, 10am–5pm. Extended hours school holidays. Ph: (03) 5356 4252

If you are looking for a few hours diversion indoors the **Grampians Cinema** at Main Rd, Halls Gap screens the latest release movies during the school holidays and long weekends. Ph: (03) 5356 4341 for session times and details.

### Heatherlie *Map 43*

Much of the Grampians allure relies on rocks — its stunning formations, dramatic peaks and plateaus affording vast views. Rock was also the basis for an important

## Aboriginal Art

Aboriginal art sites discovered in Gariwerd are of great significance. The Djab Wurrung and Jardwadjali peoples' cultures involve a diversity of customs, rituals and traditions, including expression through art. It is believed that the rock paintings served various purposes such as teaching spiritual principles, recording days or visits, assisting in retelling stories and communicating the law of the people.

Painting materials were gathered from the earth: ochre clay (rich in iron) for red and kaolin clay for white were mixed with water to form suitable paints. Some artists applied the pigment with a bark fibre brush, frayed stick or with a finger, while others used

their hand, as either a printing surface or as a stencil.

Throughout the Grampians there are an astonishing 276 recorded rock art sites, and though only 4 are open to the public, a visit to even one of these locations offers privileged insight into an important part of the culture of the local Aboriginal people. Each site is protected from vandalism and other damage by a wire cage. Please treat these places with appropriate respect.

Note: European names were assigned to the rock art sites; however, many are inaccurate (eg: 'Cave of Ghosts' is not a cave and the white figures painted there are unlikely to be ghosts). Use of Aboriginal names is preferred.

## Aboriginal rock art sites

| NAME | MEANING | EUROPEAN NAME | HIGHLIGHTS | LOCATION |
|---|---|---|---|---|
| **Northern Grampians** | | | | |
| **Gulgurn Manja** | Hands of the young people | Flat Rock | Painted bars, emu tracks and hand prints, many made by children | Start Gulgurn Manja car park near Hollow Mountain camp ground. An easy walk: 20–40min return. |
| **Ngamadjidj** | White person | Cave of Ghosts | Unusual because only white clay was used | Start Stapylton camp ground. An easy walk: 5min return. |
| **Southern Grampians** | | | | |
| **Billimina** | – | Glenisla Shelter | Painted bars, emus, emu tracks, kangaroos, and 55 human figures | Start Buandik picnic area off Red Rock Rd. A 15min uphill walk. |
| **Manja** | Painted hands | Cave of Hands | 90 excellent hand stencils, animal tracks and human figures | Start Billywing Pine Plantation car park, 10 min from Buandik picnic area. A 20min uphill walk. |

industry that occupied a page in the area's history. In the 1860s a Stawell stonemason Francis Watkins identified a valuable section of sandstone in the Grampians. After successfully crafting it for use in the Stawell Court House, Watkins persuaded others of the stone's high quality and it became widely used in government buildings in Melbourne.

Quarrying required workmen and in 1886-1887 the business employed about 100 men, warranting some basic buildings and facilities that led to the declaration of the township of Heatherlie. Its life was short lived, however, as need for such stone dwindled and by 1893 the quarry had closed. Despite a few intermittent revivals it eventually ceased completely in 1938, though some stone has been used for essential repairs to such buildings as the Melbourne Town Hall and State Library.

Today you can follow the Parks Victoria **Heatherlie Interpretive Trail** which explains the history of the impressive remnants – stone huts, old machinery, tramway and rock faces from the quarry itself. Heatherlie is located 14km north of Halls Gap along Mt Zero Rd.

### Mafeking *Map 43*

In 1900 reports of a Grampians' gold find by local timber splitters brought 4 Emmett brothers to Mt William eager to lay claim to good fortune. They were not disappointed. On 25 June one brother cycled to Ararat to register their golden discovery. Soon the rush was on and thousands of prospectors arrived from Victoria, interstate and overseas and went to the goldfields – Mafeking, Spion Kop and Ladysmith, names inspired by the Boer War (1899-1902) being fought in South Africa at the time. Shops were built, a school, photographer and hotel became permanent fixtures and the population grew to its peak of 10 000 by the year's end. However, the earth's alluvial yield was quickly depleted and by 1902 many miners had left. Some persisted with sluicing and open-cut mining until 1912 and the town lingered till the 1920s.

Though bushfires in the 1960s burnt down the few remaining miner's huts, you can still get a sense of the site wandering around the Mafeking area or taking *Brownings Walk* (1hr loop). However, beware of the hidden danger of old mine shafts. Mafeking is approximately 70km SE of **Halls Gap**, signposted off the main Tourist Rd.

### Victoria Valley *Map 41 B5*

A broad pathway bordered by abundant beauty, the Victoria Valley lies between the Victoria Range (Billawin) in the west

**Smart fishing**
In the Southern Grampians Aboriginal people dug kms of channels to divert eels into waiting nets. Today fishermen (with permits in hand) head to Lake Bellfield, Lake Wartook, MacKenzie River (at Old Mill Rd), Fyans Ck (below Lake Bellfield) and Moora Moora Reservoir to angle for trout, redfin and golden perch.

*The Pinnacle.*

and Serra Range in the east. Renowned for its river red gum forest – some of the most plentiful in Victoria – the valley also supports heath swampland vegetation and a host of wildlife.

Take the **Victoria Valley Nature Drive**, starting 9km from Halls Gap along the Glenelg River Rd, and discover a hidden world. Along the way you might sight a sacred kingfisher bird, study swamp gums with their ribbons of peeling bark (or other plants that thrive in wet winter conditions on the valley floor), scramble some rocks at **Paddy Castle** and find its micro forest of moss and lichen, or rest beside the tranquil waters of the **Moora Moora Reservoir**. For the intimate details of the drive, purchase a copy of the *Grampians Touring Guide* available from the NP visitors centre.

# Wonderful wildflowers

One of the Grampians most acclaimed natural features is its 'garden' of springtime wildflowers. In season, parts of the park are coloured a spectrum of yellow, blue, pink, white, orange, red and purple. Some species flower at other times of the year, such as the red-tendrilled flamed grevillia which blooms in winter and spring, but during the prolific months of Sep–Oct you can often see small seas of flowers.

Prime wildflower viewing tracks include:
Boronia Peak
Clematis Falls
The Piccaninny Walk
Rose Ck Rd
Sundial carpark
Mt Difficult Rd
Beehive Falls
Roses Gap Rd
Mt Zero
Heatherlie Quarry
Golton Gorge

## Wonderland *Map 42*

The Wonderland Range provides a compact, but spectacular introduction to some of the best views and walks in the NP. Take the Tourist Rd south from Halls Gap, via Lake Bellfield, turn right onto Silverband Rd then stop off at the highlights signposted along the way. **Silverband Falls, Sundial Peak, Venus Baths,** the **Grand Canyon** (Aussie style), the aptly named **Silent Street,** and the dramatic **Pinnacle** are just some of the attractions that make a camera a useful accessory (p.234 for Wonderland Walks).

An essential detour from the Wonderland is along the Mt Victory Rd up to Zumstein. Along the way, **Reed Lookout** offers views more breathtaking than any city skyline and the scenic walk to **The Balconies** passes through enchanting cypress pines stained red with lichen. As you continue your drive further

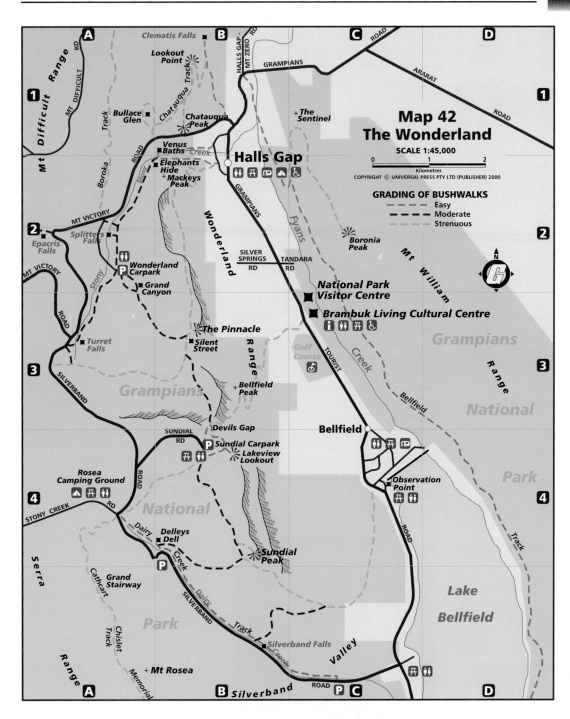

## Map 42
## The Wonderland

**SCALE 1:45,000**

0        1        2
Kilometres

COPYRIGHT © UNIVERSAL PRESS PTY LTD (PUBLISHER) 2000

### GRADING OF BUSHWALKS

– – – – Easy
– – – Moderate
——— Strenuous

west, turn off to see the generous drop of **MacKenzie Falls** before continuing on to one of the state's most famous kangaroo spotting destinations – **Zumstein**. Walter Zumstein, born in Melbourne in 1855, moved to the Grampians in 1910 to establish bee hives and a home.

You can follow a series of plaques along the signposted **Historic Walk** to tour his former property. Zumstein also planted grass to attract kangaroos and visitors today still marvel at the populous mobs that come to the field, particularly early morning and late afternoon. Please

do not feed the kangaroos, though, as our diet is not compatible with their digestion. Kangaroo-safe picnic tables, toilets and electric BBQs are located near the banks of the MacKenzie River.

## Recreational activities

Most companies operate 7 days a week, based on bookings, so please plan ahead to guarantee a place at the activity of your choice.

### Air adventure

Begin the day in spectacular fashion taking in the sights of the dew-wet Grampians from a hot air balloon, followed by a champagne breakfast. **Grampians Balloon Flights** also offer afternoon excursions and can arrange overnight and weekend packages. Ph: (03) 5358 5222 or (03) 5356 4654

Stawell Aviation Services brings the Grampians into breathtaking aerial view, offering flights over the park in a high wing Cessna aircraft. Outback Tours of 3-12 days, charter planes and flying lessons are also available. Ph: (03) 5357 3234. If hovering is more your style you can also enjoy a scenic helicopter flight with **T&M Helicopters Grampians Flyaway**. Ph: 019 685 539 or a/h: (03) 5356 6377

**Grampians Camel Tours.**

### Bushwalking

What can't be seen from the road or by air can often be discovered on foot walking one of the Grampians' lacing of trails.

On short walks make sure you have sensible footwear, appropriate clothing (including warm and waterproof gear for all but very short walks), a hat in summer, a snack (or more, depending on the length of the walk), plenty of water, and a map. It is also advisable to notify someone of your intended departure and return.

Those embarking on longer, overnight treks should also submit a Trip Intentions Form at the NP visitor centre, travel in groups of at least 3, carry a detailed, accurate map and observe any other guidelines recommended by the visitor centre.

### Camel tours

**Grampians Camel Tours**, 6km south of **Pomonal**, offer memorable camel-back journeys of varying lengths, from short or 30 min paddock rides and 1hr rides to a 4hr tour through the forest, including BBQ lunch. All rides are controlled by an experienced handler. Rides depart 8.25am and 2pm, Sat-Sun or by appt. Ph: (03) 5356 6295

### Camping

If you are planning to camp, the following NP campgrounds offer toilets, fire places and picnic facilities, though not all have water. A fee is charged per night, payable at the NP visitor centre and at the campgrounds. Availability is on a 'first come, first served' basis. For those who prefer to camp off the beaten track check first with the NP visitor centre for details of approved bush camping locations. Sites are: Northern Grampians – Plantation (tap water), Smith Mill (tap water), Stapylton (tank water), Troopers Ck (creek); Central Grampians – Boreang (creek, though dry summer and autumn), Borough Huts (tank water), Rosea (no water); Southern Grampians – Bomjinna (creek, though dry summer and autumn), Buandik (creek, though dry summer and autumn), Strachans (creek), Wannon Crossing (creek), Jimmy Ck (tank), Mafeking (tap).

## Exploring

**Grampians Adventure Services** offer outdoor action and tours led by fully qualified instructors, including rockclimbing, cycle trips, canoeing and environmental bushwalks. Located in Shop 4, Stony Ck Stores, Main St, Halls Gap. Ph: (03) 5356 4556

**Action Adventure** live up to their name. You can join them for a morning or afternoon canoe trip on Lake Bellfield, a 3hr night mountain bike ride, or a combination including both plus an introductory abseil. Ph: (03) 5356 4654

## Horseriding

Located on Schmidts Rd near Brimpaen is **The Grampians Coach House**, an accredited horseriding centre offering 1hr, 2hr and ½-day rides for beginners through to advanced riders (max. 8 per group). Bookings essential. Ph: (03) 5383 9255

Five mins from Hall's Gap on Trajul Rd, **Devil's Garden Horse Tours** take riders of all levels of experience on horseback tours through the scenic Devil's Garden SP (max. 10 per group). Children's pony rides are also available. Ph: (03) 5358 2064

## Rockclimbing and abseiling

The Grampians and nearby Mt Arapiles provide an uncommon opportunity to experience for yourself the thrill and challenge of rockclimbing with a qualified instructor.

**Action Adventures** offer a 2hr introductory morning abseil, or a 1-day rockclimbing and abseiling course. Ph: (03) 5356 4654

**Adventure Plus** provide instruction in rockclimbing and abseiling 'tailored to suit your needs'. Climbs mainly at Mt Arapiles. Ph: (03) 5387 1530

**Arapiles Climbing Guides** offer rockclimbing and abseiling action and/ or instruction for beginners through experienced climbers. Climb at the world-renowned Mt Arapiles or at the Grampians by special arrangement. Ph: (03) 5387 1284

**Base Camp and Beyond** provide rockclimbing and abseiling instruction in

*Mackenzie Falls.*

the Grampians for individuals and groups of all levels of experience. Ph: (03) 5356 4300

**The Climbing Company** run ½-day, ¾-day and 1-day climbs for all levels of experience. Most climbs are at Mt Arapiles or in the Northern Grampians. Ph: (03) 5387 1329

# Fun for the young

★ Abseiling or rockclimbing (p.233)

★ Brambuk Aboriginal Cultural Centre (p.227)

★ Bush Detectives Tour with Action Adventure (summer only). (p.233)

★ Canoeing on Lake Bellfield (p.233)

★ Halls Gap Wildlife Park and Zoo (p.228)

★ Night Bike Ride (p.233)

★ Aboriginal Art Tour (p.228)

★ The Balconies walk (pp.230, 234)

EASY = a leisurely walk along flat or gently undulating terrain
MEDIUM = may involve rock hopping and/or long steep sections
HARD = challenging terrain, rock scrambling and/or long steep sections

## WONDERLAND AND BEYOND WALKS

| | | | | |
|---|---|---|---|---|
| Venus Baths | Circuit | 2.3km | EASY | Start north end of Halls Gap camping area. Stony Creek, historic grave of Agnes Folkes, refreshing watery pools, Botanic Gardens |
| Delleys Dell | Return | 5km | EASY | Start Rosea campground or Dairy Ck carpark. Creek, shady tree ferns |
| Sundial Peak | Return | 4.2km | MED | Start Sundial carpark. Woodland, rock outcrops, stunning views of Mt William from lookout |
| Lake View | Circuit | 1.8km | EASY | Start Sundial carpark. Open woodland, Lakeview Lookout, curious rock formations |
| Boronia Peak | Return | 6.6km | MED | Start end of Tandara Rd (b/w Halls Gap and visitor centre). Messmate forest, weathered sandstone, excellent views |
| The Pinnacle *Walk A* | Return | 4.2km | MED | Start Sundial carpark. Rocky woodland, via Devils Gap, spectacular views |
| The Pinnacle *Walk B* | Return | 4.2km | MED | Start Wonderland carpark. Grand Canyon, Bridal Veil Falls, Silent Street, fascinating rock formations, stunning view (some rock hopping and ladder climbing) |
| Turret Falls | Return | 2km | MED | Start Wonderland carpark. Stony Ck, delightful falls (best Jun–Oct) |
| Splitters Falls | Return | 1.5km | MED | Start Wonderland carpark |
| Silverband Falls | Return | 1.4km | EASY | Start Silverband Falls carpark. Tall shady forest, pretty falls |
| The Balconies | Return | 2km | EASY | Start Reed Lookout carpark. Red-hued lichen covered cypress-pine, spectacular views of Victoria Valley from the 'Jaws of Death' |
| MacKenzie Falls | Return | 1.4km | MED | Start MacKenzie Falls carpark. Via view of Broken Falls, steep descent to base of MacKenzie Falls. |
| MacKenzie River Walk | Return | 7km | MED | Start 100m from Zumstein recreation area. Terraced Fish Falls, open forest, breathtaking views, peregrine falcons and wedge-tailed eagles. |
| Mt Rosea | Circuit | 11km | HARD | Start Rosea campground. Forest trail, Grand Stairway, rock formations |

*Mt Stapylton.*

## NORTHERN GRAMPIANS

| | | | | |
|---|---|---|---|---|
| Mt Zero | Return | 2.8km | MED | Start Mt Zero picnic area. Panoramic views of Wimmera plains and Mt Stapylton. |
| Mt Stapylton | Return | 4.6km | HARD | Start Mt Zero picnic area. Marked trail via Flat Rock, Taipan Wall, the Amphitheatre, steep ascent to panoramic views |
| Mt Wudjub-guyan (Hollow Mountain) | Return | 2.2km | HARD | Start Hollow Mountain campground. Diverse woodlands, iron-stained cliff face, rocky outcrops, wind-worn caves and rewarding views |
| Mt Gar (Mt Difficult) | Return | 8.8km | HARD | Start Troopers Creek campground (Roses Gap Road). Steep ascent, rock formations, sweeping views from the highest point in the northern Grampians |
| Beehive Falls | Return | 2.8km | MED | Start Beehive Falls carpark, Roses Gap Rd. Mud Hut Ck, delightful 25m waterfall, stunning springtime wildflowers |
| Briggs Bluff | Return | 10.6km | HARD | Start Beehive Falls carpark, Roses Gap Rd. From Beehive Falls (see above) steep rocky ascent, spectacular summit. NOT SUITABLE ON MISTY DAYS WHEN CLIFF VISIBILITY IS POOR. |

## SOUTHERN GRAMPIANS

| | | | | |
|---|---|---|---|---|
| Jardwadjali (Buandik) Falls | Circuit | 1km | EASY | Start Buandik picnic area. Circuit includes Aboriginal art at Billimina Shelter |
| Paddy Castle | Return | 0.5km | MED | Start Glenelg River Rd near Boreang campground. Scramble up rocks, lichen, interesting 'rock garden' |
| The Piccaninny | Return | 2.4km | EASY | Start carpark 3km from Dunkeld off Tourist Rd. Views of Mt Abrupt (Mt Murdadjoog), Mt Sturgeon (Mt Wuragarri) and Dunkeld. Wildflowers in spring |
| Mt Abrupt (Mt Murdadjoong) | Return | 6km | HARD | Start carpark on Dunkeld end of the Grampians Tourist Rd. Steep winding track to boulder strewn summit, outstanding view |
| Mt Sturgeon (Mt Wurgarri) | Return | 6.8km | HARD | Start carpark cnr Victoria Valley Rd and Grampians Tourist Rd. Woodland track, impressive views of Western district |
| Mt William (Mt Duwil) | Return | 3.5km | MED | Start carpark Mt William Rd. Steep climb to 1168m peak (park's highest), communications towers, views |

*Panoramic views of The Grampians.*

# Suggested tours – Map 43

## Natural secrets tour

### Approximate distance
630km return from Melbourne CBD

### About the tour
Sample some of the best of The Grampians' array of attractions on this 1–2 day tour starting in the southern part of the park. Dunkeld's Museum provides the historical landscape, while the Victoria Valley, Moora Moora Reservoir and Paddys Castle each exhibit a fascinating aspect of the region. Take in the view at Boroka Lookout before discovering a hidden world on a guided night walk.

### Places of interest
❶ **Dunkeld** (p.227)
❷ **Victoria Valley** (p.229)
❸ **Moora Moora Reservoir** (p.230)
❹ **Paddys Castle** (p.230)
❺ **Boroka Lookout** (p.235)
❻ **Secrets of the Forest at Night, nightwalk** (p.233)

*Mackenzie Falls.*

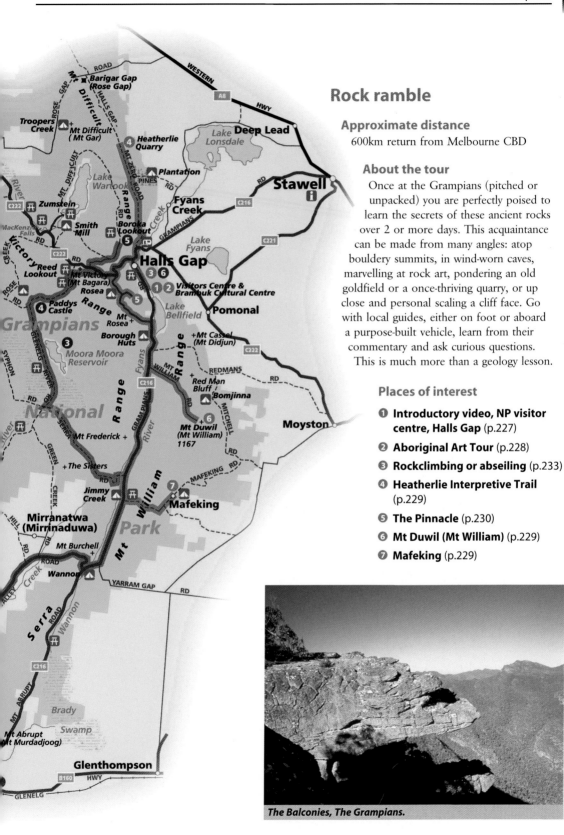

# Rock ramble

## Approximate distance

600km return from Melbourne CBD

### About the tour

Once at the Grampians (pitched or unpacked) you are perfectly poised to learn the secrets of these ancient rocks over 2 or more days. This acquaintance can be made from many angles: atop bouldery summits, in wind-worn caves, marvelling at rock art, pondering an old goldfield or a once-thriving quarry, or up close and personal scaling a cliff face. Go with local guides, either on foot or aboard a purpose-built vehicle, learn from their commentary and ask curious questions.

This is much more than a geology lesson.

### Places of interest

❶ **Introductory video, NP visitor centre, Halls Gap** (p.227)

❷ **Aboriginal Art Tour** (p.228)

❸ **Rockclimbing or abseiling** (p.233)

❹ **Heatherlie Interpretive Trail** (p.229)

❺ **The Pinnacle** (p.230)

❻ **Mt Duwil (Mt William)** (p.229)

❼ **Mafeking** (p.229)

*The Balconies, The Grampians.*

Left: **12 Apostles.**
Right: **Flagstaff Hill Maritime Museum.**

# The Great Ocean Road

In southern Victoria there is a road, not just any winding trail, but a passageway into a region renowned for its expansive blue ocean, towering cliffs, cool fragrant woodlands and lush rainforest. It is a journey via seaside towns where around the very next bend you might happen upon fantastic surfing beaches, cosmopolitan cafes, glow worm gullies or stormy tales of ships wrecked upon treacherous rocks.

The Great Ocean Rd unwinds before you offering much more than a day's diversions: you can learn the mysteries of the wave at a surfing museum, challenge your sense of balance on a board or marvel at art in the midst of a forest. There are safe sandy beaches for building a castle, taking a dip or just relaxing and kids can't be bored in a region where mountain-bike riding competes with whale watching, horseriding and time-travel back to seaports of the past.

Take the road (and your camera) further west to Port Campbell NP via the Cape Otway Lightstation, stark sentinel along a wild and windswept coast. Be among thousands of visitors awed by nature's sculptures — the 12 Apostles and other limestone landmarks etched from the cliffs, then continue, as far as your timetable permits. At the end of your journey you too will know the enchantment and spectacle of this remarkable region.

## ℹ Tourist information

**Colac Visitor Info Centre**
Cnr Murray and Queen Sts,
Colac 3250
Ph: (03) 5231 3730

**Geelong and Gt Ocean Rd Visitor Info Centre**
Stead Park, Princes Hwy,
Geelong 3214
Ph: (03) 5275 5797

**Gt Ocean Rd Visitor Info Centre**
Gt Ocean Rd, Apollo Bay 3233
Ph: (03) 5237 6529

**Lorne Visitor Info Centre**
144 Mountjoy Pde, Lorne 3232
Ph: (03) 5289 2492

**Port Campbell NP Info Centre**
Morris St, Port Campbell 3269
Ph: (03) 5598 6382

**Torquay Visitor Info Centre**
Surfworld Surfing Plaza, Beach Rd,
Torquay 3228
Ph: (03) 5261 4219

**Warrnambool Visitor Info Centre**
600 Raglan Pde, Warrnambool 3280
Ph: (03) 5564 7837

**Websites**
www.greatoceanrd.org.au
www.lightstation.com

## Must see, must do

★ **12 Apostles,**
**Port Campbell NP** (p.255)
★ **Cape Otway Lightstation**
(p.246)
★ **Flagstaff Hill Maritime**
**Museum, Warrnambool** (p.253)
★ **Qdos, Lorne** (p.248)
★ **Surfworld Surfing Museum,**
**Torquay** (p.251)
★ **Whale watching,**
**Warrnambool** (p.254)

## Radio stations

**Bay:** 93.9 FM
**Country:** 94.7 FM
**K-Rock:** 95.5 FM
**3WAY:** 100.9 FM Warrnambool
**3YB:** 882 AM Warrnambool

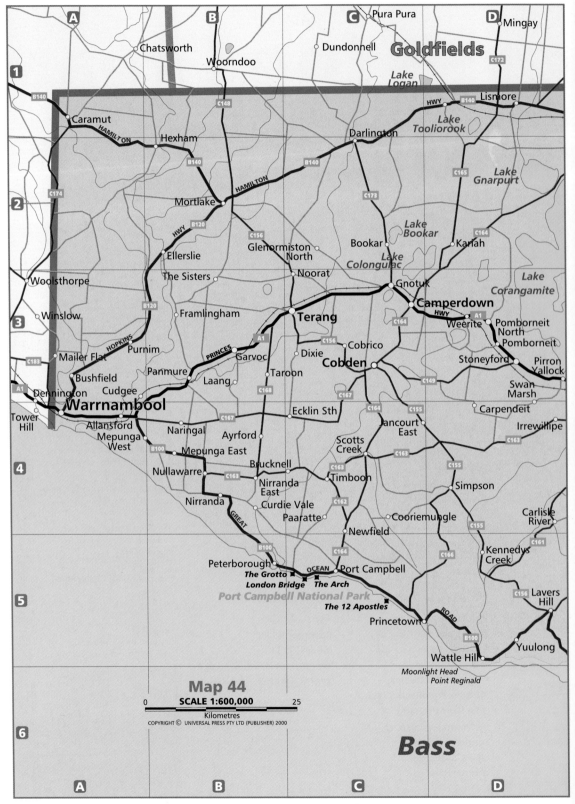

**Goldfields**

Pura Pura
Mingay
Chatsworth
Dundonnell
Woorndoo
Lake Logan
C172
Caramut
HAMILTON
Hexham
Darlington
Lake Tooliorook
Lismore
B140
HWY
B140
C174
C148
B140
B140
HWY
C165
Lake Gnarpurt
Mortlake
HAMILTON
B120
C173
HWY
Glenormiston North
Bookar
Lake Bookar
Kariah
C164
Ellerslie
C156
Lake Colongulac
The Sisters
Noorat
Gnotuk
Lake Corangamite
Woolsthorpe
B120
Framlingham
Terang
Camperdown
HWY
A1
Winslow
HOPKINS
Purnim
Weerite
Pomborneit North
C164
Pomborneit
Mailer Flat
PRINCES
Garvoc
Dixie
C156
Cobrico
Stoneyford
Pirron Yallock
C183
Panmure
Taroon
Cobden
C149
Bushfield
Cudgee
Laang
A1
C168
Swan Marsh
Denning ton
**Warrnambool**
C167
Ecklin Sth
C164
C155
Carpendeit
Tower Hill
Allansford
Naringal
Ayrford
Jancourt East
Irrewillipe
Mepunga West
B100
Mepunga East
Scotts Creek
C163
C163
Nullawarre
C163
Brucknell
C163
Timboon
C155
Simpson
Nirranda East
Nirranda
Curdie Vale
C162
Paaratte
Cooriemungle
C155
Carlisle River
Newfield
GREAT
C161
Kennedys Creek
B100
C164
C166
Peterborough
**The Grotto**   OCEAN   Port Campbell
**London Bridge**   **The Arch**
C156
Lavers Hill
**Port Campbell National Park**
**The 12 Apostles**
Princetown
ROAD
Moonlight Head
Point Reginald
B100
Yuulong
Wattle Hill

**Map 44**
SCALE 1:600,000
0                           25
Kilometres
COPYRIGHT © UNIVERSAL PRESS PTY LTD (PUBLISHER) 2000

*Bass*

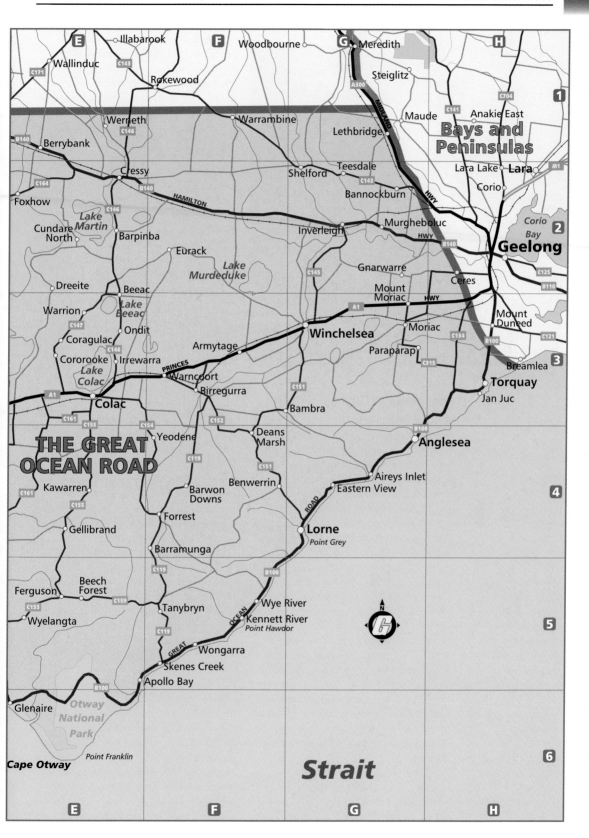

**Great Ocean Road.**

## Natural features

Descriptively named, the Gt Ocean Rd travels through some of Australia's legendary landscapes. Along the coastline, soft limestone cliffs, worn and weathered, continue to be shaped by the sea, a dynamic phenomenon best illustrated at the 12 Apostles and London Bridge.

Vegetation varies with the terrain. From Aireys Inlet to Cape Otway the sandstone peaks of the Otway Ranges provide the perfect climate and conditions for heathlands, but also for fern gullies and mountain ash forests (the hinterland town of Weeaproinah has the state's highest rainfall). Angahook-Lorne SP, Melba Gully SP and Otway NP are declared along the length of the ranges and host abundant wildlife including glow worms, kangaroos and greater gliders. West of Cape Otway, through the Port Campbell NP, mostly hardy coastal vegetation survives the assault of the ocean, though surprisingly in spring 22 varieties of orchids flourish in parts of the park.

Tower Hill, NW of Warrnambool, is a volcanic crater cradling a lake formed when molten rock reached underground water, causing a massive explosion. For thousands of years volcanoes erupted throughout this region and Colac sits at the edge of the world's 3rd largest volcanic plain. From its craters, lakes and coastal cliffs to its rising ranges, on the Gt Ocean Rd you can witness the excitement of past and present geological change.

## History

'I have seldom seen a more fearful section of coastline', explorer Matthew Flinders pronounced as he first rounded the coast near Cape Otway. The most distinctive feature of the region, the ocean has proved to be both friend and foe in the unfolding history of this stretch of the southern coast.

For thousands of years Aboriginal people lived harmoniously with the land, harvesting food from both the ocean and the forests — shell middens are particularly plentiful around Lady Bay at Warrnambool. Though the tale of the *Mahogany Ship* points to the possibility of Portuguese seamen exploring the region in the 1500s, it was not until the 1800s that whalers and sealers made regular landings, decimating the Aboriginal population in their wake.

Sailors travelling the route from Europe via the treacherous Bass Strait knew these infamous waters well. Stormy seas and human error took their toll and shipwrecks occurred with terrible frequency. Construction of the Cape Otway Lighthouse (1848) and other beacons helped ships avert the otherwise unseen dangers. The timber trade that thrived in the Otway forests through mid to late 1800s also relied on ships to transport their cargo to Melbourne as the few existing roads were rugged and often impassable in bad weather.

In 1916 the chairman of the Country Rds Board proposed that this stunning seaside region be made more accessible — his vision was of a tourist road 'of world repute, rivalling California'. Built as a memorial to those who died in WWI the road was constructed from 1918-1932 by more than 3000 returned soldiers and by 'susso' workers (paid sustenance wages) during the Great Depression. The resulting road is a more than fitting tribute.

**Mammoth discoveries**

West of Cape Otway, at **Dinosaur Cove**, palaeontologists have recently discovered fossils of polar dinosaurs equipped to survive cooler southern climates of the past. Learn more on the Web at www.pubs.usgs.gov/ publications/text/ polar.html

## Getting there
### By road
The Gt Ocean Rd can be intercepted at various points along the route, but the most common journey is taken via Geelong to Torquay where travellers continue along the length of the single-carriage road to Apollo Bay, Port Campbell or on inland to Warrnambool (which can also be reached via the Princes Hwy). Note that a few of the detours to attractions may be along partially unsealed roads, some only suitable for 2WD vehicles in dry conditions.

### By rail
V/Line trains run a daily timetable from Spencer St Stn to Geelong where a connecting V/Line coach departs several times a day, continuing the route all the way along the Gt Ocean Rd to Apollo Bay. Ph: (03) 5226 6525 (timetable, locations and bookings). West Coast Rail runs trains from Melbourne to Warrnambool 3 times a day. Ph: (03) 5226 6500

## Getting around
### By coach
Most operators take full-day Gt Ocean Rd explorer tours and several offer an overnight option to make the most of the sights: **Gray Line**, Ph: (03) 9663 4455; **Australian Pacific Tours**, Ph: (03) 9663 1611; **AAT Kings**, Ph: (03) 9663 3377; **Great Sights**, Ph: (03) 9639 2211; **Melbourne's Best Tours** (21 passenger limit), Ph: (03) 9372 8111, or for a more casual affair try **Let's Go Bush Tours**, 2-day adventure (03) 9662 3969

## Festivals and events
### Pier to Pub Swim, Lorne
Evolving out of a 1980 challenge (between Aus Olympic water polo competitor John Fox and surf lifesaver Paul Lacey) to swim the 1.2km distance from **Lorne Pier** to the front of the surf club on main beach, this is now the world's biggest blue water swim. Held early Jan, the event attracts thousands of competitors. Lorne Hotel (the Pub part of the equation) is the venue for post-event celebrations. Ph: 0412 521 577

### Wunta Food and Wine Festival
Summer is the perfect season to celebrate a 3-day fiesta of food, wine, sprawling markets, outdoor concerts, fireworks and fun. Mid-Feb at various venues around **Warrnambool**. Ph: (03) 5564 7911

### Apollo Bay Music Festival
With a growing reputation as a gathering point for musicians, **Apollo Bay** is an appropriate host for a mid-Mar tribute to the sounds of music, including jazz, folk, rock, blues and alternative, plus comedy. Venues vary from hotels and restaurants to marquees along the foreshore. Other events include street parties, markets and buskers. Ph: (03) 5237 6761

### Rip Curl Pro and Quit Women's Classic
An international Easter surf extravaganza, the event attracts the world's best male and female surfers to **Bells Beach, Torquay** to test their wave-riding skills. The action (and spectators) are mobile, moving to whichever beach offers the best waves. Ph: (03) 5261 2907

## Main localities and towns
### Aireys Inlet *Map 44 G4, 45*
A charming sea-scented township, Aireys Inlet was named after John Eyrie, a founding citizen who settled here during the 1840s. Once the terminus for Cobb & Co's coach service from Geelong, visitors today still choose to stop here to explore the rock pools, marvel at the

**Seaside volcanoes**
From Split Pt, Aireys Inlet watch out for Eagle Rock (to the east) and Table Rock (to the south). These two **volcanic rock stacks** rising out of the ocean are evidence of underwater volcanoes active in the far distant past.

*Split Point Lighthouse.*

*Surfing class, Anglesea.*

**Kanga golf**
A large population of grey kangaroos make friendly spectators at the **Anglesea Golf Course**. During spring and summer you might be lucky enough to see a joey peer out of its mother's pouch to watch the golfing action.

oceanic monuments or trek into the peace of the surrounding bush.

The town's most visible landmark is affectionately known as the White Lady. Perched out on Split Pt (so named because from a sailor's vantage the rock appears split away) the **Split Pt Lighthouse** (1891) is 65m above sea level and has a fully automatic light visible 30km out to sea. An essential investment during the shipping era, the lighthouse cost £8057 to construct. To better acquaint yourself with this patch of coastline and its vegetation, take the 300m **Split Pt Circuit Walk** or for some light refreshment stop in at the **Lightkeepers Stables** which have been converted into a tearoom and gallery.

Just before you return to the Gt Ocean Rd, take a left turn off Lighthouse Rd, following the signposted directions to the **Bark Hut**. Built from timber, brick and bark, this historic accommodation is a replica of the home of Martha and Thomas Pearce who first took residence back in 1852. The original hut survived more than 125yrs before it was destroyed in the Ash Wednesday fires. The hut is not the only memorial to the Pearce's — Thomas and Martha's **grave** overlooks the sea, marked by a cairn about 100m from Split Pt Lighthouse.

Though scouring the **rockpools** on the beach near Painkalac Ck is one popular pastime, Aireys Inlet is also a base for bushwalks, bike riding and horse treks through the northern section of the

Angahook-Lorne SP. Accessible off the Gt Ocean Rd, along the unsealed Bambra Rd (4WD necessary in wet weather), this section of the 21 340ha park is known for its flowering heathlands which are stunning in spring and early winter. **Distillery Ck Picnic Ground** is the starting point for a range of walks including the 1.7km **Distillery Ck Nature Trail**, the 5km **Ironbark Gorge Walk** , and — for the more ambitious — the 12km **Currawong Falls Walk**. Car-based camping is permitted at Hammonds Rd, and though there are no facilities, fires are permitted here except when prohibited by summer fire restrictions. No booking required.

Local artists here have flourished, inspired by the contrasts of ocean and bush. Stop in at **Eagles Nest Fine Art Gallery**, 42 Gt Ocean Rd to appreciate or purchase paintings, pottery, hand-blown glass or sculptures. Open daily summer and school holidays; Fri–Mon, May–Nov, 9am–5pm. Ph: (03) 5289 7366

### Anglesea *Map 44 G4*

A blend of bush and sandy beaches, Anglesea is a destination favoured by families. Many choose to lay down a beach towel and build a monumental sand-castle at either **Main beach** or **Pt Roadknight** — both are patrolled during the summer. Anglesea River is another focal point for fun — **Anglesea Paddle Boats** has paddleboats, aqua bikes, mini motorboats and canoes for hire, Ph: (03) 5261 3235. Picnic facilities nearby. At the end of River Reserve Rd, off Noble St is **Coogoorah Park**. During the 1983 Ash Wednesday bushfires the peat under the west riverbank topsoil caught fire and couldn't be easily extinguished. To prevent spot fires spreading from the smouldering peat, the Anglesea River was extended via a series of waterways, cutting off the fires and forming a natural sanctuary around the land. That parkland today incorporates picnic and BBQ areas, adventure playground, fishing waters and walking trails linked by bridges and elevated platforms.

Contrasting with the popularity of Anglesea's bushwalking, bike riding and other nature-based activities is the 150 megawatt **Alcoa of Australia Ltd power stn**. The plant – opened in 1965 – provides 40% of the electrical energy needed by the Pt Henry Smelter in Geelong. Although closed to the public, you can catch a glimpse of the operations from two viewing sites: at the Coal Mine Rd lookout and from the plant entrance.

For the artistically inclined **Melaleuca Gallery** offers stunning souvenirs or gifts from the gallery, 121 Gt Ocean Rd. Open Sat–Sun, 11am–5.30pm. Ph: (03) 5263 1230. **Surfcoast Arthouse and Info Centre** is more informal, displaying and selling members' work and operating as a venue for classes. During the summer months kids can paint pictures to decorate their holiday house. Ph: (03) 5221 0406. **Anglesea Cinema**, McMillan St, screens movies regularly during the summer months.

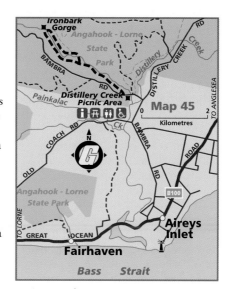

### Apollo Bay *Map 44 F5*

Listen for the sound of a sea shanty as you pass the cypress trees leading into Apollo Bay. This coastal town has the feel of a fishing village – its crescent-shaped bay curves round to the main wharf where today the local fishing fleet is moored, protected from storms by a breakwater.

Whaling opens the chapter on the town's early history. For 7yrs from 1840–1847 the Henty family from Portland ran a whaling station on the site of the present-day Apollo Bay golf course.

Trade soon turned to timber and by the 1860s there were more than 1000 cutters operating: logs were dragged down to the beach and floated out to anchored ships which transported loads to Melbourne. Forests are now regarded as environmental assets that should only be harvested at a sustainable rate. Fishing has again taken prominence, but now the staple catch is abalone, shark and crayfish. Buy some local fresh fish at the **Fisherman's Co-Op** near the pier, or take a 1hr chartered scenic cruise with **Apollo Bay Boat Charter**. Ph: (03) 5237 6214

To further orient yourself to the town and the surrounding Otway region, stop in at the outstanding **Visitor Info Centre**

*Pictureseque Apollo Bay.*

located along the foreshore. Exhibits
explore Wet and Lush Forests, Past and
Present People, Vast and Wild Coasts and
the Gt Ocean Rd. A push-button model of
the region highlights the best places to
picnic and the centre is well-stocked with
brochures. Local history is further
unveiled at the **Old Cable Station
Museum**, 1.6km east of Apollo Bay on
the Gt Ocean Rd. This quaint building
was once the entry point for a very
important underwater telephone cable –
the first connecting Victoria and
Tasmania. Photos, memorabilia and news
cuttings capture the ceremony of that
cable opening, as well as other significant
factors affecting the development of the
region. Open Sat-Sun, school and public
holidays, 2pm-5pm. Ph: (03) 5237 6505.
For an uncommon collection, stop in at
the small one-roomed **Bass Strait Shell
Museum** at 12 Noel St. Cases are lined
with a huge variety of shells, including
rare, local and overseas specimens. Sea
shell jewellery and ornaments for sale.
Open daily, 9am-8pm. Ph: (03) 5237 6395

   **Apollo Bay Community Market Inc**
operate Sat mornings, 8.30am-1.30pm on
the foreshore selling a wonderful
selection of fresh produce and local
crafts. Ph: (03) 5237 6243. During
summer you can escape the sun and take
in a movie at the temporary cinema set
up in the local hall, cnr Gt Ocean Rd and
Nelson St. Most visitors prefer the
outdoors, though, taking time to tour
some of the scenic highlights. **Paradise
Valley** picnic area, 8km west of Apollo
Bay comes highly recommended, but for
breathtaking lookouts take your camera
to any of the following: **Marriner's
Lookout**, 1km from the town off
Marriner's Lookout Rd; **Crows Nest
Lookout**, north off Tuxion Rd; or **Mt
Sabine Lookout**, 15km on Forrest Rd
(2nd highest point in Otways).

   Take a short drive to the **Otway Herb
Nursery and Cottage Garden**, Biddles Rd,
Apollo Bay (via Wild Dog Rd), where you
will discover a collection of herbs, roses,
coastal and rare plants as well as fresh
and dried herbal products. Open daily,
9am-5pm. Ph: (03) 5237 6318. For those
with a green thumb, copies of Geelong

*Cape Otway Lighthouse.*

Otway Tourism's *Garden Lovers' Guide* is
available at visitor info centres.

### Cape Otway *Map 44 E6*
In 1937 the construction of the Otway
Lighthouse Rd provided inland access to
a vital outpost on the remote Cape
Otway Cliffs – the road is still travelled
by visitors today as they search out the
history of **Cape Otway Lighthouse**, the
oldest standing lighthouse on the
Australian continent. Signposted off the
Gt Ocean Rd, along a 12km unsealed
track is the 21m sandstone tower built in
1848 to warn the heavy traffic of ships of
the unseen dangers along this treacherous
coastline. Tragic loss of life was the
catalyst for its construction, after 200
people died in the shipwreck of the *Nova*
and another 400 people in the wreck of
the *Cataraquai*. Guided tours of the
historic lighthouse and precinct operate
daily between 9am-5pm. Sleep safe from
the seas in the former **lighthouse keeper's
house**, now a uniquely situated place to
stay. Ph: (03) 5237 9240. Trails leaving
from the lighthouse entrance include the
500m walk to the **lighthouse lookout** and
a 1km trek to the **lighthouse cemetery**.

   Take Blanket Bay Rd off Otway
Lighthouse Rd to **Blanket Bay**, the
former offloading site for ship-delivered
supplies for the Cape Otway Lighthouse.
Bushwalks, picnic and camping facilities
are available in this area of the NP,

*Otway herb Nursery
and Cottage Garden.*

though if you are planning to camp during summer you will need to make a booking. No 2WD access in winter. Ph: (03) 5237 6889. If you are keen to ride a horse through this beautiful parkland, nearby **Bimbi Park Trail Rides and Caravan Park** can oblige (p.259).

### Colac *Map 44 E3*

Before heading back to the coastal road you could cut across the Otways to explore the contrasting countryside around the hinterland township of Colac. The town's name perhaps originates from the Coladjin Aboriginal tribe who once lived here along the shores of Lake Colac. Situated on the eastern edge of the world's 3rd largest volcanic plain Colac's landscape has been shaped by eruptions – Lake Colac is itself a water-filled crater and agriculture in the surrounding district has flourished in the rich volcanic soils.

Lake Colac is a popular venue for all sorts of watersports, from rowing, yachting, water skiing and swimming to fishing for a catch from its ample stocks of redfin and perch. On the banks of the lake, along Fyans St, are the picturesque **Colac Botanic Gardens**. Redesigned by famed director of Melbourne's Royal Botanic Gardens, botanist William Guilfoyle, the gardens boast more than 1000 plant specimens and several Significant Trees registered by the National Trust. The unique design includes a ring road accessible by motorists as well as pedestrians. BBQs, picnic facilities and playground are located on the foreshore. Ph: (03) 5232 9400. Enjoy public art outdoors at **Barongarook Ck Reserve Sculpture Park**, located off the Princes Hwy, just over the bridge. The sculptures were originally placed in the park in 1984–1985 and do show signs of ageing. Before departing, stop in for a sampling of local history at the **Colac Historical Centre**, adjacent the library in Gellibrand St. Open Thur, Fri, Sun, 2pm–4pm. Or head out to **Red Rock** lookout and picnic area, signposted 5km west of Colac, where you can take a long look out to the lakelands.

### Fairhaven, Moggs Creek and Eastern View *Map 44 G4, 45*

South of Aireys Inlet, the Gt Ocean Rd winds its way through a peppering of small seaside towns that fringe long stretches of sandy beach. En route to **Fairhaven**, an astonishing ensemble of homes cling to the cliffs, the handiwork of some creative and versatile architects. **Fairhaven Beach**, a 6km slice, is the longest along the Gt Ocean Rd though it is best to head to the **Surf Life Saving Club** at the eastern end – the club patrols the beach during the summer months. Just nearby, **Moggs Creek** provides some spectacular aerial displays: when the conditions are right, **hang gliders** launch from the cliffs, gliding down to the beach below. For a pleasant place to picnic, turn north into Old Coach Rd and left into Boyd Ave, till you reach **Moggs Creek Picnic Reserve**. Picnic tables, wood BBQs and walks make this a popular stopping point. For those tracing the historic trail, **Eastern View** is the site of the **Memorial Archway**, the official Gt Ocean Rd archway and a monument to WWI servicemen.

### Johanna and Lavers Hill *Map 44 D5*

Returning to the Gt Ocean Rd, the route passes through the fertile dairy farming

*Colac.*

**Largest lake**
North-west of Colac, **Lake Corangamite** is Victoria's largest inland lake, covering 23 300ha and with a shoreline of 150km. Feeding ground for pelicans, ibis and other waterbirds, the lake is 3 times saltier than sea water.

**Fishy tales**

The Surf Coast's biggest shore-fishing surf rod catch was an 18kg mulloway fish. Caught off Pt Addis Back Beach it took 4hrs to land. Pick up a copy of Surf Coast Shire's free *Torquay to Lorne Fishing Guide* for all the best locations and likely catches.

flats of Horden Vale, followed by a coastal interlude from the **lookout** at Glenaire, then rises up into the town of Johanna. Take Red Johanna Rd south for 4.5km via its trademark red coloured dunes to **Johanna Beach**, renowned for its dramatic surf, spectacular for experienced board riders but unsuitable for swimming. Perched at the highest point along the Gt Ocean Rd, Lavers Hill was once known for its place in the timber trade, though today it is known for its Devonshire teas. Only 7km west of Lavers Hill is **Melba Gully SP** a temperate rainforest retreat named after Australia's opera diva Dame Nellie Melba. In addition to its picnic area, blackwoods and ferns, the park is home to the **Big Tree**, a gigantic messmate more than 300yrs old, boasting a 27m girth. Star night-time performers in the forest are the **glow worms** — the larvae of small fungus gnats that gather in clustered colonies emitting a blue-green glow to lure their prey into sticky webs. Be aware that noise, touch and direct torchlight will disrupt their show. Inquire at the visitor info centre for glow worm tours of the park operating during the holidays.

**Lorne *Map 44 G4***

For Captain Louitit and the crew of *Apollo*, Lorne's idyllic bay provided

welcome shelter on their wool-carting journeys from Portland to Melbourne. These forays of the 1840s earned the captain a place on the map and today this fashionable coastal town is fronted by Louitit Bay, a preferred place for swimming. Local timber attracted a thriving industry during the late 1800s, but when the Gt Ocean Rd reached the region this previously isolated ocean glade was transformed into a holiday haven. Uncover the rest of the story, including the how, who, when and why of the construction of the Gt Ocean Rd at the **Lorne Historical Society**, 59 Mountjoy Pde, Sat–Sun, 1pm–4pm.

Today Lorne is dressed in cosmopolitan style — street cafes, boutique shops and fine restaurants line **Mountjoy Pde**, though all moods are catered for and you can still buy fish and chips to enjoy on the tree-lined foreshore. For an art or dining experience with a difference, take Otway St to the roundabout, then follow Allenvale Rd to no. 35 where you'll discover the remarkable **Qdos**. Set in an ever-changing sculpture garden in the Otway forest, this excellent arts complex exhibits works by national and international artists showcasing works crafted in a wide range of media, on a 2–3 week rotation. Sat night is renowned for **twilight hour concerts** featuring anything from folk, blues and middle eastern music to classical or jazz. Art workshops are also popular and during summer the **Creative Fun for Kids** program provides 2hrs of art and craft including mosaic making and claywork. Ph: (03) 5289 2182 (bookings). Open daily, 10am–6pm; closed Wed, non-holiday period. Ph: (03) 5289 1989. Also up and running in the holiday season is the **Lorne Movie Theatre**, cnr Mountjoy Pde and Grove Rd. Ph: (03) 5289 1272

Poet Rudyard Kipling visited Lorne in the 1890s and in his poem *Flowers*, paid tribute to one well-loved landmark: 'Gathered where the Erskine leaps, Down the road to Lorne'. From the Otway/George Sts roundabout, **Erskine Falls** is signposted off Erskine Falls Rd, along a route passing through fragrant

*Sun-bathed Lorne.*

*The fallen London Bridge.*

bushland. Some visitors travel no further than **Blanket Leaf Picnic Area**, popular for walks, though many take their packed picnics straight to the falls. Wooden viewing platforms offer one aspect of the 30m cascading wall of water, but to feel the spray, follow the stairs down to the base of the waterfall. Downstream are some additional sights: **Straw Falls** (approx 400m from Erskine) and **Splitters Falls** (2km). On the return trip to Lorne the **Erskine Falls Tearoom** provides welcome refreshment. For an alternative diversion take George St to **Teddy's Lookout**, where from a height you can watch motorbikes lean into the curves of the Gt Ocean Rd, framed against a backdrop of blue ocean. Picnic tables and a shady rotunda are located near the lookout. Around Lorne there are more than 50km of walking trails through the Angahook-Lorne SP. Pick up pamphlets from the visitor info centre and choose from options including **Kalimna Falls Walk** (8km), **Sheoak Falls Walk** (8.6km), a 1hr coastal **Shipwreck Walk** or various **overnight treks**. Car-based camping in the sth section of the SP is permitted at **Allenvale Mill, Sharps Track, Jamieson Track** and **Wye River Rd**, and a walker-only campsite is located on the **Cora Lynn Track**, though there are no facilities and fires are not permitted. Ph: 13 1963 for *Park Notes*.

### Moonlight Head *Map 44 D6*

One windswept stormy night in 1802, explorer Matthew Flinders, aboard the *Investigator*, peered out to the headlands just as moonlight broke through the clouds momentarily lighting the rugged cliffs in view. Affected by that moment he named the site Moonlight Head. Today this small coastal settlement situated between Lavers Hill and Princetown still carries an aura of drama. Near the cnr of the Gt Ocean Rd and Moonlight Head Rd is the privately-owned old **Wattle Hotel**, at one time a thriving guesthouse for racegoers attending the local horse running event and a stopover along the coastal coach route.

Take the unsealed road down to Moonlight Head and turn right at the forked junction till you reach a car park where a path leads down to **Wreck Beach**. Embedded in the rocks along the foreshore are the huge anchors of two ill-fated ships, the *Marie Gabrielle* (sank in 1869) and the *Fiji* (1891), silent witnesses to the graveyard of ships along these shores. Follow the left route at the junction to another burial ground where the headstones at **Moonlight Head Cemetery** record burials from 1906–1975.

### Port Campbell *Map 44 C5*

Though Captain Alexander Campbell (a whaler) took shelter from a storm in Port Campbell bay back in the 1840s, the town saw no real permanent settlement till the 1870s when salvaged shipwrecks, sea-trade and fishing soon brought this small village to life. Today you can uncover that history at several attractions. The **Loch Ard Shipwreck Museum** at 26 Lord St, houses artefacts from the *Loch Ard* and 5 other important wrecks, including the *Schomberg*, captained by the notorious Bully Forbes who boasted 'Hell or Melbourne in 60 days' (the ship was wrecked while he was below deck entertaining female passengers). The shop area offers an excellent range of suitable

**Historic trail**
Discover the tales of maritime disasters following the **Historic Shipwreck Trail** from Moonlight Head to Port Fairy. Signposts along the Gt Ocean Rd lead to coastal plaques recounting the stories of 25 shipwrecks caused by wild weather, bad judgment and even foul play.

**Fairy penguins**
During low tide at
**Thunder Pt Coastal
Reserve**, Warrnambool
you can cross carefully
to Middle Is to catch
sight of a colony of
fairy penguins. Stay on
the designated paths
and allow time before
the tide turns to return
back to the beach.

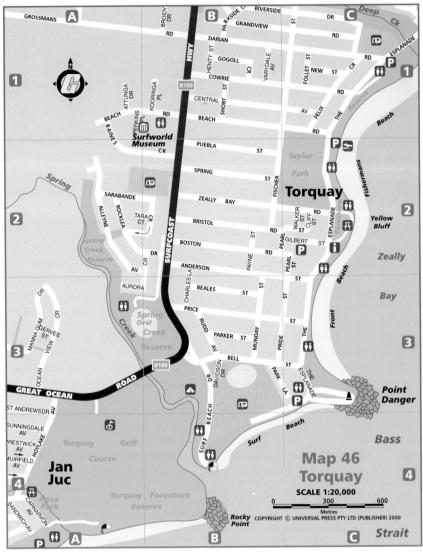

**Map 46**
**Torquay**
SCALE 1:20,000
0        300        600
Metres
**Rocky Point** COPYRIGHT © UNIVERSAL PRESS PTY LTD (PUBLISHER) 2000

souvenirs. Open daily 9am–6.30pm, Ph:
(03) 5598 6463. Local heritage has also
been preserved in photos, records and
other memorabilia at the **Old Hall
Gallery**, next door to the Port Campbell
Hotel on Lord St. Open Wed and
Sat–Sun, 12pm–4pm.

Take time to explore Port Campbell's
natural features on the 1.5hr **Discovery
Walk** starting from the steps at the western
end of Port Campbell beach. West of the
town is **The Arch**, a landform naturally
eroded into the headland at Pt Hesse.
Nearby, **London Bridge** was once a natural
double-arched walkway out to the ocean
until 15 Jan 1990 when the first section

collapsed unexpectedly, stranding 2 tourists
who were later rescued by helicopter.

**Torquay *Map 46***
Don't be deceived by Torquay's relaxed
pace and casual, sun-soaked demeanour.
Although there is plenty of fun and
frivolity on offer, this town takes its
surfing very seriously. A popular picnic
destination as early as the 1860s, the
region's surf potential was probably
discovered in 1949 by surfers Vic Tantam
and Owen Yateman. Today thousands
make their personal pilgrimage to the surf
at Torquay, as beginners, or among the
many devoted.

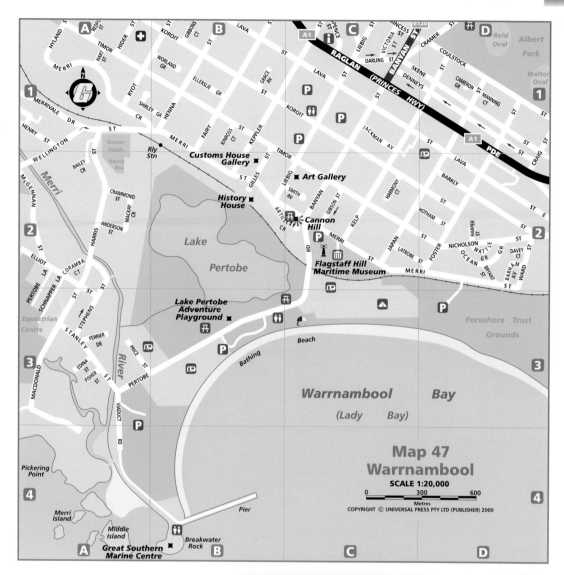

Map 47
Warrnambool
SCALE 1:20,000

0        300        600
Metres
COPYRIGHT © UNIVERSAL PRESS PTY LTD (PUBLISHER) 2000

There is no better introduction to surfing life and legends than that presented by the **Surfworld Surfing Museum**. Located at Surf City Plaza on Beach Rd, the museum is a celebration of our attempt to harness the energy of waves. The story begins with the physics of the wave's life, birth and death, continues through ancient board riding, via the history of the Hawaiian Shirt, through to today's cult of the surf. Interactive videos and displays trace the evolution of the equipment and tell the tales of the masters enthroned in the Hall of Fame. There are plenty of hands-on exhibits, including a wave making

*Surfworld Surfing Museum.*

**Miraculous memorabilia**

Washed ashore from the shipwreck of the Loch Ard was a wooden packing crate containing a 150cm porcelain peacock, seen today at **Flag staff Hill Maritime Village** (p.253).

machine and a paddling fitness test. Art on display is for sale. Open Mon–Fri, 9am–5pm, Sat–Sun and public holidays, 10am–4pm. Ph: (03) 5261 4606. You can also inquire here about **surfing lessons** (p.259), or take in a movie at the **summer cinema** operating during late Dec and Jan. Ph: (03) 5255 5666

Adjacent to the museum is a sand-coloured shopping strip that assembles outlets for all the famous brand names in the surfing gear business – Rip Curl, Quicksilver and Billabong, to name a few. Operating 7 days a week, **Surf City Plaza** provides the perfect opportunity to purchase essentials and accessories, from wetsuits and surfboards, to swimwear, shorts and sunglasses. Thus prepared, the next logical destination should be **Bells Beach** where the action is live. Named

after the Bell family who owned the surrounding land during the 1840s, the beach attracts world champion surfers each Easter to the **Rip Curl Pro and Quit Women's Classic** (p.243). This revered surfing spot is located south of Torquay, off Bells Rd. It is not for the faint-hearted or inexperienced: here spring tides combined with north-westerly winds can generate waves up to 6m.

For visitors searching for some friendly family waves, **Fishermen's Beach** is accommodating. Located along The Esplanade, near the cnr of Darian Rd, the beach foreshore boasts a special attraction – a sundial that relies on living shadows to show the time. **The Sundial of Human Involvement** is a mosaic 8m in diameter crafted from more than 120 000 glass tiles. Its patterns tell

# Beach Safety

**Hazard ratings**: 1 = safest beach, 10 = least safe beach

| BEACH | RANK | DESCRIPTION |
| --- | --- | --- |
| Fishermans Beach, Torquay | 4 | protected swimming beach, quiet surf |
| Front Beach, Torquay | 4 | showpiece beach, usually low safe surf |
| Surf Beach, Torquay | 6 | swimming, surfing, moderately safe in patrolled areas |
| Jan Juc | 7 | experienced swimmers and surfers |
| Bells Beach | 6 | world famous surfing, experienced swimmers |
| Pt Addiscot | 6 | nude beach, experienced swimmers |
| Main Beach, Anglesea | 5 | moderately safe swimming, inexperienced surfers |
| Pt Roadknight | 4 | safe swimming |
| Aireys Inlet, Aireys Inlet Sth | 6 | experienced swimmers |
| Sandy Gully, Aireys Inlet | n/av | safe swimming |
| Fairhaven | 7 | experienced swimmers and surfers |
| Surf Beach, Lorne | 5 | moderately safe swimming, Pt Grey for windsurfing |
| Wye River | 7 | experienced swimmers and surfers |
| Surf Beach, Apollo Bay | 5 | moderately safe swimming, variable surfing |
| Johanna Beach | 8 | hazardous swimming, excellent surfing |
| Loch Ard Gorge | 4 | safe swimming on beach (do not venture into Gorge) |
| Main Beach, Port Campbell | 4 | relatively safe swimming, though deep water close to shore |
| Logans Beach, Warrnambool | 7 | whale watching beach, hazardous swimming, good surfing |
| Surf Beach, Warrnambool | 6 | moderately safe at surf club, hazardous elsewhere, good surfing at The Flume |
| Merri River, Warrnambool | 4 | safe swimming, popular kid's beach |
| Shelly Beach, Warrnambool | 7 | hazardous swimming, good surfing in NE winds |

Source: A.D. Short, *Beaches of the Victorian Coast and Port Phillip Bay*. Contact Surf Life Saving Australia Ph: (02) 9597 5588 to purchase copies of the comprehensive guide.

traditional dreaming stories of the Aboriginal people of the Wathaurong area. Its creatures include Mindii the ever-watchful snake and Bunjil the Eagle, Creator and overseer. To tell the time, stand in the centre and watch where your shadow falls (don't forget to allow for daylight saving).

There is more to Torquay than surf. Follow the colourful pilot totem poles at the intersection of Blackgate Rd and Surfcoast Hwy till you spot a giant wooden pirate ship and canoeing lake. **Tiger Moth World Adventure Park** is filled with fun things for kids including mini golf, volcano maze, play park and a flying fox, but for some real flying, adults prefer to take to the skies in a 1930s WWII vintage Tiger Moth biplane, Tiger Jack, or modern passenger aircraft. This is a spectacular way to view the coastline. Aerial acrobatics are an additional option for the daring, though the more sedate may prefer a visit to the **Tiger Moth Museum**, on site. Open daily, 10am–5pm (closed Tues in winter). Ph: (03) 5261 5100

One of the region's more spectacular aspects is found 9km south-west of Torquay, off the Gt Ocean Rd at **Pt Addis** where boardwalk viewing platforms offer panoramic views of the rugged coastline. Accessible from the carpark, **Addiscot beach** is framed by rising red cliffs of sand and clay – a beautiful beach where clothing is an optional extra. Bordering Pt Addis is the **Ironbark Basin Reserve**, a natural bush habitat hosting abundant bird and other wildlife. From the visitor info centre you can pick up a copy of Mary D. White's useful **fact sheet** on the reserve's flora and fauna to acquaint yourself with some of its species. A 1km **Koorie Culture Walk** traces a signposted circuit down to the beach, highlighting the Aboriginal people's harmonious relationship with the local environment.

### Warrnambool *Map 47*

Further afield at the end of the inland stretch of the Gt Ocean Rd is a seaside haven popular with both humans and some rather larger mammals – southern right whales.

*Proudfoot's heritage boathouse, Warrnambool.*

Originally known as 'Warnimble', an Aboriginal word meaning 'between two rivers', Warrnambool is situated on Lady Bay, between the Hopkins and Merri rivers and had its beginnings as a port of call for sealers and whalers during the 1830s. Pastoral occupation soon spread into the district, and in the 1840s the Port of Warrnambool prospered as the sea proved the quickest route to Melbourne (1½ days travel v. 6 wks by bullock wagon). Today manufacturing thrives in the small city, with clothing company **Fletcher Jones** (and its scenic gardens) the most notable presence.

**Flagstaff Hill Maritime Village** on Merri St brings to life an era pivotal in the history of the southern coast. Modelled on an Australian port of the 1850s–1900s, its cluster of buildings include a lighthouse and keeper's cottage (1859), shipsmith and boat builders and port medical officer's suite. There is even an old fort and cannons built to ward off a feared Russian invasion (1887). You can explore 2 moored vessels – the *Rowitta* and the *Reginald M* – the decks are the perfect place to pose for a photo. Interesting exhibits in the Entrance Gallery add historical detail, while the movie theatre presents *Round Cape Horn* (1929) – life at and under the sea – plus an underwater film. The village also has restaurants, tearooms and kiosk. Open daily, 9am–5pm. Ph: (03) 5564 7841. After whetting your appetite for local history at Flagstaff Hill, the next stop

**Paint your wagon**
The old Jarosite Mine located in the **Ironbark Basin Reserve** was once the source of a purple-red ochre mixed into paint to colour Victoria's early red trains.

**Mills and potters to be found**

Beyond the declared Otway Park scattered mill towns remain, including **Gellibrand**, today renowned for its pottery at Old Beech Forest Rd. Open Mon–Fri, 9am–5pm, Sat–Sun, 11am–5pm. Ph: (03) 5235 8246, and **Forrest**, home of the **Feral Art Gallery**, cnr Apollo Bay and Colac Rds. Open Nov–Apr, Thur–Mon, 10am–5.30pm; May, Jun, Jul, Oct, Sat–Sun and public holidays, 10.30am–5pm; closed Aug and Sep, Ph: (03) 5236 6472

should be **History House** (1876) on Gilles St, where photos, records and memorabilia provide a more passive introduction to Warrnambool's heritage. Open 1st Sun each month (every Sun in Jan), 2pm–4pm. Ph: (03) 5562 6940. While on the heritage trail don't forget **Proudfoot's Boathouse** (1885), a National Trust classified treasure turned tearooms and restaurant, located on the Hopkins river at the end of Simpson St.

Warrnambool's waters are not only famous for ships: from Jun–late Sept **southern right whales** can be seen at the well-signposted **Logans Beach**, where the shallow seas are a nursery for females to give birth to their young. The whales swim here from the Antarctic Southern Ocean where they have spent the summer months feeding on plankton. Full-grown adults can weigh up to 60 tonnes and measure almost 15m long; the young are usually around 6m at birth. You can see the whales from the built observation point, though binoculars often prove to be a useful accessory.

One of Warrnambool's scenic centrepieces is its 8ha **Botanic Gardens**, cnr Queen and Cockman Sts. In 1877 famed botanist William Guilfoyle went to work to transform the landscape from a 'howling wilderness and rough site' to the picturesque parkland enjoyed today. Highlights include its wide sweeping lawns sheltered by towering trees, as well as its ornamental sundial, band rotunda (1913) and lone pines grown from seeds brought back from Gallipoli.

Enjoy a journey into art at the **Warrnambool Art Gallery** where visiting exhibitions complement the reputable permanent collection featuring late 19th century European works, a 1930s-1950s Melbourne modernism collection and more than 600 contemporary Australian prints. An interesting work of local historical significance is Eugene Von Guerard's *Tower Hill, 1855*, used to identify plant species during recent replanting of the Tower Hill Reserve. The gallery is located in a thoroughly modern and beautiful gallery at 165 Timor St. Open daily, noon–5pm or by appt. Ph: (03) 5564 7832. Housed in one of Warrnambool's oldest bluestone buildings in Gilles St, **Customs House Gallery** broadens the artistic array exhibiting and selling paintings, textiles, sculpture, glass, jewellery, prints and ceramics crafted by Australian artists. Some art is available for purchase. Open Wed–Sun and public holidays, 11am–5.30pm. Ph: (03) 5564 8963. Those acquainted with the work of the Swiss-born wildlife artist Robert Ulmann will be delighted to learn that the **Robert Ulmann Studio** is located only 4km east of the Hopkins River Bridge at 440 Hopkins Pt Rd. His watercolours of Australian native animals are renowned worldwide. Open most days or by appt. Ph: (03) 5565 1444

The perfect place for kids (and BBQs and picnics), the 35ha **Lake Pertobe playground** is an adventure-land filled with lots of exciting equipment including

*Beach, Lake Pertrobe.*

slides, swings, a wooden maze and balancing beams plus a series of walking trails. During summer and on weekends you can hire paddleboats, canoes or mini-powerboats to navigate the waters. There is also plenty of grass for casual cricket games.

## National Parks

### Otway NP *Map 44 E6*

Prepare for an excursion into cool mountain terrain as the Gt Ocean Rd detours from its classic coastal views through the lush green rainforests of the Otway Ranges. Steep coastal slopes, volcanic soils and generous rainfall have nurtured forests of ferns, mountain ash and eucalypts and carved trails of waterfalls and cascades. Timber cutters took advantage of the harvest and during the industry's peak more than 240km of tramways networked through the bush to transport fallen timber to the sawmills.

*Viewing platforms, 12 Apostles.*

The 12 750ha Otway NP covers a 60km section from Apollo Bay to Princetown, encompassing both rugged coastline vegetation and cool rainforest. Several unsealed roads off the Gt Ocean Rd provide a sampling of the highlights. Approx 6km SW of Apollo Bay is the road to **Elliot River** where there is a **picnic reserve**, wood BBQs and toilets, and a 500m walking track down to **Shelly Beach**. Starting from the car park, the 2hr (4km) looped **Elliot River Walk** explores the river and hardy scrub and grasslands along the coastal ridge. To appreciate nature's contrasts, take the turn off to **Maits Rest Rainforest Boardwalk**, approx 10km further along the Gt Ocean Rd. A 40min stroll along the elevated boardwalk guides you through a wonderland of giant treeferns sheltered by an overarching canopy of myrtle beech foliage. A rare resident to watch out for is the carnivorous Otway Black Snail whose surprising daily diet includes worms.

### Port Campbell NP *Map 44 B5*

In the 1759ha of NP stretching from Princetown to Peterborough, the view looking out to the 12 Apostles is the one most captured, both on film and in memory. There are, however, many other significant features here to discover and explore.

Once part of the limestone cliffs at the land's edge, the **12 Apostles** are proof of the erosive power of the waves. Persistent weathering caused the soft tertiary limestone to collapse in stages, first carving out caves, which further eroded into arches until the arches collapsed creating stacks. The 7 stacks visible from the wooden viewing platforms range from 10m–50m in height and it is unknown whether the count was higher when the Apostles were named (12 may have been a poetic flourish). For a better understanding of the rock formations tour the platforms and read the fascinating geological history in detail.

**Loch Ard Gorge** recounts again the force of the ocean, though through the tragic loss of lives in the wreck of the *Loch Ard*. Informative plaques not only point out the significance of landmarks around the Gorge, they also highlight some of the important vegetation and wildlife in the area. The **Loch Ard Gorge Walk** (1.5hrs) guides you past several other major landmarks, including the **Blowhole** (where the ocean surges down a 100m tunnel, up a 17m shaft, out to a 40m mouth), **Thunder Cave**, **Broken Head** and **Sherbrooke River**. Nearby,

*Maits Rest, Otway NP.*

*Infamous Loch Ard Gorge.*

park, however, there is a privately-run camping ground at Port Campbell.

## Other attractions

### Allansford Cheese World *Map 44 A4*

Allansford Cheese World not only offers an introduction to cheese production and its history, it also acts as an outlet to sample, savour and purchase their diverse range of products. Their products include regional wine and cheese, honey, confectionery and jam. Located only 12km east of Warrnambool, on the Gt Ocean Rd, Allansford Cheese World's on-site museum retraces regional farming history, and explains contemporary cheese making methods through an educational video. The restaurant caters for lunch, morning and afternoon teas. Open Mon–Fri, 8.30am–6pm, Sat, 8.30am–5pm, Sun, 10am–5pm. Ph: (03) 5563 2130

### Glenample Homestead *Map 44 C5*

Just outside the Port Campbell NP is a site inextricably linked with the history of the coastline. In 1867 Scotsman Hugh Gibson purchased Glenample Station. That acquisition destined Gibson to a place in history's more prominent records

**Mutton Bird Island** is also worth noting, especially Sept–Apr when the nesting colony of short-tailed shearwater (known by the early settlers as mutton birds) return to the island at dusk to feed their young. The NP also boasts an impressive range of wildflowers including 22 orchids, 14 lilies and 15 species from the pea family. Camping is not permitted in the

## The Wreck of the *Loch Ard*

On 31 May 1878 the passengers and crew of the *Loch Ard* were celebrating their near arrival in Melbourne after a long 90 days sailing from the Port of London. Visibility was poor that night and at 4am when the mists momentarily lifted it was too late to steer the mighty ship clear of the cliffs that suddenly loomed ahead and the *Loch Ard* smashed against an outlying reef off Mutton Bird Island.

As the ship disintegrated, 18yr-old Eva Carmichael was swept overboard by a massive wave. Although unable to swim she clung desperately to a section of broken mast for 4hrs till the mast caught fast on rocks at the entrance to a narrow gorge. Sighting a figure on the shore, Eva screamed for help and apprentice seaman Tom Pearce struggled back into the sea to rescue her. After sheltering Eva in a nearby cave Tom scaled the cliffs to eventually raise the alarm and obtain the help of the owner of **Glenample Homestead** (p.256). Of the 54 people on board that night Tom and Eva were the only 2 to survive. Though newspapers of the day speculated on a romance, one never eventuated — Eva returned alone to Ireland and Tom to a life at sea.

for it was in the Glenample Homestead that survivors of the wreck of the *Loch Ard* sought refuge (p.256). Today, carefully restored and classified by the National Trust, Glenample homestead serves a dual purpose – as the district's only example of a home from the 1860s and as a credible and important setting for retelling the saga of the *Loch Ard*. Located 2km east of the 12 Apostles off the Gt Ocean Rd. Open daily, 10.30am–5pm during school holidays; Fri-Mon, 10.30am–5pm at other times. Ph: (03) 5598 8209

### Timboon Farmhouse Cheese
*Map 44 C4*

Timboon Farmhouse Cheese, which is located approximately 16km north-east of Peterborough, makes a pleasant culinary interlude driving to or from anywhere. Specialising in boutique cheeses made from biodynamic milk, Timboon Farmhouse Cheese varieties include brie, washed rinds, feta, camembert and blue. Start with cheese samples from The Mouse Trap tasting room or adjourn to the gardens to enjoy a delightful cheese platter and wine, which is available for purchase. Located on Ford and Fells Rds, open daily, 10am–4pm. Ph: (03) 5598 3387

*Timboon's quality produce.*

**Mutton Bird Island.**

### Tower Hill *Map 44 A4*

Just off the Princes Hwy, 15km NW of Warrnambool, Tower Hill is a State Game Reserve cradled in the crater of an extinct volcano believed to have erupted at least 30 000 years ago. Although the reserve's history has witnessed destruction of its vegetation (some early settlers valued land and timber more than the environment), efforts have been successful in restoring indigenous plants and wildlife. This is now a prime place for sighting kangaroos, emus, echidnas, koalas and waterbirds. Visit the **Natural History Centre** for orientation, then choose from the 5 self-guided walks, including the steep **Peak Climb** (30min), an easy intro to Aboriginal foods on the **Whurrong Walk** (1hr) or a moderate **Journey to the Last Volcano** (1hr). Open daily, 8am–5pm. Ph: (03) 5565 9202

## Recreational activities

### Air adventure

For those seeking scenic aerial excursions, the region offers a variety of exciting alternatives including **Wingsports Hang gliding and Paragliding School** based at Apollo Bay, Ph: (03) 5237 6486; skydiving, acrobatics and scenic flights at **Tiger Moth World**, Blackgate Rd, Torquay, Ph: 0419 534 893; and

**Gibsons steps**

Across the road from Glenample Homestead are a series of **steps** carved into the 70m cliff-face by local Hugh Gibson during the late 1800s. Visitors today can take advantage of his handiwork to reach the treacherous ocean below.

*Mountain biking in the Otways.*

helicopter flights over the Shipwreck Coast with **Helicopter Operators Australia**, 136 Bromfield St, Warrnambool. Ph: (03) 5561 5800

### Exploring

Paddle your way into the heart of platypus territory with **Otwild Adventures** **'Paddle with the Platypus'** tour. Leaving at dawn from Forrest in groups of 2–6, you paddle 5hr in Canadian canoes, spotting a platypus colony in the wild with the help of tour guide Mark De la Warr. Morning tea is included and packaged accommodation is available. Bookings Ph: (03) 5236 2119

Discover the astonishing natural treasures of the Otways in the capable hands of a local guide. **Otway Eco-Guides** offer a variety of walks including Bushfoods and Medicine, a Koala Walk and Waterfall Walk, and from Nov–Apr Spotlight Walks, Rockpool Rambles and special eco-activities for children. Based at 58 Gambier St, Apollo Bay tours range from 1hr-full day. Ph: (03) 5237 7240. **Last Chance Tours** also run guided walks in the Otways and along the coast, departing Apollo Bay, Anglesea and Lorne. Bookings Ph: (03) 5237 7413. Another option is a self-guided tour taking the **Surf Coast Walk** from Jan Juc to Moggs Creek (south of Aireys Inlet). Although trekking the full distance takes 11hr, the walk can be done in stages. Pick up a pamphlet from the visitor info centres.

The region can also be explored on 2 wheels: **Otway Expeditions Mountain Bike Tours** offer half- and full-day rides or custom tours. Bookings Ph: (03) 5237 6529. You can also plan your own excursions hiring a bike (or canoes and surf gear) from **Go-Rats**, 73 Gt Ocean Rd, Aireys Inlet. Bikes delivered. Ph: (03) 5289 6841

### Golf

Often bordered by the ocean or the bush, golf courses along the Gt Ocean Rd are

*Golf courses along The Great Ocean Road are very scenic.*

renowned for their challenging courses and scenic views:

- **Torquay**, Great Ocean Rd,
  Ph: (03) 5261 2506
- **Anglesea**, Golf Links Rd,
  Ph: (03) 5263 1951
  (friendly free-ranging kangaroos)
- **Lorne**, Holiday Rd,
  Ph: (03) 5289 1267
- **Apollo Bay**, Nelson St,
  Ph: (03) 5237 6474
- **Peterborough**, Schomberg Rd,
  Ph: (03) 5598 5245
- **Warrnambool**, Younger St,
  Ph: (03) 5562 8528

## Horseriding

Saddle up and see the sea or the forest on an unforgettable ride.

- **Blazing Saddles Trail Rides**,
  Bimbadeen Dr, Aireys Inlet,
  Ph: (03) 5289 7149,
  1-2hr beach rides
- **Spring Creek Trail Rides**,
  245 Portreath Rd, Bellbrae,
  Ph: (03) 5266 1541,
  bushland and beach rides.
  Bookings req.
- **Wild Dog Trails**,
  Wild Dog Rd, Apollo Bay,
  Ph: (03) 5237 6441,
  1-3hr rides along beach, plus sunset rides
- **Bimbi Park**,
  Lighthouse Rd, Cape Otway,
  Ph: (03) 5237 9246,

*Surfing, Bells Beach.*

1hr-2days, Otway Ranges and coastal trails

- **Great Ocean Rd Trail Rides**,
  17 Stanley St, Warrnambool,
  Ph: (03) 5562 4874.
  Shipwreck Coast by horseback, 2hr rides.
- **Rundell's Mahogany Trail Rides**,
  Millers Lane, Dennington via Warrnambool,
  Ph: (03) 5529 2303.
  1-2hr rides or longer by appt.

## On and in the water

Make the most of the coast and learn to surf with **Go Ride A Wave**, based at 3 Harvey St, Anglesea. Classes take 2hr and are held weekends and during holidays, from 2 Nov-Easter at Anglesea, Torquay and Lorne. Wetsuits and boards supplied. Ph: (03) 5263 2111. **Westcoast Surf School** also offer 2hr lessons at Torquay, daily during summer holidays and most weekends until Easter. Ph: (03) 5261 2241. Further west you'll find the **Easy Rider Surf School** running 2hr surfing lessons at Warrnambool year round. Soft foam surfboards and wetsuits supplied. Ph: (03) 5560 5646

Weather permitting, enjoy the Shipwreck Coast sightseeing, fishing or scuba diving with **Shipwreck Coast Diving and Charters**, 457 Raglan Pde, Warrnambool, Ph: (03) 5561 6108, or with **Port Campbell Boat Charters**, bookings at the Loch Ard Museum, Port Campbell, Ph: (03) 5598 6411.

# Fun for the young

- ★ Flagstaff Hill Maritime Village (p.253)
- ★ Lake Pertobe (p.254)
- ★ Mountain-bike riding (p.258)
- ★ Horseriding (p.259)
- ★ Surfworld Surfing Museum (p.251)
- ★ Surfing lessons (p.259)
- ★ Tiger Moth World, Torquay (p.253)
- ★ Whale watching (p.254)

*Horseriding on the beach.*

# Suggested tours – Map 48

## Lighthouse and legends tour

### Approximate distance

630km return form Melbourne CBD

### About the tour

A fascinating tour in any season this journey follows the length of the Gt Ocean Rd to gain some perspective on the seafarers life of the past. Marvel at lighthouses and lookouts along the way, walk or ride the length of a beach and pause to reflect at monuments on the Shipwreck Coast. Stay 1 or 2 nights before immersing yourself in living history at the Flagstaff Hill Maritime Village, then enjoy the contrasting inland route through the countryside as you return to Melbourne.

### Places of interest

❶ **Pt Addis Lookout** (p.253)

❷ **Split Pt Lighthouse, Aireys Inlet** (p.244)

❸ **Teddy's Lookout, Lorne** (p.249)

❹ **Apollo Bay** (p.245)

❺ **Cape Otway Lighthouse** (p.246)

❻ **Port Campbell NP** (p.255) (especially the 12 Apostles and the Loch Ard Gorge)

❼ **Flagstaff Hill Maritime Village, Warrnambool** (p.253)

❽ **Colac Botanic Gardens (drive or walk through)** (p.247)

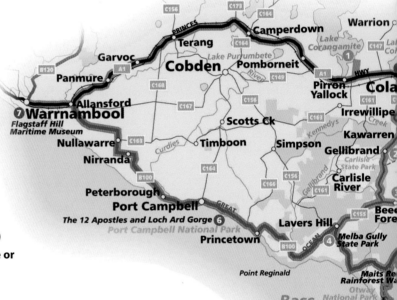

*Teddy's Lookout, Lorne.*

# Nature discovery (2-day)

## Approximate distance
470km return from Melbourne CBD

## About the tour
Leave the city behind and acquaint yourself with SW Victoria's diverse natural attractions. From volcanic plains and inland lakes to lush rainforest, dramatic limestone cliffs, heathlands and beautiful beaches, this region offers a nature study of the pleasurable sort. Visit the pelicans at Victoria's huge salty lake near Colac before crossing the Otway Ranges via Gellibrand (enjoy the pottery en route). Track back through Otway rainforest to Angahook-Lorne SP then stop off to discover the sights at Pt Addis before returning to Melbourne.

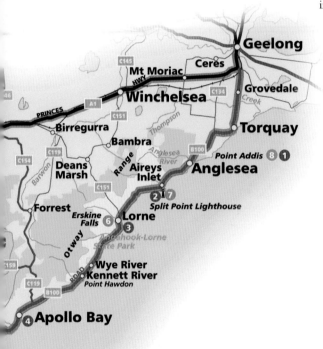

## Places of interest

❶ **Lake Corangamite, near Colac** (p.247)

❷ **Gellibrand Pottery, Gellibrand** (p.254)

❸ **Beech Forest** (ask locals about its waterfalls) (p.254)

❹ **Big Tree and glow worms, Melba Gully SP** (p.248)

❺ **Maits Rest Rainforest Walk, Otway Ranges** (p.255)

❻ **Erskine Falls, Lorne** (p.000)

❼ **Horseriding in Angahook-Lorne SP, Aireys Inlet** (p.244)

❽ **Ironbark Basin Reserve, Pt Addis** (p.253)

*Hopetoun Falls, Beech Forest.*

*Left: **View of Mt Buller from Mansfield.**
Right: **Beechworth township.***

# Legends, Wine and High Country

T his diverse region is a magnificent destination — winter or summer. The high country, with some of the most scenic countryside in Victoria, is home to both the Alpine and Mt Buffalo NPs. On offer are relaxed country rambles and active recreational pursuits: winter skiing and a variety of snow sports, as well as summer bushwalks, trail riding, whitewater rafting, and mountain fishing.

Numerous picturesque locations offer accommodation — ski lodges, B&Bs, self-contained cabins, hotels and caravan and campsites. Breathtaking views of mountainous outcrops, and lush mountain river valleys along well-made roads also make this region ideal for road touring.

You will find many historic points of interest here. The townships of Beechworth, Rutherglen, Yackandandah and Chiltern are not to be missed. As pristine examples of 19th century gold towns, many fine buildings are heritage protected, and open to the public. Whilst revealing what life was like on the frontier, they also welcome visitors to sample the pleasures of modern country life: restaurants and pastry shops, galleries and gardens, museums and musical entertainment.

Several distinct winegrowing areas, centred on the Ovens and King Valleys, and Rutherglen, cater for wine lovers' needs with winery tours, cellar-door sales, gourmet restaurants and scenic picnic areas.

## Must see, must do

★ **Beechworth township** (p.268)
★ **Bright township** (p.271)
★ **Mansfield Mountain Country Festival** (p.268)
★ **Mt Buffalo NP** (p.280)
★ **Mt Buller skiing** (p.279)
★ **Rutherglen wineries** (p.276)

## Radio stations

**3NE:** 1566 AM
**Edge FM:** 102.1 FM
**Sun FM Mt Buller:** 93.7 FM
**COFM:** 106.5 FM

## Tourist information

**Beechworth Visitor Info Centre**
Ford St, Beechworth 3747
Ph: (03) 5728 3233

**Benalla Visitor Info Centre**
14 Mair St, Benalla 3672
Ph: (03) 5762 1749

**Bright Visitor Info Centre**
119 Gavan St, Gt Alpine Rd,
Bright 3741
Ph: (03) 5755 2275

**Mansfield Visitor Info Centre**
Old Mansfield Railway Stn, High St,
Mansfield 3722
Ph: (03) 5775 1464

**Mt Buller Visitor Info Centre**
Mt Buller 3723
Ph: (03) 5777 6622

**Rutherglen Wine Region Tourism**
Jolimont Centre, Drummond St,
Rutherglen 3685
Ph: (03) 6032 9166

**Wangaratta Visitor Info Centre**
Cnr Tone Rd and Handley St,
Wangaratta 3677
Ph: (03) 5721 5711

**Victorian Snow Line**
Ph: 13 28 42

**Websites**
www.lwhc.com.au.

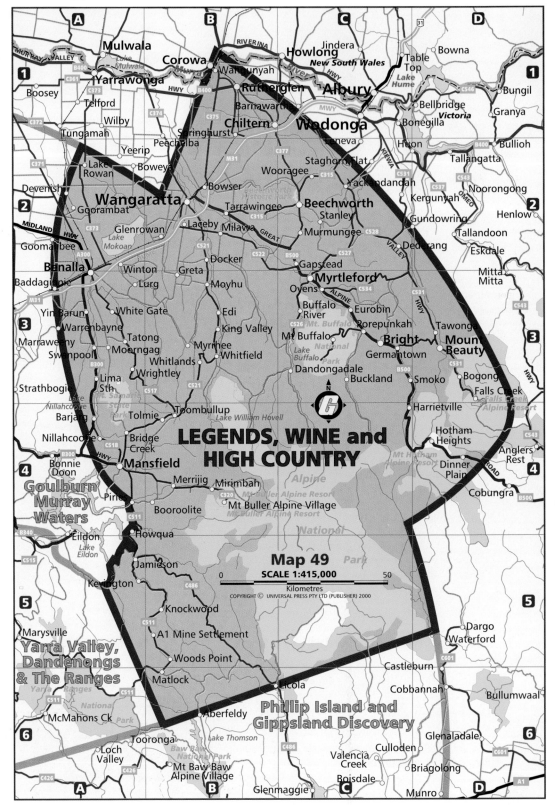

# LEGENDS, WINE and HIGH COUNTRY

Map 49

SCALE 1:415,000

0                    50

Kilometres

COPYRIGHT © UNIVERSAL PRESS PTY LTD (PUBLISHER) 2000

*Ovens Valley.*

## Natural features

The region is dominated by the Gt Dividing Range, which reaches peaks of 1600m at Mt Buller, 1988m at Mt Bogong, and 1400m at Mt Buffalo. Rugged rockfaces, glorious snow plains and valleys and foothills intermingle in this NE corner of Victoria. From Jul–Sept intermittent snowfalls provide excellent conditions for snow sports in the major alpine resorts. In spring, the high plains, accessible from Bright, Mt Beauty and Mansfield produce glorious displays of wildflowers. Fast-flowing rivers, well-stocked with trout, are another feature of the high country.

Highly productive farming land at lower altitudes follows the Ovens, King and Kiewa rivers in the north-east of the region; and the Howqua and Delatite rivers near Mt Buller in the south. In the north-east, hop and tobacco growing, cattle grazing and dairy herding, coexist with extensive vineyards. Mansfield, gateway to Mt Buller, is a centre for the high country cattlemen who herd cattle down from the high plains in autumn.

The Hume Hwy cuts a path to the Murray River and NSW border along a low-lying route which looks to the ranges in the east and runs through major sheep and cattle centres like Benalla and Wangaratta. To the west a drier climate prevails; flatter vistas meet the eye. Rutherglen, at the limit of this region, sits in the Murray River Valley.

## History

Legends, Wine and High Country, like many other regions, had an early history of sheep and cattle grazing and a period of explosive growth with the goldrushes of the mid 19th century.

Hume and Hovell explored parts of the region, cutting a course north-east across the Murray, passing through Yackandandah and the Ovens Valley and on to Wangaratta in 1824. In 1836 Major Thomas Mitchell, also crossing the Murray from the north, passed through Wangaratta and Benalla on his expedition to south-west Victoria. Grazing properties were taken up – often by squatters from the north – from this period on, along what was to become the Hume Hwy, earlier know as the Port Phillip Track.

Gold was discovered in 1852 in Beechworth and Yackandandah; 1853 at Bright, and 1858 at Chiltern. The region was alive with prospectors, both European and Chinese, often leading to angry racial disputes. After the Buckland riots of 1857, the Chinese prospectors of the Buckland goldfield decamped to Beechworth. In 1860, there were 5000 Chinese living there. Small mountain towns sprung up where none had been before. Others, like Beechworth, became prosperous and very gracious provisioning and administrative centres.

The great beauty of the alpine areas and their potential for recreational activity was recognised as early as the 1870s with

*Great Alpine Rd, Mt Hotham.*

**A spectacular tour**
The Gt Alpine Rd is a
fully sealed road from
Wangaratta on the
Hume Fwy to
Bairnsdale and beyond
in Gippsland. This
spectacular 240km
route over the
Bogong High Plains
is best taken over
several days.

**Best times to tour**
Nov–May is the best
time for road touring.
Snowfalls from Jun–Oct
may bring hazardous
conditions. For winter
road conditions,
Ph: (03) 5759 3531

expeditions to the summits of Mt Buffalo and Mt Feathertop and the formation of the Bright Alpine Club in the 1880s and the Bright Tourist Club in 1889. Mt Buffalo, Victoria's oldest NP, was declared in 1898. Today, tourism is a major industry alongside agricultural pursuits, timber logging and winegrowing.

## Getting there

### By road

The Hume Fwy is the most direct route from Melbourne, passing through Benalla, Wangaratta and close to Chiltern in the north. Rutherglen is best reached from Chiltern.

At Wangaratta, the Gt Alpine Rd heads east through the Milawa gourmet region to Mt Buffalo and Bright, and on through Mt Hotham to the Bogong High Plains. For Beechworth take the Gt Alpine Rd from Wangaratta, and head north at Tarrawingee.

The Hume Fwy is an efficient route. The more scenic but slower route from Melbourne to the High Country is via the Maroondah and Melba Hwys to Mansfield, where the roads to Mt Buller and Jamieson commence. A scenic route via Tolmie leads to the King Valley and the Gt Alpine Rd.

### By rail and coach

Trains leave regularly from Spencer St Stn for Wodonga on the NSW border, with stops at Benalla, Wangaratta and Chiltern. V/Line buses connect at Wodonga for Beechworth, Yackandandah and Mt Beauty. Buses leave Wangaratta for the Ovens Valley, stopping at Myrtleford, Porepunkah and Bright.

Buses for Mansfield in the south of the region also leave Spencer St Stn daily.

### By plane

Flights leave from Melbourne Airport, Tullamarine, daily for Albury Airport. This is the quickest way to reach the northern section of the region. Hire cars and taxis are available here. Ph: (02) 6041 1241

Flights can be chartered from Essendon or Moorabbin airports to regional airports at Benalla, Mansfield, Porepunkah and Wangaratta.

*Joyflight over Alpine NP.*

### Winter bus service

**Mt Hotham Snow Services** operates a winter bus service to Mt Hotham and other Ovens Valley destinations, departing Spencer St Stn coach terminal and Melbourne Airport. Ph: 1800 659 009. **Mt Buller Bus Lines** runs extra services from Spencer St Stn to Mansfield and Mt Buller in snow season. Ph: (03) 5777 6070

## Getting around

### By bus

During winter **Mt Hotham Snow Services** run daily bus services, picking up visitors at Wangaratta, Myrtleford, Bright and Harrietville for Mt Hotham. Ph: 1800 659 009. Timetables are available at visitor info centres. For Mt Buffalo the **Snow Bus** picks up at Myrtleford, Porepunkah and Bright during winter. Ph: (03) 5755 1988. **Mt Buller Bus Lines** run a regular service from Mansfield to Mt Buller. Ph: (03) 5755 6070

### Scenic flights

Both light aircraft and helicopter flights are a great way to see the high country. **Holiday Air Adventures**, leaving from Porepunkah Airfield, offer 3 flights – over Mt Buffalo, over Mt Hotham and the Bogong High Plains, and over the Ovens Valley. Ph: (03) 5753 5250. **Scenic and Charter Flights** offer regular scenic and charter helicopter flights over the rugged mountain terrain of the Mansfield district. Ph: 018 376 619

### Tours

**Great Getaway Tours and Picnics** offer a range of Landcruiser small group and family tours in the Bright area, including mountain tours, food and winery tours and tours of local historical towns. Great Getaway picks visitors up from their accommodation or the Bright Visitor Info Centre. Ph: (03) 5750 1814

4WD tours are a specialty of the high country. With **Lara Alpine Adventure Tours**, visitors can use their own 4WD vehicle or join a tour as a passenger. Ph: (03) 5282 2363. Small group 4WD tours depart daily from Bright with **My Life Adventures**. Ph: (03) 5759 2729.

High Country Explorer operates out of Mansfield from Dec–Easter, offering ½- and 1-day trips to Mt Stirling, Mt Buller and the southern sections of the Alpine NP. Ph: (03) 5777 3541

Trekking, snow camping and cross-country skiing tours are also available. At Mt Buffalo, **Adventure Guides Australia**, meeting at the Mt Buffalo Chalet, offer an exciting range of options, and will organise similar activities for Mt Hotham and Falls Creek. Ph: (03) 5728 1804

## Festivals and events

### Opera in the Alps

No better location could be found than the sublime Mt Buffalo for the soaring voices of Opera Australia and other well-known artists. Held on Australia Day weekend, this wonderful summer performance can be combined with a stay at the Mt Buffalo Chalet. Ph: (03) 5755 1500

### Tobacco, Timber and Hops Festival

Celebrating the traditional agricultural and forestry activities of the Ovens Valley, the pretty town of Myrtleford comes alive with musical entertainment, a market featuring the gourmet produce of the region, farm visits and exhibitions. Held over Labour Day weekend. Ph: (03) 5752 2410

### Tastes of Rutherglen

Held during vintage in early Mar, this is a 10-day festival dedicated to food and wine. Patrons collect a glass and tour the wineries, sampling Rutherglen's famous tokays and muscats, crisp whites and aromatic reds. Winery restaurants each feature a special menu, showcasing the local area's gourmet produce. Ph: (02) 6032 9127

### Beechworth's Golden Horseshoe Festival

Beechworth's Golden Horseshoe Festival, held over Easter, is a celebration of the town's history, culture and music. With a street parade, entertainment in the parks and on the streets, markets, exhibitions and historic tours, this is not only an

*Tastes of the Rutherglen.*

enjoyable occasion but an informative one as well. Ph: (03) 5728 1000

### Bright Autumn Festival

Held over 10 days at the end of Apr and into early May, Bright's fabulous deciduous trees, ablaze with colour, are the focus of this mountain festival. Featuring an open garden scheme and festivities in the streets and parks, this is one of Victoria's favourite festivals. Ph: (03) 5755 2275

### Beechworth Harvest Celebrations

On the 2nd weekend in May, Beechworth Harvest Celebrations beckons visitors to partake in the fine fruits of the earth and culinary creations for which the Beechworth area is well known. Relax in historic pubs, and under generous verandahs, tasting or purchasing the local produce and listening to music, or attend expert cooking demonstrations. Ph: (03) 5728 2077

### Rutherglen's Winery Walkabout

Rutherglen's Winery Walkabout has won 4 tourism awards, including Australian Festival of the Year. Rutherglen's 17 wineries are in close proximity and can be easily reached on foot or by the shuttle bus provided. Held over the Queen's Birthday weekend in Jun, this event is designed for all ages, with wine and food, music and children's activities. Ph: (02) 6032 9127

**A different kind of ride**
Why not try camel trekking? **High Country Camel Treks** offer short and overnight treks in the Mansfield district. Ph: (03) 5775 1591. **Linbrae Camel Farm** treks through Rutherglen's most famous wineries. Ph: (02) 6026 3452

*Cracks Cup, Mansfield Mountain.*

### Chiltern Ironbark Festival

Chiltern's famous Ironbark forests, protected in its recently proclaimed NP, give the Chiltern Ironbark Festival its name. With tours, rides, displays and concerts, it also has a strong emphasis on the area's natural heritage. Bird watching, bush walking and field naturalist activities are a special feature of this festival held mid-Oct. Ph: (03) 5728 1000

### The Myrtleford Show

Traditional agricultural shows are always a delight. The Myrtleford Show on the 4th Sat in Oct proudly displays the district's livestock, horticultural produce and country fare for judging. Showjumping, dog trials, competition billy-boiling and the Country Women's Association tea and scones are all on the agenda. Ph: (03) 5752 1727

### The Peaks Classic Car Rally

The Peaks Classic Car Rally sees more than 120 exotic and classic sports cars touring the Alpine region over Melbourne Cup weekend (last weekend in Oct). These old classics can be viewed in Beechworth before they depart for higher climes. Ph: (03) 9720 9975

### The Mansfield Mountain Country Festival

Also held over Melbourne Cup weekend, the Mansfield Mountain Country Festival, is a window onto the life of the high country and its distinctive culture. Horses feature prominently! The exciting Cracks Cup, the Melbourne Cup of the Bush, features Australia's best bush riders. There is a bush market, grand parade, dog jumping, pony rides and food stalls. Open day on Mt Buller includes free chairlift rides. Ph: (03) 5775 1464

### Bright Four Peaks Mountain Climb

Held over Melbourne Cup weekend, this event is open to the public and can be taken as a leisurely bush walk or a serious race. The 4 peaks are Mt Buffalo, Mt Bogong, Mt Porepunkah and Mt Feathertop – a peak a day. Hundreds of people participate in this exhilarating event. Ph: (03) 5755 1507

### Beechworth Annual Antique Fair

Beechworth's many antique dealers join with traders from throughout Australia to stage this fair on the 3rd weekend in Nov. Antique furniture, jewellery and other collectors' delights are on exhibition and for sale in the Beechworth Memorial Hall. Ph: (03) 5752 1944

## Main localities and towns

### Beechworth *Map 49 C2, 50*

This historic township has been described as a perfectly preserved gold town and is classified as one of Victoria's 2 'notable towns', with 32 separate buildings classified by the National Trust. Distinctive honey-coloured granite buildings line the town's wide shaded streets. Once the administrative centre of the Ovens Valley Goldfields, the struggles of the miners, the enterprise of townsfolk and the power of the Crown to order the upheavals brought on by gold fever are palpable in the town's very architecture.

The *Beechworth Touring Guide*, available from the Beechworth Visitor Info Centre, is indispensable for visitors to the town's historic attractions. The **Burke Museum**, named after the explorer Robert O'Hara Burke, who spent time in Beechworth as a policeman before his ill-fated expedition, holds a fine collection of gold-mining memorabilia, including Chinese mining

---

**The rest... is historic**

Beechworth specialises in historic B&B accommodation. Many pretty period cottages, refurbished barns and small guesthouses offer luxury and more affordable accommodation.
Ph: (03) 5728 3233

artefacts as well as Aboriginal artefacts. Open daily, 10.30am–3.30pm. **HM Prison Beechworth** stands imposingly on the edge of the town centre. It once housed Ned Kelly, and is still in use today.

The **Powder Magazine**, restored by the National Trust, is an intriguing building, especially designed to minimise the effect of any explosion, should the miners' gelignite have been disturbed. Open daily, 10am–noon and 1pm–4pm. **Beechworth Carriage Museum** is another reminder of times gone by, featuring 20 restored horse-drawn carriages once used in the Beechworth area. Open 10am–noon and 1pm–4pm weekdays and 1pm–4pm weekends. **Beechworth Cemetery** is also a must-see. Visitors can take a fascinating walk past the graves of bushrangers and

miners from far-flung quarters of the globe, including those of the significant population of Chinese miners who flocked to the mid-century goldfields. The Chinese burning towers and simple headstones with Chinese characters are testimony to the rich diversity of cultures which were part of Australia's early history.

Close by to the cemetery stands the **Golden Horseshoes Monument**, which tells the story of rival miner groups, the 'monkeys' and the 'punchers' – the 'wet diggers' and the 'dry diggers' – and how the 'monkeys' shod their candidate for State Parliament with horseshoes made of gold.

The town centre offers hours of browsing, through small galleries, the

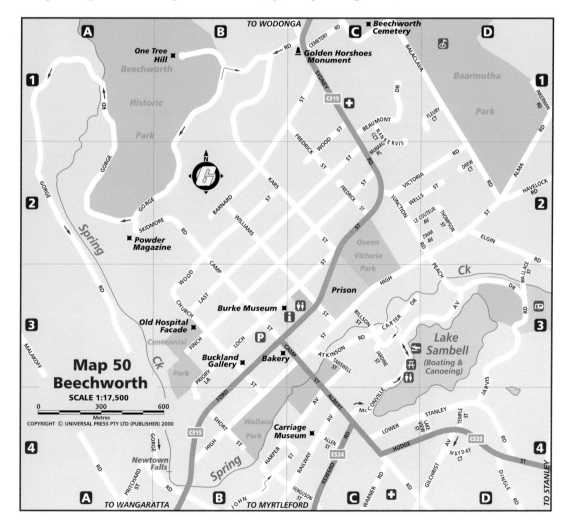

Map 50
Beechworth

SCALE 1:17,500

0          300          600
Metres

COPYRIGHT © UNIVERSAL PRESS PTY LTD (PUBLISHER) 2000

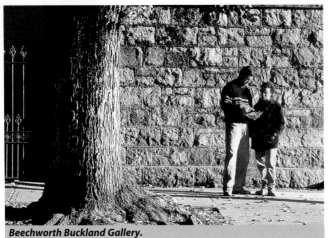

*Beechworth Buckland Gallery.*

Camp St only seats 3, for a quick coffee and nibble, but sells a fine selection of regional gourmet produce, including wine, for those wishing to buy gifts or prepare a gourmet picnic.

Numerous drives can be taken in and around Beechworth. The **Gorge Scenic Dve** takes visitors past several historical sites and along Spring Ck where the opening to the Rocky Mountain Tunnel can be seen. Picnicking is possible in Queen Victoria Park in the town centre, or at Lake Sambell, where pedal boats can be hired during summer.

Mini-bus tours of Beechworth and surrounds can be booked at the visitor info centre, or visitors might like to try the **Beechworth Stagecoach**, which leaves from the Westpac Bank in Ford St. Ph: (03) 5728 2541

**Woolshed Falls, Eldorado** and **Mt Pilot Park** (p.282) are each a short drive from Beechworth and are worth visiting. There are picnic facilities at each of these destinations.

### Benalla *Map 49 A2*

This friendly, progressive regional centre sits on the Broken River and is graced with a lovely lake around which many of the city's attractions are arranged. The intriguingly designed **Benalla Regional Art Gallery** sits on the edge of the lake. It exhibits a fine collection of Australian art, including Sidney Nolan's large tapestry 'Siege at Glenrowan', depicting the capture of Ned Kelly. The gallery is also a venue for major international and

### Sweet diversions

The Beechworth Sweet Co, at 79 Camp St, is not to be missed, especially if there are children in tow. An amazing selection of gob-stoppers, humbugs, licorice and chocolate line the walls of this old-fashioned shop.

town's 9 antique shops, bookstores, and specialty shops. The **Buckland Gallery** on the corner of Church and Ford Sts, and **Left Bank** at 93 Ford St — an artist-run cooperative — feature high-quality locally produced arts and crafts, including ceramics, textiles and woodwork. At **Beechworth Gold Gem Stone and Jewellery Merchants** the old Bank of Victoria bank vault can be viewed while browsing through a colourful display of semi-precious gemstones.

An array of cafes, restaurants, bakeries and food stores is also to be found. The historic pub, **Tanswells Commercial Hotel** at 30 Ford St, offers modern regional fare beside an open fire in its friendly bistro. The **Beechworth Bakery** is renowned for hearty lunches on its open balconies, often accompanied by a jazz band. **Beechworth Provender** at 18

*Benalla Regional Art Gallery.*

Australian touring exhibitions. Open daily 10am–5pm.

Close by, **Benalla Botanical Gardens** provide a pleasant diversion adjoining **Benalla Rose Gardens**. The gardens are a sea of colour in summer, and are the location of the **Sir Edward 'Weary' Dunlop Memorial**. A moving bronze sculpture of Sir Edward assisting two young soldiers depicts the suffering of Australian servicemen on the Burma-Thailand Railway during WWII.

Across the lake Benalla's **Ceramic Mural** provides a focal point. This fantastical terracotta creation, reminiscent of the work of Spanish architect Gaudi, is a community arts project created by local potters. Next door, at the Benalla Visitor Info Centre, a small fee is charged for entry to the **Benalla Costume and Pioneer Museum**, which has a unique display of typical 19th century dress, and several Kelly artefacts – Ned's cummerbund and the door of the old Benalla gaol to which the body of gang member Joe Byrne was tied after the shootout in Glenrowan.

Ask at the visitor info centre for its 'Lake Benalla Walk', a 4km circuit taking in various historical and cultural features, and its 'Historical Tourist Walk', which indicates Benalla's many historic buildings.

Benalla is also an action centre. The **Gliding Club of Victoria**, located at the Benalla Airport, is Australia's largest gliding centre. Visitors can take a joy flight, or enrol for lessons. Ph: (03) 5762 1058.

Weekend events at **Winton Motor Raceway** attract large numbers of spectators. The year round calendar includes the Shell V8 Touring Car Championship, the Australian Super Truck Championship and the Australian Historic Motorfest. Ph: (03) 5766 4235

Benalla is 50km from Mansfield, giving access to the high country around Mt Buller. Several good bushwalking and bike riding locations are close to Benalla, for instance **Reef Hills Park** (p.282), the Strathbogie Ranges, and **Mt Samaria SP** (p.282). Walking maps are available at the Benalla Visitor Info Centre.

## Bright *Map 49 C3, 52 C4*

Bright is a charming village nestled below the snow line in the Ovens Valley close to the foot of Mt Feathertop. The gateway to the **Mt Hotham** ski resort and Bogong High Plains, it is also the largest provisioning town close to Mt Buffalo. It is well serviced with a variety of accommodation options, from camping to B&Bs and guesthouses. With cafes and restaurants, ski and outdoor shops, craft shops and small galleries, it is a pleasant place to browse and take stock before taking off on any of the many active recreational pursuits at hand.

Planted with deciduous European trees in the late 19th century, Bright is a fiery display of colour in the autumn. Visitors can spend a pleasant hour or more strolling through the back streets and down to Centenary Park, and during Bright's Autumn Festival partake of the many additional activities, including an open garden scheme (p.267). Bright is an ideal take-off point in spring and summer for bushwalks among the wildflowers and road touring into the Alps. 4WD expeditions are another popular activity. Wineries, pick-your-own berry farms, trout farms and nut groves are some of the culinary delights of the immediate vicinity.

The towns of **Myrtleford**, **Porepunkah**, the delightful **Harrietville** and historic **Wandillagong** are close by. There are walking and cycling paths

*Bright township.*

**Bright farmgate sales**

**Gunnadoo Berries**, Gt Alpine Rd, Smoko

**Bright Fruit 'n Berries**, Roberts Ck Rd, Bright

**Crystal Waters Trout Farm**, Stony Ck Rd, Harrietville

**Rosewhite Orchards**, Gilberts Lane, Rosewhite

**Schmidt's Strawberry Winery**, Allans Flat

Get a copy of the *Legends, Wine & High Country Food and Wine Trail* gourmet guide book.

which follow the Ovens River. Many short and medium length cycling routes and easy walks are recommended to various points of historic and natural interest.

At **Morse's Creek Store Complex** in Bright, visitors can browse through intriguing local memorabilia, old wares and antiques, or view the **Bright Garden Gallery**'s collection of garden and ornamental pottery. The **Glazebrook Gallery**, 21 Gavan St, has a fine collection of prints, locally made red gum tables, and books and photographs on the region. Open noon–4pm weekdays, and daily on long weekends and during festivals. The **Bright and District Historical Museum**, located in the old railway station, houses an informative exhibition of materials from pioneer families that illuminate the town's logging, gold and agricultural past. Open Sun, 2pm–4pm, Sept–May; Tues, Thurs and Sun, 2pm–4pm during festivals and school holidays.

The town also has 2 small amusement parks, ideal for kids on a rainy day. The **Lots'afun Amusement Park** on Old Mill Rd has roller skating, trampolines, skateboarding and dodgem cars. Open daily, 9am–5pm except Tues and Wed, and all week during school holidays. **Gator Magoons** on the Gt Alpine Rd features a miniature railway – great fun for small children. Open during peak season.

**Wandillagong Maze**, on White Star Rd, Wandilligong, is a classic hedge maze which will provide hours of entertainment. It also has a licensed cafe. Open daily, 10am–5pm. Ph: (03) 5750 1311

### Chiltern *Map 52 B1*

Chiltern is a quiet historic township. Time seems to have passed it by, leaving a huddle of intact buildings dating from the town's early pioneering and gold rush days. *The Chiltern Touring Guide* outlines an informative walk. The lovely **Lakeview Homestead** should not be missed. A National Trust property, it was the home of Henry Handel Richardson, author of the Australian classic *The Getting of Wisdom*.

*Lakeview Homestead.*

Chiltern is also the location of the Chiltern Box-Ironbark NP (p.280). Short drives to Donkey Hill, Magenta Mine and the Chiltern Pioneer Cemetery within the park give a glimpse of life and death in the early days.

### Glenrowan *Map 52 A3*

Ned Kelly was captured and the members of his gang killed here after the famous siege at the Glenrowan Inn in 1879. Today, Glenrowan is a tourist town devoted to the Kelly legend. A huge Ned strides towards the road, armour on, gun in hand. There are souvenir shops and tearooms. At the **Glenrowan Tourist Centre** visitors a can watch 'Kelly's Last Stand', an animated production using computerised models in period dress, telling the story of Ned's life and death. Well-scripted, with good sets, this 'live' animated show does bring the Kelly legend to life. The show goes on daily, every 30min, from 9.30am–4.30pm. Ph: (03) 5766 2367

### Jamieson *Map 49 B5*

A pretty village on the banks of the Goulburn River, Jamieson is reached via Mansfield on the Mansfield-Woods Pt Rd, which crosses the Howqua River and skirts the south-eastern reaches of Lake Eildon. A quiet retreat for most of the year, although busy during school holidays, it is ideal spot for camping either at the local caravan park, or informally in picturesque spots along the Jamieson or Goulburn Rivers. There are many other accommodation options,

# The Ned Kelly Legend

The Ned Kelly story is not just the story of an infamous horse thief, bank robber and murderer. Not only was Kelly an ingenious thief, and a fine host if you were ever captured by him, but his legend grows out of an intriguing social history.

Historians have pointed out that stealing stock in the 1850s through to the 1870s was almost a way of life for many poor settlers. Locked out of the land deals that saw NSW and Victorian squatters grow hugely wealthy, many were forced to run their stock on the roadside, otherwise known as the 'long paddock'. Anti-authoritarian sentiment was still strong in the bush after the Eureka Rebellion of 1854, and there were many ongoing examples of preferential treatment afforded the wealthy. One was the fine, introduced by police, which squatters demanded when they impounded poor settlers' wayward stock. Settlers believed this to be a form of legalised cattle stealing or 'duffing', and responded in like kind.

The Kelly family had a history of cattle stealing. Ned was to take up the heritage, and he and his family were pursued for many years. But it was not until 1878 that Kelly and his gang were branded murderers, when they killed the 3 Mansfield policemen who had refused to surrender to the gang and had drawn their revolvers. The Kelly gang went on to rob several banks, and most famously to hold the Glenrowan Inn to siege. Despite their home-made armour, all but Ned were killed. He was tried and was hanged at the Melbourne Gaol in 1880. He departed this world after his mother is said to have told him to 'Die like a Kelly', and after he uttered the famous 'Such is life'. Four thousand supporters stood outside the gaol as Ned Kelly was hanged.

including B&Bs, affordable holiday units and motels.

Bushwalking, canoeing, fishing, horseriding and 4WD are all possible from Jamieson. Ask at the General Store for info about tracks and fishing spots. Car touring around Jamieson is especially worthwhile. The drive to Eildon is a spectacular route, twisting around the edges of the Eildon SP. For the more adventurous, the Woods Pt Rd to Walhalla, which is often closed during winter, offers a glorious forest drive past the ruins of several old goldmining settlements.

*Ned Kelly Museum, Glenrowan.*

### Mansfield *Map 49 A4*

Home of the high country cattlemen, Mansfield is surrounded by the Alpine NP and state forest. A relaxed and friendly working country town, during winter it transforms into a busy base for visitors to Mt Buller and the southern reaches of the Alpine NP. An ideal off-mountain base for skiers, it is also an ideal location in the warmer months for a variety of activities, including trout fishing, horseriding, mountain-bike riding, 4WD expeditions and bushwalking.

The full range of accommodation is available in and around Mansfield – B&B cottages, luxury lodges, and farm-stay accommodation – some offering

*Giant Ned Kelly.*

**Landscapes of pure poetry**

*The Man from Snowy River*, Banjo Paterson's famous poem, is the story of the race to find the 'son of Old Regret', a pure-bred colt escaped into the mountains. While the man from snowy river and his stocky mountain pony are laughed at by the colt's owner, they prove themselves masters of the high country.

● ● ● ● ● ● ● ● ●

**A welcome respite**

There are nearly 60 mountain huts dotted across the high country. Built by early graziers and miners, many are still used today by high country cattlemen during muster. They are also a welcome sight to bushwalkers and trail-riders.

**Best picnic spots**

Paradise Falls (p.275)

Allans Flat Recreational Reserve (p.278)

Tawonga, near Mt Beauty (p.275)

Lake Catani, Mt Buffalo (p.281)

Powers Lookout (p.274)

*Cattlemen riding the high country, near Mansfield.*

packages which include trail rides and fishing instruction.

The wild rugged country to the south and east of Mansfield is spectacular. Icy fast-running rivers, lush green mountain pastures and eucalypt forests rising to rocky mountains are the setting for Mansfield's famed mountain trail rides. Many local horsemen, including several of Mansfield's trail ride operators, featured in the film *The Man from Snowy River*, made here in 1982. What better guides into the high country could there be? Day and overnight rides are offered — visiting rustic cattlemen's huts, camping out and eating damper under the stars are all part of the experience (p.285).

To the north of Mansfield lies the Samaria SF, and through Tolmie on the Mansfield-Whitfield Rd, the scenic route to the King Valley. Tolmie is the site of the 1878 shootout between Ned Kelly and the police in which 3 troopers were killed. A monument to them stands in the centre of Mansfield. Their graves can be viewed in the Mansfield Cemetery.

**Powers Lookout**, 15km north of Tolmie, is well worth the trip from Mansfield. A spectacular view of the King Valley opens up beneath a viewing platform perched on the edge of a rocky outcrop. This was the hide-out of another bushranger, Harry Power. Visitors can get the feel of the bushranger's wild ways in this impregnable fortress. There are

picnic and toilet facilities here, and a timber shelter with a huge fireplace, well stocked with wood.

Mansfield prides itself on its high country identity, celebrated in its annual Mountain Country Festival (p.268). Mansfield's regular bush markets, featuring local produce, arts and crafts and held in Highett St, are another way to experience the life of this unique area.

**Milawa gourmet region** *Map 52 B3*

This delightful gourmet food and wine region to the east of Wangaratta, centred on the towns of Oxley and Milawa, is renowned for its wines and cheeses. Visitors can pick up a guide to the area from the Wangaratta Visitor Info Centre. The best known winery is **Browns Brothers of Milawa**. One of the leading exporters of Australian wines, Brown Brothers has superb cellar door facilities and wonderfully patient staff. Its **Epicurean Centre** offers fine food with accompanying wines.

The **Milawa Cheese Co** on Factory Rd offers tastings and is renowned for its award-winning Milawa Blue. Chef Michel Renoux offers 'creative regional food' for lunch daily, 11am–3pm. Ph: (03) 5727 3589. **Milawa Mustards** is another gourmet must, situated in the centre of Milawa. The **King River Cafe** in Oxley has an outstanding reputation as one of the region's finest restaurants, confirmed by the fact that it is often booked out! Open Wed–Sun, 10am–late. Ph: (03) 5727 3461

Milawa sits at the northern end of the King Valley, an extensive winegrowing area. A drive through this beautiful valley will take visitors past several wineries and orchards towards the Wabonga Plateau. There are several caravan parks along the river valley with scenic campsites. Whitfield's **Mountain View Hotel**, winner of the Best Country Hotel Award, has a pleasant beer garden and a hearty menu. A short drive from Whitfield onto the plateau will take visitors to **Paradise Falls**. This magnificent amphitheatre is reached by a 15min walk which provides spectacular views of the surroundings ranges. There are picnic and toilet facilities here.

### Mt Beauty Map 49 D3

Mt Beauty is superbly located at the foot of Mt Bogong, Victoria's highest peak, beside the Keiwa River. Originally built as the base for construction workers on the Kiewa hydroelectric scheme, today the town is a relaxed tourist destination. The scene, winter or summer is glorious. There are various accommodation options, and a number of good cafes and restaurants. A gateway to the Falls Ck snowfields, Mt Beauty offers access to all the mountain-based snow sports, as well as bushwalking, horseriding, 4WD touring, camping and picnicking. The **Mt Beauty Indoor Go Kart and Rock Climbing Centre** is located here and attracts families to its many fun activities.

The little town of Tawonga, 6km out of Mt Beauty, is an idyllic spot to picnic. The **Tawonga Caravan Park**, on Mountain Ck Rd, is an ideal family location scenically located by the Kiewa River. Ph: 5754 4428

### Rutherglen Map 52 B1

Close to the Murray River, Rutherglen seems a long way from the rugged high country. With its more Mediterranean climate, and its slowly meandering companion, Rutherglen's style and atmosphere is distinct. Inclined to be dusty in summer, with its verandahed shop fronts, shady trees and gold-era

*Milawa cheeses.*

pubs, Rutherglen township has an almost outback feel.

First planted with vines in the 1850s, wine has proved to be Rutherglen's enduring claim to fame. There are 17 wineries, each with their distinctive products and cellar door hospitality. Most are open daily, and many have exceptional restaurants. Rutherglen's fortified wines are world-famous, but its full-bodied whites and reds are equally delectable. Rutherglen's many wine and food events (p.267) are a great way to experience the area's gourmet food and wine produce, with winery cycling weekends, weekend musical events and harvest festivals.

*Campbells' vines, Rutherglen.*

### Wangaratta Map 52 A2

A large regional city on the Hume Hwy, Wangaratta is the gateway to Victoria's

*Mt Beauty.*

*Wangaratta Airworld.*

## Central Victorian High Country wineries

| NAME | MAP 52 ADDRESS | PHONE | OPEN |
| --- | --- | --- | --- |
| Antcliffs Chase Wines | Caveat, near Molesworth | (03) 5790 4333 | 10am–5pm weekends, or by appt |
| Delatite Winery | Stoneys Rd, Mansfield | (03) 5775 2922 | 10am–4pm daily |
| Murrindindi Vineyards | Murrindindi-Cummins Rd, Murrindindi | (03) 5797 8217 | By appt |
| Plunkett Wines | Cnr Lambing Gully Rd and Hume Fwy, Avenel | (03) 5796 2150 | 11am–5pm daily |

## Glenrowan wineries

| NAME | ADDRESS | PHONE | OPEN |
| --- | --- | --- | --- |
| Auldstone Cellar | Booths Rd, Taminick | (03) 5766 2237 | 9am–5pm Thurs–Sat and school hols, 10am–5pm Sun |
| Baileys of Glenrowan | Taminick Gap Rd, Glenrowan | (03) 5766 2392 | 9am–5pm weekdays, 10am–5pm weekends |
| Booths Taminick Cellar | Booth Rd, Taminick | (03) 5766 2282 | 9am–5pm Mon–Sat, 10am–5pm Sun. |

## King Valley wineries

| NAME | ADDRESS | PHONE | OPEN |
| --- | --- | --- | --- |
| Avalon Vineyard | Whitfield Rd, King Valley | (03) 5729 3629 | 10am–5pm daily |
| King River Estate | Whitfield Rd, King Valley | (03) 5729 3689 | By appt only |
| La Cantina | Whitfield Rd, King Valley | (03) 5729 3615 | 10am–6pm, weekends and public hols, or by appt |
| Chrismont Vineyard | Lake William Hovell Rd, King Valley | (03) 5729 8220 | 11am–6pm daily |
| Lana Trento | Cheshunt Rd, King Valley | (03) 5729 8278 | 10am–4pm Sat–Thurs |
| Dalzotto Wines | Edi Rd, Cheshunt | (03) 5729 8321 | By appt only |

## Milawa/Oxley wineries

| NAME | ADDRESS | PHONE | OPEN |
| --- | --- | --- | --- |
| John Gehrig Wines | Gehrigs La, Oxley | (03) 5727 3395 | 9am–5pm Mon–Sat, 10am–5pm Sun |
| Brown Brothers Milawa Vineyard | Gt Alpine Rd, Milawa | (03) 5720 5547 | 9am–5pm daily. |
| Ciavarella Wines | Evans La, Oxley | (03) 5727 3384 | 9am–6pm Mon–Sat, 10am–6pm Sun |
| Reads Winery | Evans La, Oxley | (03) 5727 3386 | 9am–6pm daily |
| Wood Park Estate Wine | Kneebones Gap Rd, Bobinawarrah | (03) 5727 3367 | By appt only |

## Ovens Valley wineries

| NAME | ADDRESS | PHONE | OPEN |
| --- | --- | --- | --- |
| Boytons of Bright | Gt Alpine Rd, Porepunkah | (03) 5756 2356 | 10am–5pm daily |
| Rosewhite Vineyards | Happy Valley Rd, Rosewhite | (03) 5752 1077 | 10am–5pm weekends and public hols, open daily during Jan. |
| Pennyweight Winery | Pennyweight Lane, Beechworth | (03) 5728 1747 | 10am–5pm Thurs–Tues, 11am–5pm Sun. |

## Rutherglen wineries

| NAME | ADDRESS | PHONE | OPEN |
| --- | --- | --- | --- |
| All Saints Estate | All Saints Rd, Wahgunyah | (02) 6033 1922 | Mon–Sat 9am–5pm |
| Campbells Wines | Murray Valley Hwy, Rutherglen | (02) 6032 9458 | 9am–5pm Mon–Sat, 10am–5pm Sun |
| Chambers Rosewood Winery | Barkly St, Rutherglen | (02) 6032 8641 | 9am–5pm Mon–Sat, 11am–5pm Sun |
| Cofield Wines | Distillery Rd, Wahgunyah | (02) 6033 3798 | 9am–5pm Mon–Sat, 10am–5pm Sun |
| Fairfield Vineyards | Murray Valley Hwy, Rutherglen | (02) 6032 9381 | 10am–4.30pm Mon–Sat, 12noon–5pm, Sun occasionally |
| G Sutherland Smith and Sons | Falkiners Rd, Rutherglen | (02) 6032 8177 | 10am–5pm weekends and public hols, 11am–5pm Fri and school hols. |
| Gehrig Estate | Murray Valley Hwy, Barnawartha | (02) 6026 7296 | 9am–5pm Mon–Sat, 10am–5pm Sun |
| Morris Wines | Mia Mia Rd, Rutherglen | (02) 6026 7303 | 9am–5pm Mon–Sat, 10am–5pm Sun |
| Mount Prior | Howlong Rd, Rutherglen | (02) 6026 5591 | 9am–5pm Mon–Sat, 10am–5pm Sun |
| Pfeiffer Wines | Distillery Rd, Wahgunyah | (02) 6033 2805 | 9am–5pm Mon–Sat, 11am–4pm Sun |
| R L Buller & Son (Calliope) | Three Chain Rd, Rutherglen | (02) 6032 9660 | 9am–5pm Mon–Sat, 10am–5pm Sun |
| St Leonards | St Leonards Rd, Wahgunyah | (02) 6033 1004 | 11am–3pm Thurs–Sun |
| Stanton & Killeen | Yarrawonga Rd, Rutherglen | (02) 6032 9457 | 9am–5pm Mon–Sat, 10am–5pm Sun |
| Warrabilla Wines | Murray Valley Hwy, Rutherglen | (02) 6035 7242 | 10am–5pm daily |

northern alpine areas via the Gt Alpine Rd, to the region's numerous gold towns, and to the Milawa Gourmet Region. And its name is synonymous with jazz. The **Wangaratta Festival of Jazz and Blues** is a world famous event, staged here for over a decade.

First settled in 1837, Wangaratta developed as a major service centre for the region's wool and cattle industry. With the establishment of the Wangaratta Woollen Mills in 1923 and further manufacturing development after WWII, it expanded and diversified into the modern city it is today. Located at the junction of

*All Saints Winery, Rutherglen.*

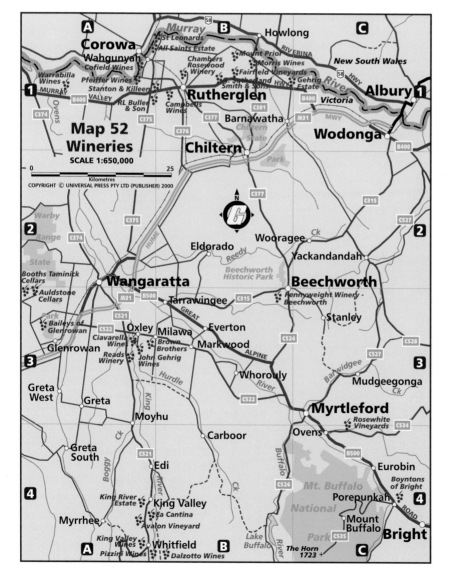

**Cranial clues of criminality?**

The headless body of Mad Dog Morgan — another of the region's famous bushrangers — is buried at Wangaratta Cemetery. Ned Kelly suffered the same fate. The heads of criminals were often studied by the medical authorities of the day for signs of criminal attributes.

the Ovens and King rivers, it is surrounded by parkland, giving excellent access to river banks and beaches. Walking and cycling paths now wend their way down leafy river banks to favourite swimming holes and ideal spots for canoeing. **Merriwa Park**, with its proud river red gums, is an ideal picnic location close to the city centre, as is **Sydney Beach**, with its sandy beachfront. A map of Wangaratta's bike paths is available at the Wangaratta Visitor Info Centre.

Guides to the city's cultural and historical features are also available. The **Wangaratta Historical Society Museum**, in Ford St, explains the pioneer and bushranging history of the area. Open Sun and public holidays, 2pm–5pm. **Airworld Aviation Museum** houses the largest collection of civil, antique and collectable aircraft in the southern hemisphere. Open daily, 9am–5pm. Ph: (03) 5721 8788

From Wangaratta it is a short trip to **El Dorado**, the hopeful name of this gold and tin mining town. El Dorado is known for its huge land-based dredge, one of the largest to operate in the southern hemisphere. Visitors can tour this mechanical giant by appointment. Bookings at the **Eldorado Museum**. Open Sun. Ph: (03) 5725 1577

**Alpine wildflowers.**

### Yackandandah *Map 52 C2*

Lined with shady trees and verandahed shops, Yackandandah is a pretty town attractive to tourists. The Australian Heritage Commission has declared a conservation area in the centre of the town, listing 5 buildings of significance: the Athenaeum, the old Courthouse, the First Bank of Australia, the former Deans Grocery Store and the town's stone bridge on Isaacs Ave.

The Yackandandah area was settled in 1837 by graziers from NSW, but exploded with a frenzy of other activities when gold was discovered in 1853. The town's fine buildings date from this period. For an experience of the goldrush, visitors can join a tour of **Karrs Reef Goldmine**, open weekends, school and public holidays. Tours at 10.30pm, noon, 1.30pm and 3.30pm or by appt. Ph: (02) 6027 1757

Yackandandah is an ideal day trip from Bright or Beechworth, a pleasant place for a lunch or afternoon tea. Visitors can picnic in the lovely **Sir Isaac Isaacs Park**, named after Australia's first Governor General, or take their pick of several cosy cafes and tearooms. Set against the Baranduda Ranges on the banks of the Yackandandah Ck, **Allans Flat Recreation Reserve**, 5km from Yackandandah, is another scenic picnic location. **Vienna Patisserie** at Allans Flat offers a fine alternative to sandwiches, serving authentic Austrian tortes, cakes and strudels. Open daily except Tues, 10am–6pm. Ph (03) 6027 1477

Several road tours are outlined in the *Yackandandah Touring Guide*. The Yackandandah Scenic Forest Dve is especially worthwhile. Leading to the Stanley SF, both 2- and 4WD routes are marked. There are several camping areas and picnic spots beside the Yackandandah Ck.

## National Parks and State Parks

### Alpine NP *Map 49 C4*

Proclaimed in 1989, the Alpine NP features mountain peaks, escarpments and open high plains. It takes in Victoria's highest mountains and offers fabulous panoramas across rugged mountain

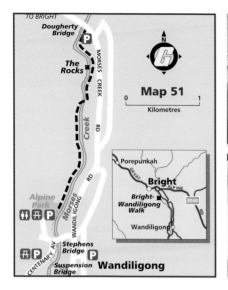

*Panoramic views of the Alps.*

ranges and magnificent river valleys. Forests, heathlands, snow gum woodlands and grasslands support a variety of wildlife. In spring and summer, the alpine meadows are a brilliant display of wildflowers. The Alpine NP is home to the rare mountain pygmy possum, thought to have been extinct, the world's only exclusively alpine marsupial animal.

The Alpine NP offers an abundance of recreational activities, including bushwalking, camping, horseriding, 4WD, canoeing, fishing and the range of snow sports. These activities cluster around the mountain resorts of Mt Buller and Mt Stirling in the south, Mt Hotham, reached via Bright, and Falls Ck, reached via Mt Beauty.

### Falls Ck *Map 49 D3*

Falls Ck Alpine Resort overlooks the Kiewa Valley, and is a 5hr drive from Melbourne. It is Victoria's most exclusive ski resort, which means that it is generally the most expensive. The ski area is 145ha and there are 22 ski lifts. Falls Ck is the only ski resort in Australia where visitors can ski directly from their lodges to the ski lifts and on to the slopes.

Some of Australia's best cross-country ski trails are found here, with Falls Ck hosting Australia's premier cross-country event – the Kangaroo Hoppet – on the last Sat in Aug. Falls Ck runs an all-year program of activities, from horseriding

and nature rambles, to musical events, photographic exhibitions and wine and food occasions. Bogong Village, on the ascent to Falls Creek, is a picturesque spot to take a rest and have a picnic.

### Mt Buller *Map 49 B4*

Mt Buller is a 3hr drive from Melbourne. Its extensive alpine village sits on the rocky ridge leading to the summit. Day and overnight trips, or longer stays are all possible. Picturesque chalets, home-style lodges, and hotels offer a range of accommodation. Lodges and hotels, with their cafes and restaurants, line the resort's main street, offering warm winter cheer, and sunny terraces, winter or summer, against the backdrop of Mt Buller's summit. Visitors can take a horse-drawn carriage ride around the village, completing the picture of a romantic mountain destination.

Victoria's largest ski resort, Mt Buller has a skiable area of 162ha, with 24 ski lifts, including a chairlift which takes skiers from the carpark to the middle of the ski runs. Slopes are graded 'beginner', 'intermediate' and 'advanced'. Snowboarding is another popular activity. Ski and snowboard hire is available, as is skiing and snowboarding instruction. A cross-country ski trail links Mt Buller to Mt Stirling.

There are designated tobogganing runs in the village area, an ice-skating

*Chalet at Mt Buller.*

rink, and various indoor sporting activities. The **La Trobe University Sports Centre** offers indoor climbing, in-line skating, volleyball and basketball, badminton, tennis and table tennis, and a fully equipped gym. It also offers mountain-bike riding and hire, outdoor climbing excursions and guided flora and fauna walks. Ph: (03) 5733 7000. For information on snow conditions ring Mt Buller Snow Report, Ph: 1902 240 523.

### Mt Hotham *Map 49 C4*

Mt Hotham village is the highest ski resort in Australia, the highest run commencing at 1840m. It has 43ha of skiable downhill area, with 11 ski lifts. While the resort is smaller than Mt Buller and Falls Ck, Mt Hotham is considered by many to be the skiers' mountain, offering some of the finest downhill runs in Victoria.

Snowboarding, including instruction and overnight snowboard camps are a specialty on Mt Hotham. There is also a ski school devoted to children. Cross-country skiing is also possible, with trails to the lovely alpine village of Dinner Plain, Wire Plain and Whisky Flat, as well as more difficult trails.

Mt Hotham offers 1st-class accommodation, good restaurants and bars, as well as a swag of ski hire and ski school operators, with good facilities for day visitors. A free village bus service operates daily in winter, 7am–10am.

*Skiing, Mt Hotham.*

**Dinner Plain**, 10km east on the Gt Alpine Rd, is well worth visiting. Constructed in the 1980s, this planned village with its weathered timber lodges in fanciful design is an architectural delight set amongst the snow gums. Dinner Plain has 1 downhill run and 16kms of cross-country ski trails. Horse rides, including rides in the snow also leave from Dinner Plain.

### Mt Stirling *Map 49 C4*

Mt Stirling is a much less developed mountain resort than its neighbour Mt Buller and is celebrated for its environmental values. The snowfalls are less reliable here, and its skiable area smaller. Consequently it is a cheaper and more relaxed option than Mt Buller. With 60km of maintained ski trails, it is best known for cross-country skiing, with fabulous tracks through alpine ash and snow gum forests, rising to open areas near the summit, which offer 360° views of the Victorian Alps.

Mt Stirling is ideal for family fun, with plenty of opportunities for snow play, including tobogganing. Snowboarding is not permitted. Ski patrols operate daily throughout winter, and facilities include a bistro and takeaway food shop, ski hire and instruction, and picnic facilities. Mt Stirling Snow Report, ph: 1902 240 523.

### Chiltern Box-Ironbark NP *Map 52 B1*

This NP encircles the historic township of Chiltern. Proclaimed in 1997, it protects one of the remaining pockets of box-ironbark forest which once dominated much of Victoria. Some of Victoria's rarest birds can be viewed here, including the regent honeyeater and turquoise parrot. In summer the wildflower displays are exceptional. Native orchids, lillies, grevilleas and pea flowers are prolific. Driving and walking tracks are marked, and there are several picnic areas with BBQs, including Donkeys Hill, Frogs Hollow and Magenta Mine. Ph: (03) 5726 1234

### Mt Buffalo NP *Map 52 C4*

Mt Buffalo NP is one of Victoria's best-loved national parks. It is a wonderland,

winter and summer, with fabulous geological formations, an abundance of native fauna, and a magnificent array of vegetation types — wet eucalypt forests, snow gum woodlands, heathlands, sphagnum bogs and snow grass plains. In spring and summer wildflowers are abundant. In winter snow blankets the mountain's higher reaches. The mountain's granite tors and rocky outcrops can be seen for kms around and are a focus for walkers and climbers.

Lake Catani, on the Buffalo Plateau, is an idyllic location for camping and canoeing. For climbers and hang gliders there are endless challenges. The north wall of The Gorge is one of a number of internationally known climbs within the park, while gliders can often be seen from Bents Lookout. Car touring along well-made roads offers fine views. *The Mt Buffalo National Park Visitors Guide* explains the various vegetation types and geological formations as visitors make the ascent by road. Many short walks to rocky outcrops and lookouts leave the main road.

The best way to explore Mt Buffalo is by foot. There are several signposted nature walks and 10 well-marked short walks to waterfalls, rock formations and across the snow-grass plains. Longer day walks of 3–8hr duration are also possible. A new remote camp area at Rocky Ck has recently been established, facilitating

a 2-day loop walk to the plateau's south-eastern sub-alpine edge. Remote camping is permitted here between Nov–Apr. Walkers must obtain a permit at the Mt Buffalo entrance station prior to setting out. Ph: (03) 5756 2328

In winter, Mt Buffalo is an ideal family location. Ski hire, lift tickets and ski instruction at Cresta Valley are remarkably cheap. Children's ski classes and over-40 classes on easy slopes are Mt Buffalo's speciality. Parents can watch their children from the comfort of the Mt Buffalo Lodge cafeteria or restaurant. There are several more difficult downhill runs.

The Buffalo Plateau's gently undulating landscape is ideal for cross-country skiing. There are 13km of marked trails, as well as 20km more remote, unmarked trails. Winter camping is also possible, at Lake Catani and Saltlick Plain. Limited sites mean booking is essential. Ph: (03) 5756 2328

Part of Mt Buffalo's charm is the **Mt Buffalo Chalet**, built in 1910. This huge chalet with high pitched gables and landscaped garden provides luxury accommodation and is an ambient watering hole for day visitors. It is also the focus of many of the mountain's activities. A full program of summer and winter activities, including ranger information sessions, nature walks, musical events and children's activities,

**The great snow shoe shuffle**
The Great Snow Shoe Shuffle is snow fun for non-skiers. Clip on your ungainly plastic 'thongs' and either join a party of shufflers or hire a pair for your own experiment. Snow Shoes can be hired at the Mt Buffalo Chalet or Mt Buffalo Lodge.

*Lake Catani.*

**Stay... for less**
There are 2 youth hostels in the region, great for both individual and family accommodation at affordable rates. For Bright YHA Lodge, Ph: (03) 5750 1180. For Mt Buller YHA, Ph: (03) 5777 6181.

**Lavender Patch, Yackandandah.**

valleys and the Alps to the east. There are 9km of walking tracks, with picnic facilities and campsites at Samaria Well, at the northern entrance to the park. A walkers-only campsite is located at Wild Dog Falls. Ph: (03) 5761 1611

### Reef Hills Park *Map 49 A2*
Five kms from Benalla, Reef Hills Park is named after the goldmining activities which took place here last century. Numerous shallow shafts can still be seen. In this open grey box and red gum forest area kangaroos are abundant. Walks, rides and driving along the many kms of track are a pleasant pastime on this gently undulating terrain. A picnic area sits in the middle of the park.

## Gardens
Indigo Shire produces a glossy pamphlet and map — available at Beechworth Visitor Info Centre — showing the location of the region's many lovely gardens that are open to the public. Of special note is Yackandandah's **Lavender Patch** 4km from Yackandandah on the Beechworth-Yackandandah Rd. This commercial lavender farm offers picnic facilities, tea rooms and nursery. A great time to visit is during the harvest festival, held over the 2nd weekend in Jan. Open daily, 9am-5.30pm. Ph: (02) 6027 1603

Beechworth is especially blessed with picturesque gardens. The **Tour-de-Malakoff Rose Garden**, 30 Malakoff Rd, is a delight, with over 2000 old-fashioned roses, and formal and informal landscapes created with crab apple, wisteria and pear walks. Open daily except Tues, from 9am-5pm. Ph (03) 5728 1107.

**Out of Town Nursery and Garden** (12km from Beechworth on the Chiltern-Beechworth Rd) is a 1.5ha garden with many romantic settings, and colour all year round. Its native birds are an additional drawcard. Open Fri-Mon, 9am-5pm Ph: (03) 5726 1554. For ideas for the smaller garden, visitors will find a shift in scale at **Duggan Garden**, 30 Mellish St. This intimate cottage garden provides a romantic setting for a historic Victorian villa. Open 2nd and 3rd

start here. Ph: (03) 5755 1500. Motel-style accommodation at affordable family rates is available at the **Mt Buffalo Lodge**. Ph: (03) 5755 1988

### Mt Pilot Park *Map 52 C2*
Mt Pilot Park, 15km from Beechworth, is a granite plateau once of special significance to the Duduroa sub-clan of the Pangarang Aborigines. While camping, picnicking, driving and nature walks are all offered here, the park is best known for its Aboriginal art site. Rock paintings 2000 years old depict the Tasmanian tiger dreaming story. The tiger was the Duduroa's totem spirit. A 45min walk has been devised that takes in several areas of significance to the people who came here for special ceremonies and to feast on the bogong moth. Ph: (03) 5728 1501

### Mt Samaria SP *Map 49 A3*
Rising to a height of 949m, Mt Samaria is 28km from Benalla, and 15km north of Mansfield. This spectacular granite plateau is forested with red stringybark, long-leaf box and narrow-leaf peppermint, and has many ferny creek-beds, with waterfalls at Wild Dog and Back Cks. The walk to the summit of Mt Samaria offers magnificent views of the river

**Prepare for the snow**
Check at ski hire shops for the latest local snow reports. Chains must be carried to all mountains in the snow season. Chains, skis, snowboards and toboggans can be hired at snow shops and also at many service stations.

weekend in Nov, or by appt, Sept–May. Ruth Duggan also takes tours of the **Beechworth gardens**. Ph: (03) 5728 1436

A celebrated newcomer is the **Black Springs Bakery Garden**. Bringing a little bit of Provence to the NE, Robert Cowell's 5-acre garden features an olive grove, lavender, a quince walk and parterre, and refurbished stone barn, now available as self-contained accommodation. Ph: (03) 5728 2565

## Recreational activities

### Air Adventures

The **Gliding Club of Victoria** based at Benalla offers joy flights and instruction in gliding. Ph: (03) 5762 1058. The **Eagle School of Hang Gliding and Microlighting** offers introductory flights and instruction at Bright and Mt Buffalo. Ph: 018 570 168

For the complete daredevil, the **National Training Centre** at Wangaratta Airfield runs parachute courses each weekend, including tandem parachuting, accelerated free fall and static line instruction. Ph: (03) 5722 9899

### Ballooning

Mansfield is a popular location for **Global Ballooning**'s exhilarating flights. The 1-hr flight takes off close to sunrise

*Horseriding in the High Country.*

over the glorious high country near Mt Buller. Ph: (03) 9428 5703

### Bushwalking

There are endless possibilities for bushwalking in this region. Check the section on NPs for details. Bright (p.271), Mt Buffalo (p.280), Mt Stirling (p.280) and the Mansfield district (p.273) offer exceptional bushwalking in magnificent

# Bogong Moths

For thousands of years Aboriginal tribes travelled to the high country in late spring and summer. They came from as far away as the coast and the south-west slopes of the mountains for intertribal corroborees, trading, marriages and initiation ceremonies. They also came to feast on the bogong moth. Huge swarms of the moth would arrive and shelter in the crevices and cracks of rocks on their annual migration from the central and north-west slopes of NSW.

A rich source of protein, the moths would be smoked out of crevices and cooked in ash or ground to a paste. They are also food for the rare mountain pygmie possum and little raven. The bogong moth continues is annual migration. Visitors to the Alps can see these large brown moths from Nov–Apr massed together in large fan-like agglomerations hanging from the cracks between rocks. At Mt Buffalo, guides identify these intriguing insects for visitors on field naturalist walks.

**Get the details**

For parks info, ring

Parks Victoria,

Ph: 13 19 63

**Bright,**

Ph: (03) 5755 1577

**Mansfield,**

Ph: (03) 5733 0120

**Mt Beauty,**

Ph: (03) 5757 2693

mountain settings. Maps and guidelines for walking and camping are available at the relevant visitor info centres.

### Camping

Caravan park campsites, roadside camping in remote areas and dispersed bush camping are all possible. Dispersed bush camping is permitted throughout the Alpine NP. Campsites with pit toilets, picnic tables and fireplaces are located at J B Plain, between Hotham Village and Dinner Plain on the Gt Alpine Rd; Buckety, Raspberry Hill and Langfords West on the Bogong High Plains, east of Falls Ck; and at Mountain Ck, at the foot of Mt Bogong near Tawonga on the Mt Beauty Rd.

### Canoeing

Many of the region's towns and cities, such as Wangaratta and Beechworth, have lakes and waterways where gentle conditions permit relaxed family canoeing. The Ovens River at Porepunkah and Bright are also ideal locations. **Rios Alpine Centre** in Porepunkah hire canoes, rafts and tubes. Ph: (03) 5756 2208

### Cycling

Easy cycling paths are to be found in many of the region's towns. Wangaratta has extensive bike paths along its waterways, a bike path joins Myrtleford to Bright, and cycling around the

*Canoeing, Ovens River.*

Rutherglen wineries is a well-practised mode of locomotion.

Mountain-bike riding is a specialty in the region, with mountain-bike hire at Bright and Mt Buller. The **Bright Audax Classic Road Bike Race,** held over Australia Day weekend, sees 100s of participants, young and old, compete in several exhilarating mountain rides. Ph: (03) 9899 6679

### Fishing

The High Country's mountain streams and rivers are famed for their trout fishing. Fly fishing instruction and guiding is available from **Braeside Flyfishing** near Mansfield. Ph: (03) 5777 5697. **Angling Expeditions Victoria** offers instruction for beginners at Falls Ck. Ph: (03) 5754 1466

The Ovens River and its tributaries are very popular, and there are endless possibilities for dropping in a line at Bright in the north, at Jamieson east of Mansfield, in the King Valley and along the Howqua and Delatite Rivers. The Ovens and tributaries are closed to fishing from the Queens Birthday weekend to the 1st weekend in Sept, but there are always fish jumping at **Bright Waters Trout Farm**, on the Gt Alpine Rd in Harrietville.

### 4WD

For the many popular 4WD routes in the region, check with local visitor info centres or the regional offices of the

*Hang gliding, Mt Buffalo.*

Dept of Natural Resources and Environment. Note that many routes are closed during winter and early spring. Near Bright, the Demon Ridge route, south of Clear Spot Lookout is especially exciting. Many other tracks extend over the high country: Mt Samaria (p.282) and the Stanley SF near Yackandandah (p.278) are other popular 4WD locations.

Mansfield Visitor Info Centre has detailed track notes on easy to moderate 4WD tracks through nearby high country.

### Horseriding

One of the delights of the region, horseriding and trail rides are widely available. **Dinner Plain Trail Rides** offers horserides across the snow plains, in the snow during winter and through the wildflowers in summer. Ph: (03) 5159 6488. At Bright, **Freeburgh Trail Rides** offers ½-day, 1-day and 3-day trail rides through mountain forest. Ph: (03) 5755 1370

The Mansfield district is exceptional for the number and quality of trail ride operators. For the authentic high country experience, you can't beat **McCormacks Mountain Valley Trail Rides** or **Chris Stoney Bluff and Beyond Trail Rides**. Chris Stoney is known locally as a 'living legend'. Ph: (03) 5775 2598. McCormack's offers 2hr and 1-day rides, taking in Craigs Hut and Mt Stirling, with river crossings at the head of the King River. Ph: (03) 5775 2886

**Beau Purcells Horse Adventures** offers short rides and small group overnight safaris. Camp out at Burnt Hut. Visitors are treated to a camp oven roast and damper. Ph: (03) 5777 5809

### Rock climbing

Excellent rock climbing is available at Mt Buffalo (p.280). **Mountain Adventure Safaris** offers a range of active recreations, including climbing and abseiling on Elephant Cliff, Mt Buller. Ph: 1800 642 234

For indoor rock climbing, the La Trobe University Sports Centre on Mt Buller offers top-class facilities (p.279). The **Mt Beauty Indoor Go Kart and**

*Wandilligong Maze.*

**Rock Climbing Centre** is open Mon–Sat 11am–5.30pm and 7pm–9.30pm. Ph: (03) 5754 1077

### Whitewater rafting

The best conditions for rafting are Jun–Dec. **Adrenalin Adventures** promises 7km of non-stop action on the King River, no experience or equipment required. Ph: 0500 531 531. The Buffalo and Howqua rivers are also popular rafting locations.

### Winter sports

Downhill skiing, snowboarding and cross-country skiing are highlights of the alpine areas within this region. See Mt Buffalo (p.280), Mt Buller (p.279), Mt Stirling (p.280), Mt Hotham (p.280) and Falls Ck (p.279).

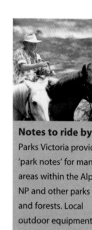

**Notes to ride by**
Parks Victoria provides 'park notes' for many areas within the Alpine NP and other parks and forests. Local outdoor equipment stores typically sell the more detailed maps needed for horseriding, mountain-bike riding, walking and 4WD tours.

## Fun for the young

★ Beginners Skiing and snowboarding at Mt Buffalo (p.281)

★ Cycling and mountain-bike riding (p.284)

★ Gator Magoons and Lots'afun, Bright (p.272)

★ Mt Beauty Indoo Go Kart and Rock Climbing Centre (p.285)

★ Playground at Centenary park, Bright (p.271)

★ Wandillagong Maze (p.272)

# Suggested tours – Map 53

## Kelly country tour

### Distance
560km return from Melbourne CBD

### About the trip
Explore Kelly country and enjoy the magnificent scenery of the Mansfield district. The drive along the Melba and Maroondah Hwys to Mansfield is a delight in itself. At Mansfield the Kelly legend begins to unfold with a self-guided tour of the town's historic monuments, including the monument to the policemen killed at Tolmie by the Kelly gang, and their graves at Mansfield Cemetery. Pick up the *Historic Town Walk* pamphlet from Mansfield Visitor Info Centre. If there is time, there is an optional side-tour in which visitors can explore the country to the east of Mansfield on the Mt Buller Rd, taking in the Delatite River Valley, Merrigig and Mirimbah. From Mansfield, the Whitfield Road winds past Mt Samaria to the mountain hideout of Harry Power, a bushranger who is said to have aided the Kelly gang, and into the King Valley. From here it is a 30min trip to Glenrowan, at the heart of the Kelly legend. From Glenrowan to Benalla is a short trip. At Benalla visit the Benalla Costume and Pioneer Museum, which holds some historical Kelly items, and the Benalla Regional Art Gallery, where you can see Nolan's Kelly tapestry (p. 270).

### Places of interest
❶ **Mansfield Visitor Info Centre and Mansfield township** (p.273)

❷ **Delatite River Valley (optional)**

❸ **Stirling Hunt Club Hotel, Merrigig (optional)**

❹ **Mirimbah picnic ground and river walk (optional)**

❺ **Powers Lookout** (p.274)

❻ **Mountain View Hotel, Whitfield** (p.275)

❼ **King Valley** (p.274)

❽ **Glenrowan township** (p.273)

❾ **Kelly's Last Stand** (p.273)

❿ **Benalla Costume and Pioneer Museum** (p.271)

⓫ **Benalla Regional Art Gallery** (p.270)

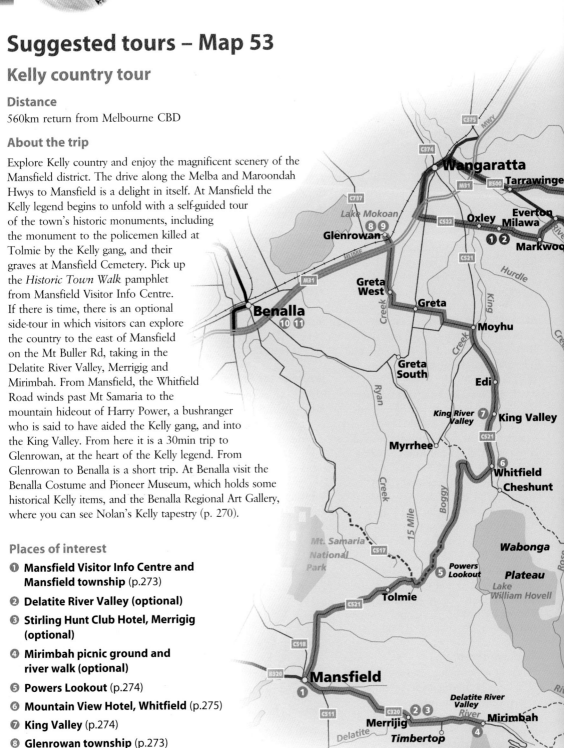

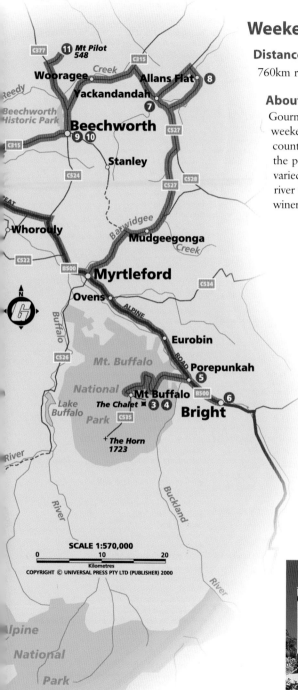

# Weekend escape tour

## Distance

760km return from Melbourne CBD

## About the trip

Gourmet food and wine, mountains and gold towns, this weekend tour takes in all the pleasures of the north-east high country. From the Oxley/Milawa turn-off near Wangaratta the pace becomes very relaxed, and the attractions many and varied. Visitors can gently potter past small townships, along river valleys and on winding mountain roads, stopping at wineries, farms, historic sites and stupendous natural features.

## Places of interest

❶ **Brown Brothers Milawa Vineyard and Epicurean Centre** (p.274)
❷ **Milawa Cheese Co** (p.274)
❸ **Mt Buffalo NP** (p.280)
❹ **Mt Buffalo Chalet** (p.281)
❺ **Boytons of Bright** (p.271)
❻ **Bright township** (p.271)
❼ **Yackandandah** (p.278)
❽ **Viennese Pattiserie, Allans Flat** (p.278)
❾ **Beechworth township and historic sites** (p.268)
❿ **Beechworth gardens** (p.283)
⓫ **Mt Pilot Aboriginal cave paintings** (p.282)

*Chalet, Mt Buffalo.*

# Index and Gazetteer

# Melbourne Digital Coverage Map

**Telstra**
**MobileNet®**
*Australia's Number 1 Digital*

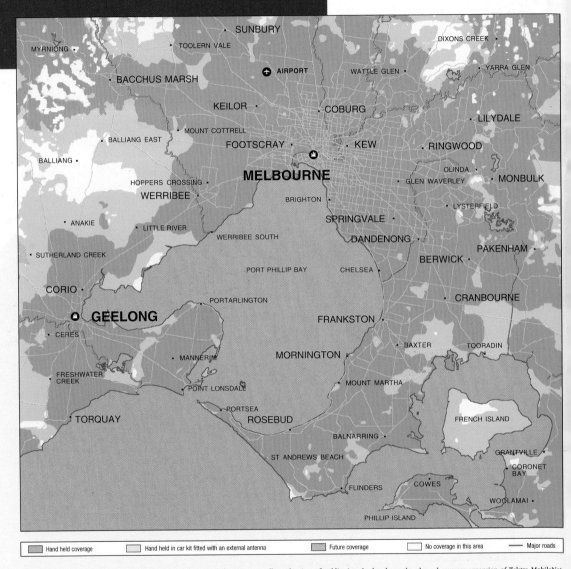

| | | | | |
|---|---|---|---|---|
| ▪ Hand held coverage | ▪ Hand held in car kit fitted with an external antenna | ▪ Future coverage | ▪ No coverage in this area | — Major roads |

This coverage map shows the extent of the Telstra MobileNet Digital service generally at the time of publication. It also shows the planned coverage expansion of Telstra MobileNet Digital service based on the targeted rollout schedule. As it may be necessary to change or modify the rollout schedule, Telstra reserves the right to do this without notice. The percentage of total land areas of Australia covered by Telstra MobileNet Digital service is about 5% and the percentage of the total population of Australia within this coverage is about 94%. As with any radio system there are places inside the marked coverage area where a mobile phone may not work due to a variety of factors. For example, radio reception can be degraded or non-existent in certain places, particularly basements, lifts, underground car parks and large buildings. However, MobileNet Digital is endeavouring to provide the best depth of radio reception practicable into such areas. Reception can also be affected by mountains, tunnels and road cuttings.

If you have any questions as to the Telstra MobileNet® service coverage please ring the Telstra MobileNet coverage information line on 018 018 888† (no call charge), or contact your local Telstra MobileNet Dealer.

http://www.telstra.com.au

For other information call Telstra MobileNet Customer Service on 018 018 111† (no call charge)

Telstra Corporation Limited A.C.N. 051 775 556
®Registered trade mark of Telstra Corporation Limited
†No call charge when call is made from a Telstra service